LIFECYCLES

LIFECYCLES

Jewish Women on
Life Passages and Personal Milestones

VOLUME 1

EDITED AND
WITH INTRODUCTIONS BY

Rabbi Debra Orenstein

WILSTEIN INSTITUTE FELLOW

JEWISH LIGHTS PUBLISHING
WOODSTOCK, VERMONT

Lifecycles: Jewish Women on Life Passages & Personal Milestones, Volume 1

Library of Congress Cataloging-in-Publication Data

Lifecycles / edited by Debra Orenstein.
p. cm.
  Includes bibliographical references and indexes.
  Contents: v. 1. Jewish women on life passages & personal milestones.
  ISBN 1-879045-14-1 (v. 1) : $24.95
  1. Jewish women—Religious life. 2. Women in Judaism. 3. Judaism—Customs and practices. 4. Jewish way of life. 5. Lifecycle, Human—Religious aspects—Judaism. 6. Life change events—Religious aspects—Judaism. 7. Fasts and feasts—Judaism. I. Orenstein, Debra, 1962-   .
  BM726.L5 1994 94-14799   296.7′4′082—dc20

First Edition

10 9 8 7 6 5 4 3 2 1

Manufactured in the United States of America

Cover art: Torah Mantle by Phyllis Kantor and Reeva Kimble
Photo: Kent Peterson
Book and cover design: Karen Savary
Page composition: Chelsea Dippel

Published by JEWISH LIGHTS Publishing
A Division of LongHill Partners, Inc.
P.O. Box 237
Sunset Farm Offices — Route 4
Woodstock, Vermont 05091
Tel: (802) 457-4000 · Fax: (802) 457-4004

To Mathilda Orenstein

*whose spirit teaches all who knew her how to mark life's moments
in joy, and whose memory is for a blessing.*

The papers included in this volume were generated as part of a
research project of the Susan and David Wilstein Institute of
Jewish Policy Studies.

The Susan and David Wilstein Institute of Jewish Policy
Studies, with a West Coast Center in Los Angeles and an East
Coast Center at Hebrew College in Boston, is an international
research center established to conduct Jewish policy analysis and
to disseminate its findings throughout the community. The aim of
the Institute is not merely to gather information and anayze it, but
also to stimulate creative thinking about important issues affecting
American Jews and to formulate strategies and become an instru-
ment for change and growth in Jewish life.

CONTENTS

Preface

About four years ago, a number of factors converged to inspire the creation of a new book, dealing with Jewish women's experiences and perceptions of lifecycle. I was just completing my rabbinical studies at The Jewish Theological Seminary. In those earliest years of Conservative women's ordination, many considered the "woman question" to have been definitively resolved. A minority, however, perceived that women's access to traditional (male) institutions was the first—not the last—stage in a long process. That minority was asking new questions: "How might the Jewish community be enhanced if it fully incorporated women's experiences and talents? What would Jewish education look like if it enfranchised women completely, both as sources of learning and as objects of study?"

Many of the women I knew were beginning to answer these questions by their own example—in the manner and content of their prayer, preaching, and teaching. There were essays of theirs as yet unwritten that I wanted to read. After hearing Pam Hoffman *daven minḥah* (lead the afternoon prayers), it was clear that she had much to contribute on the subject and practice of

Jewish spirituality. After a discussion with Eleanor Smith on inter-marriage, I concluded that her thoughts on that subject should be required reading. In the manner of the old Judy Garland/Mickey Rooney musicals, I wondered if I might assemble a group of these friends and friends-of-friends and, in person and by correspondence, "put on a book."

In 1990, I accepted a fellowship at the University of Judaism in Los Angeles and taught a class on "Introduction to Rabbinic Practice." I focused on those practices that would be most likely to affect my students' lives: Sabbath, birth, circumcision, marriage, mourning—in other words, Jewish lifecycle. Few books supplied the information I wanted to impart to my students and also entered into the cycle and symbols of Jewish life on an emotional level. Learning about and from women's perspectives on lifecycle had been my first motivation; added to that now was the need for another resource that would speak of lifecycle not only anthropologically, historically, and in terms of Jewish law, but also emotionally, spiritually, and in terms of life experience. I could not assign unwritten essays to my students. It was time to get down to business.

Rabbi David Gordis, Director of the Susan and David Wilstein Institute of Jewish Policy Studies, helped me do just that. Coaxed by his warmth and interest, I told him of my rudimentary plan to solicit women's writings for an anthology on Jewish lifecycle. I further confessed to a pipe dream: To bring together the women who would be contributing to this book, so that they could exchange ideas and inform each other's work. My conception of the book had been inspired and influenced by feminist principles: Hearing women's voices; valuing women's experience; including people of diverse backgrounds, beliefs, and affiliations; relating the intellectual with the spiritual, the personal with the political. For logistical reasons, it seemed that the book would have to be edited by a single person, with little opportunity for broader exchange. Yet if we could all meet, our work would be more cohesive, and the process of creating the book would reflect—and enhance—its content and values.

Rabbi Gordis was excited about an anthology and the prospect of a conference. He assessed as enormous the public policy implications related to changes in Jewish women's status. He also expressed the belief that academics, policy analysts, religious leaders, and laity all need to learn by example the extent and potential of women's effect on our communal agenda. Thus, the Wilstein Institute undertook the project as part of its program, and I won a supporter, mentor, and friend.

There was so much rich material that the book I imagined expanded to three volumes, and the conference, to two conferences. This first volume on life passages and personal milestones covers discrete moments—brief and extended—in life's cycle, such as birth, adolescence, midlife, and death. Volume two focuses on life themes, such as identity, sexuality, spirituality, and home. Volume three deals with Jewish holidays, including the traditional festivals, along with the holidays and holiday customs of Jewish women which may have fallen into disuse.

The two conferences were held in the summer of 1992, one at The Jewish Theological Seminary in New York City and the other at Camp Ramah in Ojai, California. These were highly participatory events, planned with the help of a committee of contributors, as well as the Wilstein Institute staff. The programming consisted of "editing groups" of five or six women, which carefully reviewed each essay that had been written by the women in that group. It also included prayer services, the planning and execution of new rituals, study sessions, shared meals, and presentations and discussions on women's perspectives and the nature of effective ritual.

The conferences were enormously instructive, exciting, challenging, and exhausting. There was a sense of something special brewing around the rare opportunity for this community of women to meet. The first night of the Ojai conference, a short presentation spontaneously erupted into three hours of ecstatic singing. The gathering was a religious experience because the time was right, and the women ready. Traditions begun by different women in different communities were gelling somehow. What started as oral Torah was ready to become the written word.

The moment the written word is released into the world, however, a new oral tradition begins. I hope that some of the atmosphere of the conferences is preserved in these pages, and that readers feel themselves to be partners in the continuing dialogue. You are invited to agree and disagree, to adopt and adapt the ceremonies, rituals, and prayers we have included. We have tried to leave room for you, and for growth, in these pages.

Creating a book, especially an anthology, is often likened to the experience of giving birth. At times, I must confess, I have felt *Lifecycles'* contractions. In the main, however, I have felt more like a match-maker than like a birthing mother. I first realized this at the conference in Ojai, where I surprised myself by greeting those in attendance with traditional words of welcome usually reserved for the Sabbath: *Bo'i khallah, bo'i khallah* (come to me my bride, come to me my bride).

I sought to match the writers of this book with topics for which they feel great passion and have personal involvement. In turn, the authors in these pages have effected marriages between instruction and inspiration, theory and personal story. Soliciting and editing essays for this book, I have tried to look into the hearts—and needs—of prospective readers, as well as of the authors. The most important match in this book is one that I hope will take place beyond the text, between the reader and the contributors.

Finding the right match is, they say, *bashert* (destined by the good will of Providence). When you look back, you see that everything was leading you to the right spot, in due time. Judaism did not come to women's inclusion first, but it is coming to it at last. Having looked, over the last several years, deep into the heart of feminism and of Judaism, I am utterly convinced that, despite any quarrels or differences, the marriage between them is one made in heaven. This book is a product of that marriage.

DEBRA ORENSTEIN
MAY 2, 1994 / 21 *IYYAR* 5754

Acknowledgments

I am grateful to the many people who saw this project through the eyes of love and helped me along the way. It would be impossible to thank everyone. The people whom it would be impossible *not* to thank are listed below:

To Yoav Ben-Horin, Dorit Gary, Rabbi David Gordis, Laura Giacomini, Aundrea Katz, and Rina Natkin of the Wilstein Institute: This project would never have been launched *or* completed without you. Thank you for your vision, for your extraordinary help with editing and organizing, and for keeping the enterprise joyous.

To my volunteers and interns: Sara Beck, Sharon Brooks, Franci Levine, Joe Mendelsohn, Linda Mendelsohn, Steve Morgan, Catherine Nelson, and Sherre Zwelling, who worked tirelessly, reliably, and cheerfully. As you have given, so may you receive.

To the donors who helped finance the conferences and the preparation of this book: The Dobkin Family Foundation, The Dorot Foundation, The Ferkauf Family Foundation, Rabbi Marion Shulevitz, Rabbi Eleanor Smith, Diane Troderman, Rabbi Sheila Peltz Weinberg, and Donna Weiss. Each is a partner in the creation of this volume.

To the individuals and organizations who helped to make the conferences a success: Rabbi Nina Beth Cardin, Rabbi Sue Levi Elwell, Rose Levinson, Rabbi Jane Litman, Rabbi Naomi Levy, Ruth Sharon, and Sherre Zwelling. Thanks especially to Catherine Coulson, whose expertise was essential in recording the Ojai conference and whose love and energy were instrumental in its planning and execution.

To friends who shared their knowledge of the world of publishing: Ellen Geiger, Joseph Mellicker, Charlotte Sheedy, Steve Sklar, and Ann Swidler. Your advice and patience were much appreciated.

To Rick Burke, Yapha Nussbaum, Harvey Schloss, and the entire library staff at the University of Judaism for your expertise and kind assistance.

To Rabbi Miles Cohen and Dr. Yona Sabar for their careful and professional help on questions of transliteration and Hebrew vocalization.

To Sharon Margolin and Rabbi Neal Weinberg of the Introduction to Judaism Program at the University of Judaism for jumping in and taking over some of my teaching and paperwork, while I was occupied with this book.

To the staff and volunteers at Congregation Beth-El in South Orange, New Jersey, who graciously allowed me to take over their office temporarily while I put finishing touches on the manuscript.

To the authors in this volume, who have given and taught more than they realize and upon whom I have called often for help and advice.

To friends and teachers who reviewed selections of the manuscript that became this book: Rabbi David Gordis, Dr. Lynn Gordon, Rabbi Lawrence Hoffman, Rose Levinson, Rabbi Margaret Holub, Rabbi Jane Litman, Rabbi Jack Riemer, and Dr. Maeera Shreiber. Thank you so much for your time, insights, and encouragement. Special thanks go to Rabbi Neil Gillman, who made invaluable comments on the entire manuscript, and to Dr. Elieser Slomovic, whose help was so frequently and generously given, that I could leave materials or questions for his review, without cover letter, and simply wait for an erudite and prompt reply. Special thanks as well, to Yoav Ben-Horin and Aviva Orenstein, who kept their editorial talents under wraps for as long as possible, but were at last found out—and then became instrumental in the editing of this book. The wisdom of all these readers made *Lifecycles 1* a better book than it would have been otherwise.

To my family, and especially my parents, who amazed the staff of the Wilstein Institute—but not me—with the degree of their caring and involvement. It is not that I have come to expect your help, it is just that you never fail to provide it.

To the entire Jewish Lights staff, including Theresa Jones Vyhnal, Wendy Kilborn, and especially Sandra Korinchak, who have been uniformly professional, skilled, considerate, and invested throughout. To my editor, Sandee Brawarsky, for her clarity, honesty, serenity, and talent. Thank you for keeping me on track and especially for your friendship. To Stuart Matlins, publisher of Jewish Lights Publishing, for the curiosity that feeds his wisdom, for his guidance at every stage along the way, and for his keen sense of aesthetics and of this book. It is a privilege to work with someone who so clearly sees the forest, the trees, and the point.

DEBRA ORENSTEIN
MAY 2, 1994 / 21 *IYYAR* 5754

Introduction

Defining Lifecycle and *Lifecycles*

There is no equivalent in Rabbinic Hebrew for "lifecycle." Yet, the ancient Rabbis understood life, in part, as a cycle. Traditional Jewish historiography sees the process and progress of the world as both linear *and* cyclical. In the midst of every cycle, we are meant to feel the finger of God pushing history to its linear destination, and every linear development is part of the grand circle.

On a macrocosmic scale, time and experience are progressive and linear in that they have a direction and a destination. Creation leads to revelation and ultimately to redemption in the messianic age. Yet, time moves cyclically as well—especially for individuals. The holidays and Torah readings cycle unendingly. Birth leads to death, which leads to eternal life. Children generally repeat the same cyclical path worn by their parents and *their* parents, marking milestones with rituals along the way. The circle of passages remains constant, but is experienced differently and anew because we constantly play different roles.

As the last example shows, lifecycle is neither linear nor wholly cyclical. Rather, it represents an approach to time in which the past is eternally present. It is this paradigm that the ancient Rabbis draw on when they tell us that we were all at Mt. Sinai, or that we must all think of ourselves as having been personally liberated from slavery in Egypt. Lifecycle rituals bend time forward, as well as back, relating each bride and groom to Adam and Eve and each wedding to the coming of the messiah. Time is seen, as it were, from God's perspective—or, more accurately, from the Rabbis' perspective on God's perspective. With God's help, they teach, Moses can travel back to the future and visit Rabbi Akiva's classroom (BT *Menaḥot* 29b).

Neither the Rabbis of two millennia ago, nor those of two decades ago, would have cited childbirth, coming out, menopause, or entering a baby girl into the covenant as life passages. Yet the Rabbis intended Jewish lifecycle classification and ritual to reflect and sanctify Jewish lives as they are lived. Thus, while some segments of the Jewish community regard innovations in lifecycle ritual as a breaking or improper expansion of the boundaries of Jewish tradition, more and more Jews have come to see these innovations as the fulfillment of its deeper purpose, and a continuation of Jewish liturgical creativity.

Feminist Jews have been instrumental in expanding the definition of lifecycle in four ways: (1) By including women in the observance of passages that formerly spoke only to and of men—e.g., establishing Bat Mitzvah (coming of age ceremony for girls), along with Bar Mitzvah (coming of age ceremony for boys), and covenant ceremonies for baby girls, along with those for boys; (2) by supplementing or altering traditional rituals related to lifecycle—e.g., supplemental divorce rituals or alternative marriage contracts; (3) by valuing as sacred and sometimes ritualizing the events of women's biological cycle—e.g., menarche, menses, childbirth, miscarriage, menopause; and (4) by sacralizing non-biological passages and milestones not contemplated by the tradition—e.g., through ceremonies celebrating elder wisdom or healing from sexual abuse. In a sense, this listing occurs in ascending order of innovation. The first category adheres most closely to the tradition and seeks both parity and uniformity in communal observances. The last uses individual lives—not tradition—as its starting point, and does not necessarily entail or expect community-wide norms. Each of these four types of expansion appears in this book, and each has had far-reaching, if differential, effects on our understanding of lifecycle.

Fifty years ago, Bat Mitzvah ceremonies were literally unheard of. Today, some form of celebration of a girl's coming of age is common, even in many ultra-Orthodox communities. Twenty-five years ago, covenant/naming rituals for girls were virtually non-existent. Today, they are widespread. The exact form and timing of covenant rituals are still in flux, but the expectation that we ceremoniously honor the entry of baby girls into the world, their families, their own names, and the Jewish covenant, has become fixed. It is startling to realize how quickly revolution becomes everyday reality.

Rituals for daughters have led to more personal prayers and parental involvement in traditional circumcision rites. Attention to menopause has led men to ask how they can mark retirement—a central and neglected passage for that half of the population that has traditionally derived its primary identity from work. We begin by asking "What does it mean for a woman to use male God language...or to study Talmud...or to wrestle with aspects of the tradition from which she is alienated?," we then apply those same questions to all Jews, and still further down the line we approach core questions about God, and learning, and a holy tradition that has been both shaped and muddied by human hands.

It is not difficult to imagine a time, in the not too distant future, when the format of girls' naming ceremonies will be more nearly standardized; when we will have communally- and religiously-sanctioned responses to miscarriage; when most Jews will become accustomed to seeing women don traditional (and perhaps feminized) prayer garments, including prayer shawl, phylacteries, and head covering. Ten years from now, it will be unremarkable for Jews to pray in the hospital delivery or birthing room—and I hope that many of the resources collected in Chapter One by Dr. Lori Lefkovitz will be used. If Rivka Haut and other activists succeed with the approach she takes in Chapter Ten, traditional Jewish divorce law will be substantially changed to balance the power between husband and wife in marriage and in divorce. In the Orthodox movement, women's increasing knowledge of traditional Jewish texts may well serve to emphasize inconsistencies between theory and practice, knowledge and behavior, and have a radicalizing effect. As the American Jewish population ages, prayers and ceremonies for menopause, retirement, elder-wisdom, and grandparenthood are likely to proliferate.

No doubt, there are other expansions of lifecycle awaiting us, which we will find surprising—at least initially. In a generation or two, some new rituals may be so ensconced in American Jewish thought and practice that Hebrew School students will assume they were given to Moses at Mt. Sinai. Others will make for an interesting historical footnote on what several Jewish women were thinking at the end of the twentieth century, but will not weather the tests of time and communal sensibilities. Of course, filling a need of the moment can be as valuable as producing literature that becomes part of the canon. The long-term challenge is to remain open to new perspectives and honor the lives of individual Jews, even as we retain traditional observances and idioms, and come to consensus about communal standards.[1]

Why Ritual?

Traditional religious ritual was designed, and continues, to meet a variety of needs that relate to life passages: The need for the individual to be acknowledged by community, the need for the community/tribe to read itself into the passages of each member, the need for bonding, which serves both individual and community, the need to (re-)enact dramatically the great stories and messages of the tradition, for the sake of individuals and of the tradition. Through rituals, we create structures that provide an element of predictability and, therefore, safety, around times of insecurity, transition, and/or loss.

Ritual has been popularized and secularized in the last few years. At the same time, there has been a flowering of ritual-writing in religious contexts as well. The impetus for this among Jews came originally from grass roots. It was women waking up to how they lived who created a cottage-industry of ritual-writing in *Rosh Ḥodesh* (New Moon Festival) groups and elsewhere.

Many of those who have been marking their lives idiosyncratically and often privately have come to want the authentic stamp of something ancient and communal. There has been a breakdown in our society both of predictable life markers and of community. Now, almost in a backlash, we sometimes want even the most personal passage—and perhaps especially that one—to be acknowledged and witnessed.

Contemporary Jewish women have had a particular need for and connection with ritual. We have needed not only to re-enact but to integrate our myths—the feminist/woman's "story" with the Jewish "story." This is often accomplished by creating and participating in rituals that take account of women as Jews, express women's perspectives on life passages, and feminize a formerly patriarchal symbolic system. Many women, and especially feminists, feel a deep harmony with the whole ritual enterprise. The women's movement has worked to achieve some of the same ends that ritual serves: Namely, to rely on and build community, while providing support and opportunities for self-expression to individuals in transition. Perhaps it should not be surprising, then, that both feminism and creative ritual have been ways "in" to Judaism for many women.

Rituals are "created" in at least three ways: By recovering traditions that have fallen into disuse (such as those Dr. Lori Lefkovitz cites in her essay on childbirth), by using an existing rite or blessing in a new context (as Rabbi Sandy Eisenberg Sasso does in her blessing following miscarriage), or by drawing on traditional texts, symbols, images, and ritual objects to create an entirely new composition (as Rabbi Nina Beth Cardin does in her ritual for marital separation). The first two methods renew the old creatively, while the last creates the new authentically. Thus, they fulfill Rav Kuk's intention that the old be made new, and the new, made holy.[2]

Invention can entail a struggle with the old. It might also mean simply finding new meanings, spaces, and places in a rich and highly interpretive and interpretable tradition. Jewish books of commentary, prayer, and lore, unlike the Bible and Talmud, were never sealed. Generating new ritual, liturgical, and midrashic material has always been permitted—and even lauded. *Vekhol hamarbeh harei zeh meshubaḥ*: Whoever tells the Jewish story more-so, we learn at the Passover *seder* (ordered readings and meal), their telling is surely to be praised.[3]

While lifecycle ritual has generated a sense of excitement and renewal, it has also provoked significant anxiety and controversy.

Some people fear that the proliferation of rituals around women's biological cycle will somehow reinforce the notion that women are linked to earth and body, and men to God and mind. If women want some of their most important private biological moments to be addressed and recognized by the community, however, that hardly means that they want *only* their biological needs to be addressed and recognized. Moreover, biology and spirit are at bottom inseparable, particularly, as the authors of this book show, in such momentous passages as childbirth, miscarriage, abortion, and menopause. The Rabbis dealt with women's biological changes, but primarily in terms of how those changes affect men—re: sexual contact and ritual purity. A Talmudic tractate *Niddah* (Menstruant) written by women would read very differently than the one we have, and some women are now trying to imagine and record it.

Some argue that ritual is debased by attaching it to relatively trivial events, such as losing a job, or completing a creative project. Triviality, like much else, is in the eye of the beholder. It might seem "trivial" to say a blessing for smelling ripe fruit, but the tradition supplies one. More important than notions of subjectivity or relativity, however, is the social assessment of familiarity. In contemporary Western culture, familiarity commonly does breed contempt. What is most available and most used is considered least interesting and essential. This contrasts sharply with the traditional Jewish emphasis on sanctifying the everyday, and with the recent focus on ritual.

Still and all, there are times, during this period of the flowering and popularization of ritual, when one cringes either at the occasion being ritualized or at the character of the ritual. I used to be judgmental of that, but I have come to see it as part of our communal creative and learning process. In any case, it is a relatively small price to pay for the benefit of an expanded tradition that, by its willingness to address the lives of Jews as they are lived, remains both relevant and viable. The "price" is also temporary: In the end, rituals that speak to the needs of the Jewish community will last, and those that do not will fall into disuse.

Women, Feminism, and Judaism

This book is concerned with three under-told stories: That of contemporary Jewish lifecycle, that of Jewish women, and that of the intersection of the two. It is quite common to discuss "women and Judaism," as if they were entirely separate entities.[4] In the words of the Rabbis,"*nashim am bifnei atzman hen*" (women are a nation unto themselves [BT *Shabbat* 62a]).

One essential goal of feminist Jews is to foster environments where love of the People Israel and of Woman can both flourish. Being asked to give up one or the other half of this dual birthright, is, as Rabbi Laura Geller remarks in these pages, like having to choose between your heart and your liver.

Feminist Perspectives In large measure, feminism inspired the creation of this book, and informs its essays. As we ponder the classic question—is it (in this case, feminism) good or bad for the Jews?—we have to remember that half the Jews are women. Feminism benefits both halves of the Jewish population—and Judaism itself. Even as feminism addresses the lack of attention, opportunity, respect, and education that Jewish women have suffered, it also calls our attention to a lack in the tradition. When women's concerns are omitted or excluded, our understanding of Judaism is skewed and incomplete. The equation of "Jew" with "Jewish male" can cause simple factual errors in historiography ("elementary Jewish education in the Talmudic period was universalized"), lifecycle studies ("the covenant is sealed in the flesh of every Jew"), and other areas. Beyond individual mistakes, it also leads to a fundamental corruption of the disciplines and of our thinking.[5]

By the same token, when women's participation, scholarship, and leadership are embraced, the tradition is enhanced. Feminists and feminist methods can generate alternative readings of classical texts (as in Rabbi Sheila Peltz Weinberg's essay on midlife), and develop aspects of the tradition which have languished (as in Rabbi Einat Ramon's essay on marriage). Thus, to my mind, strengthening Judaism and embracing feminism are complementary goals. Full inclusion of women makes Judaism bigger, not smaller; more true, not less.

Women's Perspectives It is now largely accepted that men and women generally have different perspectives—probably mostly, if not entirely, due to differences in conditioning and socialization—and that there is much to learn by taking account of *both* vantage points. Women's perspectives are not necessarily identical with feminist perspectives; obviously, there are non-feminist women and feminist men. Feminist theorists have generally argued not for eliminating or ignoring gender differences, but for valuing traditional female styles, as well as traditional male styles, and for allowing individual choice, rather than dividing roles, responsibilities, or feminist identity, along gender lines.

Because normative Jewish perspectives are often equated with male perspectives and vice versa, it can be difficult for women to find a point of entry into the Jewish cultural conversation. This book provides a still rare forum for the perspectives of Jewish women and an opportunity to hear directly their needs, rituals, prayers, and dreams. Allowing women simply to collect their thoughts, as they literally do in these pages, constitutes a necessary step which we are often tempted to skip in our rush to resolve problems, set policy, and even apply feminist hermenutics and principles. (Ironically, however, inviting women's expressions without demanding that they speak in a feminist idiom fulfills the feminist principles of inclusivity and the valuation of personal story and perspective.) In short, the recent information explosion on Jewish women and the rapid changes in our roles need to be digested, and responded to. This means setting aside time and creating occasions for women to name their experience.

There are two male contributors in this volume, and each is part of a husband-and-wife-team. Rick E. F. Dinitz and Dr. Lawrence Baron comment, respectively, on childbirth and adoption following infertility—intimate areas, where couples experience "the same thing," and yet have profoundly different biological—and, often, psychological and spiritual—experiences. When being male is taken to be part of the natural Jewish order, men are deprived of dealing with issues of Jewish masculinity. By marginalizing women, we have created the illusion that only Jewish women—and not men—have a gender. Every subject treated in this book would benefit from men's perspectives and responses, and contributors do touch on men's issues in relation to such passages as childbirth, adopting a child, circumcision, and intermarriage. However, this is a book of women's expressions.

Access and Influence in Feminist Judaism The relationship between feminism and Judaism has evolved significantly over the last two decades, amidst the remarkable developments in Jewish women's studies, practices, and roles. In every arena of change—from synagogue life and liturgy to communal leadership, from Jewish feminist scholarship to lifecycle rituals and Jewish family life—there are two essential issues: Access and influence. Access means wanting "in"—to rabbinical school, to positions of leadership in Federation, to the mysterious world of Talmud study, to *minyanim* (prayer quorums) and ritual life generally. Influence means informing, critiquing, and helping to shape those very institutions to which we have sought access. Once women are admitted to rabbinical school the question "Can I become a rabbi?" may be replaced by "What should male and female students study—and are women represented in the curriculum?" As women begin to achieve high positions in the Federation hierarchy, they ask not only "Where are the women?" but also "Does this sort of graded hierarchy foster the kind of communication and leadership that we want?" Once girls and women are allowed to study Talmud, they ask new questions, applying feminist interpretive methods to Rabbinic texts and Rabbinic principles and insights to women's concerns. Many women who have gained equal status in their praying communities come to advocate sensitivity to gendered-language in the liturgy of those communities.

Access and influence are not neatly separable stages. It is obviously possible to struggle with God-language whether or not one prays in an egalitarian *minyan*. The fact that women are ordained as rabbis in the Conservative movement, but not accepted as witnesses by all camps in that movement, demonstrates the complexity and the long-term relevance of access issues. Yet, for both strategic and psychological reasons, we typically deal first with issues of parity and access as they relate to a particular topic, and only later move on to explore questions of influence. As questions of access are resolved, still greater attention is likely to be paid to questions of communal structure and priorities, and of deep psychic change in relation to sex-role fantasies, expectations, and stereotypes.

Feminist scholars of higher education use the ironic term "add women and stir" to characterize an unnamed, but widely used "recipe" for women's full inclusion and participation in various endeavors. Many assume that "adding" women to Judaism will do nothing to change the dish that has been cooking on the stovetop these last few-thousand years. Such an assumption implicitly asks women to gain access, but not influence, and to replicate and validate *in toto* the male perspectives that have shaped Jewish institutional life. These demands not only require women to deny a part of themselves, they also compromise the tradition, and cut it off from legitimate, potentially enriching influences.

In the stage of access, the primary goal is for women to achieve that which Judaism has valued—including Torah learning, ritual skills, and religious leadership. In the stage of influence the primary goal becomes to value that which Jewish women have achieved and can contribute—including authoring personal prayers, conceiving and perpetuating folk customs, and providing new readings of sacred texts. Initially, we ask "What does Judaism have to say about women?" and we search for clues in legal, literary, and historical texts. Increasingly, we also ask, "What do women have to say about Judaism?" Thus, women have come to comment on and influence not just "women's issues in Judaism" narrowly defined, but the whole of Jewish life. Certainly, the women writing in this book address a wide gamut of concerns, including issues of influence as well as access.

With the increasing prominence of influence questions, we are interested not just in Jewish women and men adopting a pro-woman stance, but in the tradition itself incorporating that stance and being transformed by it.[6] In that pursuit, we open ourselves to unforeseen and unforeseeable possibilities. Moreover, the resolution of influence questions is both less predictable and less absolute than that of access questions—which in the end must be decided one way or another. It is hard to anticipate how women's words—in one sense, nearly fifty percent new input—might change the tone and terms of Jewish dialogue. It is not unreasonable to be excited—or afraid.

Rabbi Neil Gillman, when once accused of espousing "dangerous ideas," assured his critics, "I am not strong enough to topple Judaism." The phrase charms me, and easily applies to Jewish women and feminists who have been accused of endangering the tradition by exploring questions of influence. It is clear we cannot topple Judaism. We may, though, by asking the right questions, be able to help sustain and renew it.

The Historical Moment

It is difficult to conceive of this book being written even as recently as ten years ago. Its orientation and content depend significantly on questions of influence that have been raised in the last decade and on the developments in Jewish women's studies. Ten years ago, Jewish women were not ready to undertake a comprehensive and collaborative treatment of the entire personal and communal lifecycle, as the *Lifecycles* series attempts to do. We were still examining individual pieces of the puzzle, still learning to own all parts of the lifecycle as our own. A decade ago, feminist Jews spent more of our energy on questions of access, contending with women's political and religious exclusion, and responding to critics. Because of the gains made, the contributors to this book have the luxury of focusing on women's spiritual concerns, relatively undistracted by the need to react to something or someone else.

Because of the historical moment in which *Lifecycles 1* was conceived and written, it functions as both a secondary and a primary source. As a secondary source, it is a resource for readers to use in exploring the cycle of Jewish and human life. A woman who has suffered a miscarriage, a man going through marital separation, a gentile with an interest in Jewish cosmology, a Jew who is studying mourning rituals—all will find practical and theoretical treatments of their areas of concern in these pages. As a primary source, *Lifecycles* provides insight into the concerns, compromises, convictions, and transitions of the early generations of Jewish feminists. It supplies raw data toward answering the question, "What do and will women do differently?" I am often asked this specifically in relation to women rabbis. Women in the rabbinate are a group we have all heard a great deal about, and relatively little *from*. This book is a partial corrective to that. It includes eighteen rabbis—five Reconstructionist, five Reform, seven Conservative, and one with private ordination—along with leaders in the Orthodox movement.

Diversity and Common Themes

As the above statistic shows, this book is trans-denominational. In a single chapter, a Reform rabbi chooses an Orthodox divorce, and an Orthodox leader responds to the divorce practices of her movement in a fashion that should shake its rabbinic establishment to the very core.

Contributors are diverse not only in terms of movement affiliation, but also in terms of profession, experience, sexual orientation, and approaches to Jewish and women's issues. Age ranges from fourteen to seventy-something. While most contributors are upper middle class Americans, one Israeli, one Canadian, and several Jews from lower-class backgrounds are included. Sources cited by the authors range from the Babylonian Talmud to Germaine Greer. Contributors create poetry, personal essays and narratives, rituals, prayers, blessings, bibliographic summaries, interpretations of Jewish texts and philosophy, social analyses, and guided visualizations.

On the subject of diversity, Bernice Johnson Reagon of the singing group "Sweet Honey in the Rock" has said, "If you're in a coalition and you're comfortable, you know it's not a broad enough coalition."[7] Many of the contributors were uncomfortable with each other's ideas, and this book does not present a neat and uniform set of conclusions. Rather, it reflects the variety of women's perspectives and concerns—some of which may cause discomfort.

For all the diversity, there is a unity of purpose: The validation and incorporation of women's experience in the Jewish enterprise, and the validation and revitalization of the Jewish enterprise on the basis of its spiritual relevance to the lives of *all* Jews. A number of themes repeat and reverberate throughout the book. Authors report a sense of shame or of being criticized for who they are— whether single, intermarried, childless, lesbian—and reclaim their identities with new attitudes and new rituals. Jewish women "come out" and declare themselves not only as lesbians, but as survivors of abuse, as Jews by choice, as feminists. (Several contributors mention abuse and recovery from victimization as essential components in women's life journeys.) Contributors name and validate multiple roles and aspects of Jewish women's identity. At the same time, they face the reality that women must often decide whether, when, and to whom to reveal their fullest identity, and must judge their own safety in doing so.

In addition to coming out, becoming is also a theme. Women do not all at once come of age, come of *old* age, come to terms with an abortion, choose Judaism, release their children to independence, or mourn a loved one. The essays dealing with these and other issues reflect the cyclical aspect of lifecycle—the opportunities life offers to visit and revisit important passages and themes, and thus to be constantly in the process of learning and becoming.

Another shared concern is community. Contributors stress the importance of creating community, of being acknowledged and honored in community, of fostering communal and family structures that support women. Perhaps the dominant theme is a need and determination to be seen and heard, to communicate our experience and put women's concerns on the communal agenda. This applies to everything from gender issues in marriage law, to the religious acknowledgement of weaning children, to Jewish women's issues in midlife. Finally, the authors share an excitement about being a Jewish woman in this time of transition. Their essays consider not only women's challenges, but their contributions, opportunities, and internal resources, as well.

A Note on Translation, Transliteration, Foreign Terms, and Abbreviations

The translations in *Lifecycles* are those of the authors unless otherwise indicated. Where translations are more than creative, and actually adapt the original, this is indicated by the word "after," as in "after Psalm 150:1." In order to remain accessible to readers of all backgrounds, it is the policy of Jewish Lights to translate a foreign term the first time it appears in any given chapter. Readers can find definitions of commonly used terms in the glossary, as well.

The transliteration system is intended to meet the needs of scholars, while serving as a pronunciation guide for those who do not read Hebrew, Yiddish, and/or Aramaic. The system is similar to one used in the *Encyclopedia Judaica*, and entails the use of *e* to represent *sheva na*, *ḥ* to represent *ḥet*, *kh* to represent *khaf*, *i* to represent a *ḥirik*, *u* to represent a *shuruk* and *kubbutz*, *e* to represent *tzereh* and *segol*, *ei* to represent a *tzereh* followed by a *yud*, *a* to represent *patah* and *kamatz*, and *ai* to represent *patah* or *kamatz* followed by a *yud*. No distinction is made between *alef* and *ayin*, but apostrophes are used to separate the two consecutive English vowels that appear when an *alef* or *ayin* is in use (e.g., *da'at*). Apostrophes are used to separate vowels in the English even in the case of a *patah ganuv*, as in *shome'a* or *shavu'a*. Letters are doubled in the case of a *dagesh hazak*, except when a prefix or article or the letter *shin* is used. The system differs from that used in the *Encyclopedia Judaica* in three main ways: the letter *tzadik* is represented by *tz* rather than *z*; there are no hyphens between prefixes or articles and words; the letter *h* is added to words that end in *he* and take an "ah" sound, as well as to words that end in an "eh" sound, whether the final letter is *he* or *alef*.

Several exceptions to the transliteration system are made for words that have common spellings: the reader will see *brit* and not *berit*, *mazal tov* and not *mazzal tov*, *bnei mitzvah* and not *benei mitzvah*. When foreign words are anglicized, they do not appear in italics (e.g., davening or halakhic).

BT refers to the Babylonian Talmud, and JT to the Jerusalem Talmud.

Finally, Rabbis refers to the Talmudic sages (sometimes called the ancient Rabbis), while rabbis (lower case) refers to religious leaders from subsequent generations.

1

Beginnings

The vast majority of Jewish lifecycle classifications begin with circumcision. It seems odd, even absurd, yet it is standard. Fifteen or twenty years ago, many Jews began to include some form of welcoming a baby girl into her name and the Jewish covenant as part of life's beginning. Only recently have we begun to distinguish that life begins as early as birth.

The failure to take ritual notice of childbirth seems especially incongruous, given the traditional Jewish emphasis on family, procreation, teaching the next generation, and national/religious continuity. Yet the neglect itself stems from two traditional sources. First, Jewish law is quite cautious on the subject of birth, being keenly sensitive to the potential for both mother's and baby's undoing. In some traditional Sephardic communities and among all non-Orthodox Jews, women *bentsh gomel* (recite a prayer of

thanksgiving for coming through danger in safety) after giving
birth.[1] According to popular custom—both Ashkenazic and
Sephardic—the names of baby boys are not uttered publicly until
their circumcisions, nor are any supplies for Jewish babies bought
until after their birth. Most tellingly, a baby under thirty days old
who dies is not mourned as a "full person" under traditional
Jewish law. (This has sometimes led to a sense of isolation on the
part of the bereaved parents and siblings—a subject taken up in
the next chapter.)

A second cause for the neglect of childbirth is more basic, and
relates directly to the calling of this book: Childbirth is women's
domain. Not only that, it is women's domain at its most mysterious, powerful, and frightening. During childbirth, life or death—
and maybe both—will be given by God and seemingly by Woman,
as well.

Dr. Lori Hope Lefkovitz attributes the paucity of childbirth
observances in common Jewish practice, in large measure, to the
Rabbis' ambivalence toward women, women's power, and childbirth. She uncovers prayers and rites that have fallen into disuse,
recovers and feminizes biblical images of creation, and chronicles
contemporary attempts to fill the liturgical gap. Through her
review and explanations of the literature, Dr. Lefkovitz enables the
reader to make appropriate use of available resources. She also
names patterns and categories in the literature and offers her own
innovations, such as the possibility of building childbirth ceremonies around laughter, or the idea of sacralizing screams.

Thus, Dr. Lefkovitz clears the way for the introduction of
entirely new material, which can now be understood in context.
Following her essay is a compendium of never-before-published-
work by ten authors, arranged according to the chronological
stages of the pregnancy and birth process.

Rick E.F. Dinitz and Tina D. Fein Dinitz present the blessings
they created to be recited upon learning the results of a pregnancy
test. Dr. Chava Weissler, an ethnologist and expert on Jewish
women's petitionary prayers, provides original translations for
two such prayers related to pregnancy and childbirth. Dr. Tikva
Frymer-Kensky, a biblical scholar and Assyriologist, draws on
Rabbinic and other ancient texts in crafting liturgical poetry
around birth. I have culled selections from Psalms to create a

prayer for parents of children born with disabilities. Poets Carol V. Davis and Merle Feld provide snapshots of birth, as it is remembered, marked, and perceived after the fact. Davis' poem explores the traditional postpartum immersion in a ritual bath. Both poems highlight how much being born *and* giving birth can connect us to our mothers.

Most of the authors feature mothers more prominently than fathers, partly because of women's dominant biological role and partly because the opportunity to reflect on women's experience of childbirth is so new. The work of naming it, much less integrating it fully with male experience, has only just begun.

The chapter concludes with a section on adoption, which may take place at the time of birth, or later, but always constitutes a happy beginning. Bonnie Ellen Baron and Dr. Lawrence Baron describe their odyssey from fertility treatments to the acceptance of their infertility and ultimately to the adoption of their son. They also outline some of the major issues associated with Jewish adoption. Rabbi Sandy Eisenberg Sasso provides a prayer for adoptive parents, which could be recited when they first bring their child home, or during a circumcision or naming ceremony.

Writings on birth and adoption necessarily focus on the parents' point of view, rather than the baby's. But the book begins here because childbirth was the beginning of life on earth for each of us. Moreover, the baby's experience is contemplated and valued throughout the chapter, e.g. in prayers that request the baby's welfare and *"kashrut"* (kosher laws; fitness; in this case, moral fitness). Babies are the focus, as well, when Dr. Lefkovitz and Feld "remember" their own births in the stories their mothers used to tell. Giving birth is a life passage that only some women will experience. But being born—the imprinting of our birth experience and, equally important, the *story* of our birth—is a passage we all, literally, traverse.

Obviously, birth is the critical experience upon which every other passage depends. And arguably, every subsequent passage re-enacts the original in a sequence of familiarity and stability (symbolically being in the womb), followed by tearing away from stability and travelling through a transition (symbolically traversing the birth canal), followed, in turn, by a reconstitution and rebirth of the self (symbolically emerging into the world). With these stages in mind, birth—and subsequent passages—can be seen as a tearing away from mother *and* a grasping toward the world, a leaving behind of all Torah wisdom (known, according to lore, *in toto* before birth) *and* an entering into an orchard of learning and lessons.

If the writings in this chapter are any indication, we are, at long last, on our way toward assigning birth its due.

Sacred Screaming:
Childbirth in Judaism

LORI HOPE LEFKOVITZ[2]

*"...Convert, O God! my pain into delight at the lovely sight of a
living, well-formed and healthful babe...."*

—FANNY NEUDA, UNTITLED PERSONAL PRAYER,
PUBLISHED 1878

When Debra Orenstein first called to invite me to contribute an
essay on "Childbirth in Judaism," she did not find me at home: I
was, as it happens, in the throes of childbirth. It was a mixed
omen: Though I had the recent experience of childbirth, Judaism
was not officially present at the occasion. I was struck by the irony
of Judaism's absence from one of the only occasions that I would
dignify with the language of religious experience: "Awesome,"
"transformative," "at once terrible and wonderful," and "miraculous." The expression "religious experience" does not do much for
me, but more than anything else in my life the births of my daughters, Ronya six years ago, and Samara, a year ago, invite this designation. I have privately treated these occasions in what might be
considered religious ways: I return in my imagination to the births
of my children regularly, as one returns to a mantra, recalling the
initial pangs, the feelings of anxiety and anticipation, the long car
rides to the hospital on country roads, the specific ways my
spouse supported me, details and more details to the emergence
of the baby herself, and then the phone calls, the order in which I
made them, the words said.

Through tireless mental review, I retain the memory—to pass
these stories on to my children as my birth story was passed on to
me. Also, these commemorations calm and uplift me. They are a
private version of public rituals of remembrance like the Passover
seder (ordered readings and meal) or *Yizkor* (memorial service) that
offer both comfort and inspiration. Although pregnancy and labor
happen routinely and require less deliberate effort than some
other tasks (such as writing assignments), giving birth felt like a

---

Dr. Lori Hope Lefkovitz, associate professor of English at Kenyon College, teaches and writes about fiction, critical theory, and Jewish feminism.

personal triumph ("I did this!?!"), as unique as the babies themselves. Yet for all this religious language, there was nothing
markedly Jewish in my response, not so much as a *Sheheheyanu*
(blessing for reaching a new or momentous occasion) to acknowledge the newness of it all.

I take my Judaism seriously enough to honor ritual observances and time-honored practices, such as those prescribed by
the dietary laws; seriously enough to be interested in liturgical
innovation, contemporary invention of *midrash* (Rabbinic genre of
lore often based on biblical texts), and other strategies of engagement with the tradition which enable women to reclaim a classically patriarchal heritage. Judaism's unselfconscious absence at
the births of my daughters was, therefore, remarkable.

Judaism made its appearance in Ronya's life first with her
Simhat Bat (girl's naming ceremony; literally, the joy of a daughter), a welcoming ceremony that my spouse and I composed for
her with much care. When Samara was born, we invoked Judaism
earlier in the newborn's life, with Rabbi Sandy Eisenberg Sasso's
prayers for homecoming; Ronya recited the sibling prayer, and my
spouse and I said prayers for our expanded family.[3] But we recited
no Hebrew to acknowledge conception, or at the onset of labor, or
in the delivery room. For the event of childbirth itself we knew no
legal, ritual, or liturgical mandate, and we did not think to discover or invent one. With the assignment of this essay I wondered
how it is that someone with my Jewish commitments, married to a
rabbi, and dedicated to feminist innovation in Judaism could have
neglected to sanctify Jewishly my most sacred events.

My own neglect is consistent with a historical neglect of childbirth both in institutionalized Judaism and in Jewish writing. This
negligence is not due to an absence of customs and sources, but
rather to their underutilization and, in some cases, to their having
been forgotten. One explanation for the neglect can be found in
the overall treatment of women and women's bodies in Judaism
and another in the nature and history of childbirth itself.

Childbirth: Noticeably Absent, Conspicuously Central

Historically, responses to childbirth are characterized by ambivalence—terror of death beside holy awe in the hope for new life.
Women's prayers, such as the *tkhine* (petitionary prayer for

and/or by women, traditionally written in Yiddish), from which my epigraph was taken, capture this ambivalence. Neuda begins her prayer in awe and then begs pardon and confesses her dread and anxiety. She pleads for courage and makes the poignant request that the life of her child not be her own death. "Mercy" is the poet's ultimate plea.[4] In general, *tkhines* characterize childbirth as curse and blessing, and they represent women as both vulnerable and strong, their voices close to God's ear.

Childbirth is the subject of contradictions: That which is most distinctively female and most in the image of the divine (the power to create life) is represented biblically as God's curse to Eve and to the generations of women. The curse functions in marked tension with childbirth represented as blessing: The command to be fruitful and multiply (the first biblical commandment) and the fervent prayers of the matriarchs and the other "barren" mothers of biblical heroes. At the same time, levitical purity laws identify the postpartum mother as impure (Leviticus 12:1-8), and most sources from the Rabbinic through the medieval periods focus on purity questions, with special anxiety about how to respond to the death of the mother. (We learn that she must be buried in her bloody clothes.)

When I raised the question of childbirth's low profile in Judaism with my father-in-law, whose training was from a classical Lithuanian *yeshivah* (traditional academy of Jewish learning), he suggested that once the powerful system of purity laws kicked in, it would have interfered with imagining the childbearing woman as anything other than a vessel of impurity. I argued: Judaism has codified rules, rituals, and blessings for everything; we have a blessing to recite if we see a rainbow. Surely something should be muttered in awe, thanksgiving, or petition if you are present to see a human head emerging from a vaginal opening. He reminded me that the Rabbinic prohibition against looking at "that place" would have precluded any blessing.

This attitude towards female sexuality and the categories of classical Judaism may have obscured the female religious expressions that are available to us in our textual tradition. When we avoid dependence on patriarchal models of liturgy and ritual and that which has the force of law, we can begin to hear women's voices: Sarah's laughter when informed of her pregnancy, Hannah's apparently drunken muttering as she prayed for a child, the screams of our grandmothers as they pushed our parents into the world. We can find powerful Jewish images and symbols in such things as breast milk, menstrual blood, and amniotic fluids. We can thus discover alternative categories and images both for reviewing the traditional place of childbirth in Judaism and for investing childbirth with sanctity in the present.

The process of developing Jewish responses to childbirth facilitates the perception of its already pervasive presence. For example, laws govern procreation, intercourse, and postpartum behavior; stories in Bible and *midrash* connect childbearing, women, and God; the liturgy around childbirth includes *berakhot* (blessings)—ancient and modern—a rich tradition of *tkhines* and psalms recited before and after birth. In addition, there are folk traditions and rituals—again, both ancient and modern. The work of recovering, reinventing, and instituting appropriate Jewish responses to childbirth has begun in earnest, significantly in middle-class America in the 1990s, as fathers now regularly enter the delivery room and as childbirth has become safer than ever before.

"Adding childbirth to Judaism" means adding it for Jewish men, as well as Jewish women. For example, once childbirth is reclaimed as a Jewish event and theme, *Rosh Hashanah* (New Year), the birthday of the world, can serve as an invitation to reimagine God as a laboring mother. The metaphor can be sustained: God's creative strategy—a classification system that makes meaning by separating this from that—is also like human birth, a process of separations. Developing the analogy of divine creation to birth, Orenstein has observed that individuated life begins with a physical tearing away of one body from another and that psychological health requires further successful acts of separation. She has also noted that a feminized version of the morning prayer *Barukh She'amar* ("Blessed is the One who spoke and the world came into being"), yields a line which can be translated "Blessed are You who has mercy on the earth" or "Blessed are You who wombs (i.e. whose water breaks) over the earth."

The tradition has resisted establishing an affinity between God's work and maternity, as God's labors have been masculinized. Sanitized by myth, the birth of the first human creature is a startlingly bloodless and painless event: God takes Adam from the earth (Genesis 2:7). Closer to subsequent human experience, and, at the same time, a reversal of it, woman is brought forth from man's body (Genesis 2:21-22). The birthing of life—in human experience an activity in the provenance of the female—is represented as the work of a male divinity and then seems to be given over to the man until another story intervenes to give childbirth to the future generations of women. Perhaps jealous of woman's procreative powers, patriarchal religion posits a creative male God and gives childbirth to women not as a gift, but as a curse.

Maternity and Blessing: Following Sarah, Our Mother

However powerful the curse in Eden (the focus on pain possibly standing as silent acknowledgment of the potential for death in childbirth), Genesis also represents maternity as the most important fact of woman's existence, *the* blessing for which she prays. Perhaps overcompensating for the fear of death in childbirth, biblical heroines often feel their lives are meaningless without children. Curse that childbirth may be, barrenness is worse, and pregnancy is devoutly wished for by all the "barren mothers" of Scriptures. The convention of the "barren mother" reasserts divine prerogatives over creation because when heroes, such as Isaac, Samson, and Samuel, are born to barren mothers, God necessarily and miraculously enters history.

The instance of Sarah, the first matriarch, may be the most dramatic. Sarah is old when she overhears that she will have a child, and she laughs enigmatically. In delight? ("Finally!"); terror? ("Can I do this?"); bitterness? ("So late in life"); cynicism? ("You are kidding"). Sarah's laughter may be the laughter of wonder, anger, nervousness, or some combination of the many emotions that laughter can express. God asks why Sarah laughed, and when Sarah fearfully denies having laughed, God—who evidently sees what we do, but like Freud after him, is at a loss for an interpretation when it comes to women's motivations—says, without apparent reproach, "But you did laugh."

Sarah's response rings with the laughter of women across times and places who may well have reacted to the news of a baby in their future with mirth, scorn, or as they say, "God knows what." I too laughed when I became aware of my pregnancies, and I walked around laughing inside for a long time. Whether one's pregnancy came easily or with difficulty, whether planned or not, it is surely among the moments in life (to those who are inclined to think in these terms) when one feels the other world impinging on this one, either miraculously or demonically. So Sarah laughs. She utters no blessing. She performs no ritual. We know that circumcision was the sign of God's covenant, and we even learn about the weaning celebration that Abraham held for Isaac, but the details of this first birth to the first matriarch and patriarch are omitted: When did Sarah go into labor? Did she scream? Did Abraham feed her ice chips? More realistically: How close did the aged mother come to death? Did she greet her baby with pleasure or depression? Did her milk come in easily? The text does not imagine any parental response at all: No prayer, no ritual of thanksgiving, nothing upon which future generations of parents can base a liturgical, ritual, or other Jewish response to childbirth.

Yet I imagine the possibility of using Sarah's laughter as part of new pregnancy rites. Sarah's laughter is central to our self-definition as a people. Sarah and Abraham name the child born of God's extraordinary promise *Yitzḥak* ("he will laugh"), not only in memory of laughter but with the promise of laughter to come. As such, we are all heirs to Sarah's laugh. This story allows me to imagine prayers with Sarah's laugh as a governing metaphor, and rituals that incorporate stylized and choreographed laughter. In response to this "imagining," Orenstein has written a brief prayer:

> As parents, we pray for our child's complete fulfillment. May s/he have all the blessings we have had and more; may s/he be blessed with gifts we have not yet imagined. As God laughed when the rabbis surpassed even divine expectation, may we, too, laugh delightedly and say, "My children have surpassed me. My children have surpassed me" (after BT *Baba Metzi'a* 59b).

Fruits—and Religious Acknowledgments—of the Womb: A Review of the Sources on Childbirth

Until very recently, few birth ceremonies were practiced. Susan Weidman Schneider, in her now classic book, *Jewish and Female*, writes with reference to giving birth that "there has been scant traditional ritual around the women in the picture—whether as mothers or daughters." She echoes Blu Greenberg's question: "Could it be that if men had been giving birth all these centuries, some fantastic ritual would have developed by now?"[5] Instead, Arlene Rossen Cardozo's *Jewish Family Celebrations* and Jacob Neusner's *The Enchantments of Judaism* are exemplary in that they identify themselves as comprehensive of the stages of Jewish life and begin describing life rituals not with fertility, conception, pregnancy, labor, or even birth itself.[6] These books and others like them begin with *Brit Milah* (covenant of circumcision ritual) and sometimes with the conferral of a name for a daughter. Given high rates of infant mortality, Judaism may have cautiously waited to celebrate birth at *Brit* when one could be more confident in the baby's viability.

Psalms and Blessings The mandate of the tradition around birth has been limited. Psalm 126 has long been associated with birth, likely due to the verse "Those who sow in tears will reap in joy" (Psalms 126:5). Psalm 118 which begins "Out of the narrow place I called upon God, who answered me in spaciousness" has been paraphrased in Yiddish and recast as a *tkhine* for childbirth. It tells of coming close to death, but not succumbing, and of trusting in God.[7] Brief blessings of thanksgiving at birth itself are increasingly usual in Orthodoxy: The birth of a son commands the blessing *Hatov Vehametiv* (naming God as good and doer of the good), and a daughter is greeted with the *Sheheheyanu* prayer, expressing gratitude for sustaining the lives of the parents to this moment. Postpartum, a mother, or her spouse on her behalf, *bentshes gomel* (recites the prayer of thanksgiving for coming through danger in safety) in the synagogue.

Traditions and Conception While the legal mandate is small, folk traditions have been sustained through the ages. Monthly ritual immersion can be understood as signifying readiness for motherhood. In addition, Jewish mystical tradition encourages lovemaking on Friday night, and considers a conception on the Sabbath particularly blessed, since *Shabbat* (Sabbath) is said to reunite the male and female aspects of God. From the fervent prayers of the barren mothers of Scriptures, until our own century, Jewish women have maintained traditions of petition to God for conception. Women hopeful of fertility have long invoked the names of Rachel and Hannah, the classic "barren mothers," and have wept beside Rachel's tomb in Israel.

Women's Prayers before the Enlightenment Recent years have seen the publication of women's prayers that focus on childbirth in its many stages: Prayers for conception, for each of the months, for the beginning of labor, for the stages of childbirth, and for the postpartum. Books such as Nina Beth Cardin's translation *Out of the Depths I Call to You* and Tracy Guren Klirs' collection *The Merit of Our Mothers* have again brought to light poetry and prayers which women shared for several centuries, but which fell into virtual darkness during the Enlightenment.[8] These prayers have provided source material for recent efforts of Jewish women to sanctify childbirth in ways authentic to both Judaism and women's history.

Chava Weissler, an expert on *tkhines*, observes that the male Rabbinic tradition "collapses all women into Eve" and makes much of the association between sin and childbirth. The *tkhines* that seem to be authored by women, in contrast, plead for the health and safety of mother and infant and address the question of suffering. As Weissler writes, attention is paid to "the physical discomfort, pain and danger women experience in menstruation and childbirth. The authors of the *tkhines* want to know why women suffer, not why they bleed."[9]

Contemporary Liturgy and Ritual *Tkhine* literature nourishes contemporary efforts to produce liturgy and rituals for childbirth. In *The New Jewish Baby Book*, Anita Diamant reprints Judy Shanks's beautiful *tkhine* written in a modern idiom. Shanks prays for the health of her child, the health of the world, and the ability to love and nurture.[10] Jane Litman's "*M'ugelet*: A Pregnancy Ritual" uses a cord that had been wrapped around Rachel's tomb. A group of women recite adapted *tkhines* and pass the pregnant woman around a circle, chanting personal blessings as she becomes entwined by the cord to which she may later cling while giving birth. This ceremony resonates with some older customs recorded by Douglas Weber and Jessica Brodsky Weber in the *Jewish Baby Handbook*; they write that a woman in difficult labor was sometimes given the keys of the synagogue to clutch or the cord that binds the Torah.[11] Along with Litman's ritual, Elizabeth Resnick Levine's *A Ceremonies Sampler* includes a Yemenite postpartum celebration, welcoming ceremonies for new babies, a weaning ceremony, and Sasso's personal prayers mentioned earlier.[12] Women have also borrowed images from the Jewish wedding in creating childbirth rituals. In *Reconstructionist*, Shoshanah Zonderman describes a ritual that she designed for twelve women on the last full moon of her pregnancy; it included a ceremony parallel to the wedding and a document parallel to the *ketubbah* (wedding contract). The women used symbols and fruits, breathing exercises and chanting, and they completed a Jewish mandala upon which the mother focused during labor and which now has a permanent place in the family home.[13] Dr. Tikva Frymer-Kensky has drawn on a variety of ancient traditions—Jewish and non-Jewish—in creating liturgical poems for pregnancy and childbirth.[14] Schneider in *Jewish and Female* includes Nechama Liss-Levenson's and her husband's simple ritual for conception: The couple marked their decision to stop using contraception by making *Kiddush* (blessing over wine on Sabbath or holidays) and reciting the *Sheva Berakhot* (seven marital blessings) to reestablish the traditional connection between marriage and childbirth, and to sanctify their choice to wait until they were ready to conceive.

Several women who have created new prayer and ritual shift focus from the birth of the baby to the birth of a "mother." Zonderman writes that she

> ...thought of her advancing pregnancy as a passage through a constricting tunnel to emergence with a revitalized, fuller identity as a Jewish mother—a birth image. This is also the metaphor of the Exodus from Egypt—*mitzrayim* (Egypt) being a narrow (*tzar*) place of oppression—when the Israelites passed through the (birthing) waters of the Red Sea to accept new ethico-religious obligations at Mt. Sinai. In becoming a mother, I was accepting new responsibilities and a commitment to the future of the Jewish people.[15]

The Trends in New Rituals

These new religious expressions of gratitude are particularly effective in their appropriation of feminine biblical metaphors. The exodus from Egypt through the parted Red Sea is the central moment in the drama of the Israelite past, and it remains the central metaphor for Jewish redemption. Only recently have we stressed that it is a birth metaphor, the passage of people into a new life of trials and triumphs through parted waters, after which nourishment in the form of manna is bestowed like mother's milk, various in its taste, and supply generated by demand. The practice of ritual immersion might be reimagined in analogous ways by invoking, for example, Miriam's well, the source of water for the Israelites in the desert. Amniotic waters can be seen as analogous to the *tohu vavohu* (hurly burly) out of which God labored in birthing the world. The bringing of first fruits to the Temple also finds a new vitality as a feminine image of birth *per se* when it is brought back to the experience of childbirth in new rituals and prayers.

New as these compositions are, they can be especially poignant when they speak with the force of tradition. For example, in many Jewish families, including my own, it is customary to add a candle to one's Sabbath candelabrum for each new family member. A *yartzeit* (anniversary of a death) candle is burned when a Jew dies and annually on the anniversary of a family member's death. A *ner neshamah* (soul candle) is often lit at *brit* and naming ceremonies. Recognizing the candle as a Jewish symbol for the soul, a group of contemporary women liturgists has suggested a rite of conception in which an unlit candle is introduced to the Sabbath candelabrum.[16] In the unfortunate event of a failed pregnancy, this candle would be ritually burned, like a *yartzeit* candle, as an act of mourning. An abortion is marked by submerging the lit candle in water. Under happier circumstances, on the first Sabbath following the birth of the baby, the unlit candle becomes a light among its companions and its place is permanently filled on the candelabrum. The pregnancy rite speaks in a Jewish idiom that extends itself and assimilates naturally into Jewish practice.

Reclaiming "The Body" of Tradition

Contemplating how childbirth can connect us to our foremothers
has reminded me of one of the few details that I know about my
paternal grandmother, who gave birth to eight children. My
father, who was second oldest, recalls that the older children were
made to leave the house when his mother delivered. Still, she
screamed loudly enough that the frightened boy could hear. I
screamed my heart out when Samara was born and hoped at that
moment that my grandmother's screaming may have been like
my own: Liberated, defiant of pain, awe-struck, thrilled. I have
come to think of my screams as my foremothers' and my
Judaism's presence in the delivery room. The work of naturalizing
and assimilating women's responses to childbirth is in progress.
And there is much work still to do—to honor the laughter of
Sarah, to sanctify the screams of our mothers, and to bequeath
powers of articulation to our daughters as they labor in the creation of worlds to come.

Prayers and Poems for Pregnancy, Childbirth, and "Afterbirth"

A Holy Moment—Pregnant or Not

RICK E.F. DINITZ AND TINA D. FEIN DINITZ

"Three partners create a child—the Holy One, the father and the mother."

—BT *NIDDAH* 31A

In another era we would have had to wait to be certain. But in our time an accurate and convenient home pregnancy test would confirm or disprove our suspicions in a matter of minutes. How would we mark the special holiness of that moment of certainty?

In July of 1992, we composed two blessings and prepared to recite the appropriate one upon learning the results of our pregnancy test.

For a negative test (no pregnancy), we would say:

בָּרוּךְ אַתָּה יי אֱלֹהֵינוּ מֶלֶךְ הָעוֹלָם, הַבּוֹחֵר בְּשָׁעָה טוֹבָה.

Barukh attah adonai eloheinu melekh ha'olam, haboher besha'ah tovah.

Blessed are You *Adonai* our God, Ruler of the universe, who chooses a good hour.

In traditional Jewish circles, one does not respond to news of an expected child with *"mazal tov"* (congratulations) which is the usual response when someone shares good news. One responds instead with *"besha'ah tovah"* ([may it happen] in a good hour),

---

Rick E. F. Dinitz is a writer, artist, lay cantor, and father. **Tina D. Fein Dinitz** is a landscape designer and a mother. Their son, Nathan Pardes Fein Dinitz, arrived just in time for Passover 5753 (Spring 1993).

expressing shared joy and good wishes, but also acknowledging the uncertainty inherent in childbirth.

We incorporated this phrase into our *berakhah* (blessing) for a negative test result to acknowledge that same uncertainty. The ultimate hour and conditions of childbirth are a mystery to us even when pregnancy is known. How much more so when even the time of conception lies in the future.

The blessing acknowledges that God chooses the right time for every child to enter the world, and that the time is apparently not yet right. We cannot know why—that is God's province. This *berakhah* would tacitly express our disappointment, and our hope that the right time would come soon.

Although we both were eager for a positive result, we wanted the blessing to reflect the fact that not everyone desires a positive result at any given time. The blessing for a negative result is worded to reflect feelings of relief as well as sadness or frustration. People who hope for a negative test result can use this *berakhah* to thank God for waiting until a good hour.

Still others are ambivalent about pregnancy. Perhaps they desire a child, but have trepidations about how their lives will change. Maybe they are unsure about having another child at this time. These same words speak to both their concerns and their hopes, and the thought that another hour might find them more confident of their own desires.

We could have recited the same *berakhah* for a positive test result. After all, at such a result we would rejoice that God had chosen this time for our good news, and we would look forward to the birth, hoping it, too, would come in a good hour. But instead we wrote a second *berakhah* to reflect the profound difference between "pregnant" and "not now pregnant." When we learn that we are *not* pregnant, we glimpse our future for another month; next month may bring other news, but for now we do not mentally prepare for childbirth and parenthood. In contrast, when we learn that we *are* pregnant, we glimpse our future for the next nine months, and slowly bring into focus the new patterns of our lives for the next twenty years and beyond. Perhaps we even imagine ourselves as grandparents, or dimly perceive the garland of generations stretching out into the future.

It is the same future that Abraham and Sarah saw—children

bearing and raising more Jewish children, keeping God's covenant generation after generation. So, for a positive test (confirming pregnancy), we would (and did) say:

בָּרוּךְ אַתָּה יי אֱלֹהֵינוּ מֶלֶךְ הָעוֹלָם, מְקַיֵּם אֶת הַבְּרִית.

Barukh attah adonai eloheinu melekh ha'olam, mekayyem et habrit.

Blessed are You *Adonai* our God, Ruler of the universe, who fulfills the covenant.

God's covenant with Abraham is to make his descendants (the Jewish people) exceedingly fruitful—as numerous as the stars in the sky, as plentiful as the sand. Each birth (and each pregnancy) is a partial fulfillment of that covenant. So our *berakhah* for learning of a positive test result explicitly praises God's continuing role in a perpetual covenant.

The language of covenant also emphasizes the value that Judaism places on children. It evokes generations past, as well as those to come, and the special relationship with God that we enjoy and pass on to our progeny. Covenant implies responsibility, and this *berakhah* reminds us that we, too, have a covenantal role to fulfill. The child to be born will depend on us as welcomers, nurturers, teachers and guides. God is entrusting a new child to our care, and we acknowledge our responsibility with appropriate awe, knowing that our strength to fulfill it also comes from God.

Tkhine 100 from *Seder Tkhines Uvakoshes*

Translated from the Yiddish and introduced by **CHAVA WEISSLER**

*"Send me the good angel to wait in the womb to bring the seed
before you, Almighty God, that you may pronounce: 'From this
seed will come forth a righteous man and a pious man, a fearer of
your Holy Name, who will keep your commandments and find
favor in your eyes and in the eyes of all people, and will study
Torah day and night....'"*

—*SEDER TKHINES UVAKOSHES, TKHINE 93*

Tkhines *are prayers in Yiddish written for and sometimes by women.
Books of* tkhines *in early modern Yiddish were published in Germany
and the Netherlands from the middle of the seventeenth until the end of
the eighteenth century. These books were anthologies of prayers to be said
on occasions of a woman's life, such as lighting Sabbath candles, visiting
the cemetery, confessing sins, blessing the New Moon, menstruation,
pregnancy, and childbirth. The early collections of* tkhines *were almost
all published anonymously, and we do not know for certain whether they
were written by women or men. In the mid-eighteenth century, in
Eastern Europe, older Yiddish anthologies were reprinted, and new*
tkhines, *often written by women, began to appear. These texts confined
themselves to a smaller range of subjects, preeminently the Days of Awe,
the Sabbath, and the blessing of the New Moon.*

With the decline of Yiddish, the tkhines *were largely forgotten.
These prayers are firmly rooted in the realities and the consciousness of
the seventeenth and eighteenth centuries, in many ways foreign to our
way of thinking. Nonetheless, we may find that they have the power to
surprise and move us.*

The tkhines *translated in this chapter are taken from* Seder
Tkhines Uvakoshes *(The Order of Supplications and Entreaties). This
comprehensive anthology, published anonymously in Fürth in 1762,
draws upon at least four earlier collections.*

A woman should say this *tkhine* evening and morning in the

Dr. Chava Weissler, Philip and Muriel Berman Professor of Jewish Civilization at
Lehigh University, writes about the religious lives of eighteenth century
Ashkenazic women.

prayer of the Eighteen Benedictions...from the time of her seventh month: My God and God of my fathers, have mercy upon all of the daughters of Israel who are giving birth, including your handmaiden _____ daughter of _____. Behold, I lay my supplication before you, O merciful and gracious One, for your mercies are all-merciful. And in your hand, O Lord, is the key of vitality, and it is not [given over] to the hand of a messenger. And so, remember your mercies and your lovingkindness, Lord our God, who desires...to visit mercy upon me. May I give birth with room to spare to healthy and kosher offspring, from the Holy Side. May there be fulfilled for me the verse, as it is written by King David, peace be upon him: "From out of the straits I called unto you [O Lord]; he answered me with great spaciousness. The Lord is on my side; I have no fear" (Psalms 118:5-6). The one who heard the prayer of [David] King of Israel will hear my prayer, and by the merit of my forefathers and foremothers, the one who [answered] our holy fathers [sic] Sarah, Rebecca, Rachel, and Leah and all the righteous and pious and proper women, He will answer me.

At a Caesarean

TIKVA FRYMER-KENSKY

"God took [us] out...with a mighty hand and
an outstretched arm...."

                                                    —DEUTERONOMY 4:15

Sometimes a woman cannot give birth without medical intervention, and a caesarean section may have to be performed. Many women are disappointed, fearing that technology has deprived them of a sacred birth. However, the caesarean is no less sacred than a vaginal birth, and the

---

Dr. Tikva Frymer-Kensky is the director of biblical studies at the Reconstructionist Rabbinical College and the author of *In the Wake of the Goddesses: Women, Culture and the Bibilical Transformation of Pagan Myth* (The Free Press, 1992) and the forthcoming *Motherprayer.*

divine Presence is as present in the hands of the surgeon as in the birth canal of the mother. The power of God resides in human hands and human minds.

> Some things,
> we are taught,
> You alone and only do:
> You brought Israel forth from the Land of Egypt
>> "not by means of an angel,
>> not by means of a seraph,
>> not by means of an agent."[17]
> You provide rain for Israel.
>> "not by an angel
>> and not by means of an agent"[18]
> In all other matters you have your workers,
>> "Moses received Torah from Sinai
>> not from the mouth of an angel
>> and not from the mouth of a Seraph
>> but from the mouth of the King of king over kings
>> the Holy One Blessed be He."
> But we, the people, received them from Moses,
> God's mediator, God's agent.[19]

> No child is created
> without a man and a woman.
> God, a man and a woman,
> three partners in the birth
> and sometimes also:
>> Wise women
>> doctors
>> nurses
>> midwives
>> angels
>> seraphs
>> and agents.

> There is much to be done
> to create a person.

Tkhine 103 from *Seder Tkhines Uvakoshes*

Translated from the Yiddish by **CHAVA WEISSLER**

"Yah is my strength and is become my salvation...I shall not die,
but live, and declare the works of Yah."

—PSALMS 118:14, 17

When she comes out of childbed, she says this: Lord of all the
world, You hear all the prayers of those who call upon You
wholeheartedly, and who fear You. Lord God, I thank You as a
Lord that you have caused me to escape from the great, bitter
pains of childbirth, and You give me milk to nourish the child,
and strength to arise today from the bed to return to the service of Your holy Name...Lord of all the worlds, accept my
speech and my prayer and my calling upon Your holy Name
from the bottom of my heart as if they were the [Temple] altar
and the offering. Protect me further from all evil, along with
all Israel who trust in You. Continue to give me strength, and
also to my husband, that we may be able to raise this child and
the other [children] easily according to the desire of our hearts.
And also give [us] your help that the child may serve Your
Name at all times with truth and with love. God our Lord,
may this come true in Your Name, Amen.

A Prayer for Parents of
Babies with Disabilities

DEBRA ORENSTEIN

"Even when we fall, we will not go headlong, because Adonai sup-
ports our strength. Adonai knows the lives of the innocent; their
portion lasts forever. Guard the innocent. Watch the upright, for
there is a future—and descendants—for the person of integrity."

—AFTER PSALMS 37:18,24,37

Rabbi Debra Orenstein, editor of *Lifecycles,* fellow of the Wilstein Institute of
Jewish Policy Studies, and instructor at the University of Judaism in Los Angeles,
regularly writes and speaks on Jewish spirituality and gender studies.

Our fantasy of birth is that all goes well, that giving or witnessing birth is a high and completely happy point in our lives, that mother and child emerge healthy and "perfect." For parents who have a child with disabilities, many of the standard phrases and cliches—the counting of toes and fingers, the wish for a future filled with Torah learning—ring hollow, or even sound cruel. Yet the exceptional child is created in God's image, and tradition teaches that God's hesed (steadfast love) for us has nothing to do with physical prowess or mental agility, and everything to do with the simple fact that we are.

The birth of an exceptional child affects each family—and each family member—differently. A family with predispositions to genetic disorders, one that has known of a problem early on in the pregnancy, or one that adopts a child with disabilities, will have had at least some time to consider their situation and process their emotions. Regardless of the circumstances, parents will probably feel shock, rage, protectiveness, love, tenderness and despair—variously directed toward themselves, their partner, the child, and God.

The following selections from the Book of Psalms evince sadness and struggle as well as hope and the beginning of acceptance. Psalms that may speak to the gamut of emotions associated with having an exceptional child include numbers 13, 37, 103, 115, 127, 130, 143 and 147.

I remember the days of old;
I meditate on all Your works;
I contemplate the work of Your hands.

I stretch out my hand to You: My soul thirsts after You, like a
thirsty land. Make haste and answer me, Lord. My spirit
faints.
Do not hide Your face from me, lest I be like those who go
down into the abyss.

Cause me to hear Your words of steadfast love in the morning,
for I have put my trust in you. Cause me to know the path I
should take, for I lift up my soul to You. Teach me to do
Your will, for You are my God.
Let your good spirit lead me to level land.

God is Healer of the brokenhearted, Binder of their wounds,
who counts the number of the stars, calling them all by
name.

God has not treated us according to our sins, nor requited us
   because of our iniquities. Rather, as the heavens stand high
   above the earth so God's love prevails over all. As far as east
   is from west, so far has God removed our transgressions
   from us.
As a father has mercy on his children, so does *Adonai* have
   compassion for us.

Praise God who covers the heavens with clouds, prepares rain
   for the earth, makes grass grow on the mountains. God
   gives food to the beast, and to the young ravens that cry.

It is not the strength of a horse that God delights in, nor the
   swiftness of a person's legs that the Lord desires. *Adonai*
   desires those who revere God, those who hope in God's
   steadfast love.

   —*after Psalms 103:10-13; 143:5-8, 10; 147:2-11*

The Waters[20]

CAROL V. DAVIS

Traditional Jewish law dictates that a woman immerse in the mikveh
*(ritual bath) after childbirth in order to regain a ritually pure status,
after the bloody experience of birth.*[21]

   Nine months she was cushioned in the waters
   and then the floodgates open
   and the rush of birth.
   Now, weeks later, I am compelled
   to visit the *mikveh*.
   Descending the four precise steps
   to immersion, my feet sink
   onto tiles concentrated as the waves
   which lap at the Haifa shore.

   ———————————

Carol V. Davis is a widely published poet and the author of a chapbook, *Letters
from Prague* (Paper Bag Press, 1991).

What compels me to this act,
so bewildering to my husband?
Not just the commandment, but
the submersion and the chant of prayers.
To have a daughter:
This link to my grandmother
and hers, who, on some Petersburg sidestreet,
entered a secret door and also walked
down four steps into the waters.
As now, crying, I see my doctor
for the final visit. It's not, as she says,
that we've been floating side by side
on icebergs for nine months and then I move on
and wave to her, as I shield my daughter
from the glare of sun on snow.

I remember a Ḥasidic tale of the Holocaust.
A rabbi was told to jump over an open pit.
If he made it, his life would be given to him.
Later he was asked by a nonbeliever,
How did you do it?
I was holding on to my ancestral merit, he said.
Holding on to the coattails of my father, and my
grandfather, and his father, of blessed memory.

As now, I place my daughter beside me and
descend alone the stairs to immersion.
And I see my mother, young and healthy, not
as in her last years, with eyes turned
inward by illness and full of ambivalence
towards this ritual of her heritage.
Her tenderness washes over me
as I immerse three times, saying the blessing.
And as I rise, it merges with the voice
of my doctor and the murmurs of my infant,
filling this room, seeping through the crevices,
drifting slowly up and up.

Happy Birthday Merle[22]

MERLE FELD

October, late afternoon
soft FM music on the kitchen radio
feeding the baby supper
feeling warm, peaceful, complete
cards and phone calls
everyone's checked in—
Happy Birthday Merle!
and yet

Strange, not to talk
to my mother on my birthday
she who created all birthdays
small, bustling, ruddy
always running
I remembered her running

Running to buy me a watch
for my sweet sixteen
(after work, after groceries
before laundry)
she tripped and fell
down the stairs to the IRT
required several stitches
just above her eyebrow
she bore the scar ever after
long after the watch
thrilled me, marked time for me
joined the other broken watches
in my drawer

Merle Feld is an award-winning playwright, a poet, a political activist, and a
long-time Jewish feminist.

Faint surprise
an awareness in my stomach
it's been seven years already
what would I tell her
if I could?
what she always hoped to hear
I'm happy, Ma. Finally.
Really happy with my life.

Once on my birthday
I sent her a dozen roses
I got the idea from a Dear Abby
but I never told her that—
she was already dying
And actually,
the last time we talked
the night she slipped into a coma
I sat on her bed
and she told me about
the morning I was born:

It was such a beautiful autumn day, crisp, clear,
the leaves turning, brisk morning chill.
I called Dr. Rubenstein—he lived across the street—
and I said, "I'm in labor, I'll be walking over to the
hospital now." He was so upset. He just wouldn't have
it—he insisted on driving me. I was sorry really.
It was such a beautiful morning, and I love to walk.

Happy Birthday Merle.

On Adoption

A Jewish Adoption

BONNIE ELLEN BARON AND LAWRENCE BARON

*"Positive talk about adoption emerges from feeling good about it,
from feeling that your baby came into your life as a matter of
much-welcomed destiny."*
                    —MARI MENNEL-BELL, "TALKING ABOUT ADOPTION"

We were both thirty-nine years old and had been married for seventeen years before we tried to have a baby. Like so many professional couples, we had put our careers ahead of building a family, confident that we could do the latter whenever we chose. Unfortunately, we had not consulted our bodies. After a brief pregnancy which ended in a miscarriage, we encountered the monthly cycle of hope and disappointment which is the lot of most people undergoing infertility treatment. The emotional wounds inflicted in this process, especially on the woman, are compounded by the hormonal shifts produced by infertility drugs and the loss of control in the most intimate area of one's life. After four years, our aging reproductive systems convinced us that it was time to end our quest for having a biological child. Despite the development of new medical technologies which may have helped us, we refused to continue to endure the psychological, physical, and financial burdens that accompany such treatments for infertility.

Bonnie Ellen Baron, LCSW, conducts adoption home studies and supervises adoption placements in San Diego for Vista Del Mar Child and Family Services of Los Angeles.
Dr. Lawrence Baron is the director of the Lipinsky Institute for Judaic Studies and the Nasatir professor of modern Jewish history at San Diego State University.

Releasing Old Dreams

Before we could move ahead and decide between being childfree or becoming parents through adoption, we needed to bury our dream of ever having a biological child. In our eyes, not doing so would have been tantamount to not acknowledging the death of a loved one. Moreover, we worried that if we pursued adoption without mourning the loss we had experienced, then we might project the traits of our fantasized biological child onto our adopted one. It is difficult enough to grow up to be yourself, let alone someone else!

We searched for relevant Jewish customs and prayers to help ease our pain and assist us in making this transition. Since so much of Jewish communal life takes having children for granted, traditional Judaism provides little guidance to comfort those who have not been blessed with their own offspring.

Thus, we decided to write our own ceremony. For three consecutive days, we cloistered ourselves in our home, seeking relevant passages from the Bible, prayerbooks, and books on infertility. We drew upon traditional and new Jewish prayers, rituals, and stories that deal with the themes of barrenness and procreation, death and life, bondage and liberation, despair and hope, and the inevitable transitions that lead from one to another. The intensity of "creating" this ritual together provided us with a catharsis more healing than we ever expected. We titled our ceremony "Seder Kabbalat Akrut" meaning the order of the acceptance of infertility. Through prayer and ritual, we cried out against, consoled ourselves about, and ultimately accepted the finality of our infertility.

On a warm California day, we gathered with relatives and friends for an oceanside ceremony. We began by quoting Rachel's anguished cry to Jacob: "Give me children or I shall die" (Genesis 30:1). We spoke about how difficult it was to end infertility treatment in light of constantly emerging high-tech procedures and the lingering possibility that conception might occur the next month. Consequently, we sought to symbolize physically that we were releasing all hopes of a biological child. To do this, we borrowed from the *tashlikh* (casting out) ceremony and cast our qualms and dim hopes in the form of breadcrumbs into the ocean, just as one casts breadcrumbs, representing sins, into water at the Jewish New Year. The connection with *Rosh Hashanah* (New Year) also augured the promise of a new beginning following an unhappy ending.

To us, the most significant portion of our service entailed enumerating the "Ten Plagues" of infertility which had oppressed our spirits during our years of trying to have a baby: Denial initially about having an infertility problem; anger over the injustice of infertility; shame about our inability to procreate like a "normal" couple; marital stress caused by infertility; isolation from friends and relatives with children; reproductive regimentation required for medical treatment; uncompensated medical costs since infertility treatment is viewed as an elective procedure by most insurance companies; depression brought on by fertility drugs and the situation; loss of control in being forced to place all your plans "on hold"; death of the dream of the first born. Following the custom practiced at the Passover *seder* (ordered readings and meal), as each plague was named, we each took a drop of wine out of our cup.

To demarcate the transition from our dark years of infertility to the lighter years of either becoming parents through adoption or choosing to be childfree, we recited the *Sheheheyanu* (blessing for reaching a new or momentous occasion) and then performed *Havdalah* (distinction-making ritual that separates the Sabbath or holiday from weekday), which distinguishes between light and dark as well as Sabbath and weekday.[23]

Facing New Challenges

It was only after the writing and sharing of our service that we felt able to face the vicissitudes of the adoption process. Since we were forty-four years old by then, we ruled out adopting through public agencies which generally favor placing infants with younger couples. We also decided against seeking an international adoption because many adoption experts now believe that it is psychologically healthier for an adoptee's sense of identity to know who his or her birthparents are and to have some continuous or future contact with them. Therefore, we chose to adopt independently through a lawyer. She asked us in detail about the criteria we had for our prospective child: Did we want only a Caucasian baby or would we be open to a transracial adoption? Was gender a consideration? Did the child have to be a newborn or might a toddler or older child be acceptable? Would we be willing to adopt a child with a mental or physical disability or whose birthmother abused drugs, drank alcohol, or smoked during the pregnancy? While our lawyer advised us not to compromise on the child we wanted, she also warned that the more selective we were, the longer the adoption process might take. All of this reminded us of how much more complicated adoption can be than going home from the hospital with a healthy biological bundle which nature bestows.

We quickly discovered that being Jewish would limit the pool of birthparents who might consider relinquishing their child to us. When we prepared a resume and ad describing ourselves to potential birthparents, we wondered whether or not to mention that we are Jewish. Our lawyer recommended not doing so because birthparents who felt strongly about the adoptive family's religious affiliation would make this known in their initial response to our ad. She also sought to minimize the possibility of religion becoming an obstacle to a potential adoption by placing our ad only in venues which have cosmopolitan and liberal reputations. Nevertheless, we had one conversation with a birthmother that ended abruptly when we revealed our Jewishness.

Encountering Jewish Attitudes

During our search for a child, we also learned that Jewish attitudes towards adoption are mixed. On one hand, the Bible and Talmud contain many examples of adoption-like arrangements. When he feared he would die childless, Abraham designated Eliezer as his heir (Genesis 15:2-3). In an act that resembled modern surrogacy, Abraham fathered Ishmael with Sarah's handmaiden Hagar (Genesis 16:1-4). Mordecai assumed the guardianship of Esther when her mother and father died (Esther 2:7). Michal raised her sister's five sons (2 Samuel 21:8). Regarding Michal's story, the Talmud teaches, "Anyone who raises an orphan in his home, scripture considers him as if he gave birth to him" (BT *Sanhedrin* 19b).

On the other hand, while the Bible appears to sanction surrogacy in Abraham's story, it subordinates the status of Ishmael in favor of Isaac, the son Abraham subsequently fathered with Sarah. This is dramatically symbolized by Sarah's banishing of Hagar and Ishmael into the wilderness (Genesis 20:9-14). More generally, Jewish law lacks a formal procedure for adoption because of the primacy it accords biological kinship in determining a child's inheritance rights and religious and tribal status.[24] An adopted gentile child must be converted to Judaism through a *tevilah* (immersion) ceremony in a *mikveh* (ritual bath) or natural body of water. For reasons of religious freedom, adopted gentiles retain the right to renounce Judaism until they reach Jewish adulthood, twelve years old for girls and thirteen for boys (BT *Ketubbot* 8a). Thus, there is some ambiguity in the official status of adopted children.

The Judaic stress on biological lineage apparently still exerts a lingering influence on the attitudes of relatively secular Jews. In a recent survey of college students, 80 percent of Jewish males, compared to 41 percent of Catholic males and 31 percent of Protestant males, indicated that it was "very important" to them that their future children be conceived by themselves and their spouses rather than adopted. Only 7 percent of these Jewish males considered themselves "very religious."[25]

Finding Joy and Expressing Gratitude

After ten months, our quest for a child ended successfully with the adoption of our son, Ari Isaac. His Hebrew name, *Avraham Yitzhak*, not only recalled the memory of a departed grandfather and uncle, but also his own history as the first son of a couple who, like Abraham and Sarah, had experienced infertility. At his circumcision, we recited a prayer of gratitude to his birthmother for entrusting him to us, and committed ourselves to respect both her wishes and the best interests of our son, in facilitating their future contact. Having endured and grieved our own loss of the dream of a biological child, we can empathize with the sacrifice she made and the sadness she must feel. We firmly believe that the Hagars of today are allies to be incorporated in mutually agreed-upon ways into the family, rather than competitors who must be banished from it.

Prayer for an Adopted Child

SANDY EISENBERG SASSO

*"Adonai is mindful of us, will bless us; will bless the house of
Israel; will bless the house of Aaron; will bless those who revere
Adonai, the little ones and the big ones together."*
—AFTER PSALMS 115:12-13

We have been blessed with the precious gift of this child. After so much waiting and wishing, we are filled with wonder and gratitude as we call you our daughter/son. Our daughter/son, our child, you have grown to life apart from us, but now we hold you close to our hearts and cradle you in our arms with our love. We welcome you into the circle of our family and embrace you with the beauty of a rich tradition.

We pledge ourselves to the creation of a Jewish home and to a life of compassion for others, hoping that you will grow to cherish and emulate these ideals.

God of new beginnings, teach us to be mother and father, worthy of this sacred trust of life. May our daughter/son grow in health. May s/he be strong in mind and kind in heart, a lover of Torah, a seeker of peace. Bless all of us together beneath your shelter of *shalom* (peace), and grant our new family, always, the harmony and love we feel today.

Rabbi Sandy Eisenberg Sasso, parent, spiritual leader, storyteller, was the first woman to be ordained by the Reconstructionist Rabbinical College and is author of two books that help children and their parents encounter God, *God's Paintbrush* and *In God's Name* (Jewish Lights Publishing, 1992 & 1994).

2

Infertility and Early Losses

I nfertility is a very private and individualized kind of anguish. It can occur in a cycle with miscarriage, stillbirth, medical procedures, adoption, simple failure to conceive, or a decision not to have children; it can also end with the birth of one's own biological child.

Likewise, pregnancy losses take various forms, and are experienced in diverse ways. Some miscarriages—particularly for people who are young, healthy, fertile, and in the earliest stages of pregnancy—may be understood as a "correction of nature," rather than a tragic loss. No authority can "permit" or "require" grief. Moreover, there is no reason to expect that a woman's initial response and grieving process will necessarily match those of her partner. In fact, significant conflict between partners in the nature and timing of their reactions is itself another factor in how couples experience, and heal from, their loss.

This chapter speaks to those women and men who feel the need to mark and mourn infertility, miscarriage, and stillbirth. Those who are largely at peace with their circumstances and choices will have little, if any, use for liturgical intervention in this area.

Traditional Jewish responses to infertility and pregnancy loss are inadequate and even problematic for many Jews today. This is so in part because of technological advances. Many contemporary Jews who suffer miscarriage, even early in a pregnancy, have seen an ultrasound "picture" of their fetus. And our increased expectations of pre- and neo-natal care make their limitations in individual cases all the more devastating. Jews of our generation hope and struggle for fertility—sometimes for years—in circumstances that would have been final and decisive for earlier generations. As a result, our generation has greater need for a continuing liturgical response.

It is not just the state of modern medicine, but also the tradition itself that creates a dilemma for Jews who suffer infertility and pregnancy loss. The great value placed on children in the Jewish tradition becomes painful for infertile couples precisely because they, too, value children. Moreover, "barrenness" has significant negative biblical associations. It is a punishment for certain sexual crimes (Leviticus 20:20-21). It is also seen, for the most part, as a woman's failing, a woman's sorrow, and a basis for competition among women. Think of Sarah in relation to Abraham and Hagar (Genesis 16, 21), Rachel in relation to Jacob and Leah (Genesis 29:31-30:25), Hannah in relation to Elkhanah and Peninah (I Samuel 1-2:10). Barrenness is frequently used in the prophetic writings as a metaphor for Israel's exile, defeat, and disgrace. It also contravenes the first biblical commandment: "Be fruitful and multiply" (Genesis 1:28). According to many Rabbinic interpretations, a man who was married for ten years to a wife who did not conceive had to divorce her and/or take another wife, in order to pursue the commandment of fertility (BT *Yevamot* 64a).[1]

The fact that great figures like Isaac, Samuel, and Samson were born to "barren mothers"—whose "delivery from" infertility showed the hand of God at work—may eventually become a comfort to those who, despite early difficulties, are able to conceive and bring a child to term.[2] Formerly infertile couples often identify with biblical heroines and feel that God has answered their prayers. However, the image of the barren mother is of no comfort to those who remain infertile. In fact, one could infer from the biblical stories that couples who cannot have biological children are not righteous enough—or the children who might have been born to them, not heroic enough—to merit divine intervention.

The traditional Jewish response to miscarriage and stillbirth can be equally problematic. Ritual acknowledgment of losses during pregnancy and up until a baby is thirty-one days old is severely limited under Jewish law, because babies younger than one month—and certainly fetuses—are not accorded full human status. This is not simple insensitivity on the part of the Rabbis. There were reasons for it in their time (high rates of pregnancy loss and infant mortality), and there continue to be reasons today (mourning rites for a fetus imply a stance on life's beginnings and on abortion that many women and most feminists are not willing to take). The motivation of the law was largely to spare women pain. However, the result today is that many Jews are left without a communally-sanctioned way of mourning what feels like a death in the family.

Traditionally, there are no mourning or burial rites for a fetus less than five months old. A fetus up to forty days old is considered, by law, "merely water" (BT *Yevamot* 69b). And, in fact, many women who miscarry this early in a pregnancy do not even realize that they are pregnant. Fetuses three months old and up are counted as "babies" in a few technical ways.[3] However, there is no precedent for burial of a fetus before it has "a human shape," a criterion that has been interpreted by some as corresponding with the fifth month.[4] It is customary to bury older fetuses, as well as stillborns and babies under a month old, either in family plots or together with other fetuses and young babies, on the outskirts of the cemetery. No formal service is held for fetuses.

Many of the mourning customs and procedures are omitted for stillborns and sometimes newborns who live less than a full thirty days. For a stillborn, we wash the body ritually, bury it in a box or casket, recite *El Maleh Raḥamim* (memorial prayer asking God to guard and keep in peace the departed soul), and give the baby a Hebrew name at a graveside funeral service, which parents are encouraged to attend. However, parents neither rend their garments in mourning nor perform *Tzidduk Hadin* (proclamation of God's justice in the face of tragedy), which is shortened or eliminated for babies who die anytime within the first year of life. Many rabbis encourage parents to say *Kaddish* (mourner's prayer) at graveside, but it is not required, and a few rabbis forbid it. It has long been customary to circumcise stillborn and infant boys who die without being circumcised. The optional circumcision is performed during ritual washing before burial, without blessings or ceremony.

If a baby is born alive and dies before reaching the age of one month, many contemporary rabbis either allow or require full burial and mourning rites. Jewish law favors full rites particularly if the baby has reached full term. Recently, the Conservative movement legitimated the position that all burial and mourning rites are proper for infants who die within their first thirty days.[5] Whatever one's stance on the legalities, the Mishnah sets an unmistakable example with regard to compassion: "A one day old infant who dies is, to his father and mother, like a full bridegroom" (Mishnah *Niddah* 5:3).

The authors in this chapter do not address the technical and legal issues summarized here. Instead, they provide Jewish ways of grieving and of acknowledging human pain. Though some, particularly Rabbi Amy Eilberg, make use of burial and mourning rites, none equates pregnancy loss with death. Many of the writings on stillbirth and miscarriage may be suitable or adaptable for abortion, particularly if abortion is medically indicated. However, voluntary termination of a pregnancy is an issue in its own right, and will be taken up in Chapter Six.

Rabbi Lynn Gottlieb provides a response to infertility that not only mourns the loss of a possibility and a dream, but also celebrates the creative powers that women own and exercise, regardless of their fertility. The structure she devises is flexible enough to express and heal the range of feelings that infertile people, with various life circumstances, may experience. Her ritual is also useful for fertile women or men who decide not to have children. Prayers by Rabbis Nina Beth Cardin and Sandy Eisenberg Sasso put words to the private pain of couples who have difficulty conceiving or suffer miscarriage or stillbirth. In the poem "Hold Me Now," Rabbi Vicki Hollander lays bare her vulnerability and draws strength from her faith in God and growth, following a miscarriage. Rabbi Eilberg draws on Psalms and traditional mourning customs in the creation of a full ritual response to miscarriage and stillbirth. The last paragraph of her ritual can also be adapted for use as a *mi sheberakh* (blessing recited on one's behalf) for the synagogue, if the family wishes acknowledgement and support from the larger community. Although infertility is suffered privately, infertile couples may wish to be sustained in community, and the community has an obligation to rally, and help them through their painful passage.

The Fruits of Creation

LYNN GOTTLIEB

"I am come into my garden aḥoti kallah (my sister, my bride).
Sisters I am come into my garden, I have gathered myrrh, crushed
and blended spices, eaten honeycomb with honey, and prepared
sweet wine to drink. Eat at my table, beloved friends. Feast on the
abundance of my table."

—AFTER SONG OF SONGS 5:1

This Fruits of Creation ceremony was created as a response to not giving birth which is sometimes, but not always, a choice. It is offered as a way for women to grieve the fact that they will not enjoy fruits of the womb. At the same time, it offers women the opportunity to celebrate the fruits of their creative labors. The name "Fruits of Creation" also alludes to the tale of Eve eating the fruit of knowledge and her sudden awareness of death and loss of innocence. In reframing the story of Eden as it has mostly been told, we allow ourselves to tell the story of women's experience of suffering and of the creative powers of transformation, which women discover and offer the world. Eve eats the fruit and gains knowledge. She uses her knowledge of life and death to acquire wisdom, to seek beauty, and to facilitate these pursuits for all her kin, just as contemporary women seek to lead conscious, authentic lives.

Now for the Rabbinic question: Why this ceremony? Women without children—married or unmarried—are especially in need of receiving communal acknowledgment, both of the sadness they may feel at being childless and of their own creativity and achievements.

Rabbi Lynn Gottlieb, spiritual leader of Congregation Nahalat Shalom in Albuquerque, New Mexico, was among the first women to serve as a rabbi.

FRUITS OF CREATION *SEDER*
(Ordered Readings and Meal)
An Order of the Ceremony in General Outline

Setting up the Space
We designate a place in our homes, out of doors, or in a synagogue or other public place for the ritual to happen. Using cloth, greenery, special ritual objects related to this event, candles, bread, wine or juice, and a washing bowl, we create a kind of altar which acts as a visual focus for prayer.

Gathering as a Community
People come together 15-30 minutes before the official beginning of the ceremony to help with final preparations and to make the transition from mundane to sacred time.

Beginning the Ceremony
The recommended timing of the ceremony is *Rosh Ḥodesh* (New Moon Festival), the beginning of a Hebrew month, which is designated as a women's holiday. We call ourselves to enter sacred time with a traditional or contemporary poem or prayer which speaks to the theme of the ceremony. This is followed by singing and playing music.

Lighting Candles
We consecrate time by kindling a flame in honor of *Rosh Ḥodesh*.

Performing the Ritual Act
We create a ceremony of song, story, prayers, dances, ritual washing, anointing, sacred vessels, or *mikveh* (ritual bath immersion) to honor the fruits of our creation.

Closing

We offer final prayers to bring the ceremony to a close.

Sharing Food

We say the blessings over the fruit of the vine and the bread and share informally till the evening's close.

Fruits of Creation Ceremony: "Deborah"'s Story Breathes Life into the Outline As she grew into womanhood Deborah always imagined she would be mother to many children. She used to dream of living on a farm surrounded by barn cats, milk cows, the smell of fresh hay, and at least six children. Over the years, this dream gave way to a feeling of desperation as marriage did not occur. Deborah became a therapist and eventually moved to the Southwest where she began a relationship which culminated in marriage six years later, at the age of forty-two. She also devoted much time to the pursuit of her pottery. Shortly after the marriage, Deborah was diagnosed with breast cancer, from which she has successfully recovered. However, she underwent menopause as a result of the treatment. After a period of depression around not being able to bear children, Deborah asked her *Rosh Ḥodesh* group to help her compose a Fruits of Creation ceremony. Her goal was to honor her body's courage and health and to turn her sights forward.

For the ceremony, Deborah set up an altar made up of three bowls which she crafted for the occasion. The first bowl was for ritual washing, the second for mourning her losses, and the third for honoring her life and creativity. We convened the ceremony with a selection from the Song of Songs and placed a special *tallit* (prayer shawl), used by our community on New Moon Festivals, over Deborah's shoulders to designate her an *eshet kallah* (literally, woman of *kallah*). The word *kallah* is usually translated as "bride," so that this phrase might be rendered "wife of the bride." However, the Hebrew root k.l.h. means fullness, wholeness, or completeness. Thus, in a feminist context, the term *eshet kallah* implies a woman's completeness within herself, rather than within marriage. I use the translation "Woman-in-Her-Fullness."

The ceremony took place outside, on the banks of the Rio Grande. As Deborah lit the candles and recited a blessing welcoming the new month, she offered a spontaneous prayer and gave thanks for the healing light of creation.

Then we went around the circle and spoke our Hebrew, Yiddish, or Ladino names and sang two Hebrew songs related to healing. Using the first bowl and a washing cup, Deborah ritually washed her hands and feet. She spoke of the waters of *Shekhinah* (close-dwelling Presence of God, associated with the feminine) healing and regenerating her soul.

The second bowl, the bowl of lamentations, was filled with sand from the banks of the river. First Deborah and then all of us performed a kind of *tashlikh* (casting out) of our losses. Modeling our ritual after the *tashlikh* ritual for the New Year, we took a handful of sand, named our losses and then threw the sand in the river. Then we spontaneously formulated a "litany of grief":

> *Shekhinah,* She who dwells within all being: I mourn the loss of the child I never bore. I mourn the loss of the mothering I envisioned. I mourn the loss of my ability to bear children. I mourn the loss of....

We began wailing to a tune Deborah composed until our tears flowed, our hearts were opened, and our spirits felt a release from grief. We filled the (now empty) washing bowl with water and passed it around, washing each other's faces and giving each other a blessing. Then we recited a calmer, more peaceful listing.

> *Shekhinah,* She who gives and takes away: I release the feelings of rage I have because I could not birth a child. I release my anger at my husband and forgive him for the times we struggled over our yearning for children. I release my feelings of inadequacy over not being physically able to conceive and forgive myself for difficult times. I release....

We made the transition to the last stage of the ritual by holding up the third bowl, which was quite large. Each of us had been asked to bring a token/gift which expressed some special quality we admired in Deborah. As we placed the gift in the bowl, each of us, in turn, named the quality that inspired her gift and related a small story which exemplified it. Thus, Deborah began another litany:

Shekhinah, She who eternally creates and renews: I celebrate
my devotion to becoming a potter in the face of hardships. I
celebrate my ability to grow an abundant garden. I celebrate
my relationship with....I celebrate my gratitude for....I celebrate
my courage to....

Then we danced in a circle to a *niggun* (wordless melody) until we
were ready to bless the food. We concluded the ceremony with a
blessing:

Shekhinah, we give thanks to you for the ever-present Mystery
dwelling within all being, who gives and takes away, who
eternally creates and renews life for the good.

Deborah brings her bowls to Fruits of Creation ceremonies, for
other members of our community, and we continue to use them
for healing, lamentation, and the offering of blessings.

Prayer for Those Having
Difficulty Conceiving

NINA BETH CARDIN

*"God heals the broken-hearted and binds up their wounds, counts
the number of the stars and calls them all by name."*
                                              —PSALMS 147: 3-4

*This prayer is phrased in the plural and written in the voice of a married
couple. It is easily adaptable for an infertile person to say on her or his
own.*

On our bed at night, we sought the one our hearts ached for;
we sought, but did not find, that one.
How lovely you would be, so we imagine, how lovely!
Every part of you would be fair; no blemish would mar your
coming.

Rabbi Nina Beth Cardin is advisor to students in the Rabbinical School of The
Jewish Theological Seminary and editor of *Sh'ma* magazine.

Who is the one that shines through like the dawn,
Beautiful as the moon,
radiant as the sun,
awesome as hosts draped in their colors?
Who is the one that our hearts wait for,
wait for, as the watchman for the morning light?

In You, God, our ancestors trusted,
In You they trusted, and You answered them.

We will trust in God, for God's goodness is never-ending;
God's mercy is without bounds.
We will trust in God, for God is our help and our shield.

May the God who made heaven and earth, hear our plea and
grant us a child.

—*Based on verses from Song of Songs and Psalm 22*

Prayer After a Miscarriage or Stillbirth

SANDY EISENBERG SASSO

*"Seeing our days are determined, the number of our months are
with You, You set limits that we cannot pass."*

—AFTER JOB 14:5

God, we are weary and grieved. We were anticipating the birth of
a child, but the promise of life was ended too soon. Our arms
yearned to cradle new life, our mouths to sing soft lullabies. Our
hearts ache from the emptiness and the silence. We are saddened
and we are angry. We weep and we mourn. Weep with us, God,
Creator of Life, for the life that could not be.

Source of healing, help us to find healing among those who care
for us and those for whom we care. Shelter us under wings of love
and help us to stand up again for life even as we mourn our loss.

Rabbi Sandy Eisenberg Sasso, parent, spiritual leader, storyteller, was the first
woman to be ordained by the Reconstructionist Rabbinical College and is author
of two books that help children and their parents encounter God, *God's
Paintbrush* and *In God's Name* (Jewish Lights Publishing, 1992 & 1994).

בָּרוּךְ אַתָּה יי, זוֹכֵר יְצוּרָיו לְחַיִּים בְּרַחֲמִים.

Barukh attah adonai, zokher yetzurav leḥayyim beraḥamim.

Blessed are You, Eternal our God, whose compassion renews us unto life (from the High Holiday *Amidah* [standing prayer]).

After a Miscarriage: Hold Me Now

VICKI HOLLANDER

Hayotzer, *one of seventy names of God, is translated roughly as "One who fashions, forms, creates."*

Hayotzer,
One who shapes,
Who formed us out of moistened clay,
Who rolled and pinched and sculpted the world,
hold me now.

You who enable wisps of seeds to grow,
Who partnered the life which grew inside me,
shelter me.

Life was gifted.
Life removed.

Hayotzer,
shape me a place where I can weep,
and mourn the loss,
and let the blackness inside
cry.

Rabbi Vicki Hollander weaves together the creation of ritual and poetry with rabbinic work at Congregation Eitz Or, hospice work, and single parenting.

Help me say goodbye
to the child
who was growing within me,
to the dreams I bore,
to the love I held within for that budding soul,
plucked away.

Let my voice ring,
a mother's call,
wild to the universe,

And You,
stand by me,
stand at my side,
and watch my tear fall and touch the earth.
Hear my pain and
hold me.

Hayotzer,
You who shaped me,
Heal my body and my soul.
Mend my spirit.
Thread new life among my bones.

Help me to find ground again.
To feel the earth beneath my toes.
To smell the beckoning scent of rich soil.
To see shoots of green emerge through winter beds,
determined hands grasping life.
To hear the sap rushing within.

I kneel to plant.
A seed of life.
An act of faith.

Hayotzer,
Sower of life,
Take my hand and, for a time,
hold it tight.

A Grieving Ritual Following Miscarriage or Stillbirth

AMY EILBERG

*"Like a father who says, 'My sons, my sons' or like a mother hen
who cries for her brood, so God declares, 'Look away from Me, I
will weep bitterly'(Isaiah 22:4)."*

—*TANḤUMA DEBEI ELIYAHU,* 154-155

*This ritual is intended to take place in a rabbi's study or in the couple's
home, in the presence of a small, trusted group. The couple is encouraged
to sit on hard chairs, reflecting our traditional mourning customs and
the hard place in which they find themselves.*

Mourning the Loss

All present may chant:

מִן-הַמֵּצַר קָרָאתִי יָהּ, עָנָנִי בַמֶּרְחָב יָהּ.

Min-hametzar karati yah, anani bamerḥav yah.

Out of the depths I call to You, O God; you hear me fully when
I call (after Psalm 118:5).

Rabbi or Lay Leader: We had hoped to gather soon with
you, [parents' names], to celebrate the birth of a baby.
Instead we are with you today to join in your sadness.
There was in your womb, [mother's name], the stirring
of life. This baby grew inside you, and so, too, in both of
you grew dreams and hopes and longing, images of
who this baby would be, and of your future with this

Rabbi Amy Eilberg, the first woman ordained by The Jewish Theological
Seminary, currently serves as the director of Kol Haneshama, the Jewish Hospice
Program of the Jewish Healing Center.

child. Now there is emptiness and pain as you acknowledge that this seed of life could not grow into a child.

"Out of the depths I call to You, O God; You hear me fully when I call. God is with me, I have no fear. I was hard pressed, about to fall; God came to my help. God, You are my strength and my courage. I will not die, but live, and yet tell of the deeds of God. I thank You for having heard me; O God, be my deliverance" (Selections from Psalm 118).

At this point the couple may share their own words about the meaning of this loss for them. When they have said whatever they wish to say, the rabbi or lay leader offers his/her hand to the couple, inviting them to stand and symbolically rise from the low hard place of mourning. At this time a loved one brings forward a baby's receiving blanket, or other piece of cloth associated with the couple's yearning to nurture a new life.

Rabbi or Lay Leader: Although this child left this world before he/she lived with us, he/she will always live on in our memory. We shall remember this child by the Hebrew name [insert name] *ben/bat* (son/daughter) [mother's name] *ve-* (and) [father's name].

When we lose someone close to us, something is torn inside. As Jews, we symbolize that experience by tearing a piece of cloth and wearing it over our heart, reflecting what is happening within. The being inside you never grew into life outside the womb. You did not know this baby, except as a stirring, a dream, an invisible presence (*for a stillbirth:* an all-too-brief presence) in your lives and your hearts. Still, part of you is torn inside, as you acknowledge the end of this potential life that could not be. To reflect the pain you feel on this day, we tear this baby blanket, reciting the time-honored words:

יי נָתַן, וַיי לָקָח, יְהִי שֵׁם יי מְבֹרָךְ.

Adonai natan, va'adonai lakah, yehi shem adonai mevorakh.

God gives, God takes away. Blessed be the name of God (Job 1:21).

The rabbi or lay leader and those assembled may chant here:

אֶשָּׂא עֵינַי אֶל הֶהָרִים, מֵאַיִן יָבֹא עֶזְרִי. עֶזְרִי מֵעִם יי, עֹשֵׂה שָׁמַיִם וָאָרֶץ.

Essa einai el heharim me'ayin yavo ezri. Ezri me'im adonai oseh shamayim va'aretz.

I lift my eyes to the mountains; where is the source of my help? My help comes from *Adonai,* Creator of heaven and earth (Psalms 121:1-2).

Choosing Life Again

Rabbi or Lay Leader: To sanctify this moment of transition to the next phase of your lives, we invite you to take part in the life of our people by choosing the *mitzvah* of *tzedakah* (sacred practice of charity), even in this time of pain.

The couple may explain their choice of a gift. (Appropriate charities might include a local Jewish Family Service, expressing the couple's devotion to family, or a tree planted in Israel.)

All respond: וּבָחַרְתָּ בַּחַיִּים.

Uvaharta bahayim.

May you continue to choose life (Deuteronomy 30:19).

Communal Support and Blessings

Rabbi or Lay Leader: At this time I ask all of you except the parents, to form two lines. [Insert parents' names] will walk between the lines, as is customary for Jews at a time of bereavement. Feel free to offer words of condolence as they pass between you. *(When the couple has passed through:)* Together, we offer ancient words of comfort to our friends in their sadness.

All say to the parents: "*Hamakom yenahem etkhem,* May God grant you comfort."

Rabbi or Lay Leader: May God who blessed our ancestors, Abraham, Isaac and Jacob, Sarah, Rebecca, Rachel, and Leah, grant to this family *refu'at hanefesh urefu'at haguf,* a full healing of body and spirit, abundant blessing from loved ones, and an awareness of God's presence with them in their pain. As for the baby that was not to be, shelter this spirit, O God, in the shadow of Your wings, for You, God of parents, God of children, God of us all, guard and shelter us. You are a gracious and loving God. Guard our coming and our going, grant us life and peace, now and always, for You are the Source of life and peace. May we as a holy community support and love our friends in times of pain as well as times of joy. And as we have wept together, so may we soon gather to rejoice. Amen.[6]

All present may conclude by singing Oseh Shalom *or another appropriate hymn.*

3

Welcoming Children into Name and Covenant

"Welcoming children into name and covenant" is, I think, an apt phrase. It describes the purpose and tone of a distinct passage, includes both boys and girls, and takes account of three separate, though related, components: Welcoming, naming, and entry into religious covenant.

Traditionally, a variety of rituals for infants accomplished some combination of these three. Practices, more-or-less-commonly observed, include *Shalom Zakhor* (welcome to the boy-child), a gathering held on a boy's first Sabbath which both celebrates his arrival and, to a lesser extent, mourns the loss of all the Torah he is said to have known *in utero* (BT *Niddah* 30b); *Leil Shimmurim* (eve of watchfulness), a study vigil/party held the night before circumcision to comfort baby boys over their impending surgery, and guard them from attack by demons who may seek to prevent the fulfillment of *brit milah* (covenant of circumcision); *Shavu'a/ Yeshu'ah Haben* and *Shavu'a/Yeshu'ah Habat* (week/salvation of son and daughter), ambiguous phrases describing an imperfectly remembered custom, probably a week-long celebration after a birth, similar in nature to the traditional week-long celebration after a wedding; *Hollekreish* (translation unknown) or *Shem Arisah* (cradle or crib name/naming), an Ashkenazic custom dating from the fourteenth century, in which children circle the cradle of a newborn, lift it up three times, and pronounce the baby's secular name; and *Zeved Habat* (gift of a daughter), the Sephardic prayer for baby girls, recited in synagogue upon a daughter's naming, during the first Torah service which a mother attends after the birth.[1]

Despite this plethora of rituals and customs, *Brit Milah* (covenant of circumcision ritual) is so dominant that even the most judicious chapter title cannot keep our minds from jumping to *"the"* covenant ritual. So great is the connection between circumcision and covenant, that ritual circumcision is known in common parlance as *brit* (covenant), rather than *milah* (circumcision). Moreover, the Hebrew verb for making or entering into a covenant, *likhrot*, translates literally as "to cut."

Whereas the term *Brit Milah* means that boys are covenanted through the act of circumcision, the term *Brit Banot* (covenant ceremony for daughters) offers no act or mechanism for girls' entry to the covenant. Another popular term for a girl's naming ceremony, *Simhat Bat* (joy of a daughter), does not attempt to connect the ceremony with the notion of covenant at all.

The connection with covenant is vital, because the connection to God *through* covenant is one of the cornerstones of Jewish religion and self-definition. We are the people with whom God made a covenant, and we are eternally bound to God by covenant. Biblical and Rabbinic literature use a variety of metaphors to express this relationship: Parent to child, Ruler to subject, Husband to wife. In each case, the partners are traditionally understood to have different degrees of power and freedom, but their relationship is always considered caring and mutual. Obligations, promises, love, and loyalty are implied. In the Jewish idiom, God is a maker and a keeper of covenants. This serves as inspiration even in darkest times, for we have faith in God's faithfulness.

Brit Milah is the ultimate case-study for women's perspectives on Jewish lifecycle because it raises questions that are supremely challenging and rich with potential: What is the purpose of this most ancient and basic—some would say primitive—mark of the covenant? What does it mean that women can never have it? If and when parity is not possible, what does equality between the sexes look like? What is the meaning of "covenant?" What are the connections among the various biblical covenants between God and humans—e.g. the covenant of circumcision (Genesis 17:2f); the covenant of divisions in which God promises Israel's ultimate dominion, following enslavement (Genesis 15:18); the covenant after the Flood (Genesis 9:9f); the covenant at Sinai (Exodus 34:10); the future covenant in which God's teaching will be inscribed on our hearts (Jeremiah 31:33)? How shall we understand the fact that God made a covenant with Abraham and not Sarah, that the covenant is "cut" on males and not females, that Moses addressed men, and not women in preparing the people to receive Torah and covenant at Sinai (Exodus 19:15)?[2] Given the scriptural and biological impediments, is it now possible for women to be full partners in the covenant, and, if so, how?

In addressing such questions, Rabbi Laura Geller sets aside the physical component of circumcision, and focuses on the liturgy. Words and symbols connect the child to kin, patriarchs, and national saviors, thus transforming him from a nameless, rootless babe into a titled and covenanted member of the Jewish people. Rabbi Geller considers how and why *Brit Milah* is so effective a ritual, and argues that its spiritually transformative aspects are more important religiously—and more easily applicable to girls—than the surgery itself. She reviews a variety of approaches to naming and covenant ceremonies for baby girls, and advocates the use of blessings for the new moon in the creation of a liturgy that parallels *Brit Milah* by connecting girls to kin, matriarchs, and national saviors.

Rabbi Geller makes, I believe, the best possible argument for a purely liturgical response to the challenge of *brit milah*. Still, men have a *mitzvah* (commandment) and physical sign that "accompanies them for life," and women do not. Boys and men enter into the covenant of Abraham; girls and women do not.[3]

Dr. Shulamit Magnus and Treasure Cohen do not resolve those lingering disparities with respect to *Brit*, but they mitigate them by providing additional rituals that can be used equally for boys and girls. Dr. Magnus creates the *Simḥat Lev* (rejoicing of the heart), a ritual for entering children into the House of Israel. She bases the text, symbols, and timing of the ritual on traditional sources. Cohen draws on an ancient custom of planting trees in honor of the birth of one's children, and invests it with new vitality. She also connects her "tree-dition" to the spectrum of Jewish lifecycle, especially to death, growing up, and the *Tu Bishvat* (New Year for Trees) holiday.

Not surprisingly, the authors for this chapter have negative associations with circumcision. All three point out that parents, and mothers particularly, are hardly prepared for a major celebration just eight days after a birth. Rabbi Geller and Dr. Magnus both mention that circumcision is considered child abuse by some parents and activists. The authors agree with those who consider circumcision abusive on one essential point: Circumcision is an imprinting experience. However, they regard it as imprinting boys with peoplehood and covenant, rather than pain or parental uncaring. Thus, none of the authors doubts the power of *Brit Milah*, nor would any abandon this four-thousand-year-old ritual. Instead, they seek to plumb its mystery and to create parallel or supplementary rituals for welcoming girls, as well as boys, into name and covenant.

Brit Milah and *Brit Banot*

LAURA GELLER

"You say there are no words to describe this time, you say it does not exist. But remember, make an effort to remember. Or, failing that, invent."

—MONIQUE WITTIG, *LES GUERILLERES*

Our lives are shaped by both biology and culture. Nowhere in the cycle of life is this clearer than at birth. Every human being comes into the world in the same way, but cultures mark this entrance idiosyncratically, imposing values on the individual and the community through particular rites of initiation. For traditional Judaism, that rite is *Brit Milah* (covenant of circumcision ritual). What is the meaning of this rite in its own terms, and how might its form and content be applied to baby girls?

The covenant of circumcision is first mentioned in Genesis 17:9:

And God said to Abraham..."This is my covenant which you shall keep between me and you and your seed after you; every male among you shall be circumcised. And you shall circumcise the flesh of your foreskin and it shall be a token of the covenant between me and you. And he that is eight days old shall be circumcised among you, every male in your generations...."

The tradition makes it clear that circumcision is not merely a surgical procedure. It is a sign of the eternal promise and relationship between God and the Jewish people, sealed in the flesh of Jewish males. Maimonides explains the reasons for *Brit Milah* as follows:

Circumcision...gives all Jewish people a common bodily sign. There is much mutual love and assistance among people who are united by the same sign...Circumcision is also the symbol of the covenant which Abraham made in connection with the belief in God's unity. So every person who is circumcised enters the Covenant of Abraham to believe in the unity of God.

(*GUIDE TO THE PERPLEXED*, III, 49)

Rabbi Laura Geller is the executive director of the American Jewish Congress, Pacific Southwest Region, which includes the AJ Congress Feminist Center.

Fears and Objections

For non-traditional Jews, the decision to enter sons into the covenant of circumcision is often a difficult one. For some, traditional explanations like that of Maimonides seem less compelling than the fear of hurting a healthy infant.

Some go so far as to consider circumcision a form of child abuse.[4] Yet, despite this concern, most Jews continue to have their sons circumcised either through *Brit Milah* or through a hospital circumcision—surgery without ritual.

Those who are satisfied by medical arguments about the benefits of circumcision or the baby's relative insensitivity to pain, or those willing to carry on the tradition at the cost of momentary pain, may well have other objections to the ritual. From a feminist perspective, it appears totally phallocentric; obviously it does not give "all Jewish people a common bodily sign"—it gives that sign only to Jewish males. *Brit Milah* excludes female Jews in the most powerful of ways. Women cannot in and of themselves fully participate in the covenantal relationship and bodily sign that connects God and the Jewish people.

The Draw of Tradition

Why is this ritual so compelling in spite of the critique it evokes? Why do Jews who respond to few other *mitzvot* (commandments) want their sons to bear this bodily sign? Why do some Jews continue to celebrate *Brit Milah* even as they allow feminist critique to shape other dimensions of their Jewish commitments?

Perhaps the power of *Brit Milah* comes from its danger and antiquity. To witness a *Brit Milah* is to experience a primitive enactment of a very ancient understanding that this child belongs not only to his parents, but also to God—and God wants what parents cannot fully understand. Through the *Brit Milah*, the child is wrested from his parents in order to fulfill the ancient demand. Parents are often uncomfortable with the message that their children do not belong completely to them, but it is a lesson that they must eventually learn in order to allow their children to become themselves.

All this attention to a baby's penis forces his parents to acknowledge that this little one will be connected primarily to his family of origin only for a limited time, that he will grow up and likely use his penis to create a family with another human being, and that his parents need to help him become ready for this. That the sign of the covenant is located on the male organ of generation has powerful implications for the centrality of sexuality and reproduction.

Another way to understand the power of *Brit Milah* is as a bonding between the father and son. Perhaps the father relives his own *Brit* through the *Brit* of his son. Or perhaps the *Brit Milah* is the father's experience of giving birth. Just as the mother's experience of birth was painful and bloody, so too the father's experience of giving birth is painful and bloody—painful and bloody for the child who may grow up to be a father reexperiencing this moment with his own child. Perhaps this is why the primary commandment is for a man to circumcise his sons, not to *be* circumcised. Only failing a father's ability to circumcize his own sons(s) does a *mohel* (ritual circumciser) act on his behalf. Just as fathers can be present to comfort mothers as they birth their children, perhaps the most women can do is to comfort fathers as they symbolically give birth to their sons through the *Brit Milah*. The power of this ritual for our patriarchal tradition is also its major problem from a feminist perspective. It ritualizes for us a disturbing inequality of our tradition: Mothers give birth and fathers give tribe. Mothers birth babies and fathers birth Jews.[5]

Brit Milah as Effective Ritual

Lifecycle rituals, including circumcision, are transformative. Not only does the boy emerge physically different after the *Brit Milah*, but he is also transformed from baby to covenanted Jew; from an infant with no history, to a person with a past and a future. In the process of ritual, the individual passes through a moment when he or she is separated from a prior status and not quite incorporated into the new one, no longer what s/he was but not yet what s/he will become. That period of "betwixt and between"—what anthropologists call "liminality"—is a time when the individual merges with all other individuals, sharing characteristics of innocence, vulnerability, paradox, and renewal.

Rituals are performed. They are like theater in that they are effective not because they make rational sense but because we somehow believe them. The *Brit Milah* has such players as the *mohel*, the *sandak/sandakit* (person holding the baby during ritual circumcision), the parents; such props as Elijah's chair, the knife, the cotton dipped in wine. The procedure itself is full of drama.

Finally, lifecycle ritual asserts the idea of a life. *Brit Milah* communicates that this baby boy is in some profound way the same person who will go to school, stand under a *ḥuppah* (wedding canopy), and one day, die. Even though the eight-day-old infant bears little resemblance to the eighty-year-old man he may become, he remains, at core, the same.

Seder Brit Milah: **Order of the Service**

As the baby is brought into the room, he is greeted with words that simultaneously welcome him and Elijah, the forerunner of the messiah.[6] The child is placed upon an empty chair, designated as the chair of Elijah in tribute, according to many, to the prophet who criticized the people for forsaking the covenant (I Kings 19:10) and was rewarded with the privilege of attending every *Brit Milah*. The clear message of the ritual is that this child could be messiah, or, perhaps at least for the moment, is messiah.

After the *mohel* says the blessing and performs the circumcision, the father responds: "You are blessed, *Adonai* our God, ruling over time and space, who has sanctified us by Your commandments and commanded us to enter him into the covenant of Abraham our father." Those present respond with a text, that appears in the Talmud (BT *Shabbat* 137b): "Just as he has entered to the covenant, so may he enter to Torah, to *ḥuppah* (marriage canopy), and to good deeds." Thus, the ritual asserts the idea of a life and a set of values for baby, parents, and all assembled. A custom which symbolizes this linking is the adornment of a *wimpel* (swaddling cloth that envelopes the baby at his *Brit*) which is donated to the synagogue to be used as a Torah binder at his Bar Mitzvah ceremony.

Then covenant is invoked. After a blessing over wine, the following passage is recited:

You are blessed, *Adonai* our God, ruling over time and space, who did sanctify the beloved person from the womb, impressing Your statute in his flesh and marking his descendants with the sign of the holy covenant. Eternal God our Stronghold, because of this, for the sake of the covenant You did impress in our flesh, deliver our dearly beloved from destruction. Blessed are You, *Adonai*, author of the covenant.

(BASED PARTLY ON BT *SHABBAT* 137B)

Who is the "dearly beloved," sanctified from his mother's womb? Obviously it is the child. And yet, who are his descendants? Rabbeinu Tam says that *yedid* (beloved one) means Abraham; Rashi explains that it must be a reference to Isaac. The Tosafot conclude that it is Abraham, Isaac, and Jacob (See BT *Menaḥot* 53b and *Shabbat* 137b).

Why the confusion? Who is this child just entered into the covenant but not yet named? This is the moment of liminality when the child is "betwixt and between." All Jewish history flows through this child, who is simultaneously Abraham, Isaac, Jacob, and the hoped-for messiah; his father, his grandfather, and every Jewish man who ever was or ever will be. Wholeness is possible; rebirth is possible; redemption is possible. And this moment is ended with the giving of his name:

"Our God and the God of our fathers and mothers, preserve this child to his father and mother and let his name be called in Israel _____ the son of _____ and _____ ....May this little one become great."

Even more than the circumcision, it is the granting of the name that transforms and brands a Jew. This becomes most clear through the folk tradition of not speaking the child's name until after the *Brit Milah*. Until the moment of the *Brit* he is simply "the baby." During that moment he is Abraham, Isaac, and Jacob, his father, grandfather, and the messiah. After the naming, he becomes himself—a Jew linked through ritual to covenant and messiah, and transformed through ritual into so-and-so the son of his particular parents within the context of the Jewish people. Thus, the power of *Brit Milah* is spiritual, as well as physical. The infant is transformed, named, given tribe and history, roots and purpose, baggage and wings. As the infant is transformed so are we, the community gathered for the ritual, who have relived again the biblical stories of our ancestors and the messianic promise of our redemption, in the process of welcoming another Jew into our covenantal community.

Where Are the Girls, and Where Should They Be?

What do we learn from this about rituals for entering our daughters into the covenant? Should a covenant ritual for daughters be modeled after *Brit Milah*? If so, how closely ought they be parallel? If not, how do we create covenant ceremonies for girls that are authentically Jewish?

If the primary source of the power of *Brit Milah* were the physical marking of the infant boy, it would be almost impossible to create a parallel ritual. But we have seen that the power of *Brit Milah* is not only physical. While a *Brit* for a daughter cannot physically parallel the circumcision, it ought to be transformative in a similar way: The child must change from baby to Jew; the child must become Sarah, Rebecca, Rachel, and Leah, as well as messiah; she must be named and given tribe and history; and the community gathered for the ritual must be different because of the ritual.

While boys are named at the *Brit Milah*, girls are traditionally named in synagogue on the Sabbath after their birth. Typically, the father is called to the Torah and receives a blessing in which the child is named. Another blessing prays for the healing of the mother. Most often, neither the child nor the mother is present.[7] Naming, then, has none of the power that we observed in connection to *Brit Milah*; there is no connection to covenant or a messianic future, only the ceremonial conferring of a name on the (usually absent) child.

"On the Birth of a Daughter," one of the first published covenant rituals for girls, included variations of the seven blessings said at Jewish weddings, as well as a version for girls of *Pidyon Haben* (ceremony symbolically redeeming first-born males, born vaginally, from Temple service), celebrated one month after the birth.[8] Among the innovations of this early ceremony is a *berakhah* (blessing) for entrance into the covenant: "Praised are You

Adonai, Our God, Lord of the Cosmos, who has made us holy through Your commandments and commanded us to bring our daughter into the covenant of the People of Israel."

Since this ceremony, there have been many others. Early ceremonies tended to be closely modeled after *Brit Milah* in that they were set on the eighth day after birth and used much of the traditional imagery and blessings.[9] In the early 1970s, Mary Gendler proposed that the parallel to *Brit Milah* ought to involve the ritual breaking of the infant girl's hymen[10]. This would incorporate the blood ritual and genital elements of *Brit Milah* and, at the same time, free the baby girl from the strictures of virginity. Here, as in *Brit Milah*, the sign of the covenant would be located in connection to the organ of generation. Gendler's suggestion, while provocative, has not been followed.

Other alternatives involve blood, for example tapping a girl's cheek[11] to evoke the folk tradition of a "menstrual slap" which a mother gives her daughter when she reaches menarche. Proponents of blood rituals argue that in a boy, blood is made to flow unnaturally through circumcision, but in a girl blood will flow naturally when she gets her period. A problem with this type of ceremony is the possible implication that the girl's entrance into the covenant is somehow incomplete until she begins to menstruate and, arguably, ends when she reaches menopause.

More recent ceremonies foresake *Brit Milah* as the model. They operate from the assumption that, because *Brit Milah* focuses on the physical maleness of the boy, there can be no parallel ritual for girls. Instead they propose that a *Brit Banot* (covenant ceremony for daughters) ought to celebrate female spirituality. This, of course, raises the provocative question: What are the sources of female spirituality in Judaism?

Two symbols have become popular in *Brit Banot* ceremonies: Water/ritual bath immersion and moon/lunar celebrations and blessings. The Me'iri, a medieval commentator, suggests that when Abraham was circumcised, Sarah underwent ritual immersion in order to enter the covenant (BT *Yevamot* 46a). So ritual immersion seems to be the feminine equivalent of circumcision as a sign of *brit*. Both immersion and, in the case of males, circumcision are required of converts to Judaism who take on the covenant. This connection between immersion and covenant led to the creation of a ceremony by Rabbi Michael and Sharon Strassfeld which replaces circumcision with immersion in the *mikveh* (ritual bath) for a baby girl.[12] Immersion is most commonly done after a woman's menstrual period, so that this ceremony, like *Brit Milah*, evokes associations with blood, as well as covenant. The problem is that this ceremony resembles baptism too much to "feel Jewish," although in fact the Christian tradition of baptism is an adaptation of the Jewish tradition of ritual immersion.

A less problematic ceremony, also associated with water, is called *brit reḥitzah* (covenant of washing) and was created by Rabbi Ruth Sohn and others.[13] It evokes the biblical story of Abraham's welcoming the three angels who visited him after his circumcision by washing their feet. The ceremony welcomes the girl child into the world and covenant by washing her feet and employs a new *berakhah*: "Blessed are you *Adonai* our God, Ruler of the universe, who is mindful of the covenant through the washing of the feet."

The second, and in my view, more powerful, alternative to immersion rituals relates female spirituality to the cycles of the moon. *Rosh Ḥodesh* (New Moon Festival) is designated in the tradition as a woman's holiday. The mystical tradition links women and the moon and suggests that in the world to come women will be restored to their rightful position as equal to men, just as the moon will be restored to her equal position with the sun.[14] There is also an obvious connection between the menstrual cycles of women and the cycles of the moon.

Using the connection between women and the moon as the organizing principle of the ritual determines its timing. It no longer occurs on the eighth day but on the *Rosh Ḥodesh* after the birth. It moves the ceremony from the day to the night.

A most interesting ritual flows out of the tradition of *Kiddush Levanah* (blessing of the moon).[15] Traditionally observed on a Saturday night after *Havdalah* (distinction-making ritual that separates the Sabbath or holiday from weekday), between the third and the fifteenth of the month, the ceremony offers fitting opportunities for a covenant ceremony for daughters. It involves singing, chanting, and movement; a liturgy filled with images of renewal, regeneration, and creation; and most importantly, a powerful messianic thrust. For example, the liturgy includes "Long live David, king of Israel," an obvious messianic reference, and Song of Songs 2:8-9, a more subtle one.

A *Brit* ritual which begins with *Kiddush Levanah* celebrates female spirituality in an authentically Jewish way. It evokes the liminal—the possibility that this child is messiah, and that she is connected to the women of our tradition who celebrated the cycles of the moon.

SEDER BRIT KIDDUSH LEVANAH
Order of the Service

Entry into the Covenant

The girl is entered into the covenant with a new berakhah based on the blessing offered at a circumcision:

בָּרוּךְ אַתָּה יי אֱלֹהֵינוּ מֶלֶךְ הָעוֹלָם, אֲשֶׁר קִדְּשָׁנוּ בְּמִצְוֹתָיו וְצִוָּנוּ
לְהַכְנִיסָה בִּבְרִיתָם שֶׁל אַבְרָהָם וְשָׂרָה.

Barukh attah adonai eloheinu melekh ha'olam, asher kiddeshanu bemitzvotav vetzivvanu lehakhnisah bivritam shel avraham vesarah.

Blessed are you God, Ruler of the universe, who has sanctified us with the commandments and commanded us to enter our daughter into the Covenant of Abraham and Sarah.

The community responds: "As this child has been entered into the covenant, so may she enter into a life enriched by Torah, a warm and loving relationship, and a commitment to create a better world."

The baby is linked not only to the cosmic future and redemption, but also to her own individual future, as the ritual asserts the idea of a connected life.

Welcoming and Naming

Before _____ was formed in (her mother's) womb, the Holy One gestured to the angel in charge of the winds

and said, "Bring me the wind which is in the Garden of
Eden and whose name is _____ bat (daughter of)
_____ ve (and) _____." Immediately the angel went
and brought the wind _____ before the Holy One
shaking and trembling, and the Holy One said to the
wind: "_____, enter into that sperm and that egg."
And the wind _____ opened her mouth to speak: "I
am quite satisfied living in the garden of Eden. Why
must I leave? I am holy and pure and formed out of
Your own holiness." And the Holy One replied, "The
place where I am sending you will be even more pleasant than the Garden of Eden. And when I created you it
was just for this purpose." The Holy One dispatched the
wind _____ and the angels placed her in her mother's
womb. There she was fed by two angels, and they
guarded her and kept her safe. And in there a candle
burned over her head and by its light she saw from one
end of the universe to the other. There are no days in a
person's life more enjoyable than those days in the
womb, and by the light of the candle the angels taught
_____ the entire Torah. After nine months the angel
announced that the time had come to enter the air of the
world. _____ protested: "Why do I have to leave? I am
just fine in here!" But the angel replied, "Whether you
like it or not, you are going. And mark my words, when
your time comes to leave that world outside, you will
not want to go." And the child _____ entered the air of
the world. And the angel tapped her on the upper lip,
leaving a mark, and the candle went out and _____
has forgotten all that she had seen and known.[16]

The rabbi or a parent then says: Tonight is the beginning of
_____'s remembering. We give her, her first word of
Torah—her own name.

Like the "dearly beloved" of the *Brit* liturgy, the soul about to
enter the world is no longer what she was but not yet who she will
become. It is especially powerful to use portions of the *Zeved Habat*
(gift of a daughter), the traditional Sephardic welcoming blessing
for a baby girl, in the naming:

May God who blessed our mothers Sarah, Rebecca, Rachel, and Leah, Miriam the prophet, Avigail and Esther, the queens, bless this lovely little girl and let her name be called in Israel _____ the daughter of _____ and _____ at this favorable moment of blessing.

May she be raised in health, peace, and tranquility to study Torah, to stand under the *ḥuppah*, to do good deeds. May her parents merit to see her happy, blessed with children, wealth and honor, peaceful and content in their old age. May this be God's will. Amen.[17]

So this little girl, at once the wind from the Garden of Eden, the hoped-for messiah, Sarah, Rebecca, Rachel, Leah, Miriam, Avigail, and Esther, becomes a particular person with a particular history, the daughter of her mother and her father. The baby is entered into the covenantal community, endowed with both cosmic and personal history.

Creating a Future of Continuity

The time has come for our tradition to mark the entrance of girls as well as boys into the world and our people. *Brit Banot* can be powerful, transformative and authentic. Someday a mother will look into the eyes of her baby girl at her child's *Brit* and see her own mother looking into her own eyes. And when that chain goes back for generations, we will know we have succeeded.

Simḥat Lev: Celebrating a Birth

SHULAMIT MAGNUS

"It is for this child that I prayed."

—I SAMUEL 1:28

In the last few decades, feminist Jews have devoted enormous energy to creating ceremonials marking the birth of Jewish girls. Yet, despite the discomfort of many feminists with *Brit Milah* (covenant of circumcision ritual), there has been little effort to construct new rituals for the birth of Jewish boys. At most, feminists have tinkered with the *Brit*, notably adding the mother's name in the naming section and occasionally giving a woman the honor of holding the infant during the circumcision.

Doing a *Brit* the way it is usually done—a public ceremony with a *se'udat mitzvah* (sanctified meal)—itself is problematic. There is the pain to the infant, and while I have seen some infants with moderate responses, I have seen many others writhe, shriek, and turn purple with pain. As I contemplated the birth of my own child and the possibility that it would be a boy, celebrating this seemed sick. When else would you hurt your child in public and make a party out of it? And the sexism: *Brit Milah* is, after all, a celebration of the penis. I did not want to participate in and perpetuate this in my own, new family circle.

Still, there was no way that my husband and I would forego a *Brit Milah*: We were not prepared to make such a statement of disconnection from our ancestors and the present community. This left us with very negative feelings about the *Brit*, no possibility of abandoning it, and no good way to celebrate the birth of a boy.

Creating new rituals for girls but leaving the established, sexist one for boys falsely implies that feminist Judaism is for females only. At the same time, much as I believe in birth rituals for girls, it seems to me that nothing done for girls (yet) approximates the power of the *Brit*: Its antiquity, its universality in the Jewish world and, yes, the power of carving of identity into flesh ("the *brit* You

---

Dr. Shulamit Magnus teaches modern Jewish history and Jewish women's history at Stanford University.

have sealed in our [sic] flesh," as the Grace After Meals proclaims). Thus, I faced two unhappy prospects: Doing a *Brit* with all its hoary recognition for a boy and any of the rituals I knew for a girl; rejoicing at the ritual for the girl but detesting (or absenting myself from) that for the boy.

All this passed from the theoretical to the practical when I gave birth to a boy. Since I considered the *Brit* unredeemable, I did not want to feminize it. The only alternative was to de-emphasize it radically. We invited no guests and made no celebration; interestingly, *Brit Milah* does not require a prayer quorum. It was just the *mohel* (ritual circumciser) and us.

A month later, however, was a different story. My husband and I had decided that, boy or girl, the real celebration would come about a month after the birth, by which time we hoped to have recuperated from the birth and the freneticism following it, and be able to participate in and enjoy a ceremony.[18]

Traditionally, a month is a significant marker. The rabbis considered an infant *bar kayyamah* (viable outside the womb) only after a month of life (Numbers *Rabbah* 3:8). Having had several miscarriages, I was very grateful that this child had stayed with me, and marking that felt important. But my reading of a rabbinic commentary on the significance of a month in the biblical census made this feel like an appropriate time even for someone without my history.[19] Doing a ceremony at one month is reminiscent, of course, of the *Pidyon Haben* (ceremony symbolically redeeming first-born males, born vaginally, from Temple service), yet with obvious differences: This celebration is for all Jewish children, whatever the birth order or sex. It would also be appropriate for an adopted child.

I called the ceremony *Simhat Lev*, meaning, "rejoicing of the heart." The numerical value of the letters which make up the word *"lev"* is thirty-two—a reference to the approximate number of days since the baby's birth. The centerpiece of the ceremony was special Torah readings.[20] The Torah is our covenant with God, and children, according to the well-known Rabbinic teaching, are its guarantors (Song of Songs *Rabbah* 1:24). What better way to celebrate the birth of a Jewish child and proclaim our commitment to raise a Jew, than with Torah?

We decided to hold the *Simhat Lev* on the *Rosh Hodesh* (New

Moon Festival) following the baby's first month of life, since the New Moon is a festival in itself, with a joyous chanting of *Hallel* (Psalms of praise) as part of the morning service. As is mandated for *Rosh Ḥodesh*, we read four Torah portions.

The first was the creation story (Genesis 1-2:3). To me, God is first and foremost Creator who, as the Rabbis say, "renews daily the work of creation." I had experienced the truth of those words in the development of this child in my body and since the birth. I rejoiced in that and would give it voice.

The second and third readings were some of the most moving words about Torah and being Jewish: "Standing all of us before God—the high and the lowly, women, men, children—we become a people before God...Torah is not hidden nor far off, not in heaven nor beyond the sea but near to us, in our mouths, in our hearts" (paraphrasing our readings, Deuteronomy 29:9-15 and 30:11-16). Enigmatically, these verses also include "those present this day and also those not here with us this day" (29:14)—a reference, on the day we bound our child to the generations of Israel, to those who came before us and those who would follow.

The reading ordained for *Rosh Ḥodesh* (Numbers 28:1-15) was the fourth segment.[21] We honored loved ones with the first three *aliyot* (honors of reciting the blessings before and after the Torah is read). For the fourth, my husband and I were called to the Torah together with the baby, called ceremoniously by his full name. In preparation for that *aliyah*, we honored a cousin with a ritual wrapping of the baby in a *tallit* (prayer shawl), whose strings and knots have the numerical value 613, the number of *mitzvot* (commandments). The wrapping symbolized our hope that the baby would live a life enveloped in *mitzvot* and comforted by the embrace of Torah.[22] It also satisfied the need for a dramatic physical act—one that is nurturing and loving. After the service, we had traditional joyous music and a *se'udat mitzvah* at which I explained what we had done and why, and discussed the baby's name. The service itself included blessings based on biblical, liturgical, and Talmudic texts. Phrased here for a boy, these can easily be adapted for girls.[23]

BLESSINGS

1. הַיּוֹם אָנוּ מִתְחַבְּרִים לְתוֹלְדוֹת יִשְׂרָאֵל. אֶל הַנַּעַר הַזֶּה הִתְפַּלָּלְנוּ. יי נָתַן אֶת שְׁאֵלָתֵנוּ. עָלַץ לִבֵּנוּ בַּיי.

Hayom anu mithabberim letoledot yisra'el. El hana'ar hazeh hitpallalnu. Adonai natan et she'elatenu. Alatz libbenu badonai.

Today we join the generations of Israel. It is for this child that we prayed. We were granted our desire and our hearts rejoice (I Samuel 1:28 and 2:1).

2. יי אֱלֹהֵי יִשְׂרָאֵל, תִּשְׁרֶה עַל יְלָדֵינוּ שְׁכִינָתֵךְ, תְּחֶזַקְנָה יָדֵינוּ לְגַדְּלוֹ לְתוֹרָה, לְחֻפָּה, וּלְמַעֲשִׂים טוֹבִים.

Adonai elohei yisra'el, tishre al yeladenu shekhinatekh, tehezaknah yadenu legaddelo letorah, lehuppah, ulema'asim tovim.

God of Israel, shelter our baby in your *Shekhinah* (close-dwelling presence of God, associated with the feminine) and strengthen our hands to raise him to Torah, the marriage canopy, and good deeds (adapted from BT *Shabbat* 137b and the liturgy for *Brit Milah*).[24]

3. זֶה הַקָּטָן, גָּדוֹל יִהְיֶה. יי אֲשֶׁר הִתְהַלְכוּ לְפָנֶיךָ אִמּוֹתֵינוּ וַאֲבוֹתֵינוּ, הָרוֹעֶה אוֹתָנוּ מִנְּעוּרֵינוּ עַד הַיּוֹם הַזֶּה, הַמַּלְאָךְ הַגּוֹאֵל אוֹתָנוּ מִכָּל רָע, בָּרֵךְ אֶת הַנַּעַר, וְיִקָּרְאוּ בוֹ שְׁמוֹתֵינוּ וּשְׁמוֹת אִמּוֹתֵינוּ וַאֲבוֹתֵינוּ.

Ze hakatan gadol yihyeh. Adonai asher hithallekhu lefanekha immoteinu va'avoteinu, haro'eh otanu mine'ureinu ad hayom hazeh, hamalakh hago'el otanu mikol ra, barekh et hana'ar, veyikkare'u vo shemoteinu ushmot immoteinu va'avoteinu.

This little one, may he grow great. God before whom our ancestors walked, God who has been our shepherd all our lives until this day, the angel who redeemed us from all ill, bless this boy and let our names and the names of our mothers and fathers be upon him (adapted from the *Brit Milah* liturgy and Genesis 48:15-16).

4. _____ , יִתֶּן לְךָ הָאֱלֹהִים מִטַּל הַשָּׁמַיִם וּמִשְׁמַנֵּי הָאָרֶץ.

_____, yitten lekha ha'elohim mital hashamayim umishmannei ha'aretz._

[Child's name], may God give you of the dew of heaven and the fatness of earth (after Genesis 27:28).

5. תָּאִיר תּוֹרָה דְּרָכֶיךָ וּתְהֵא דַּרְכְּךָ נֹעַם. סוּר מֵרָע וַעֲשֵׂה טוֹב, אֱהֹב שָׁלוֹם, וּרְדֹף שָׁלוֹם, וְהָבֵא שָׁלוֹם לָעוֹלָם.

Ta'ir torah derakhekha uteheh darkekha no'am. Sur mera va'aseh tov, ehov shalom, uredof shalom, vehaveh shalom la'olam.

May Torah light your path and may your way be one of pleasantness. Shun evil and do good, love peace, pursue it, and help bring peace in the world (after Proverbs 3:17, Psalms 34:15, and Mishnah _Avot_ 1:12).

6. הֱיֵה אָח נֶאֱמָן לְאַחֶיךָ וּלְאַחְיוֹתֶיךָ בֵּית יִשְׂרָאֵל. עֲשֵׂה צֶדֶק עִמָּהֶם וְעִם כָּל יוֹשְׁבֵי תֵבֵל.

Heyeh aḥ ne'eman le'aḥekha ule'aḥyotekha beit yisra'el. Aseh tzedek immahem ve'im kol yoshevei tevel.

Be a loyal brother to your sisters and brothers in Israel. Do justice to them all and the inhabitants of the world (after Psalms 98:9).

7. יי אֱלֹהֵי אִמּוֹתֵינוּ וַאֲבוֹתֵינוּ, קַיֵּם אוֹתוֹ. תַּעֲמֹד שְׁכִינָתֵךְ לִימִינוּ וְלִשְׂמֹאלוֹ, לְפָנָיו וּלְאַחֲרָיו וּמֵעַל רֹאשׁוֹ.

Adonai elohei immoteinu va'avoteinu, kayem oto. Ta'amod shekhinatekh limino velismolo, lefanav ule'aḥarav ume'al rosho.

God of our mothers and fathers, sustain him. May Your spirit stand at his right and his left, before him and behind him and above his head (adapted from the Prayer Before Retiring for the Night).

יְשִׂימְךָ אֱלֹהִים כְּאֶפְרַיִם וְכִמְנַשֶּׁה. יְבָרֶכְךָ יי וְיִשְׁמְרֶךָ. יָאֵר יי פָּנָיו אֵלֶיךָ וִיחֻנֶּךָּ. יִשָּׂא יי פָּנָיו אֵלֶיךָ, וְיָשֵׂם לְךָ שָׁלוֹם. אָמֵן, כֵּן יְהִי רָצוֹן.

Yesimkha elohim ke'efrayim vekhimnasheh. Yevarekhekha adonai vey-ishmerekha. Ya'er adonai panav elekha vihunnekka. Yissa adonai panav elekha, veyasem lekha shalom. Amen, ken yehi ratzon.

May God make you like Efraim and Menashe (Genesis 48:20; traditional Sabbath blessing recited by parents over sons). May God bless you and protect you. May God illuminate you with Her countenance and send you grace. May God raise up Her countenance to you and give you peace (after Numbers 6:23-27).[25] Amen, may it be Your will.

The following blessings are to be recited over wine or grape juice. In addition to being said at a Simḥat Lev, *they could be recited immediately after the birth.*

1. בְּרוּכָה אַתְּ יי אֱלֹהֵינוּ מַלְכַּת הָעוֹלָם, בּוֹרֵאת פְּרִי הַגָּפֶן.

Berukhah att adonai eloheinu malkat ha'olam, boret peri hagafen.

Blessed are You, our God, Sovereign of the universe who creates the fruit of the vine.

2. בְּרוּכָה אַתְּ יי אֱלֹהֵינוּ מַלְכַּת הָעוֹלָם, הַמְחַדֶּשֶׁת בְּטוּבֵךְ בְּכָל יוֹם תָּמִיד מַעֲשֵׂה בְרֵאשִׁית.

Berukhah att adonai eloheinu malkat ha'olam, hameḥaddeshet betu-vekh bekhol yom tamid ma'aseh vereshit.

Blessed are You, our God, Sovereign of the universe, who in Your goodness renews daily the work of creation (adapted from the morning prayers).

3. בְּרוּכָה אַתְּ יי אֱלֹהֵינוּ מַלְכַּת הָעוֹלָם, אֲשֶׁר יָצְרָה אֶת חַוָּה בְּחָכְמָה, וּבָרְאָה בָּהּ רֶחֶם. גָּלוּי וְיָדוּעַ לִפְנֵי כִסֵּא כְבוֹדֵךְ, שֶׁאִילּוּ לֹא נִסְתַּם הָרֶחֶם וְלֹא נִפְתַּח, אִי אֶפְשָׁר הָיָה לָלֶדֶת וּלְהִתְקַיֵּם לְפָנַיִךְ. בְּרוּכָה אַתְּ יי, רוֹפֵאת כָּל בָּשָׂר וּמַפְלִיאָה לַעֲשׂוֹת.

Berukhah att adonai eloheinu malkat ha'olam, asher yatzerah et ḥavvah beḥokhmah, uvar'ah bah reḥem. Galui veyadu'a lifnei khisseh khevodekh, she'illu lo nistam hareḥem velo niftaḥ, i efshar hayah laledet ulehitkayyem lefanayikh. Berukhah att adonai, rofet kol basar umafli'ah la'asot.

Blessed are You, our God, Sovereign of the universe, who has fashioned Eve in wisdom and created in her a sheltering womb. It is known before Your throne of glory that were the womb not to stay sealed, and then not to open in its appointed time, there would be no birth and no existence before You. Blessed are You, God, who heals all flesh and acts wondrously (adapted from the blessing over bladder and bowel function).

4. הָפַכְתָּ מִסְפְּדִי לְמָחוֹל לִי, פִּתַּחְתָּ שַׂקִּי, וַתְּאַזְּרֵנִי שִׂמְחָה. בְּרוּכָה אַתְּ יי אֱלֹהֵינוּ מַלְכַּת הָעוֹלָם, הַגּוֹאֶלֶת מִצַּעַר.

Hafakhta mispedi lemaḥol li, pittaḥta sakki, vate'azzereni simḥah. Berukhah at adonai eloheinu malkat ha'olam, hago'elet mitza'ar.

You have transformed my lament into dancing; You undid my sackcloth and girded me in joy (Psalms 30:12). Blessed are You, our God, Sovereign of the universe, who redeems us from anguish.[26]

5. בְּרוּכָה אַתְּ יי אֱלֹהֵינוּ מַלְכַּת הָעוֹלָם, שֶׁגְּמָלַתְנוּ כָּל טוֹב.

Berukhah att adonai eloheinu malkat ha'olam, shegemalatnu kol tov.

Blessed are You, our God, Sovereign of the universe, who has granted us all manner of goodness (*Birkat Hagomel*, prayer of thanksgiving for coming through danger in safety).

6. בָּרוּךְ אַתָּה יי אֱלֹהֵינוּ מֶלֶךְ הָעוֹלָם, יוֹצֵר הָאָדָם.

Barukh attah adonai eloheinu melekh ha'olam, yotzer ha'adam.

Blessed are You, our God, Sovereign of the universe, who fashions humankind.

7. בָּרוּךְ אַתָּה יי אֱלֹהֵינוּ מֶלֶךְ הָעוֹלָם, אֲשֶׁר יָצַר אֶת הָאָדָם בְּצַלְמוֹ, בְּצֶלֶם דְּמוּת תַּבְנִיתוֹ, וְהִתְקִין לוֹ מִמֶּנּוּ בִּנְיַן עֲדֵי עַד. בָּרוּךְ אַתָּה יי, יוֹצֵר הָאָדָם.

Barukh attah adonai eloheinu melekh ha'olam asher yatzar et ha'adam betzalmo, betzelem demut tavnito, vehitkin lo mimenu binyan adei ad. Barukh attah adonai yotzer ha'adam.

Blessed are You, our God, Sovereign of the universe, who fashioned humans in your image, the image of Your likeness, and made of them a building for eternity. Blessed are You, God, who fashions humankind.

8. שׂוֹשׂ תָּשִׂישׂ וְתָגֵל הָעֲקָרָה, בְּקִבּוּץ בָּנֶיהָ בְּתוֹכָה בְּשִׂמְחָה. בָּרוּךְ אַתָּה יי, מְשַׂמֵּחַ צִיּוֹן בְּבָנֶיהָ.

Sos tasis vetagel ha'akarah, bekibbutz baneha betokhah besimhah. Barukh attah adonai mesammeah tzion bevaneha.

The barren rejoice and exult through the ingathering of their children in their midst in gladness. Blessed are You, our God, Sovereign of the universe, who gladdens Zion through her children.

9. שַׂמֵּחַ תְּשַׂמַּח רֵעִים הָאֲהוּבִים, כְּשַׂמֵּחֲךָ יְצִירְךָ בְּגַן עֵדֶן מִקֶּדֶם. בָּרוּךְ אַתָּה יי, מְשַׂמֵּחַ הָאֵם בִּפְרִי בִטְנָה וְהָאָב בְּיוֹצֵא חֲלָצָיו.

Sammeah tesammah re'im ha'ahuvim kesammehakha, yetzirkha began eden mikedem. Barukh attah adonai mesamme'ah ha'em bifri vitnah veha'av beyotzeh halotzav.

Gladden the loving companions as You gladdened Your creatures in the Garden of Eden long ago. Blessed are You, our God, Sovereign of the universe, who gladdens the mother in the fruit of her womb and the father in his offspring (the above four blessings are adapted from the *Sheva Berakhot* [seven marital blessings] and from the liturgy of *Brit Milah*).

10. בָּרוּךְ אַתָּה יי אֱלֹהֵינוּ מֶלֶךְ הָעוֹלָם, שֶׁהֶחֱיָנוּ וְקִיְּמָנוּ וְהִגִּיעָנוּ לַזְּמַן הַזֶּה.

Barukh attah adonai eloheinu melekh ha'olam sheheheyanu vekiyyemanu vehiggi'anu lazeman hazeh.

Blessed are You, our God, Sovereign of the universe, who has kept us alive and sustained us and brought us to this day.

This ritual was a way to begin addressing the challenge of non-sexist child raising in a Jewish context. Having done it, I was surprised by how right and real, how "new/old" it felt. Thank God, we had a beautiful child; we had formally brought him into the House of Israel.

Creating a Tree-dition

TREASURE COHEN

"Just as our parents planted for us, so must we plant for our children."
                        —*MIDRASH TANHUMA KEDOSHIM* 8

The idea came to us before the baby. During those quiet nights before the arrival of our firstborn when we had to be concerned only with the theoretical aspects of child-rearing, we focused on a creative problem: How could we mark the occasion of bringing a new life into the world in a personal and spiritual way, at a time when we would be able to participate in the service and savor the occasion? Although circumcision (for a boy) or naming (for a girl) would provide traditional opportunities to celebrate, we were concerned that since these ceremonies usually take place so soon after the physical and emotional trauma of birth, it would be very difficult for us to involve ourselves fully. It was also important for us to develop a ceremony that would express joy and gratitude for our child in the same symbolic terms, whether that child be female or male.

The Genesis of the First Ceremony Our decision was to plant a tree in our child's honor and watch the child and tree grow together. We would celebrate life with life, involve our child as well as ourselves, and nurture a living reminder of the ceremony and its importance in our lives. This idea was rooted in Jewish tradition (BT *Gittin* 57a). In ancient Israel a tree was planted when a child was born, a cedar for a boy and a cypress for a girl. As children grew up, they cared for their own trees. When they married, the bridegroom and bride stood under a canopy made of "their" branches.[27]

In due course, Judah Michael was born that August by emergency caesarian section. It is fortunate that we did not put our creative efforts into making *Brit Milah* (covenant of circumcision ritual) more personally meaningful, since we were still in the hospital, and the ritual turned out to be entirely sterile. The hospital *Brit* room was dusted out, and the *mohel* (ritual circumciser) was

---

Treasure Cohen is a Jewish family educator, a teacher of young children, and a mother of four.

assisted by two nurses as a number of friendly observers clustered behind a glass window. My husband and I felt like outsiders to our child's initiation into Jewish life.

Our disappointment was tempered by the prospect of the special tree-planting ceremony which we had conceived. However, it took us months before we felt strong and resourceful enough to contemplate anything more abstract than feeding, burping, and changing the baby. Since by then the New England soil was locked into a deep winter freeze that promised to extend into early spring, we scheduled our tree-planting for May, when Judah would be eight months old.

Planning the ceremony was another act of creation. We hand-picked the tree, a small pink-flowering dogwood, which promised to be hardy and pretty. We studied the practical aspects of tree planting and researched biblical, liturgical, and historical allusions to trees. We compiled a service and wrote a prayer. And involved in all these activities was Baby Judah, either accompanying us in the many preparations or getting in the way, always making his presence very much felt.

We had every intention of actually planting the tree at the ceremony—until we went to pick it up at the nursery. Who would have believed that the skinny five-foot sapling would be so heavy and unwieldy! So we dressed in our grubbiest jeans and left Judah with a sitter (for fear that the wrong baby might end up in the hole). Then we drove to the site of the tree-planting with the tree sticking out of our Chevrolet's trunk like a leafy tail. We dug and dragged and pushed and huffed and puffed, finally connecting the tree to the hole. We piled some layers of soil over the roots, leaving the final layer to be filled in at the ceremony.

Two hours later—fingernails scrubbed, clothed in our best attire—we were ready. Judah was polished and tucked in a backpack, as we shared with friends and relatives the readings we had prepared on trees and children. Our service concluded with a *Sheheḥeyanu* (blessing for reaching a new or momentous occasion) and a *Kiddush* (blessing said over wine on sacred occasions). Then, we "planted" the tree and asked everyone to shovel soil onto the tree's roots.

How a Tradition Grows Judah grew and so did the tree. By *Tu Bishvat* (New Year for Trees), he was singing and romping over snowdrifts to wind paper streamers around his tree. In time, we moved to another community. Although we could no longer watch the tree grow from day to day, we would get long-distance reports from friends on our tree's progress and, once a year, we made a pilgrimage to measure Judah's growth against the tree's. It was like making notches in a wall that grew faster than the child.

In the years that followed, we added three daughters to our family tree, and our tree-planting ceremony became a tradition rather than an innovation. With each act of creation, we re-created the service to reflect our evolving expectations about life and growth and our understanding of the uniqueness of each child. Every time a baby was born, each of her older siblings had a role in creating the tree ceremony and welcoming the child's new tree into the world. Grandparents too had their parts, reflecting the Talmudic ideal of planting trees so that our grandchildren can see them grow to fruition (BT *Ta'anit* 23a).

When Jessica, our youngest, was born, we added a new piece to our tree planting ceremony. As we were celebrating Jessica's birth, we were mourning the loss of my mother Jessica who had died the previous year. Grandma Jessie had been an integral part of our family's life and our tree planting ceremonies. She had created a personal memory for each of Jessica's siblings by writing a poem for their tree plantings. Now we needed to include her memory in our service. We told the story of Baby Jessica's name— capturing the essence of what made her grandmother so special and expressing our hope that this legacy would continue. As we planted the tree's roots in the soil, we understood that Jessica's roots in the family tree had been nourished by her namesake. As each participant shoveled dirt onto the tree, we were reminded of the custom of personally shovelling dirt on the coffin of those who have died, and felt the symmetry and circularity of Jewish lifecycle.

All of our children cared for and about their trees. In their own small way, they became *shomrei adamah* (guardians of the earth). It became a yearly custom in our house to have a *Tu Bishvat* birthday party when the children would invite their friends over to decorate their trees with bows and streamers.

When we planted the trees, we were aware that, as with any living organism, there was a chance that the tree would not live out the length of its days. And although we intended the parallel between trees and children to reflect celebrating life with life, not every tree that we planted survived. In its fifteenth year, Shira's beautiful peach tree endured a difficult winter. It saddened us to watch the vibrance drain from its sturdy frame until there was no chance for survival. After mourning its loss, we knew we had to replant. We told Shira that we would celebrate her sixteenth birthday with another tree-planting. This time, *she* planned the ceremony. She invited her best friends, including her siblings, to read a poem of their choice about trees. She even included the poem her Grandma Jessie had written for her fifteen years before. She let her father read the prayer we had written for her at her first tree planting. Our eyes brimmed with tears, as we saw how much of our prayer had already come to fruition and we softly said our own *Sheheḥeyanu*. I added my own blessing for our almost-grown daughter:

> Shira, we pray that the tree we plant today has a long life. As it grows, so may you grow too. This time you will fly away to new worlds and new adventures, leaving your tree behind. May you go and grow in peace, but do not forget to come back to the place where your roots are planted.

Our children and our trees are now approaching a new stage of life. They are on the verge of maturity, and we, the parents and planters, no longer need to tend them so vigilantly. As they reach upward and outward, we hope that their roots and traditions will continue to nourish and sustain them until and beyond the day when they too can plant their own family trees.

ORDER OF THE TREE PLANTING CEREMONY

Welcome

Welcome to our tree planting! We plant a tree in our child's honor and watch the child and the tree grow together. In this way we are able to celebrate life with life, to involve our children as well as ourselves, to cherish a living reminder of this new birth, and to mark its importance in our lives.

Custom of Tree Planting

In ancient Israel, a tree was planted when a child was born—a cedar for a boy, a cypress for a girl. As the children grew up, they cared for their own trees. When they were married, the bridegroom and bride stood under a canopy made of branches cut from the trees that had been planted in their honor years before. Thus, the Jewish tradition formed a strong bond between birth and marriage, and helped to develop a love for trees and a sensitivity to the wonders of nature.

Etz Ḥayyim (Tree of Life)

Our Torah is a Tree of Life to those that hold tight to it and everyone who upholds it is happy. Its ways are ways of pleasantness, and all its paths are peace (after Proverbs 3:17-18, and Torah Service).

The above may be sung in Hebrew, using traditional or modern melodies.

Responsive Reading[28]

And God said: Let the earth put forth grass, herb yielding seed, and fruit trees bearing fruit after its kind...And it was so... And God saw it was good (Genesis 1:11-12).

When a tree is wantonly cut down, its voice rings from one end of the earth to another (*Pirkei Derabbi Eli'ezer* 43).

When you besiege a city, do not destroy the trees thereof. You may eat of them but you must not cut them down (Deuteronomy 20:19).

A person's life is sustained by trees. Just as others planted for you, plant for the sake of your children (*Midrash Tanḥuma Kedoshim* 8).

If you had a sapling in your hand and were told that the Messiah had come, first plant the sapling, then go out to greet the Messiah (*Midrash Avot Derabbi Natan* 8, 31).

Build houses and dwell in them; plant gardens and eat the fruit of them (Jeremiah 29:5).

You shall be like a tree planted beside a river; that brings forth its fruit in season, whose leaf does not wither; and whatsoever you do shall prosper (after Psalms 1:3).

Zion shall no more be termed forsaken; neither shall the land be termed desolate any more (Isaiah 62:4).

For the pastures of the wilderness are green with grass, the tree bears its fruit; the fig tree and the vine do yield their strength (Joel 2:22).

Be glad, O land, and rejoice, for the Lord hath done great things (Joel 2:21).

The Story of the Planter

While walking along a road, a sage saw a man planting a carob tree. He asked him: "How long will it take for this tree to bear fruit?" "Seventy years," replied the man. The sage then asked: "Are you so healthy a man that you expect to live that length of time and eat its fruit?" The man answered: "I found a fruitful world because my ancestors planted it for me. Likewise I am planting for my children." (BT *Ta'anit* 23a)

Family Tree: The Story of the Name

This is the opportunity to share the heart and spirit of the person/people the child was named after. It is the child's living history—the roots from which s/he will grow and the legacy s/he carries.

Siblings and Grandparents
Welcome the New Baby and the Tree

Using poem, picture, or story, immediate and extended family offer words of welcome, blessing, and advice to the baby.

Our Prayer for Our Child and Her/His Tree

Dear God, we stand before you in awe as we witness these miracles of your creation—this young tree and our baby. Both are unique and original, unlike anything that ever was before or will be. Each began with a single seed, concealing a complex potential that miraculously unfolds with each passing day.

We pray that the roots of this tree will gain hold and spread deep, drawing nourishment from the fertile earth. So may our child draw nourishment from her/his own roots—family, heritage, and the Jewish tradition.

We pray that the trunk will grow healthy and strong, withstanding the harsh forces of nature and able to support its canopy of branches and leaves. So may our daughter/son possess a healthy body and a strong moral spirit, holding steadfast to her/his own integrity and withstanding the tempests and temptations that could weaken or deter her/him.

We watch these branches bud and blossom, giving shade and beauty for all to enjoy. So, too, may we watch our child bud and blossom to be a blessing and support to family, friends, and community, and to make her/his unique contribution to the world.

Help us to nourish and nurture this tree and our child so that they may both mature and prosper, fulfilling to the greatest extent possible the potential for which God placed them on earth.

Final Blessings and Planting

בָּרוּךְ אַתָּה יי אֱלֹהֵינוּ מֶלֶךְ הָעוֹלָם, עוֹשֶׂה מַעֲשֵׂי בְרֵאשִׁית.

Barukh attah adonai eloheinu melekh ha'olam, oseh ma'aseh vereshit.

Blessed are You, *Adonai* our God, Ruler of the universe, who continually does the work of creation (blessing traditionally recited upon seeing wonders of nature, including sunrises, shooting stars, vast deserts).

בָּרוּךְ אַתָּה יי אֱלֹהֵינוּ מֶלֶךְ הָעוֹלָם, שֶׁהֶחֱיָנוּ וְקִיְּמָנוּ וְהִגִּיעָנוּ לַזְּמַן הַזֶּה.

Barukh attah adonai eloheinu melekh ha'olam, sheheheyanu vekiyyemanu vehiggi'anu lazeman hazeh.

Blessed are You, *Adonai* our God, Ruler of the universe, who has kept us in life, and preserved us, and enabled us to reach this season (blessing for reaching a new or momentous occasion).

The tree is planted.

4

Adolescence

Adolescence as we know it is an invention, some would say a luxury, of modern Western society. In societies where twelve and thirteen year olds have adult responsibilities to earn a living, or where it is normative for teenagers to marry and bear children, the passage between childhood and adulthood is neither so discrete nor so lengthy as it is in our privileged setting.

A major theme of adolescence is rebellion: Finding one's way in opposition to the known and defining oneself against the norm. Adolescence is also a time of experimentation—with sex, self-image, identity, and group affiliation. It is marked by obvious biological changes and less obvious psychological and spiritual ones. Adolescence is known for its contradictions: Massive indifference and uncompromising idealism; approach *and* avoidance of sexuality, responsibility, and parents.

In the Jewish tradition, boys come of age at thirteen and a day, girls, at twelve and a day. These are the ages of *mitzvah* (commandment, or, more figuratively, commandedness). At the age of Jewish majority, one is no longer just the son or daughter of one's parents; one becomes, also, the son or daughter of the commandments themselves (the literal meaning of *bar* or *bat mitzvah*). While becoming a Jewish adult does not happen all at once, the Bar or Bat Mitzvah (coming of age ceremony) is an important marker along the way, especially in light of the preparation and public ritual.

As much as adults remember the strength of their feelings during adolescence, it is hard to recapture exactly what it was like to live in that state between childhood and adulthood. And it is too rare that we trust adolescents—even as experts on their own experiences. Recently, Carol Gilligan and others have listened intently, via a series of interviews with pre-adolescent and adolescent girls, over a period of years. Their research shows that adolescence is a particularly difficult and dangerous time for girls—a time when they may become caught between "conventions of female goodness" that suppress self-fulfillment and "values...of self-sufficiency in North American culture" that suppress human connections and inter-dependence.[1] It is at this time that many girls deny or forget what they know, and give up their dreams in an effort to meet contradictory social expectations. Sensitive adults can help girls overcome harmful social strictures. The Jewish community, in particular, has a responsibility and interest in helping girls move safely and powerfully from childhood to Jewish and female adulthood.

Elana Rosenfeld Berkowitz, fourteen, looks back on her Bat Mitzvah and reflects on its meaning for her future as a Jewish woman. Her voice, her respect for women and the tradition, and the conscious and connected nature of her spiritual self-assessment will, I hope, serve as models for other young Jews. Berkowitz's message also holds lessons for Jewish adults. She points out that the question "What kind of Jewish woman do I wish to be?" is more complex than ever before, since this next generation of women and feminists faces challenges that are harder to define than those of past generations.

Fifty years ago, it was virtually unheard of for a girl to celebrate a Bat Mitzvah publicly and liturgically. My mother was the second girl in her congregation to have a Bat Mitzvah on Friday night and recite the *Kiddush* (blessing said over wine on sacred occasions). Twenty-five years later, I was the second girl in my congregation to have a Bat Mitzvah on Sabbath morning and read from the Torah. Now, twenty years after that, Sabbath morning Bnot Mitzvah are the norm in Reconstructionist, Reform, and Conservative synagogues. Many modern Orthodox, and a few ultra-Orthodox, communities have parties and/or religious celebrations in honor of girls who reach the Jewish age of majority. In light of all this, Norma Baumel Joseph shares her experience of coming of age, and speaks to both the miracle, and now the normalcy, of Bat Mitzvah.

The prayer upon menstruation which I wrote with Berkowitz addresses the major biological change that adolescent girls undergo. It stands in line with the Jewish tradition's proclivity to sanctify what could be regarded as simple bodily functions. (For example, eating is sanctified by keeping kosher and reciting blessings over food, just as going to the bathroom is elevated to an occasion for thanksgiving by a blessing.) Our prayer upon menstruation also serves to "assert the idea of a life" (a subject Rabbi Geller addresses in Chapter Three), by connecting the girl who gets her period for the first time with the woman she will become—the woman who may resume menstruating after a stretch of amenorrhea during pregnancy and nursing, the woman who will eventually undergo menopause.

In the final essay for this chapter, Rabbi Patricia Karlin-Neumann calls attention to the diversity of religious and secular options on college campuses and to the multiple points of entry—feminism included—that students have into Judaism. She also reflects on late adolescence as a time for questions of meaning and affiliation, and for Jewish identity formation. Clearly, the process of coming of age—growing up religiously, intellectually, and otherwise—continues well past puberty and, in various forms, throughout one's lifetime.

At Age Fourteen

ELANA ROSENFELD BERKOWITZ

*"With gladness and rejoicing shall they be brought. They shall
enter into the king's palace."*
                                                    —PSALMS 45:16

As I sat staring at my blank computer screen, I wondered how I
could summarize my passage from childhood to womanhood
given that I have not completed this trip nor had much time to
reflect on events. What many people think is the culmination of
the earliest phase of the transition from child to adolescent, the Bat
Mitzvah (coming of age ceremony for girls), was for me only the
beginning of what I hope will become a life of ritual and spiritual
events. I believe that becoming a Jewish woman takes much more
than a Bat Mitzvah ceremony; it involves more than just chanting
and explaining Torah and *Haftarah* (prophetic readings). To make
this change one must go through a series of events and at each
step pick up a little more wisdom.

Community Influence

I have had an experience different from that of many Jewish
women because I grew up in an egalitarian community where I
did not have to battle much religious sexism. (I thank my elders
for making it easier to be a Jewish feminist by virtue of their
example and contributions.) I was also brought up in a household
and taught in a school that had firm egalitarian values. Because
my whole Jewish experience was and is different from that of the
many others who wrote for this book, I face different struggles
ahead.

The first step on my road to womanhood was one which I did
not even choose. At the tender age of eight days I became the
youngest congregant at Minyan Ma'at on the Upper West Side of
Manhattan in New York City. I am still a member of this commu-

---

Elana Rosenfeld Berkowitz lives on the Upper West Side of Manhattan and is in
the ninth grade at Hunter College High School.

nity today. It was in this egalitarian setting that I developed a sense of self-worth both as a religious being and in a secular sense. My participation also offered gifts and opportunities (comfort with traditional texts and public speaking, for example) that have not always been readily available to other women. Unfortunately, I began to take these wonderful things for granted and not as rights that generations of women before me had to fight for. From an early age I thought it was natural for women to wear a *tallit* (prayer shawl) and to participate fully in synagogue life.

During and after Bat Mitzvah

My Bat Mitzvah took place on a cold November day in 1991, on the exact day that I turned twelve years old. I was rather apprehensive as I took my seat, waiting for the first *aliyah* (honor of reciting the blessings before and after the Torah is read), so that I could chant the Torah. On this day, I was nervous, but not because I did not know my Torah or *Haftarah* portion. Rather, it was because I was not sure of exactly why I was having my Bat Mitzvah—beyond the fact that my parents would kill me if I did not. I knew that I had grown both of body and, in some ways, of mind, but I still had questions.

I think that many young people experience this due to the erosion of traditional Jewish values and culture among American Jews. The focus of many Bat Mitzvah celebrations is a large, overly extravagant party, rather than the changes that let a woman mature and find her own path to God. I think that it is important to make the child and the Torah the focus of the Bat Mitzvah, not the party. Even though my Bat Mitzvah had more Jewish content than most, it still lacked the spiritual connection I wanted. Nevertheless, on the day of my Bat Mitzvah I started taking on some responsibilities. I became responsible for telling my grandparents' numerous friends that giving me checks or cash was not appropriate on *Shabbat* (Sabbath).

It was frustrating to me that I could not in a flash of light have the meaning of my Bat Mitzvah revealed to me. Instead, I came to realize that public moments must be discrete in time while personal development is continuous. My evolution as a Jewish woman has just begun and my family has taught me that it will take many years to complete. Until my Bat Mitzvah I felt little Jewish responsibility; I would spend much of the *Shabbat* service scampering around or reading. (As I got older I sat through more and more of the services.) While I feel that a spiritual turning point did not occur at my Bat Mitzvah, it was certainly a significant ritual marker in my transition from child to woman.

It seemed that the repercussions of this event hit my parents before they hit me. Almost immediately after my Bat Mitzvah my father decided to *bentsh* (say the blessing) after every meal as a way of thanking God for what he had, and now I was included as a participant in this prayer. My parents felt as I did, in that they saw my Bat Mitzvah as a link in a chain to God, rather than a monumental change. Therefore, my father's interest in bentshing related to my Bat Mitzvah because he saw the event as a step in strengthening his—and the whole family's—relationship with God and the Jewish people. After my Bat Mitzvah my parents took me and the new rituals I was to observe more seriously. This in turn made me examine the event more closely, searching for its meaning.

Still, it was not until a while later that I began to try in earnest to understand the meaning of going from child to woman and consciously to assume more adult responsibilities. It was as though my Bat Mitzvah, the ritual passage, was a springboard into my inner spiritual passage. Why did it take a year or more for a change referable to the Bat Mitzvah to be felt? Maybe at the time of my Bat Mitzvah I was simply not mature enough to handle the *mitzvot* (commandments), or perhaps the ritual provided a context and body of knowledge which I needed to make my spiritual decisions.

At the time of my Bat Mitzvah, I experienced community as an obligation. I had the burden of knowing how much this event meant to my parents, family, and community. In particular, my Bat Mitzvah was a big event because I was the first child born into the Minyan Ma'at to reach the age of Jewish majority. Since the time of my Bat Mitzvah ceremony, I have begun to realize how much my community means to me. The community is made up of people who know me and are always there for me, who encouraged me when Bat Mitzvah preparation—and later synagogue participation—was getting tough. These were the people who helped me with the cantillations, rehearsed a *devar torah* (Torah explanation and homily) with me, or just listened to my nervous complaints. I still do not think that I fully understand the meaning of the Jewish community that has supported me. Just as those who have both parents take that fact for granted, I took my community—people who protect me and help me learn and grow—as a given. My community is a second family. Like my parents, it will shelter me and eventually release me. Then I will find my way back. Joni Mitchell said, "You don't know what you've got till it's gone," and I will probably not fully understand the power of my community until I am away from it, in college.

Making Choices as a Jewish Woman

It was my third summer at Camp Ramah in the Berkshires and the summer after my Bat Mitzvah when I decided that I wanted to start to wear a *tallit* and to become more a part of the Jewish community. To this day, I am not exactly sure what made me decide to wear a *tallit*. The uniqueness of my wonderful egalitarian community was brought home to me when I went to buy my first one. In a Judaica shop, I tried on a big *tallit* which reached to my calves and covered me in rainbow stripes. As I tried to master the art of keeping the *tallit* on my shoulders, I noticed the reactions of five people in the store. There was a couple who were choosing a decorative *ketubbah* (marriage contract); judging by the questions they were asking my family and the shopkeeper, they did not seem to know much about Jewish tradition. They were laughing when they saw me, as if my struggle with the *tallit* were hilarious. An ultra-Orthodox woman, shopping with her small son, seemed uncomfortable and puzzled. Lastly, there was a lone woman browsing through the extensive book section, who reminded me of my aunt. She gave me a comforting smile as she noticed my obvious discomfort at being looked at. She seemed to understand all the different emotions racing through me. That is when I realized that my community is important because they understand me and allow me to be the sort of Jewish woman I am without exacting a price. My community was not the norm, as I had earlier thought it was. It was more of an aberration or at least something very different and special.

Along with my interest in wearing a *tallit*, my interest in learning about Jewish women started at Camp Ramah. To escape the mid-day heat I would dart into the camp library. It was there that I started to read from a weathered Bible and to look into the life of the first Jewish woman role model, Sarah. After I returned home, I decided to write a *devar torah* on the roles of Jewish women in the Bible and today. For me presenting a *devar torah* was an unnamed right of passage which was, in some ways, more powerful than my Bat Mitzvah. For the first time I was thinking and speaking not in the childish voice of my Bat Mitzvah speech, but in a more mature voice that was trying to understand the plight of Jewish women. It was almost like a second Bat Mitzvah because I was now doing one of the rituals voluntarily (as opposed to my Bat Mitzvah when I was pushed to do it). And I felt its power more.

Over the years I have tried to do things that reinforce and celebrate my Jewish and feminist identities. I joined the women's issues group at my school; I began to read more literature by women; and I started working at NARAL (National Abortion Rights Action League). I have also studied Jewish texts—biblical and modern. In addition, I helped start a group called the Student Holocaust Education Group which seeks to promote learning about the event from a Jewish perspective.

My Foremothers, Myself

My ability and freedom to study sets me apart from my mother, grandmother, and great-grandmother. It is only as the beneficiary of their Jewish struggles that I can now rejoice in my identity as a Jewish woman. My maternal great-grandmother raised ten kids and ran the family distillery so her husband could study Jewish texts all day. On her deathbed she made her husband swear before all the family that half of all his learning would go up with her to heaven. My great-great-aunt struggled for years before she became the first woman doctor in the Austro-Hungarian empire. My grandmother on my father's side spurned the limitations of salaried professions for women. Instead, she devoted herself to volunteering for and leading numerous Jewish causes. My mother, Dina Rosenfeld, did many things to help the Jewish women's movement. She was one of the founders of a Jewish women's group called Ezrat Nashim. She also worked toward the goal of women's ordination as rabbis. While it is hard to reflect on the gifts my mother has given me thus far, for I am still so young, it is already evident to me that she has been, through her example, particularly influential in the shaping of my identity as a woman and as a Jew. My mother has instilled in me respect for myself and for all others. She has taught me the importance of *tzedakah* (sacred practice of charity) and social activism and has fostered a love for family and the Jewish people. A child of Holocaust survivors, she has also taught me the importance of remembering the Jewish past and celebrating the present. I enjoy hearing the family stories of brave, smart, and empowered women, but sometimes I wonder what struggle is left for me.

It seems as if my foremothers bulldozed roads on which I can now just stroll. While I am not disappointed that I missed out on certain struggles and oppressions, I think the lack of turmoil for me as a Jewish woman has made it harder to define myself as a Jewish feminist. For the most part, I have fit, although not seamlessly, into my ready-made Jewish community. Nevertheless, by no means do I think our struggles are over, just that our struggles are harder to define. We still have a long way to go before we reach equality in many arenas. Ironically, because of women's advances in Judaism, teenage girls have gained the right to be as thoroughly apathetic as boys toward Judaism and its personal meaning. I do not want to be apathetic; I want to join battles with all women and revel in the spoils of all the wars hard won.

On Becoming a *Bat Mitzvah*, or When Do I Get to Say Today I Am a Jew?

NORMA BAUMEL JOSEPH

"Women's Otherness is not just a matter of social and religious marginality but of spiritual deprivation."
                    —JUDITH PLASKOW, *STANDING AGAIN AT SINAI*

I received my high school bulletin today. Usually, I rush to read the alumni section, but this time, my attention was caught by the column of news from the middle school. In it I read of the grade six and seven school celebration in honor of all the girls who came of age religiously. The *mazal tov* (congratulations) column listed the names of girls, as well as boys, who had reached Jewish majority. What a difference a few decades makes!

In 1956, my female classmates and I turned twelve. On our respective birthdays we each became a *bat mitzvah* (juridical Jewish adult), obligated to commandments according to Jewish law. We understood the new level of ritual performance expected of us; now, for example, we had to fast on *Yom Kippur* (Day of Atonement). The world of Jewish ritual observance descended upon us completely and quietly. We underwent this potentially momentous change in our lives and status privately. The only public sign of change was our complete absence from the men's section of the synagogue. Although most of us had long ago stopped sitting with Daddy, I felt sad when I was no longer welcome at my grandfather's side in the synagogue; when I could no longer hide under my father's prayer shawl.

The transition to adult status was so "quiet" that I do not remember anyone ever saying "*mazal tov!*" Did anyone ever teach us about being "twelve and one day," about all those ritual responsibilities? How did we learn about being required to pray, to give charity, to accept our obligation to the laws?

The following year, at age thirteen, the boys in our class expe-

---

Norma Baumel Joseph is a member of the faculty in the Department of Religion at Concordia University, Montreal.

rienced the same legal ritual transformation in a radically different form. In fact, to say that the transformation was "the same" in this context is absurd. Each boy was publicly tested and feted, proclaimed adult by the adult world, religiously and socially acknowledged as having entered the community of Jews. In every conceivable way the Bar Mitzvah (coming of age ceremony for boys) differed from the Bat Mitzvah (coming of age ceremony for girls), while supposedly meaning the same thing.

I cannot honestly say that I felt left out then or that I was aware of how much I was missing. Boys and girls were different— we all knew that. I was certainly proud that I could fast all day and that I was an adult one year before those immature boys. I enjoyed being a woman in the women's section, as I still do today. But of that momentous change, I expected no recognition and got none.

The school I went to is today considered more traditional and less progressive than it was in my day. Yet, the girls in that school are now taught about being *bnot mitzvah* and are publicly recognized with school ceremonies and parties, which of course still differ from the boys' Bar Mitzvah celebrations. The school always acknowledged that girls as well as boys need to learn Torah. Now it is identifying girls as adults who, though differently obligated than boys, must be ritually active also. Today, the Jewish world abounds with a variety of public Bat Mitzvah celebrations. Without great fanfare or revolution, all segments have been affected by a concern for women's religious experience and public involvement. A change in status was always part of the ancient tradition (BT *Baba Kamma* 15a). Only the recognition is new. No longer invisible, girls have a variety of opportunities to publicly proclaim: "Today, I am a Jew."

Prayer upon Menstruation

ELANA ROSENFELD BERKOWITZ AND DEBRA ORENSTEIN

"One is not born a woman, one becomes one."
                    —SIMONE DE BEAUVOIR, *THE SECOND SEX*

There have been many attempts to create a "menarche ritual," i.e. some sort of religious response to, for, and by a girl or young woman getting her period for the first time. Putting this particular event in a Jewish context is especially important because of the negative associations many Jews have to menstrual blood, to the biblical and Rabbinic attitudes toward menstrual impurity, to the folk custom of slapping a first-time menstruant, or to all of the above. While the intention of sacralizing our milestones is one we hold dear, we have found that a ritual, in this case, does not serve. Girls often feel embarrassed at the time of menarche. The last thing they want is public acknowledgment, and even a private ritual among family or friends feels uncomfortable. There may also be physical discomfort. In addition, there is often competition among peers around who is first, and who second, to get her period. Therefore, for young women, menstruation may be more of a nuisance than a cause for celebration. It often seems that the people who most want a ritual for this occasion are the mothers of teenage daughters, who are remembering their own adolescence and wishing, through a lifecycle ceremony, to connect both with their own past and with their daughters' current experience.

Mothers do have something to offer their daughters at this juncture: Practical advice, tales of their own experiences with menstruation early on, a hug (rather than a slap), a special mother-daughter outing or gift, a jointly recited *Sheheḥeyanu* (prayer recited on reaching a new or momentous occasion).

The prayer that follows is meant to be recited upon menarche and subsequent menses. Its references to a new month and its

------

Elana Rosenfeld Berkowitz lives on the Upper West Side of Manhattan and is in the ninth grade at Hunter College High School.

Rabbi Debra Orenstein, editor of *Lifecycles,* fellow of the Wilstein Institute of Jewish Policy Studies, and instructor at the University of Judaism in Los Angeles, regularly writes and speaks on Jewish spirituality and gender studies.

attendant blessings echo the *Birkat Haḥodesh* (blessing recited in anticipation of the New Moon Festival), and fit the occasion of a monthly menstrual cycle that has ties to the moon. Invoking the matriarchs in response to a uniquely female experience is also appropriate. The text is open enough that it can take on a variety of meanings, depending on the situation in which the woman reciting it finds herself. It can celebrate a marriage, a good grade in school, a new job, or it can offer comfort in the case of an illness, a break-up, a death in the family. The original version of this prayer was written by Rabbi Nina Beth Cardin for women with fertility problems, trying to conceive.[2] This version would still be applicable to infertile women. Saying the blessing every month would only give it extra meaning for the times when it is recited after unsuccessful attempts to get pregnant.

The wording might be altered slightly to create a menopause prayer, thus responding to another moment in women's biological cycle that has been overlooked by traditional liturgy. A menopause prayer similar to this menstruation prayer would implicitly validate middle age and the cessation of fertility as equal in worth to youth and the potential to have children. It would also serve to connect women's biological cycle as a single whole.

Finally, in addition to all these real and potential benefits, the prayer upon menstruation also has the advantages of being short, *un*ceremonious, and unembarrassing.

A woman says the following upon first getting her monthly period:

May it be Your will, Our God and God of our mothers, Sarah, Rebecca, Rachel, and Leah, to renew our lives in this coming month. May it be a month of goodness and blessing, healing and vitality, fruitfulness and abundance, joy and happiness, deliverance and consolation; a month which fulfills all our hearts' desires. Just as You took account of Sarah, answered Rebecca, saw the pain of Leah, and remembered Rachel, so may You tend me. Amen. Selah.

A Rabbi's Encounter with Jews Coming of Age on Campus

PATRICIA KARLIN-NEUMANN

"God, you know I have no space to call my own./I am a wandering ship, my anchor still stowed safely in its hold./My doorways are always changing,/my homes always temporary,/I have no constancy save myself and You./Let this token remind me/that whether I am entering into my quiet domain/or entering the world beyond my room,/You are with me, part of me, part of my shifting life./ Help me to be a portal for love, and Torah,/and an opener of doors."

—MIRIAM LIPPEL BLUM, "MEDITATION UPON ENTERING MY DOORWAY," 1985[3]

In my years as a Hillel director at several campuses, my one constant observation was that change characterizes college life. As student Miriam Lippel Blum recognized in the above *tkhine* (petitionary prayer for and/or by women, traditionally written in Yiddish), each year—sometimes each semester—brings with it new residences, new teachers, new subjects, new methods of inquiry, perhaps new roommates and friends. In college, students learn about other ways of being and investigate differences. Vision is expanded, and long-held assumptions are challenged. Boundaries are for crossing. Yet, in this place and time of exploration, students encounter and solidify the commitments and beliefs which will shape their adult lives.

What is the place of a tradition which values roots, rituals, continuity, enduring truths, and a dedication to the past, amidst the swirling opportunities of change and difference? The answer depends in part on the individual student and his or her Jewish background. Some students are exposed to Judaism for the first time while in college. Others come to college wishing to escape their Judaism. Some will find safe haven from the storm of campus politics, while others grapple with a Jewish pluralism that challenges orthodoxies.

Rabbi Patricia Karlin-Neumann, the rabbi at Temple Israel in Alameda, California, has worked with Jewish students at the Claremont Colleges, University of California, Los Angeles, and Princeton University.

For Judaism to join the conversation of college students, it must be represented with both breadth and depth, in all its complexity. Captivated by the variegated and enlivening world of the campus, students may assume that the pediatric Judaism of their youth is all that exists.

Viable Jewish campus communities have multiple points of entree, a veritable Chinese menu of Jewish choices: Social gatherings, Israel action committees, Torah learning, prayer services, Jewish feminist study groups, associations of Jewish business, law, or medical students. The programmatic sweep of an active Hillel addresses the head, the body, and the soul of Jewish students.

Yet, along with variety, a Jewish campus community also offers constancy. Every *Shabbat* (Sabbath) morning, the UCLA *minyan* (prayer quorum) studied Torah with the wisdom of many disciplines. Friday night dinners in my home were, for many students, the first experience of a Judaism lived and examined. At retreats with thoughtful Jewish academic and religious leaders, we regularly raised serious Jewish questions, and left plenty of time for discussion. Every Wednesday, at the Claremont Colleges, students from six different campuses gathered to lunch and schmooze with other Jews, in a program we half-jokingly dubbed "the ritual gathering of the clan." With the uncertainty and many possibilities of campus life, I, along with the students, came to value ritual gatherings on Wednesdays *and* Saturdays for religious, cultural, and other reasons.

Students expressed a variety of Jewish concerns. They came to me with questions about an academic paper, or because of an encounter with a Christian fundamentalist roommate, or a love relationship with a non-Jew. I spoke with students about the complicated and highly charged world of identity politics. Often, they were uncertain of their identity as Jews, Zionists, and members of a minority community. I did my best to help them navigate the maze of issues surrounding sexuality, freedom, and responsibility.

The students most enriched by their Jewish encounters were often those who had been utterly secular. I worked with Jewish feminists in creating a feminist Passover *seder* (ordered readings and meal) and other rituals marking sacred Jewish space, precisely because anger at their exclusion energized them to address their heritage. They demanded a place—and explored the tradition they were critiquing in the process. I studied with students who encountered *Shabbat* (Sabbath) for the first time and were engaged forever. Just as students often leave campus with friends for life, they also leave campus with commitments for life—some of which may be born of their Jewish encounters.

It is unpredictable which Jewish students will leave the campus with strong Jewish identities. Among my Hillel colleagues and faculty are dedicated and powerful models of Jewish life, who help to shape the next generation of Jews. With a multiplicity of Jewish and secular possibilities in the open world of the campus, Jewish college students make the first independent religious choices of their lives. It can be a difficult, confusing time of life. Our job, as I see it, is to facilitate a meaningful encounter with the tradition that gives due credit and respect to Judaism and to the students themselves. The possibilities and the diversity of *both* are inspiring.

5

Being Single

M en and women, in their teens or early twenties, once commonly moved, overnight, directly from their parents' home into a marital household. In contemporary American Jewish society, such a pattern is now uncommon, and single life has been extended. Moreover, increasing numbers of American Jews never marry. For some, this is a deliberate choice. Others regard it as their default decision or even their fate. Singlehood was once presumed, especially for women, to be a passage that had its terminus in marriage. Today, marriage is likelier than ever before to terminate in divorce and, at least for a time, in singlehood.

In a Jewish community that stresses family and builds so much of its continuity on family rituals performed around the dining table, single and childless people are often made to feel out of place. Many Jews and Jewish institutions operate out of a popular (and unconscious) "chain-letter-theory" of Jewish lifecycle: Marriage leads to birth which leads to naming, which leads to *Bar* or *Bat Mitzvah,* which leads back to marriage, until an unmarried and/or childless offspring "breaks the chain." Put so starkly, this "theory" becomes laughable, but it is shocking to realize how often we behave as if we believed it.

Modern attitudes may have their roots, in part, in Jewish tradition. The Rabbis regard failure to marry as just that—a failure (BT *Kiddushin* 29b). However much we may disagree, few Jews would reject the traditional affirmation and valuation of family and children.

This leads us to ask: What of single people in our communities who may not have any close relatives? How might we more fully include singles—those who have not married, as well as those who are single again because of divorce or the death of a spouse—in our vision and definition of "family" and "community?" What of single parents? What of childless singles during holidays which emphasize children and nuclear families? What occasions have we crafted (or might we now craft) for single adults to celebrate their milestones Jewishly?

While single people, in general, have lacked sufficient acknowledgment, respect, and opportunity for self-expression in a Jewish context, Jewish women have been more alienated than Jewish men. Single women generally suffer a greater stigma than male counterparts. Men are bachelors; women, spinsters. Men who assert their disinterest in marriage are inveterate bachelors; women who express similar disinterest are often considered man-haters. Venues for the unmarried in the Jewish community—from personal ads, to singles events, to retirement communities—all convey the impression, for reasons demographic, psychological, and sexist, that single men are in demand, and single women, "flooding the market." Women are still defined primarily through home, relationships, and family, rather than through work, and so the "failure" to marry and bear children is particularly incriminating. The idea that women, even more than men, *"should"* have a family is supported by Jewish cultural programming, though not by Jewish law.

Many of these stereotypes and sex-role divisions are losing their hold on a logical level. Yet they still retain a psychic grip.

Interesting and accomplished single men and women with high self-esteem may live their lives with a sense of being "on hold." (Meanwhile, ironically, unhappy people in bad marriages are waiting until...for life to begin in earnest.)

Jewish rituals marking the seasons of single life are lacking, especially for women. Married couples re-live and build on their own life passages through their children. Single men can, to a lesser extent, see themselves honored in the happy fuss that is universally made over an eight-day-old male, a thirteen-year-old male, a male who leads a congregation in prayer or completes the study of a tractate of Talmud. Single women, at least for now, have fewer role models and possibilities for identification.

Rabbi Pamela Hoffman addresses the need for personal passage celebration in the lives of single Jews with an annual celebration of adult personhood. Drawn from traditional sources and suitable for *any* Jew, it honors individual growth on one's birthday. To set this ritual in context, Rabbi Hoffman uses a celestial analogy, recognizing each of us as stars in our own right, as well as members of various constellations.

Rose L. Levinson focuses unflinchingly on the shame we apportion to single women—and the shame they internalize. Her writing both notes and demonstrates that the experience of being single may have divergent meanings for different people, or even for the same person over a period of time. Jewish singles are sometimes accused of being fickle. They wish to be "set up," and want special programs and attention in the Jewish community. Also—and sometimes alternately—they want their status to be irrelevant, and ask for full inclusion in everything from programming to religious observances to synagogue membership applications. Levinson's essay invites the reader to look beyond any apparent contradictions and ask: What is the source of pain to which both alternatives are responding, and what is the need of the person standing before me?

"Childlessness: A Conversation" transcribes a heartfelt exchange that took place at a conference for contributors to this volume. Not every unmarried woman is childless, and not every childless woman is unmarried, but there is significant overlap in the two groups. And not having children, or waiting to have them, is one of the most difficult aspects of being single for many Jewish women. This selection, besides illuminating the topic, also conveys a sense of the camaraderie and caring that developed in preparing this book.

The continuing challenge for the Jewish community is to address the needs and often the pain of single Jews, without condescension, sexism, or rigid and exclusive definitions of family.

A final word: Women, more often than men, have a stretch of singlehood as widows. Widows have different concerns than women who have never married, and are not the focus of this chapter. However, widows and singles are both marginalized to the outer boundaries of a family-centered tradition, and much of what is said here will apply. (For more on widowhood, see Chapter Fourteen.)

On Being Single

PAMELA HOFFMAN

*"Then I said, 'I will bring a scroll which contains my story. To do
Your will, my God, is what I desire. Your teaching is deep inside me.'"*
—AFTER PSALMS 40:8-9

If ritual, in general, is the drama by which we superimpose our sense of cosmos in an often wild, unruly universe, then it is the ritual surrounding lifecycle events, in particular, that casts each and every one of us—at different times—as stars in this cosmic ordering. In the presence of these stars, our faith in the indestructibility of the covenant is renewed. The distance between here and Sinai seems, after all, not so far. An eight-day-old baby, a young adolescent called for the first time to the Torah, a couple standing under the wedding canopy—each is transformed by ritual into a for-this-moment luminary who sheds light on the present Jewish community and on our mythic past and future.

Stars, however, do not exist on their own. They form part of a larger constellation. So, too, every person celebrates lifecycle events within the context of a broader community. One star among the many will soon make way for and witness other celebrants as they, in their turn, become the focal point. Unfortunately, Jewish singles, and particularly Jewish single women, are rarely celebrated by the community.

Communal Celebration: A Family Affair

Lifecycle events are not only communal occasions, but also family affairs. In Judaism, as in many traditions, the growth of the individual is measured largely through life-generating acts. In many ways, birth, childhood, and adolescence form a kind of one-directional corridor leading ultimately to the wedding canopy. At birth, the community projects its aspirations onto every newborn (male) child with the blessing: *Letorah, lehuppah, ulema'asim tovim.* "May

---

Rabbi Pamela Hoffman serves as spiritual leader to the Jewish community of Halifax, Nova Scotia and teaches Jewish spirituality to recovering alcoholics and drug addicts in New York City, through her "Rabbinate Without Walls."

[he] be privileged to learn Torah, to arrive at the wedding canopy, and to do good deeds." The echoes of this ancient blessing reverberate throughout the twists and turns of life's lengthy passageway, and find their fulfillment under the wedding canopy.

With marriage, the "I" of the individual persona begins to recede into the background—at least as far as Jewish tradition is concerned. A script is already set: Soon the young couple will bear a child. The community will once again gather. Some of the cast will be the same. New faces will have been added to the circle. Familiar faces will bear the passage of time. The same words will be recited anew, the same ritual acts performed. And we, the community of family and friends, will be comforted with the momentary assurance that this new offspring will embark upon the same long corridor, accompanied by the same echoes of that ancient blessing: *Letorah, leḥuppah, ulema'asim tovim.*

Now all of this constitutes a grave problem for me and many other "non-attached" Jewish adults. For we, perhaps more than any other population in the Jewish community, find ourselves in a kind of "no-man's" land where, because structure is utterly lacking, chaos prevails. With what communal recognition do I, as a non-married person, celebrate a committed human relationship, avail myself of opportunities for maternal nurturing, participate in ritual events which acknowledge my standing in the community as a vital contributor to its time-honored values? Sadly, the answer is: None.

As a single woman, I have had ample cause to think about the lack of a ritual of personhood in Jewish lifecycle observance. Jewish theology finds its articulation in rituals which embrace both the "macro events" of its mythic history as well as the microcosmic signs of God's providence—which is to say, its family events.

But I, too, have a history that calls for acclamation, a present in need of celebration, and a future demanding to be renewed by the power that ritual can provide. I look for a natural pausing point where I might recognize the contours of my own life—with its achievements, struggles and steppingstones; where I might celebrate my own acts of generativity in the world—for I have given birth to dreams, and I have created and nurtured ideas that have since taken on a life of their own. I have in my more sanguine, less anxious moments, watched and helped my garden grow.

Honoring Individual Growth

My guess is that I am not alone in this search for a ritual expression of adult personhood, unrelated to family status. It is no accident that the last several years have witnessed the proliferation of Adult Bat Mitzvah (belated coming of age ceremony). Nor is it surprising that significant numbers of these celebrants are single professional women who seem to be seeking a way of honoring their personhood within a community that has become highly important to them. This innovation, however, is not the kind of ritual expression that I am speaking about. First, the Adult Bat Mitzvah is a one-time-only event. Also, it is an inadequate substitute for the rituals of married adulthood because, happily, more and more young women are celebrating a Bat Mitzvah at age twelve or thirteen. My own Bat Mitzvah occurred some two decades ago and has since receded to a place somewhere in my distant "primordial" past. In contrast, the type of celebration I am proposing could operate throughout the life of every Jew, and would not be contingent upon being either parent or spouse. Like other lifecycle events, it would mark a transition and thereby become an occasion for examining that complex process we call living.

For some time I have contemplated appropriating the occasion of my birthday and investing it with a ritual ceremony and structure. Admittedly, the recognition of a birthdate is distinctly foreign to Jewish observance. In fact, the only mention of a birthday observance in the entire Torah is that of Pharaoh, the archgentile.[1] We Jews have been good at *yartzeit* (anniversary of a death), at celebrating a life in retrospect, rather than as it is being lived. Birthdays evoke associations with transition—even with anxiety or chaos—especially, though not exclusively, for the single and unattached. It is a boundary in time that thrusts itself upon us, uninvited. It is the most individualized marker that we are given, and like it or not, it summons us to engage in personal inventory and reflection. Navigating our way across this boundary can be a turbulent business. Hence there is much that "good ritual" could do to transform chaos into cosmos, to keep this highly-charged time from violently erupting. Formulated in the positive, there is also much that "good ritual" could do in celebrating that piece of the divine image with which we are entrusted at birth, to do good works in the world just as we are.

The celebration would ideally take place in the warmth of one's home, amidst close family and friends. It can be used to acknowledge passages, goals, and contributions in any Jew's life, though the celebration fills a special need for the non-married. Herewith, then, are the "raw ingredients" of a ritual of personhood, to be celebrated yearly on the occasion of an individual's birthday. More important than the specifics of the ritual is the value that we will, I hope, learn to assign to all our lives, whether they are lived in marriages or in other constellations.

ORDER OF THE ANNUAL RITUAL

Verses for Song/Study/Interpretation

Emphasis should be placed on verses that have to do with the passage of time, the celebration of life, the individual's connection with God and the world, as in the selections from Psalms, below:

אֹרֶךְ יָמִים אַשְׂבִּיעֵהוּ, וְאַרְאֵהוּ בִּישׁוּעָתִי.

Orekh yamim asbi'ehu, ve'arehu bishu'ati.

I will satiate you with length of days; I will show you My salvation (after Psalms 91:16).

אַךְ טוֹב וָחֶסֶד יִרְדְּפוּנִי כָּל-יְמֵי חַיָּי, וְשַׁבְתִּי בְּבֵית יי לְאֹרֶךְ יָמִים.

Akh tov vahesed yirdefuni kol-yemei hayyai, veshavti beveit adonai le'orekh yamim.

Surely goodness and lovingkindness will follow me all the days of my life; and I will dwell in *Adonai*'s house for the length of my days (Psalms 23:6).

אָשִׁירָה לַיי בְּחַיָּי, אֲזַמְּרָה לֵאלֹהַי בְּעוֹדִי.

Ashirah l'adonai behayyai, azammerah lelohai be'odi.

I will sing out to *Adonai* with my life; I will sing out to praise my God with that which is yet in me (Psalms 104:33).

Traditionally, each Hebrew name has a biblical verse associated with it. The verse begins and ends with the same letters as the name. Many prayerbooks provide a listing of verses for each possible combination of Hebrew letters, and it would be most appropriate to study the celebrant's "name verse."[2]

Teaching of Text

The following are sample texts for teaching and personal reflection. The first is taken from the writings of Rebbe Naḥman of Bratzlav, who advocates that each person see him/herself as constituted of "points of goodness" containing her/his life force. It is by connecting the dots, so to speak, that we revitalize this vital energy. The second selection is from the Zohar (premiere Jewish mystical text) and concerns "entering our days."

1. A person's soul should find rejuvenation and joy in the *me'at hatov*—that little bit of good—that she finds within herself, some *mitzvah* or *davar tov*—some good thing—that she has done in her days. And in that same way, she has to continue to search within herself and find yet another bit of good. Even if that good thing is tainted with impurities, in spite of this, she must draw forth its *nekuddah tovah*—its good point. And as she continues to search and gather together other good points within herself, *niggunim* (wordless melodies), are made. Only then is she able to pray and to sing and to express gratitude to God. This is the way she celebrates and revitalizes herself. It is certainly appropriate that this is the way she intensifies her joy, by gathering together each point of her being that emanates from the holiness of being a Jew. This is what the Psalmist meant when he said, "*Azammerah*—I will sing!"—that is to say, I will sing the melodies and songs that come into being as I gather together my *nekuddot tovot*, the good points of my being.[3]

2. It has been taught: When a human being is created, on the day s/he comes into the world, simultaneously, all the days

of her life are arranged above. One by one, they come flying down into the world to alert that human being day by day.

Come and see: When those days draw near to the Holy King, if the person leaving the world is pure, s/he ascends and enters into those days, and they become a radiant garment for her soul! But only her days of virtue, not her days of fault.

Happy are the righteous, for their days are pure and stored up with the Holy King. When they leave this world, all their days are sewn together, woven into radiant garments for them to wear in the world that is coming.[4]

Inscribing the Scroll of Days

The inspiration for writing a scroll comes from Psalms. "Then I said I will bring a scroll which contains my story. To do your will, My God, is what I desire. Your teaching is deep inside me" (after Psalms 40:8-9). The idea is for celebrants to make a scroll to which they could add year after year. One possibility is for the celebrant to inscribe newly achieved "points of goodness" that reflect the growth of the last year.

Blessings by Friends

These can be offered orally or included in the "Scroll of Days."

Prayer of the High Priest

The prayer of the High Priest, which is said at the conclusion of the *Avodah* (Temple worship) service on *Yom Kippur* (Day of Atonement), could be recited in the singular by the birthday celebrant as s/he prays for the blessings of a new year. The following is a version of that prayer translated by Rabbi Debra Orenstein and adapted for a birthday celebration:

May it be your will, *Adonai* our God and God of our ancestors, that this year now coming upon us, be for me and for all Your people, a year of abundance; a year of blessing; a year of good decrees and good tidings; a year

of grain, wine, and oil; a year of growth and success; a
year of assembly in Your sanctuary; a year of prosperity;
a year of good and happy life before You; a year of dew
and rain and warmth; a year in which choice fruits ripen
and sweeten; a year of atonement for all my sins; a year
in which my food and drink, both, will be blessed; a
year of good business; a year in which I may enter
Jerusalem's Holy Temple; a year of plenty and pleasure;
a year in which You will bless the fruit of the womb and
the fruit of the land; a year in which You will bless my
going out and my coming in; a year of salvation for me
and my community; a year in which Your mercies shall
be moved toward me; a year of peace and serenity; a
year in which You may bring me rejoicing to Zion; a
year in which Your treasures will be opened to me; a
year of independence in which You will set a blessing
upon all the work of my hands.[5]

Standing Alone at Sinai: Shame and the Unmarried Jewish Woman[6]

ROSE L. LEVINSON

"...And [Hannah] was in bitterness of soul, and prayed to God, and wept sore."

—I SAMUEL 1:10

To be a woman in Judaism is to be less than. To be an unmarried, childless woman is to be even more diminished. To be an unmarried, childless, middle-aged Jewish woman is to move dangerously close to invisibility.

All this might be bearable—or less unbearable—if inside ourselves we women somehow felt it was all right to be unmarried. But many of us do not. Words like "spinster" and "old maid" burn in our psyches, even in these days of feminism. The result of our internal struggle is a wounding, paralyzing sense of shame.

We are ashamed that we have not been chosen by a man. We are ashamed that we stand alone—too dominating, too unlovely, too conflicted, too screwed up, too whatever—to have been picked. We are ashamed that we come before God without a husband by our side.

Of course, this does not apply to every unmarried woman. There are other choices, other views. I write for those, like myself, who wrestle with the shame beast.

The Shame Beast

What is shame? The definitions range from those which describe shame in terms of body phenomena (sweating, blushing, casting the eyes down, etc.) to those which describe an emotional state.

In fact, it is early in Genesis that we first encounter the concept. Prior to eating of the forbidden fruit, neither Adam nor Eve knew shame. But when the link with the Source was broken, the world became external and shame made its first appearance.[7] This notion of splitting, of losing wholeness and contending with an alien, external other, ties in with journalist Susan Miller's simple,

---

Rose L. Levinson continues her search for God, Meaning, and Other in the context of her life as Conservative Jew, radio host, writer, aunt, sister, and friend.

powerful definition of shame: "An experience of the self as diminished....before another and potentially visible to another."[8]

Another view of shame suggests that it is "a violation of expectation, of incongruity between expectation and outcome, resulting in a shattering of trust in oneself, even in one's own body...and in the world one has known."[9]

Putting theory aside, we all know what shame is: It is our little girl standing vulnerable, embarrassed, frightened, stripped in front of some "other." It is our foremother Rachel ashamed because she is barren and her sister Leah ashamed because she was not chosen, making up for being unlovely by bearing child after child. It is each of us who has ever said, "I am too fat; I am too old; I am too loud; I am too much or too little."

On Being Seen and Judged

As Jewish women, we stand before others all the time. At the heart of Judaism is community, intertwinement, accountability. We stand before God, we stand before peers, we stand before institutions, we see and are seen because to be a Jew is to be part of an expanded collective.

But we women are more seen than see-ers. The eyes that view us, the people who judge us, the peers who define us, the ones who name us are male. And woe to those of us who are not "prime marriage material." For then the internalized messages of see-ers and namers tell us that we do not count for much; we are shadow figures.

The social hierarchy in Judaism places successful, moneyed males at the top of the pyramid (extra points for being married), followed by married couples of any socio-economic level who have children. Next come married couples without children (at least they are married, but they may contend with the shame of barrenness). Unmarried Jewish males, of whatever age, are next on the pyramid; their unmarried status is assumed to be a matter of choice. At the bottom of the structure are unmarried Jewish females, presumably waiting to be chosen. The Talmud implies that "a woman would rather be impoverished and married than wealthy and unmarried."[10]

To be involved in any aspect of Jewish communal life is to be in a world where family and children are central values, where it is a given that these comprise the heart and soul of Judaism. In the swirl and joy of Jewish life, home—with spouse and children—is where God resides.

On Judging and Seeing Ourselves

Even for high-powered, successful, attractive Jewish women, feeling diminished if one is not married is often a core reality. What is wrong with me? How did I fail? Why am I left out? On some level, the woman feels unchosen and unworthy. She feels that she cannot partake fully in the community nor share equally in the covenant because she has not fulfilled a fundamental criterion for acceptance: She is not married.

Given this set-up, it is no wonder that so many unmarried Jewish women retreat from Jewish communal life. Why bother? Why participate as a second- or third-class citizen? Why feel even more marginalized?

The point of all this is not to challenge the power of connection that wifehood and motherhood can bring. Nor does this challenge the possibility that marriage and family can foster a heightened relationship with God. In fact, here is the really tough part: I believe in marriage. I tend toward the view that marriage does, in fact, provide the playing field on which we mortals replicate our relationship to the divine. I subscribe to the notion that through marriage a woman finds new and deeper connections to her ancestors, her descendants, her God. I am ashamed that I am not married.

So why make all the fuss? Why shine a light on shame and disturb it as it sleeps over there in its dark corner? Because shame cripples; it robs us of energy and joy. It makes a hard task even harder. For if our task is to keep searching—for Meaning, for Other, for Husband, for God—we need all the strength we can muster. And if we fail to find any of these things or find them only partially, then we must reconcile the deeper fears and disappointments that lie buried beneath our shame.

It is enough to be lonely and not know who will recite the mourner's prayer for us. It is a waste of precious energy to mask the true pain with feelings of shame. Shame is less real than what it conceals. Once it is moved aside we can, perhaps, confront our deeper darkness and begin to move beyond it.

Childlessness: A Conversation

ARLENE AGUS, BARBARA BREITMAN, TIKVA FRYMER-KENSKY, DEBRA
ORENSTEIN, ELLEN M. UMANSKY, AND CHAVA WEISSLER

*"Once, in my early twenties, I saw that I was a speck of light in
the great river of light that undulates through time."*

—JANE KENYON, *CONSTANCE*

*The following is an edited transcript of a conversation at one of two con-
ferences held for contributors to* Lifecycles. *The paper under discussion
was on midlife.*

Arlene Agus: There is a certain invisibility to women who are
not married or women who don't have children. When I read
essay drafts written for this book—even essays that describe fairly
universal life moments—somehow we are not fully a part of it,
because there is a part of our pain that is not seen or acknowledged. We are very careful to talk about all kinds of lifestyle differences and take into account all kinds of permutations, and yet
not having children is rarely mentioned. So, you feel as though
you dropped off the map somewhere, but you don't want to say
so. It requires you to feel and announce your own alone-ness and
alienation, and you don't want to betray yourself in that way. At
the same time, you want somebody to acknowledge the existence
of this kind of pain.

Ellen M. Umansky: Reaching midlife without children in a
Jewish context is both difficult and important. So are all the permutations: Having children, not having children, having young
children, grown children, aging parents, parents who have died—
all of that significantly changes how we view midlife.

Arlene Agus is the founding director of the Poretsky Foundation.
Barbara Breitman is a feminist therapist in private practice in Philadelphia, an
instructor at the University of Pennsylvania School of Social Work, a trainer on
issues of cultural, racial, and ethnic diversity, and a long-time activist in the
Jewish Renewal Movement.
Dr. Tikva Frymer-Kensky is the director of biblical studies at the
Reconstructionist Rabbinical College and the author of *In the Wake of the
Goddesses: Women, Culture and the Bibilical Transformation of Pagan Myth* (Free
Press, 1992) and the forthcoming *Motherprayer.*

Tikva Frymer-Kensky: The difference between childlessness in midlife and childlessness earlier is the profound realization, once you have reached midlife without children, that you are *never* going to have them.

Barbara Breitman: I thought of that last night. I am staying at my mother's this weekend. A few weeks back, she gathered all the eight-millimeter films that my father had taken—literally from the time of my birth until he died, which is when I graduated from college. She had all the film transferred to videos. We had not seen these films for twenty years, and we sat down and we watched them. It took four hours to run the footage. I looked at myself change from being a toddler searching for the right end of a lollipop, to being a senior searching for my place in the graduation line. And I was crying, and we were laughing, and my mom and I both felt the entire gamut of emotions as we reviewed the first twenty-one years of my life together. When I went to bed, my one thought was, "What am I going to do with these films? I have no one to give them to." That's the experience. I was lying in bed, thinking, "Which of my friends' children am I close enough to, that I could give them these videos? Who would look at these images and laugh about the little baby who became this woman?" And then I realized that nobody was ever going to look at them the way my mother and I did. There would be no daughter of mine, no granddaughter to cherish these frozen moments, to wonder over the mystery of this time together. And I thought, "Well, maybe I'll ask in my will, which I have to write now because I just bought a house for the first time, maybe I'll ask that they bury the videos with me."

Arlene Agus: Do you continue to hope that your life will work out in a normative way (i.e. being married and having children), which is a way that you might have preferred? Or, do you

---

Rabbi Debra Orenstein, editor of *Lifecycles*, fellow of the Wilstein Institute of Jewish Policy Studies, and instructor at the University of Judaism in Los Angeles, regularly writes and speaks on Jewish spirituality and gender studies.

Dr. Ellen M. Umansky is the author of numerous essays and books on women and Judaism, including the co-edited *Four Centuries of Jewish Women's Spirituality: A Sourcebook* (Beacon Press, 1992).

Dr. Chava Weissler, Philip and Muriel Berman Professor of Jewish Civilization at Lehigh University, writes about the religious lives of eighteenth century Ashkenazic women.

begin to try to adjust to something that you don't want to face? Or, in avoidance of these options, do you live simultaneously with both possibilities? That is what most of us do, and in some ways that is the most painful choice.

In the Jewish feminist culture, the word "nurturing" is used so often, and every time I hear it, it's like an arrow through my heart, because it is so closely associated for me with motherhood. I do not know if I want to describe that in too much detail; maybe I want to gloss over it just to keep myself sane.

Chava Weissler: I am thinking of what you said about "Who could I leave these films to?" For me, some years ago, there was a moment of realization when I wondered which of my friends' children was going to visit me in the nursing home. And immediately I realized that I could not count on any of them. Of course, one cannot absolutely count on one's own children, either. But, there was a moment of saying, "No, they are not my children."

Debra Orenstein: We are talking about being single and not having children, and invisibility is central to that issue. Part of feeling or being "invisible" is that everyone else looks very "seen" and large and pronounced to you. A contributor was originally going to write about home for this volume: The place of the Jewish woman in the home, Jewish women as the keepers of *kashrut* (kosher laws) and *Shabbat* (Sabbath), how home relates to work if you are a modern Jewish woman, etc. And she found that all she could come up with was her tremendous resentment against the Jewish community, for not supporting the Jewish home, for making schools and camps astronomically expensive. She pointed out that we are—appropriately—reaching out to unaffiliated and intermarried Jews, but meanwhile ignoring or shunting aside families who are already committed, who can't go to Jewish events because there is no childcare, and can't have another child because who can afford it with the price of a day school education? I think of that conversation juxtaposed with this one because it strikes me that we—the various "we's"—experience ourselves as part of a community that does not see us, that looks right at us, whoever we are, and just does not see. Somehow, the "community" never approves or takes in the people who really make up its membership, but serves this mythical Jewish family, which no longer exists, if it ever did.

Ellen M. Umansky: I never felt so young.

Debra Orenstein: I never felt so old.

Chava Weissler: I never felt so single.

Tikva Frymer-Kensky: I never felt myself so much a mother.

6

Invisible Life Passages

"Invisible life passages" is, essentially, the subject of this book. Feminist Jews have noticed the invisibility of women and many of their life stages, and this has led to a broader awareness of the need for all Jews to name and mark their hidden milestones. So much of what we face in life, we necessarily face alone, and each life has its private significant moments. Yet there is much that ritual and community can do to acknowledge and support us.

Rabbi Leila Gal Berner broaches two private and painful passages: Abortion and healing from sexual abuse. By telling the stories of women who have gone through these experiences, she renders the people and the life stages, real and visible. (She also renders them "heard"; the title of her essay is "Our Silent Seasons." Passages and women have not only been invisible, but unheard— or made mute—as well.) Rabbi Berner then guides the reader through the process of addressing these passages ritually: With poetry, song, and dance, and in community. The need for ritual responses to the particular passages she covers was brought home to me at the conference for contributors to this volume. Three of the five women randomly placed in Rabbi Berner's editing group had either had an abortion or been sexually abused.

While Rabbi Berner models a method for creating new rituals, Amy Bardack suggests applying an existing liturgical text, the *Eshet Ḥayil* (poem about a valiant woman found in Proverbs 31) to new and newly-charted milestones. Examining the context and meaning of *Eshet Ḥayil*, she argues for the feminist usage of a traditional text that many have regarded as sexist. The two authors' approaches, of course, are not mutually exclusive. Rabbi Berner uses liturgical innovation to address exactly the singular character of particular experiences. Bardack capitalizes on a form that is already familiar, resonant, and legitimized in order to mark, with a single text, a variety of passages. Both methods attempt to fill some of the blank spaces, for which we have wanted and lacked a religious vocabulary.

Many passages are, still, largely invisible. New rituals have recently been created—some published for the first time in this book—but the practices are neither standardized nor widely observed. Nor is a new ritual, or an old ritual applied in a new way, desirable in every case. Sometimes, a blessing is called for; sometimes a sermon, story, or change in public policy; sometimes an honor in the synagogue; sometimes a private meditation, or simply a pause.

In general, liturgical and homiletical innovation are permitted and encouraged under Jewish law. Traditional law does prohibit the use of *shem umalkhut* (traditional blessing formula which names *Adonai* as Ruler of the universe) for new blessings. Since that formula states that God commands us to perform the act or ritual described in the blessing, it is considered improper for a case of innovation, which cannot be "commanded." However, many modern rabbis hold that we can take on a sense of commandedness for new blessings, and that the traditional language is necessary to create legitimized and effective liturgy. Moreover, many of those who oppose the use of *shem umalkhut* still believe that the proliferation of new writings is all to the good.

If individuals create rituals, prayers, or readings so novel or idiosyncratic that they are not appropriate for the wider community, they will simply not be adopted. For the moment, the danger is less that we will become irrelevant by addressing individual needs too minutely, than that we will become irrelevant by failing to address individual needs closely enough. When I lecture, I sometimes ask my audiences to name occasions which they would like (or would have liked) to mark somehow in a Jewish context. The following is a selection of such occasions:

- Embarking on or completing a creative project
- Becoming a grandparent
- Giving birth
- Nursing
- Weaning
- Forgiving yourself for a sin you have committed
- Celebrating a time of family closeness/reunion
- Miscarriage
- Menses (especially first period)
- Menopause
- First love
- First sexual experience
- First apartment
- Planning a wedding
- Publishing a book
- Deciding to leave (or stay with) a love partner
- Letting go of an adult child/children leaving the nest
- Recognizing yourself as the caretaker of elderly parents
- Coming out as a lesbian
- Deciding to conceive or adopt a child
- Deciding not to have (more) children
- Acknowledging that you or someone you love is terminally ill
- Finding out the biopsy is negative
- Mastectomy
- Other surgery
- Leaving a batterer
- Reconciling with a friend or relative
- Taking a new name
- Having an abortion
- Cooking a special family dish using your *bubbe*'s (grandmother's) recipe
- Retiring
- Celebrating age with croning rituals and *Simhot Hokhmah* (celebrations of elder-wisdom)
- Acknowledging the pain during times of transition or crisis
- Moving to a new home or apartment
- Making *aliyah* (immigrating to Israel)

- Entering a nursing home
- Recovering from addictions
- Healing from sexual abuse
- Celebrating key achieve-
  ments in your work life

- Changing careers
- Discovering Jewish
  feminism

I hope that this list and this chapter encourage Jewish women and men to honor each moment of their lives, and to interpret both incremental changes and major transitions as part of Jewish living.

Our Silent Seasons

LEILA GAL BERNER

*"The need for a feminist Judaism begins with hearing silence. It
begins with noting the absence of women's history and experiences
as shaping forces in the Jewish tradition."*
                    —JUDITH PLASKOW, *STANDING AGAIN AT SINAI*

Twenty years ago, I supported a friend as she made the difficult
decision to have an abortion. We found a kind, reputable physi-
cian and I accompanied her to his sterile office. I waited in the
outer-room as the "procedure" was carried out. On the way home,
we sat in silence. Then she thanked me for being there, and I went
home.

It was not until about a decade later that my friend finally
talked about her painful decision and the loneliness of her grieving. It all felt like a sad dream, she said, with no reality other than
the scars (both physical and emotional) that she bore. It felt as if
something was still unfinished from that time. Ten years after her
abortion, my friend and I cried together, and I recited a *mi sheberakh* (blessing recited on a person's behalf). We sang a song of healing, honoring her difficult choice. Finally, we marked this "silent
season" in my friend's life. The power of this first experience with
creating a ritual (however unconsciously conceived) has stayed
with me since.

Fast forward a few years: I am attending a workshop on spiritual healing and a young Jewish woman speaks up:

> I am a survivor. I have endured the terror of a man who sexu-
> ally abused me and forced me to keep the filthy secret. I have
> endured the shame, the near-annihilation of my soul, the ter-
> ror of being touched and the invasion of all my sacred spaces.
> Sometimes I feel as though I have gone through the Holocaust.
> And each year, on *Yom Hasho'ah* [Holocaust Memorial Day],
> when the six million of my people who died are remembered,

Rabbi Leila Gal Berner is a congregational rabbi, an historian of medieval
Jewish history, a composer of Jewish music, a liturgist, and a teacher on Judaism
and feminism.

I consider it to be my day of remembrance as well. But, unlike them, *I am still alive. I have survived.* I am strong, unashamed and undefeated—and I want a celebration![1]

Responding Ritually and Jewishly to Real-Life Needs

My friend and the young woman at the workshop both needed some kind of ritual to help bring closure and healing to their experiences. In Gertrud Mueller Nelson's words, each needed "a place to officially engage in [their] sorrows, a healthy way to suffer."[2] Each needed a "vessel" into which to pour into her most profound feelings. The one needed a sense of closure and containment; the other needed a communal affirmation and celebration of her emotional victory over abuse.

The Book of Ecclesiastes tells us that "To everything there is a season and a time for every purpose under the heaven" (3:1). And yet, so many of our "seasons" are observed silently—unmarked and unaddressed by our liturgical tradition—because our tradition does not hear the silence. *Mima'amakkim*, from the depths of that silence, I offer two rituals that I believe address these needs. The first may be used by a woman upon making the decision to have an abortion, or after having undergone the procedure, and the second is for women who have endured the violation of sexual abuse and walk the healing journey with courage and strength. I do this with a humble heart knowing that no ritual is exactly right for every individual and that lifecycle rituals in particular are most compelling when shaped for and by the people using them. Still, I hope they will serve as catalysts for others to begin their own exploration around which to sculpt more personally customized rituals.

I address these lifecycle moments from a woman's perspective. I am not suggesting that men do not feel the loss of an abortion or the painful memory of sexual abuse, but my focus here is on the woman. It has been my experience that many women prefer to observe rituals for such private and biologically-oriented subjects in the company of women. The language of the rituals assumes an all-female gathering, but men could obviously be included.

Not every Jewish woman goes through these particular experiences, but many do. We deserve a place within Judaism to address the emotional and spiritual needs that emerge from our experiences. By ritualizing the full breadth of our life experiences, Jewish women enfranchise ourselves.

Mah tovu oholekhah ya'akov, mishkenotekhah yisra'el: How goodly are your tents, O Jacob, your dwelling places, O Israel (Numbers 24:5). Even the home of the whole Jewish people is referred to as the tent of *Jacob*, and the dwelling place of the generic male collectivity Israel. Too often, Jewish women have felt like outsiders standing hopefully at the entrance of the Jewish tribal "tent," awaiting an invitation to enter. Only when Judaism begins to "hear the silence" and fully include women's experience in the organic and natural flow of the ritual life, will the tent welcome all, and the homeless come home.

In his introduction to Arnold van Gennep's *The Rites of Passage*, Solon T. Kimbala writes that "One dimension of mental illness may arise because an increasing number of individuals are forced to accomplish their transitions alone and with private symbols."[3] That Jews (women or men) should have to experience some of their most important life passages in aloneness, using private symbols rather than collective sancta is inconsistent with Jewish tradition. In a culture so imbued with a sense of collective consciousness, there must be room for a communal marking of *all* life's seasons.

A ritual for women survivors of sexual abuse, in particular, may serve to "gather in the exiles." For far too long, victims of sexual violation have been isolated or even banished, because of a "dirty, shameful secret" that is not theirs. It is hard to acknowledge that sexual abuse happens within one's own community, and perhaps even harder for Jews who carry a pride of peoplehood based on being "a light unto the nations." Yet we must acknowledge the dark side that resides within our community. While the Jewish community all too often engages in collective denial, the victims remain in spiritual and emotional *galut* (exile).[4]

As we welcome survivors of sexual abuse home from exile, we ease their aloneness and affirm what Mordecai Kaplan has called the Jewish "we" feeling.[5] We also offer a clear and unequivocal message that a sexually abused Jewish woman is not a pariah, cut off from the life of her people, for it is not *she* who bears any responsibility or shame because the abuse occurred.

Finally, rituals offer us an important opportunity to release the "toxins" from our souls. In a recent conversation, a friend who was raped several years ago spoke of her "spiritual dilemma": "I believe deeply that maintaining my faith and holding on to the light is far healthier than allowing the 'dark side' [of memory of the rape] to take over. But I have so much anger, so much bitterness about the attack, so much hatred toward the attacker. I need to find a way to get rid of the poison, so I can heal." We are considering a trip to the beach, to a quiet, isolated place where she can scream her pain and send her anger out to sea. We may even bring a few sturdy pillows for her to punch. Just contemplating the possibility of creating a ritual has begun to help my friend deal with the demons inside.

Edward Whitmont has written that "any affect or emotion which in its raw and unaltered form is too intense to be controlled by will alone may need its ritual....Ritual brings about containment and acceptance, control of intensity...."[6] I hope that the rituals presented here will assist many Jewish women in containing and accepting, healing and recovering.

The "How" of Creating Rituals

A word about method: In designing each ritual, I have tried to honor our people's ancient and new voices. I have incorporated elements derived from a variety of traditional Jewish sources, and attempted to choose or create contemporary sources that build on and resonate with the tradition. Songs and chants are included because using our breath enhances and enriches the experience of a ritual. Other elements that might be included are dance and physical movement.[7]

A word about liturgical language: For decades, Jewish feminists have sought to develop prayer that is egalitarian and inclusive. Marcia Falk's formula, "*nevarekh*" ("Let us bless") to replace "*barukh attah adonai*" ("Blessed are [masculine] You, Lord") and "*ein haḥayyim*" ("Source of life") to replace "*melekh ha'olam*" ("King of the universe"), has led the way in this regard. Many others have engaged in similar work, suggesting "*ḥei ha'olamim*" ("Life of the worlds and of eternity") or "*ruaḥ ha'olam*" ("Spirit of the world") in place of traditional masculine language. In the rituals that follow I have kept the traditional masculine formulation for the sake of simplicity and accessibility. I encourage each woman to choose the language that speaks most genuinely to her own heart, and I welcome any alternative suggestions.

Abortion: A Ritual upon Termination of a Pregnancy

I am indebted to Rabbi Amy Eilberg, my friend and colleague, who shared with me the rituals she recently created to address the voluntary termination of a pregnancy:

1. a "grieving ritual" to address "a strong sense of the loss of parental hopes and dreams for [the] baby;"

2. a "letting go ritual—for use when the primary pastoral issue is guilt: The termination was chosen, but ambivalently, and uncertainty and doubt remain...;"

3. a "ritual of renewal offered to those women who primarily seek a traditionally Jewish expression of rebirth and renewal following the painful experience of the termination;" and

4. a ritual that "addresses the specific occasion of termination of pregnancy following an act of sexual violence."[8]

Women who decide to terminate a pregnancy for medical reasons often feel as if they have suffered a death in the family and need to mourn the "child-soul" that they have lost, just as one would mourn the death of a fully living human being. Penina V. Adelman suggests use of the *El Maleh Raḥamim* (memorial prayer asking God to guard and keep in peace the departed soul). She points out that this seems especially appropriate because of the word *"raḥamim,"* which has its root in the Hebrew word *"reḥem"* (womb) and can be poetically translated as "God who is full of wombs."[9]

The *Birkat Hagomel* song included in this ritual was written to express the belief that all things in the universe are divinely inspired and filled with godliness—the good and the bad, the light and the dark, the joyful and the tragic. I do not suggest that God "wills" tragedy, injustice, painful choices or evil into being, but I do believe that these, too, are part of the flow of godliness in the universe, and part of what God is all about. Even within darkness and evil, deepest despair and most painful decision making, there is God.

The blessing is designed to be sung in addition to, or in place of, the traditional *Birkat Hagomel* (prayer of thanksgiving for coming through danger in safety), which is recited after a life-threatening experience (including childbirth), serious illness, imprisonment, or dangerous journey. The Talmud instructs us to give thanks for our survival so that we may understand that God is the Source of life and safety (BT *Berakhot* 54b). Deciding to terminate a pregnancy and undergoing the abortion procedure are "perils" worthy of the recitation of *Birkat Hagomel*.

I have woven several Jewish images into the Hebrew and English words of this blessing:

- a reference to God as *ein haḥayyim* (Source of life);

- a reference to the *Yotzer* blessing which follows the *Barekhu* prayer and speaks about God's creation of light and dark. The end of the prayer as found in our liturgy ("[God] creates all things") is a modified form of Isaiah 45:7, where the text actually reads *uvoreh ra* ("[God] creates evil");

- a reference to Psalms 23:4 ("Yea, though I walk through the valley of the shadow of death, I will fear no evil, for You are with me");

- a reference to the *Modeh Ani* prayer, based on BT *Berakhot* 60b, recited upon awakening ("I thank You, living and eternal God, for returning my soul to me in compassion").

HEALING FROM ABORTION
Order of the Ritual

Opening

The ritual begins with one woman inviting all to take a few deep breaths. She then begins a *niggun* (wordless melody). Participants stand in a circle.

Creating Supportive Space

The "focus" woman, for whom the ritual is being conducted, steps into the center of the circle, with one or two women near her to hold her hand and comfort her, and says:

Hinneni—Here I stand alone, as before, when I made my decision about childbearing in the uniqueness of my personal choice.

All other participants approach and tighten the circle around the "focus" woman to support her. Women say together:

You are not alone now. In aloneness you made your choice, and in community you will be sustained.

Affirming One's Choices

One woman says: It is the blessing and the curse of being human that we have the capacity to make choices. Sometimes the choices can make our lives rich and beautiful. Sometimes the choices are filled with pain, or it feels as though we have no choice at all. Nothing can make the ending of a pregnancy easy. We affirm you in your painful and difficult choice.*

Women say together: Blessed are you, Creator of the Universe, who sustains us in times of decision. You have made it possible for us to consider with wisdom our lives and the lives of our loved ones, and you have granted us courage and intelligence to make choices about childbearing.

As you have been with us in times of past decisions, so
may you be with us today as we affirm the difficult decisions _____ [and her family] has [have] made.[10]

"Focus" woman says:

בָּרוּךְ אַתָּה יי אֱלֹהֵינוּ מֶלֶךְ הָעוֹלָם, אֲשֶׁר נָתַן לַשֶּׂכְוִי בִינָה לְהַבְחִין
בֵּין יוֹם וּבֵין לָיְלָה.

*Barukh attah adonai eloheinu melekh ha'olam, asher natan lasekhvi
vina lehavhin bein yom uvein lailah.*

I bless you, Holy One, Sovereign Spirit of the Universe, who
has enabled me to distinguish between night and day, who has
given me the ability to make wise choices (BT *Berakhot* 60b and
traditional morning liturgy).[11]

Women respond: Amen.

Sharing the Pain

One woman says: We know that there is deep sadness
within you. We know that you feel loss and sorrow and
regret. We mourn with you.

*"Focus" woman is invited to share her own words about her
grief. She may also wish to express any regret, guilt, doubt,
uncertainty, or resentment that arose while making the decision to terminate the pregnancy. The intention here is for the
focus woman to be heard and to "let go."*

*Option A: In the event of a medically-recommended abortion,
one woman says*: We know the Torah teaching: When we
must choose between a being not yet born and the life of
a mother, the choice is very clear. The being you were
carrying could not be. No human hand caused this to
happen; no human act could have allowed this being to
emerge in health and wholeness. Still, in the shadow of
such a choice, we feel small and limited and out of control (adapted).*

Women say together: We who stand with you today are
witness to the terrible choice that was no choice at all.
We affirm you in choosing life. You made a choice,

choosing life for you. We grieve with you over the loss
of this seed of life, and we affirm your essence, as a person gifted with the ability to nurture other life—within
yourself, in your love for others, and in your connections to family, friends, and community (adapted).*

One woman chants an adapted El Maleh Raḥamim:

אֵל מָלֵא רַחֲמִים, שׁוֹכֵן בַּמְּרוֹמִים, הַמְצֵא מְנוּחָה נְכוֹנָה תַּחַת
כַּנְפֵי הַשְּׁכִינָה, אֶת נִשְׁמַת הַתִּינֹקֶת/הַתִּינוֹק שֶׁלֹּא נוֹלְדָה/נוֹלַד
לְעוֹלָמֵנוּ. אָנָּא, בַּעַל הָרַחֲמִים, הַסְתִּירֶהָ/הַסְתִּירֵהוּ בְּסֵתֶר כְּנָפֶיךָ
לְעוֹלָמִים, וּצְרוֹר בִּצְרוֹר הַחַיִּים אֶת נִשְׁמָתָהּ/נִשְׁמָתוֹ, יְיָ הוּא
נַחֲלָתָהּ/נַחֲלָתוֹ, וְיָבִיאֶהָ/וְיָבִיאֵהוּ לְשָׁלוֹם. וְנֹאמַר אָמֵן.

*El maleh raḥamim, shokhen bameromim, hamtzeh menuḥah
nekhonah taḥat kanfei hashekhinah, et nishmat hatinoket/hatinok
shelo noldah/nolad le'olameinu. Anna, ba'al haraḥamim, hastirehah/
hastirehu beseter kenafekha le'olamim, utzeror bitzror
haḥayyim et nishmatah/nishmato, adonai hu naḥalatah/naḥalato,
veyavi'eha/ veyavi'ehu leshalom. Venomar amen.*

O God filled with womb-like compassion, who resides in the
high places, grant perfect peace in Your sheltering Presence, to
the soul of this being who was not born into our world. Please,
compassionate Mother-God, shelter her/him beneath Your
protective wings for all eternity and bind her/his soul to the
Bond of Life. The Holy One is now her/his home and will
bring her/him eternal peace. And let us say: Amen.

*Option B: In the event of a decision to terminate the pregnan-
cy for reasons other than medical, women say together:* May
You who share sorrow with Your creation be with
_____ now as she experiences the loss of potential life.
We are sad as we think of her painful decision, and support her as she and we imagine what might have been.

Life is a fabric of different emotions and experiences.
Now, O God, while _____ experiences life's bitterness
and pain, be with her and with us, and sustain us. Help
us to gather strength from within ourselves, from each
other, and from our wider community. Blessed are You,
Divine Presence, who shares sorrow with Your creation.[12]

Affirming One's Self

(After option A or B continue here.) "Focus" woman says:

אֱלֹהַי, נְשָׁמָה שֶׁנָּתַתָּ בִּי טְהוֹרָה הִיא. אַתָּה בְרָאתָהּ, אַתָּה
יְצַרְתָּהּ, אַתָּה נְפַחְתָּהּ בִּי, וְאַתָּה מְשַׁמְּרָהּ בְּקִרְבִּי. . . .

Elohai, neshamah shenatatta bi tehorah hi. Attah veratah, attah yet-
zartah, attah nefaḥtah bi, ve'attah meshammerah bekirbi....

My God, the soul You have given me is pure. You created it,
You formed it, You breathed it into me (BT *Berakhot* 60b and
traditional morning liturgy).

I know that I am created *betzelem elohim*, that a divine spark
resides within me. I know that I am free to make choices—
about my body and my future. I have made my choices,
painful as they may be, in harmony with the divinity that
dwells within me. I affirm my freedom, I affirm my self, and I
honor my choices in the face of enormous complexity and still-
lingering questions.

בָּרוּךְ אַתָּה יי, שֶׁעָשַׂנִי אִשָּׁה. בָּרוּךְ אַתָּה יי, שֶׁעָשַׂנִי בַּת-חוֹרִין.

Barukh attah adonai, she'asani ishah. Barukh attah adonai, she'asani
bat-ḥorin.

I bless You, Holy One, who has made me a woman. I bless
You, Holy One, who has made me free (adapted from BT
Menaḥot 43b and traditional morning liturgy).

Surviving and Being Thankful

"Focus" woman says: The Holy One "heals the broken in
heart and binds their wounds..." (Psalms 147:3). I have
survived a sad journey—with peril to both body and
soul. I thank You for sustaining me and bringing me
through the peril in wholeness.

"Focus" woman reads or sings (Hebrew or English, as is com-
fortable for her): Birkat Hagomel *(dedicated to Ira*
Silverman, of blessed memory) (Hebrew and English are both
to be sung to the melody of the traditional American folk song,
"The Creole Girl")

אֲבָרֵךְ אֶת עֵין הַחַיִּים   יוֹצֶרֶת טוֹב וָרָע.   אֲקַדֵּשׁ אֶת חֵי הָעוֹלָם
יוֹצֵר אֲפֵלָה וְאוֹרָה.   עָבַרְתִּי בְּגֵיא צַלְמָוֶת   וְאַתָּה עִמָּדִי.
מוֹדָה אֲנִי לָךְ   שֶׁהֶחֱזַרְתִּינִי בְּשָׁלוֹם.

*Avarekh et ein haḥayyim yotzeret tov vara. Akaddesh et ḥei ha'olam
yotzer afelah ve'orah. Avarti begei tzalmavet ve'attah immadi.
Modah ani lakh sheheḥezartini beshalom.*

I shall bless the Source of Life who fashions good and evil. I
shall bless the Holy One who brings dark and light to all people. For I have walked in the valley of the shadow of death.
And You, and You were with me then, with every painful
breath.

Seeking Healing

*"Focus" woman moves from her place in center of circle. All
women greet and embrace her. They respond to her* Birkat
Hagomel *by repeatedly chanting in Hebrew Moses' prayer
for Miriam's healing, as long as the power of the chant moves
them:*

אֵל נָא רְפָא נָא לָה . . . אֵל נָא רְפָא נָא לָה . . .

El na refa na lah...El na refa na lah...

Please God, heal her please...Please God, heal her please...
(Numbers 12:13).

*Chanting subsides and women flow right into singing Debbie
Friedman's adaptation of a traditional prayer for healing:*[13]

*Mi-she-beirach
Mi-she-beirach i-mo-tei-nu
M'kor ha-bra-cha l'a-vo-tei-nu*

May the source of strength
Who blessed the ones before us,
Help us find the courage
To make our lives a blessing,
And let us say, Amen.

*Mi-she-bei-rach i-motei-nu
M'kor ha-bra-cha l'a-vo-tei-nu,*

Bless those in need of healing
With *r'fu-a sh'lei-ma*
The renewal of body,
The renewal of spirit,
And let us say, Amen.

After a moment of silence, one woman says: "Thank you all for sharing your love and support with _____ at this difficult time."

HEALING FROM SEXUAL ABUSE
Order of the Ritual

Opening
The ritual begins with one woman inviting all to take a few deep breaths. She then begins a *niggun* (wordless melody). Participants stand in a circle.

Creating Supportive Space

The "focus" woman, for whom the ritual is being conducted, steps into the center of the circle, with one or two women near her to hold her hand and comfort her, and says:

Hinneni—Here I stand, alone in the depth of my pain, in the uniqueness of my anger. *Then* there were no limits, no boundaries, no safety. *Then* there was no one to whom I could turn. *Then* as I stood powerless against the abuse and violation, I felt terror gnawing at the depths of my soul. I was so afraid.

All other participants approach and tighten the circle around the "focus" woman to support her. Women say together:

You are not alone now. We are here, encircling you with gentleness and support. This is a circle of unending love, a safe space for you. Now *you* set the limits and the boundaries. You can turn to *us*. *Now* you have power. Once you were so afraid. *Now* you have nothing to fear.

All sing: *Kol Ha'olam Kullo* (words attributed to Reb
Naḥman of Bratzlav)

כָּל-הָעוֹלָם כֻּלוֹ גֶּשֶׁר צַר מְאֹד, וְהָעִקָּר לֹא לְפַחֵד כְּלָל.

Kol ha'olam kullo gesher tzar me'od, veha'ikkar lo lefaḥed kelal.

All this world is a very narrow bridge, and the essential point
is not to fear at all.[14]

Acknowledging the Anger

One woman says: After the pain and terror, after the complete violation you have endured, you must feel deep
anger. We invite you to speak of your anger.

"Focus" woman reads:

You mean to tell me
that i,
powerless little
i
can have
big, scary
anger?
You just told me
that i
am allowed to be mad.
i can complain
i can write
and not feel guilty.
i don't have to make excuses
for those who hurt me?
i
can express my anger,
i
can tell people
about my experiences
and expect to be listened to?
Lowly little
me

can have anger.
Oh.
i'm angry.

   —Marta Metz[15]

"Focus" woman speaks about her anger, if she wishes.

Women say together:

You have been hurt, attacked, violated. But we are here
to tell you that you are loved with an unending love.

You are embraced by arms that find you
even when you are hidden from yourself.

You are touched by fingers that soothe you safely
even when you are too proud for soothing.
You are counseled by voices that guide you
even when you are too embittered to hear.
You are loved with an unending love.

You are supported by hands that uplift you
even in the midst of a fall.
You are urged on by eyes that meet you
when you are too weak for meeting.
You are loved with an unending love.

Embraced, touched, soothed, and counseled...
ours are the arms, the fingers, the voices;
ours are the hands, the eyes, the smiles.
And we are all loved with an unending love.[16]

Blessed is the Holy One, Source of Love, who
loves each of us in our uniqueness.

Surviving and Being Thankful
(See page 130)

Seeking Healing
(See page 131)

Affirming One's Self

"Focus" woman says:

אֱלֹהַי, נְשָׁמָה שֶׁנָּתַתָּ בִּי טְהוֹרָה הִיא. אַתָּה בְרָאתָהּ, אַתָּה
יְצַרְתָּהּ, אַתָּה נְפַחְתָּהּ בִּי, וְאַתָּה מְשַׁמְּרָהּ בְּקִרְבִּי . . . .

Elohai, neshamah shenatatta bi tehorah hi. Attah veratah, attah
yetzartah, attah nefaḥtah bi, ve'attah meshammerah bekirbi....

My God, the soul You have given me is pure. You created it,
You formed it, You breathed it into me (BT *Berakhot* 60b and
traditional morning liturgy).

I know that I am created *betzelem elohim,* that a divine spark
resides within me. *Hinneni*: Here I stand, no longer alone, on
my way to becoming fully unafraid, knowing that I can create
safe space for myself, knowing that I have a circle of loved and
loving ones who will support and protect me, knowing that I
am sheltered beneath the wings of *Shekhinah* (close-dwelling
presence of God, associated with the feminine), knowing my
own power.

בָּרוּךְ אַתָּה יי, שֶׁעָשַׂנִי אִשָּׁה. בָּרוּךְ אַתָּה יי, שֶׁעָשַׂנִי בַּת-חוֹרִין.

Barukh attah adonai, she'asani ishah. Barukh attah adonai, she'asani
bat-ḥorin.

I bless You, Holy One, who has made me a woman. I bless
You, Holy One, who has made me free (adapted from BT
Menaḥot 43b and traditional morning liturgy).

After a moment of silence, one woman says: Thank you all for
sharing your love and support with _____ at this difficult
time.

A Final Prayer

May the time come, speedily and in our days, when every season and every purpose under heaven in Jewish women's (and men's) lives will be embraced by an evolving Jewish tradition. May the time come, speedily and in our days, when the seasons of Jewish women's lives will no longer be silent and when the most profound moments of their life experiences will no longer be mute in the liturgical repertoire of our people. Amen.

Praising the Work of Valiant Women:
A Feminist Endorsement of *Eshet Ḥayil*

AMY BARDACK

"Give her credit for the products of her labor and let her works praise her in the gates."
                                                      —PROVERBS 31:31

Friday night, the candles have been lit, the table set, the meal cooked by the wife. The husband, having just returned from *shul* (synagogue), sits at the table. *"Shalom Aleikhem"* is sung, welcoming the Sabbath angels. The husband then sings to his wife *Eshet Ḥayil* (The Valiant Woman, Proverbs 31:10-31), a poem praising a wise, righteous woman for her accomplishments in business, education, and household management.

When I first encountered *Eshet Ḥayil*, I felt alienated by the overemphasized domesticity of its setting.[17] Sung at the Sabbath table, where the only visible signs of the woman's work are the products of housework, the message is clear: Domestic chores are central to her worth. *Eshet Ḥayil* can thus be read as a gesture to the housewife, tacit recognition of the meal she has cooked and the house she has cleaned, in compensation for her exclusion from public worship. Unlike the dynamic protagonist of *Eshet Ḥayil*, her real-life referent is silent and passive, dependent entirely on her

---

Amy Bardack is a rabbinical student at The Jewish Theological Seminary in New York.

husband to praise her. Thus, the ritual seems to glorify the stereo-typical Jewish wife and mother, catering selflessly to her family, denying herself—or being denied—opportunities for public and self-recognition.

But the contemporary ritual does not fully express the richness and complexity of the text. The Book of Proverbs, in which *Eshet Hayil* is found, is a compendium of teachings and aphorisms which give practical advice regarding ethics and day-to-day conduct. Removing *Eshet Hayil* from this context and restricting it to home and hearth has diluted the power of the poem. It deserves a second look, unfettered by its history of interpretation and ritualization.

The text praises the Valiant Woman for far more than "house-work" in the modern sense. Although the Valiant Woman works from her home, she is by no means confined by its boundaries. She is in charge of a successful home-based economy—selling tex-tile products of wool and flax (v. 24, 13), and using the income to buy a field where she plants a profitable vineyard (v. 16). That her work extends beyond the home is clear: "She is like a merchant fleet, bringing her food from afar" (v. 14).

In addition to her economic contributions, the Valiant Woman is responsible for management of a large household, which includes teaching morals and ethics (v. 26, 30). Her moral con-science is evident in acts of social justice (v. 20); she is generous with the needy, rather than hoarding the profits of her labor. Her work is impressive enough to bring recognition at the city gate (v. 31), the locus of business and political activity from which most women were excluded.

Like the male heroes in Psalms, the Valiant Woman is known for her praiseworthy accomplishments, above beauty or pedigree. A comparison to male heroic warriors is further suggested by the pervasive military imagery in the text. For example, the word *"hayil"* denotes power and strength in a military sense. Numerous phrases with double meanings referring to war are complemented by several references to her physical strength.[18] The battle imagery signifies that her work is as vital to the survival of the community as that of a male heroic warrior.

This portrayal of a strong, active woman derives further sig-nificance from its location at the end of Proverbs. Such placement suggests that women's work is representative of the wise, right-

eous activities commended in the rest of the book. In her embodiment of practical knowledge, the Valiant Woman is not simply
capable, but pious as well. Proverbs makes clear that wisdom is at
once mundane and holy since it is a quality bestowed upon us,
and shared, by God. The Valiant Woman's tasks—which are manifestations of wisdom—take on some of the luster of God's own
labor.

In the first nine chapters of the Book of Proverbs, wisdom is
personified and deified as a woman. Numerous correlations
between Wisdom, who opens the Book of Proverbs, and the
Valiant Woman, who closes it, suggest that the authors and editors
of Proverbs drew a deliberate analogy between the two figures.[19]
We learn that the Valiant Woman's "mouth is full of wisdom" (v.
26) and that she is "a woman who fears God" (v. 30), a quality
which the Books of Proverbs and Psalms deem a prerequisite to
wisdom.[20] Fear of God is also associated with the knowledge
Wisdom bestows on her followers (1:29, 8:13). Both Wisdom and
the Valiant Woman are deemed more valuable than rubies, and
each recognizes her own worth.[21] Both figures seek and receive
attention at the city gates (1:21, 8:3, 31:31). These parallels are but-
tressed by the passages' physical placement as brackets surrounding the Book of Proverbs: The book opens with Wisdom personified as female, and closes with a woman who is wise.

The connection of the Valiant Woman with the figure of
Wisdom signifies that women, through their daily activities,
exhibit the shared human-divine characteristic of wisdom. The
analogy with Wisdom places the public functions of the Valiant
Woman on a par with her roles as wife and mother. Her worth is
not dependent upon the praise of her family; rather, her works
speak for themselves. The Valiant Woman is good to her husband
and children, but it is by virtue of her activities—in business,
teaching, household management, and charity to the poor—that
she is wise. And her wisdom does not just earn her praise; it is,
above all, a vehicle for holiness.

Despite these positive messages, some feminists see in the
poem an endorsement of "superwoman," the unattainable, and
therefore oppressive, ideal of a woman who can do everything
well. Thus, *Eshet Ḥayil* is perceived as supporting the unreasonable expectations which society places upon women. Others think

Eshet Ḥayil should be rejected outright insofar as it is a product of a patriarchal world view: That the Valiant Woman is a wife and mother implies a sanctioning of that lifestyle above others; that she is praised by her husband suggests that her worth is defined by him.

These criticisms are based, I believe, in a reading and experience of *Eshet Ḥayil* outside its biblical context. I choose not to abandon the ritual, but to extend its application, so that it can function as an appropriate tribute to contemporary women and do justice to the text. *Eshet Ḥayil* becomes more powerful when it is not sung exclusively by a husband to his wife.

In some communities, including some Orthodox circles, single, divorced, and widowed women recite *Eshet Ḥayil* and/or "receive" its recitation. Just as the Valiant Woman's works sing her praises, just as Wisdom promotes herself confidently, more women should feel free to sing it to themselves and to one another. As lesbian partners, unmarried heterosexual couples, and single women adopt *Eshet Ḥayil*, it becomes a celebration of all women, not only wives.

I am not suggesting that we dispense entirely with the ritual of a husband singing to his wife. The meaning of *Eshet Ḥayil* need not necessarily be distorted in a domestic setting. As women's productivity in private and public arenas is acknowledged, the image of a wife in the home will conjure fewer associations with oppression and limited opportunity, and a husband's singing *Eshet Ḥayil* to his wife at the table might resonate differently. Also, some women reciprocate their male partner's recitation of *Eshet Ḥayil* with their own recitation of Psalm 112, which praises a Godfearing man for many of the same qualities with which the Valiant Woman is credited.

In keeping with Proverbs' conception of wisdom as encompassing all facets of life, the setting of the ritual should be expanded beyond the Sabbath table to mark other occasions in which women excel with valor. It could be sung in the synagogue, in honor of a woman's first time leading services or reading Torah. It could be sung in celebration of a creative endeavor, job promotion, or graduation. Even our most secular pursuits are appropriate to be sanctified in this manner. *Eshet Ḥayil* could be a vehicle for rendering visible women's invisible passages.

In order to reinforce the holiness of the Valiant Woman's activities, *Eshet Ḥayil* could be framed by Wisdom passages from Proverbs, such as the following:

> Wisdom cries aloud in the street, raises her voice in the squares: "Receive my instruction rather than silver, knowledge rather than gold. Mine are counsel and resourcefulness; I am understanding; courage is mine. Whoever finds me finds life, and receives favor from God."[22]

New tunes could be composed, incorporating Wisdom passages, and *Eshet Ḥayil* could be complemented by verses which a woman, her family, or her friends choose or write.

Given difficulties with the poem and how it is used, some might opt to start anew with an original text. There is, however, tremendous value in re-imaging, and thereby reappropriating, a traditional text. The words of an ancient text carry with them the power of history and heritage. They connect us to a past which, despite its devaluation of women in certain areas, did nonetheless recognize and celebrate women's accomplishments. By endorsing *Eshet Ḥayil* today, we rediscover and redeem that strain in Jewish tradition which praised women for their independent achievements and saw in women's work manifestations of God-like wisdom. Taking our place among the generations of commentators who read *Eshet Ḥayil* in light of their own experience, we make our mark on tradition.

7

Coming Out

C oming out is obviously not part of the traditional Jewish lifecycle classification. Coming out ceremonies, commitment ceremonies for same-sex couples, and syn- agogues that have predominantly gay, lesbian, and bisexual memberships are all new on the Jewish scene, and most segments of the Jewish community remain uncomfortable or even opposed to them.

Jewish legal objections to homosexuality stem from the Levitical laws which label two men lying together as an abomination (Leviticus 18:22, 20:13). For that reason, there are fewer halakhic (Jewish legal) problems for lesbians than for gays, and less attention is paid in the law to female than to male homosexuality. That les- bians are relatively un-seen by the tradition cuts both ways—they are more ignored, but less condemned than gay men.[1]

Orthodox law continues to prohibit lesbian and gay sexual practices. The Reform and Reconstructionist movements have accepted Jewish homosexuality as a viable alternative, and they ordain gay men and lesbians as a matter of policy. As of this writing, the Conservative movement is still in the process of re-evaluating its stance, as part of a general rabbinic study of human sexuality.

A variety of legal arguments have been marshalled to permit gay and lesbian sexual behavior. For example, some contemporary rabbis reassess the prohibition against male homosexuality on the grounds that it was intended to outlaw exploitative and/or idolatrous homosexual sex, and not loving same-sex relationships. Others use *ones* (literally, force), the principle that people are not responsible for violations of Jewish law over which they had no choice, to validate gay and lesbian sexuality, on the assumption that no one chooses her or his sexual orientation. In Rabbinic terms, *ones patreh raḥmanah* (God, the merciful Divine self, holds harmless those who are under *ones*).[2] Of course this interpretation of the law does not validate gay and lesbian partnerships equally with heterosexual unions, and many find it condescending.

For the moment, these halakhic arguments are relevant principally for the Conservative movement. The Orthodox movement has not yet taken up this question. The Reform and Reconstructionist movements have already resolved it, and, in any case, do not consider *halakhah* binding. Most American Jews see the Jewish debate on homosexuality, like the secular one, in terms of civil rights and/or "family values," rather than *halakhah*.

In this chapter, Rabbis Rebecca T. Alpert and Jane Litman do not engage in legal debate. Rather, they look to the experiences of Jewish lesbians and gays and to their contribution—past and future—to the Jewish community.

Rabbi Alpert draws on her own life experience to explore the process of coming out as a lesbian and the particular dynamics of being a lesbian in the Jewish community. While Jewish lesbians proudly consider themselves thrice blessed—as Jew, woman, and lesbian—they also recognize that they are thrice marginalized.[3] Rabbi Alpert proposes a blessing and a ceremony for coming out to address this challenge. Her article suggests that the continuing commitment of Jewish lesbians despite their extreme marginalization holds a lesson for the general Jewish community: One key to overcoming prejudice and denigration, whether external or internalized, is to answer it with a brave and persistent attachment both to freedom and to an integrated identity. This message invites all Jewish women to be true to themselves, risk disapproval and prejudice, become "too visible," and cast off unhealthy constraints, whether self- or other-imposed.

Rabbi Litman offers the observations of a spiritual leader on what distinguishes her gay/lesbian/bisexual congregation from mainstream congregations. In a joyful and appreciative tone, she notes some of the special programs, needs, and gifts of this and other gay/lesbian/bisexual communities. At the same time, she points to the vast degree of similarity between this *shul* (synagogue) and every other, reminding us that what we share as Jews is greater and more important than what divides us.

Coming Out in the Jewish Community

REBECCA T. ALPERT

"There was no one else about when Joseph made himself known to his brothers. His sobs were so loud that the Egyptians could hear...."
—GENESIS 45:1-2

As a child reading the Bible, I was deeply touched by the story of Joseph and his brothers. I was moved to tears when Joseph, having hidden his true identity, was finally able to tell his brothers who he really was, and to be reconciled with them after years of estrangement.

It was not until I was much older that I identified Joseph's story as similar to my own. Like Joseph, I hid part of my identity for many years. And also like Joseph, revealing that hidden dimension of myself made me feel whole. Joseph hid his identity as a Hebrew. I hid my identity as a lesbian.

I grew up knowing that I was strongly attracted to members of my own sex. But everything I saw in society—movies, popular songs, my parents' relationship, Bible stories—pointed to heterosexuality as the norm. I often had crushes on girls and women teachers, and I had sexual relationships with girlfriends in high school. Yet as an adolescent I would never have called myself a lesbian; I assumed I was going through a stage. When I was growing up, lesbians were found in bars, underground magazines, and pulp novels. They were assumed to be poorly adjusted women who wanted to be men, not courageous women who dared to be different. I did not want to be one of them.

My experience in Hebrew school reinforced my own discomfort with my sexual feelings. Lessons about the importance of marrying a Jewish man and raising Jewish children were well taught, and I wanted desperately to belong. There was nothing in the Judaism of my childhood that indicated a possible acceptance of lesbians.

For me, focusing on Jewish identity provided a perfect alternative to exploring my sexual identity. I married, became a rabbi, and had two children. Despite my wishes to the contrary, the strong

---

Rabbi Rebecca T. Alpert is the co-director of the Women's Studies Program at Temple University in Philadelphia.

erotic attraction I felt towards women never left me. After a while I began to think of myself as bisexual. But at some point it became clear to me that I needed to make a choice. It was then that I left my marriage and developed a primary relationship with a woman.

Coming Out: A Gradual—and Difficult—Process

Coming out to myself, calling myself a lesbian, was not easy. I had achieved status and visibility in the Jewish world as a rabbi, and I was afraid that if I came out I would have to give that up. I was concerned that my co-workers would be uncomfortable around me, or that they would no longer respect my ideas and judgments.

But at a certain point I developed a strong conviction that it would be better if people knew, and that I would not worry about whether or not they did—at least, not most of the time. I came out because I got tired of hiding and lying; it had a corrosive effect on my soul. In coming out I experienced a sense of pride in being lesbian. I gained peace of mind and a sense of freedom unattainable in the closet. Passover took on new meaning, for I had truly experienced the journey through the narrow straits of *mitzrayim*[4] (Egypt) to freedom. And I finally knew what Joseph felt like when he revealed his identity to his brothers.

But this was the beginning, not the end, of a story. Coming out is a process—not a one-time event.

After I took the step of coming out to myself, I was ready to face identifying as a lesbian in the lesbian community. When I was growing up in the 1950s, no such possibility existed. But as a result of the gay and feminist movements in the 1970s, gay and lesbian culture has flourished. In most big cities around the world there are institutions and organizations with which gay and lesbian people can affiliate. Before I came out, I never felt completely comfortable at a gay bookstore, coffee house, or synagogue. What if someone thought I was a lesbian? After coming out, it was easy to enter predominantly gay or lesbian spaces. I became interested in listening to the local lesbian radio program and reading the lesbian and gay press. I volunteered to deliver meals to a man with AIDS. I excitedly contributed an article to *Twice Blessed* (Beacon Press, 1991), an anthology on gay and lesbian Jews. Proudly, my lover and I attended a national march for lesbian and gay rights as part of a group sponsored by New Jewish Agenda.

It was also important to integrate my lesbian identity with the other dimensions of my life by coming out at work and to my family and friends. For most gay men and lesbians, coming out to our families is the hardest part of the process. In my case, I waited until both of my parents died to come out, so great was my fear of their disapproval or rejection. As an only child, I did not have to face coming out to siblings. My children were very young when I left my marriage. I have been fortunate that their father has been most supportive and understanding of my life choices. I have worked hard to give my children an understanding of my lesbianism. It means a great deal to me when they proudly identify as part of a lesbian family.

As a rabbi, coming out at work was exceedingly difficult. The Jewish institution where I worked had an open lesbian on its staff, but when I came out it was made clear to me that it was time for me to leave; one was enough. While looking for another position I felt constrained from writing or speaking publicly about being a lesbian, or discussing the issue with students. I knew that, at least for the time being, the possibilities of my finding another position in the Jewish community where I could be open about being a lesbian were remote.

Continually Integrating a New Identity

Now that I no longer work full time as a Jewish professional, it has been easier for me to be more public about my lesbian identity in the Jewish community, and to explore the connections between being a lesbian and being a Jew. Like many other Jewish lesbians, I have experienced similarities between homophobia and anti-Semitism. Both Jews and lesbians have the option to deny our identities, to "pass" as non-Jewish or heterosexual. For members of both groups it often takes courage to admit to difference in public, to ask friends and colleagues not to wish you "Merry Christmas," to tell people at a wedding that you do not wish to "be next," at least not with a man. This kind of coming out is common to both, and is experienced doubly by those who identify as lesbian and Jewish. Hitler persecuted gay men and Jews. Jews were forced to wear yellow stars, and gay men had to wear pink triangles. Gay Jews often wear pins that combine both symbols. This act reclaims pride and unites our two identities in a powerful way. There are other, happier commonalities, as well: Shared emphasis on community, identity-formation through reading and bookstores, a group humor and culture.

Despite similarities between anti-Semitism and homophobia, it is much less threatening in most regions of the United States to reveal that you are Jewish than to reveal that you are gay or lesbian. Moreover, gay and lesbian people, unlike Jews, experience legal discrimination as a class. We are denied housing and jobs, the right to marry (and thereby receive benefits from our partners, or access to them when they are hospitalized), the right to serve openly in the military, the right to adopt children and in many states, the right to have sexual relations in the privacy of our homes.

We also must learn to live with our own internalized homophobia. I have written and spoken publicly as a Jewish lesbian for several years. As comfortable with my sexual orientation as I have become, the fear that someone I respect might disapprove of me still surfaces on occasion. For example, when I spoke on being lesbian and Jewish at a conference sponsored by the (New York) Jewish Women's Resource Center, I never expected to run into Doris, an older woman who had been an informant for my dissertation research fifteen years earlier. I must admit that I did not tell her what I was doing there, and honestly hoped she had not read the program. I did not want her image of me as a "proper Jewish woman" to change. I understand this as my own homophobia, and continue to work to overcome it.

What gives me the courage to work for gay and lesbian visibility in the Jewish community is knowing that I am part of a movement. As more and more gay and lesbian Jews have come out and demanded to be taken seriously, things have begun to change. The development of gay and lesbian synagogues and their acceptance into the Union of American Hebrew Congregations and the Federation of Reconstructionist Congregations and Havurot, the willingness on the part of the Reconstructionist Rabbinical College and the Hebrew Union College-Jewish Institute of Religion to ordain openly gay and lesbian students, the courage of some rabbis and other Jewish professionals to come out, the publication of books and articles on Jewish and gay and lesbian themes have all helped to increase gay visibility in the Jewish community, and to lessen the presumption of heterosexuality in Jewish contexts.

Of course, the process is only beginning. There is much work that needs to be done for gay and lesbian Jews to achieve full acceptance. One important change will be the creation of lifecycle

ceremonies for the unique passages of lesbian and gay Jews.
Coming out ceremonies are crucial for this process.

Coming Out as a Life Passage and a Ritual

Coming out is the central passage in the lives of lesbians and gay
men. It marks a change of identity and a change of status in the
world. Like other life passages, it is both exciting and dangerous.
A coming out ritual can provide the opportunity to make this
important life change in the context of a community, and with its
blessing.

For some lesbians and gays, commitment ceremonies celebrating the loving relationship between two same-sex partners have
taken on the role of coming out ceremonies. Although these ceremonies are not common, they are occurring with increasing fre-
quency in Jewish lesbian and gay circles, and some rabbis will
officiate at them. Commitment ceremonies offer an opportunity to
acknowledge a relationship publicly, joyously, and in community.

However, lesbians also need coming out rituals which
acknowledge us as individuals. It is crucial to recognize women as
lesbians when they are single as well as when they are in relationships. A woman does not have to be having sex with a man to
define herself as heterosexual, and this principle also holds true
for lesbians. Lesbians without partners do not cease to be lesbians.
And coming out is not only about being in a sexual relationship
with a partner of the same sex, or the possibility of being in such a
relationship. It is also about establishing a new identity and a
sense of self in the world. For many women, being a lesbian
means participation in a new culture. It may involve a new hair-
cut, or wearing jewelry with women's symbols. It can involve
reading different newspapers, magazines, and books. It will probably involve attending communal gatherings—pride parades, concerts of lesbian comics or musicians, or political rallies. It may
involve visiting places where lesbian identity is openly accepted,
places like Provincetown, San Francisco, or the Michigan
Womyn's Music Festival.

Since there is no definitive moment of coming out (although for
many lesbians, telling parents may be the most crucial point in the
process), it is difficult to pinpoint a precise moment for a coming
out ritual. I would therefore like to offer three different possibilities.

COMING OUT CELEBRATIONS

A Blessing

As coming out is a continual process, it is fitting to say a blessing or a prayer each time the process is furthered. Even when we have been public about our identities for years, we are faced time and again with the decision of whether or not to make ourselves known in particular circumstances, and we experience the fears that arise when we need to make that decision. Whether we are telling a co-worker about our identity or marching in a demonstration for gay and lesbian civil rights, we can acknowledge our courage by saying a blessing:

נְבָרֵךְ אֶת עֵין הַחַיִּים, אֲשֶׁר נָתְנָה לִי הָעָצְמָה לָצֵאת מִן הַמְּצָרִים.

Nevarekh et ein hahayyim, asher natnah li ha'otzmah latzet min hametzarim.

Let us bless the source of life for giving me the strength to come out.[5]

Mi Sheberakh

While such a blessing fills an important religious need, it remains a private, individual form of expression. Many gay and lesbian Jews may also feel a need to have a public ritual in the synagogue. The ritual could be very simple, consisting of the recitation of the above blessing followed by a special *mi sheberakh* (blessing recited on one's behalf) which the service leader or rabbi could recite on the occasion. The form for women follows:

May the One who blessed our ancestors, Sarah, Rebecca, Leah, and Rachel; Miriam and Ruth; Abraham, Isaac, and Jacob, Moses, Aaron, and David, bless _____ bat (daughter of) _____, who has come forward bravely to proclaim her lesbian identity to this congregation. May she grow in self-understanding and rejoice in her newly claimed identity. May her courage be a model for others who yearn to reveal hidden parts of themselves. May she receive love, warmth, and support from her community, family, and friends. May her public act inspire us to deepen our commitment to work for a time when gay men and lesbians will no longer suffer from hatred and prejudice, and when all will live in harmony and peace. Amen.

This *mi sheberakh* could be recited at any synagogue service, but would be most appropriate during a Torah service, when the woman coming out could have an *aliyah* (honor of reciting the blessings before and after the Torah is read). Having an *aliyah* followed by a *mi sheberakh* echoes the Bat Mitzvah (coming of age ceremony for girls), the occasion of a young woman's first *aliyah*. Coming of age means making the transition to being a responsible Jew, and taking on a new identity as a Jewish woman. Similarly, coming out is a lifecycle event that makes demands and proclaims a new identity. The link is most appropriate.

Shabbat Shirah

A third option for celebration is to link the coming out ritual to a specific aspect of Jewish history as it is marked on the Jewish calendar. As I have noted, the experience of *yetzi'at mitzrayim*, going out of Egypt, resonates powerfully with a public coming out for a Jewish lesbian. It is thus reflected in the language of the prayer I have formulated. The Hebrew for coming out, *latzet min hametzarim* (literally, to come out of narrow places) hints at the theme of coming out of *mitzrayim*. Jewish tradition demands that each Jew must experience herself as coming out of Egypt (Mishnah *Pesaḥim* 10:5). The historical event is a celebration of freedom, of emerging from a restricted life as a slave into life as a free person. For the Jew this freedom is not merely individual liberation, but also the acceptance of responsibility for claiming a Jewish identity and living as a Jew in the world. When a lesbian comes out, she too leaves the restrictions of the closet behind to experience the joy and freedom of a new identity, and to assume the weight of responsibility that this new identity entails.

These themes of exodus from Egypt are evoked not only on Passover but also on *Shabbat Shirah* (Sabbath of Song, which generally falls in February) during which we read the Torah portion about crossing the Red Sea. It is that moment of transition that best exemplifies the experience of coming out, because of the courage necessary to cross the sea into a new life of freedom, and because of the exultation experienced when the crossing has been completed. The *Haftarah* (prophetic reading) for *Shabbat Shirah* contains Deborah's

Song of Victory, just as the Torah portion contains Miriam's song of rejoicing, so that there are several women's voices heard on *Shabbat Shirah*. It is a most fitting time for lesbians to come out.

Readings in the service could include stories of courage from Jewish and gay literature. The *midrash* (Rabbinic legend) about Nahshon, the first Israelite to cross the sea (BT *Sotah* 37a), is felicitous: When the other Israelites held back in fear at the raging sea, Nahshon stepped into the water, an action based on faith and the courage to dare. He had to wade into the sea until the water reached above his nostrils; only then did the miracle of the parting occur. The following passage from Adina Abramowitz's story, "Growing Up in Yeshiva," would also be appropriate:

> In December 1980, I attended the founding conference of New Jewish Agenda and signed up for the lesbian and gay affinity group. That may have been my first conscious act of self-acceptance and pride. I was twenty-two years old and had been carrying around the conflict between my Jewish and lesbian identity for five years. Just being in a room with over thirty people who put the words "gay" and "lesbian" together with "Jewish" was immensely healing....After all of the years of debate, I decided on New Year's Eve, 1980, to try calling myself a lesbian for one month. Almost immediately I felt enormous relief. Although my struggles with my sexual orientation were by no means over, I have not questioned my lesbian identity since that moment.[6]

The person who is coming out should define her own role in the service. She could give a talk on the meaning of this change in her life. She could also read Torah, or perhaps write a *midrash* filling in new words for Miriam's rejoicing as she crossed the sea. She might, following Miriam's example, lead a song or dance to celebrate her new status. At a minimum, she should recite the blessing for coming out and be called to the Torah for an *aliyah*. The special *mi sheberakh* may be recited after the *aliyah*.

The ritual might conclude with some joyous song, such as "*Siman Tov Umazal Tov*," to reflect the mood of celebration. As the Israelites sang at the sea, so should the Jewish community sing when anyone of us chooses to liberate him or herself from old enslavements.

Communal Support and Individual Courage

It is crucial, when someone celebrates coming out in so public a way, that the community clearly and unequivocally manifest its support. At this point, the risk involved in coming out is still great, and the person who celebrates this ritual will probably feel a mixture of pride and vulnerability. Members of the community may wish "*mazal tov*" (congratulations), write a note, sponsor a celebratory meal or *oneg shabbat* (reception following Sabbath services), or make a contribution to a worthy cause in the person's honor, preferably to an organization that works for gay and lesbian rights. While the primary goal of these ceremonies is the celebration of an individual life passage, a secondary benefit is that they will educate the community about gay and lesbian issues and, one hopes, play a role in encouraging the Jewish community to work for gay and lesbian liberation. Increasing the visibility of gay and lesbian Jews within the Jewish community will only have a positive effect on our status.

Jewish lesbians will be comfortable celebrating coming out with a communal ritual only when the Jewish community becomes more supportive of people making choices to live as lesbians. Until the stigma is lessened, many lesbians and gay men will remain in the closet. Some will also choose to come out selectively to individuals, but ask those individuals to keep the information confidential.[7] It is important to understand that deciding to come out is difficult for most of us who discover we are gay or lesbian, and the process is individual to each of us.

The expectation that increased visibility will ultimately lead to increased acceptance has been a major factor in helping lesbians to take the risk of coming out. In many ways, it is easier to remain closeted. You do not fear other people's negative assessments, you do not worry that you will lose your job or promotion or the love of parents or other family members. It is hard work to educate others about how to relate to you if they have problems; it is not comfortable to disagree with your friends' or colleagues' assessment of your life. It is so comfortable to blend in, to be just like everybody else, as we are also often tempted to do as Jews.

Coming out is not easy, but it is vital for the health of individuals, of the lesbian community, and of the Jewish community. This is so because—on every level—denial of who we are ultimately compromises who we are. In a world where people still encounter hostility merely because they are different, it is wonderful to realize that lesbians increasingly have models for their process of self-discovery, as well as public spaces—Jewish spaces—in which they can feel at home.

On Serving a Gay/Lesbian/ Bisexual Congregation

JANE LITMAN

"Your people will be my people and your God will be my God."
—RUTH 1:16

For the last three years, I have been the rabbi of Kol Simcha, the gay/lesbian/bisexual congregation of Orange County, California. Our congregation is open to all who wish to participate, and there are a few heterosexual members who feel that the open and tolerant atmosphere best suits their spiritual needs. We are a small *haimishe* (homey) congregation of fewer than one hundred households, located in Laguna Beach, a liberal seaside artists' colony in a fairly conservative section of the state. In most respects the congregation has the same concerns and operating issues as any small congregation—i.e., budget, dues, programming, logistics, and publicity. It is much more similar to other congregations I have served than it is different from them. There are, however, a few areas in which the special nature of the congregation is particularly evident.

Tzelem Elohim: Recognizing the Image of God in Oneself

The Jew who chooses a gay/lesbian/bisexual synagogue asks a question commonly posed by American Jews: Will this congregation and rabbi respond to my spiritual, social, and communal needs? But far more than Jews who attend mainstream synagogues, the members of my congregation tend to arrive with personal histories that have generated feelings of disenfranchisement from the Jewish community. At the same time, many of the Jews

---

Rabbi Jane Litman is on the faculty of California State University at Northridge and serves as spiritual leader of congregation Kol Simcha of Orange County.

who attend gay/lesbian/bisexual synagogues also have stronger feelings of commitment to their heritage.

Why is this? Gay Jews experience a great deal of marginalization and delegitimation in the Jewish community because of their sexual orientation. Jewish communal life tends to be geared toward nuclear heterosexual families with children; many who do not fit that model experience a sense of being less than central to the Jewish collective enterprise. This is true of childless couples, single people, divorced people, non-traditional families, and gays. Gay Jews must also confront the history of Jewish scriptural homophobia (vis. Leviticus 18:22).

It is easy to allow these biases to become a barrier to Jewish life and practice. In addition, the strong gay community can often serve in the stead of a Jewish community. Because gay congregations are generally not neighborhood synagogues, and because many gays and lesbians do not have children, the need to find a nearby religious school is not a major incentive for synagogue affiliation. Thus, gay and lesbian Jews who choose to affiliate most often do so from conviction and commitment rather than routine, external pressure, or convenience for the family.

These Jews have special needs. The most important are inclusion and self-esteem. When I teach or lecture, I make a special effort to discuss important Jewish gay/lesbian/bisexual people in history such as Harvey Milk, Gertrude Stein, Emma Goldman. I make use of the gay male love poetry of the Jewish Golden Age in Spain.[8]

On Passover, we read the Song of Songs homo-erotically, in same-sex pairs, as well as hetero-erotically. I teach kabbalistic (Jewish mystical) passages about homo-eroticism and mysticism. Since, in many ways, gay life is not about whom gay people have sex with, but about whom they love, I also emphasize Jewish material about same-sex love which may not be sexual, such as the biblical stories of Ruth and Naomi or David and Jonathan. In addition, I make sure to draw the parallels between Jewish identity in the face of intolerance and gay pride. I seldom give a sermon or teach without some reference geared toward establishing positive Jewish gay identity.

Torah and Tefillah: Study, Ritual, and Prayer

In part, Jewish identity means partaking in traditional Jewish practices. However, the structures of gay life (and increasingly in the United States, of non-gay life as well) often demand flexibility and change in Jewish tradition. The children of my congregation need positive Jewish educational material which speaks to their reality, such as the stories of Leslea Newman or Rabbi Julie Greenberg.[9] When these children celebrate their Bnei Mitzvah (coming of age ceremonies), I must be sensitive to the fact that they may well have two mommies or two daddies or a divorced heterosexual parent who might be somewhat uncomfortable in our congregation.

My congregants require rituals and ceremonies which affirm their lives and choices. On Passover, we compare homophobia and gay-bashing to the oppression of our Jewish forebears. On *Yom Hasho'ah* (Holocaust Memorial Day) we remember those in the camps forced by the Nazis to wear pink triangles, as well as those made to wear the yellow star. National lesbian and gay pride marches often coincide with *Shavu'ot* (Festival of the Giving of the Torah), and we rejoice in the Torah of freedom as well as the Torah of wisdom.

One of the most controversial duties of a rabbi of a gay/lesbian/bisexual congregation is officiating at same-sex commitment ceremonies. Committing one's life to another person, starting a new family within the people Israel, is a sacred and, traditionally, public event. Same-sex relationships should be accorded the respect and religious sanction they merit. This is a key test of tolerance and equal rights. If love and relationships are holy, created by God, then same sex-couples are entitled to a Jewish ritual of bonding.[10] That ritual may or may not be called a wedding, usually depending on the couple's political perspective towards weddings.[11] Regardless, a communal celebration affirms not only the powerful coming together of the two lovers, but also the entire worth of gay/lesbian/bisexual existence.

Kelal Yisra'el and *Tikkun Olam*: Community Relations and Social Action

As a result of their position in society, gay Jews tend to be fairly sophisticated about publicity and community relations. My congregation and the other gay congregations with which I am familiar all have speakers' bureaus. We particularly promote outreach and education to the mainstream Jewish community and to schools.

Recently, we had an incident of almost fatal gay-bashing in

Laguna Beach, which is about thirty percent gay. This incident proved to be a catalyst for a strong alliance between our congregation and the local Jewish Anti-Defamation League. Kol Simcha and ADL have since collaborated on several educational forums.

Bikkur Ḥolim: AIDS

My congregants live in a sub-culture which has been profoundly shaken by AIDS. Although relatively few congregants have been stricken, every member, including myself, has lost at least one close friend who literally wasted away and died in terrible pain. This epidemic creates new religious demands for hospital, hospice, and home visitation; buddy programs; and survivor support. It also revives an old religious question: What kind of God would allow such a thing? Mortality is a much closer and more intimate religious concern of a predominantly gay/lesbian congregation than of a mainstream one of otherwise similar demographic make-up.

Tzedek, Tzedek Tirdof: The Pursuit of Integrity

Coming out necessarily involves risk. Members of a gay congregation put themselves at risk in service to personal integrity. It is my privilege to pray and study with a group of people who are clear about who they are—as lesbians, gay men, bisexual people, and Jews. This community has challenged and affirmed my own personal sense of honesty and honor.

Being true to ourselves gives us strength to respect the other. Kol Simcha is one of the most tolerant and accepting groups I have ever known. They practice genuine *ahavat yisra'el* (love of Jews and the Jewish people). Perhaps that is due, in some measure, to Kol Simcha's size, perhaps to the values of Laguna Beach's liberality, or to the diversity of its members. Certainly it is due in large part to a commitment to survive anti-gay discrimination and intolerance, and to flourish. Because of the courage of its members, Kol Simcha has lived up to the meaning of its name: It is truly a "voice of gladness and joy."

8

Marriage

Getting married is not the same as being married. A wedding lasts one day; a marriage, we hope, a lifetime. Yet the way one chooses to get married sets a tone and a precedent for the enduring marital relationship. For Jews who care about the full inclusion of women in ritual life, this is both good news and bad news: Good news because many rabbis and laypeople have already begun to look critically at the wedding ceremony and to equalize it; bad news, because, in its classical form, the Jewish wedding seals and celebrates acquisition of a woman by a man.

Most girls are still raised to dream of their wedding day. But, in addition to envisioning tulle, satin, and sprays of gentle flowers, contemporary Jewish girls and women may well fantasize about double-ring ceremonies or breaking *two* glasses under the *ḥuppah* (marriage canopy). Times have changed!

Yet, the authors in this chapter and the next find many elements of the wedding ceremony unsettling. For example, the declaration of consecration recited by the groom is one-sided and has the consequence of binding the bride, but not him, to exclusivity; the traditional Jewish wedding does not accommodate same-sex couples who wish to sanctify their commitment to each other; the custom of *kinyan* (pulling on a handkerchief or other object to signify the transfer of ownership or the conclusion of a transaction) physicalizes the wedding's basis in acquisition law and conveys that the bride is now "owned" by the groom. While the Rabbis are careful to distinguish between acquiring a wife and all other types of purchases and acquisitions, the foundation of marriage in acquisition law remains (e.g., BT *Kiddushin* 12a).

Despite all this, even the most progressive feminists are cautious about making changes. We have great attachments to and nostalgia for the Jewish wedding ceremony as a whole. The *Sheva Berakhot* (seven marital blessings) are breathtakingly beautiful and, except for masculine God language, completely non-sexist. Even "politically incorrect" aspects of the wedding may be quite moving. For example, the traditional *ketubbah* (marriage contract) is not a mutual document; it presumes to, but does not, negotiate divorce settlements in advance; and it offers more money, upon the dissolution of the marriage through death or divorce, to a virgin-bride than to a non-virgin. Yet, I value the *ketubbah* for the antiquity of its language, the continuity of its usage, the artwork and calligraphy that it has inspired over the centuries, and the fact of its acceptance by all segments of the Jewish community—from ultra-Orthodox to classical Reform.

The authors of this chapter are duly respectful of the tradition, but there is a consensus among them that change is necessary. Rabbi Einat Ramon draws on methodologies used by Rabbis Mordecai Kaplan and Abraham Joshua Heschel to retrieve and build on the original purpose of the *ketubbah*, as well as the biblical understanding of marriage. She reinstates the tradition of creating *tena'im* (marriage conditions) that supplement the *ketubbah* and spell out in concrete terms the commitments that each marriage partner makes to the other. She stops short of eliminating any reference to acquisition law in the ceremony, and opts instead to retain most of the traditional terminology while investing it with new meaning, based on early usage.

Founding a marriage on the acquisition of a woman by a man may be considered offensive or irrelevant in the case of heterosexual couples. It can only be considered absurd for lesbians who wish to make use of the traditional Jewish ceremony and thus to sanctify their relationship. Rabbi Leila Gal Berner and Renee Gal Primack confront key questions for lesbians and gays who seek to affirm their commitment to each other in a Jewish context. What are the similarities and differences between lesbian/gay marriages and traditional Jewish marriages? How much do the language, symbols, and philosophical assumptions of a traditional wedding ceremony speak to same-sex couples? What can be reclaimed or understood newly? What must be discarded, and what, invented? These last three questions are exactly those addressed by Rabbi Ramon and, in the next chapter, by Rivka Haut. All four authors take seriously the notion that marriage ritual binds two partners in a sanctified relationship, and, precisely for that reason, they care deeply about the nature of the relationship which marriage ritual names as holy.

Rabbi Ramon and Haut both quote Rav Kuk's injunction to renew the old and sanctify the new. This is most appropriate, as the Jewish community is engaged in both endeavors, in its process of rethinking Jewish marriage. So far, we have no conclusive answers. Some liturgists and theologians are leaning toward the creation of a single marriage ritual, which would be appropriate for gays, lesbians, and heterosexuals, and which would treat the partners as equals. Theologian Rachel Adler suggests that all sanctified unions should be based on Talmudic laws of partnership, as opposed to property, and on traditional interpretations of covenant.[1]

Yiḥud (brief seclusion of a couple immediately after the wedding ceremony) is one example of a traditional wedding practice that is completely compatible with the emotional and spiritual needs of modern couples. *Yiḥud* provides the opportunity for privacy and quiet reflection in the midst of a public and boisterous celebration. The ritual I offer in this chapter attempts to revitalize the practice and invest it with added significance.

Rabbi Debra Cantor describes the day-to-day challenge and joy of Jewish partnership. Her personal and inspirational words help to clarify what makes a good Jewish marriage—and what lasts after the wedding day.

All four essays portray marriage as a sanctified, challenging, loving relationship, and, at the same time, as a social structure that affects and is affected by the larger community. Our private partnerships are opportunities for intimacy, for *tikkun olam* (repairing the world), and for managing the balance and integrity of public and private life.

A Wedding in Israel as an Act of *Tikkun Olam*

EINAT RAMON[2]

"The desirable relationship between man and woman...can only be achieved when the man and woman know how to live their own selves....Then each of them will know how to enrich and deepen his or her essence through the essence of the partner."

—AHARON DAVID GORDON, *CLARIFYING OUR IDEA FROM ITS FOUNDATION*

When we decided to marry, my husband and I envisioned a ceremony that would embrace our love for Rabbinic Judaism as well as our dedication to feminism, liberal values, and secular Israeli culture. Finding theoretical and practical methods to harmonize these, sometimes conflicting, commitments and traditions was a major challenge. In addition, we anticipated a technical obstacle: We were two newly ordained rabbis—he Reform and I Conservative—who planned to marry in Israel, where Jews can ordinarily marry only via the Orthodox establishment. Our situation necessitated a creative approach both to *halakhah* (Jewish law) and to Israeli bureaucracy. On the third of Tammuz, 5750 (July 6, 1989), we were married in Jerusalem, my hometown and the place where Arik and I hope to settle eventually. Planning our wedding was the beginning of what will, we hope, become the enterprise of our life: A constant struggle for the "renewal of the old and the sanctification of the new," in Zion and in the world.[3]

We understood our marriage through the kabbalistic (Jewish mystical) paradigm, according to which the union of male and female is a catalyst for *tikkun olam* (repairing the world).[4] In an age when women are becoming equal partners in shaping cultures and societies, this paradigm can finally be fully realized. We were guided by the thought of two modern Jewish thinkers, Mordecai Kaplan and Abraham Joshua Heschel, in transforming the wedding ceremony and interpreting the laws of marriage. We wanted the ceremony to reflect the Bible's vision of marriage as a covenant

---

Rabbi Einat Ramon, Ph.D. candidate at Stanford University and part-time rabbi in Missoula, Montana, was the first Israeli woman to be ordained.

formed by a man and a woman created in the image of God (Genesis 1:27) who become "one flesh" (Genesis 2:24) and who regard one another as friends and companions (Malachi 2:14). We felt that the literal interpretation of the *halakhah*, according to which a woman was symbolically "purchased" by a man through the act of marriage, violated these biblical and kabbalistic visions.

Historical and Halakhic Background

The greatest intellectual and emotional challenge lay in our effort to write our *ketubbah* (marriage contract) and *tena'im* (marriage conditions). The *ketubbah* is a prenuptial agreement instituted by Rabbis in the first century to grant women economic protection within the marriage and in case of its dissolution. In a time when it was easy to expel a woman from her husband's household (Mishnah *Gittin* 9:10),[5] the *ketubbah* ensured that "he shall not regard it as easy to divorce her" (BT *Yevamot* 89a). The *ketubbah* was not a mutual contract but rather the husband's one-sided promise to his wife, witnessed by two men. Traditionally most women were not considered autonomous beings. Until she married, a woman was under the auspices of her father. The wedding of a woman who was not a divorcee or widow marked the transition from her father's to her husband's possession (Mishnah *Ketubbot* 4:5). The Mishnah (*Kiddushin* 1:1) perceived a betrothal partially as a financial transaction through which the man symbolically "acquired" the woman by giving her an object. Though modern scholars and traditional apologists have argued that acquisition of the woman is limited to a husband's claim for exclusive conjugal rights, the "right" and expectation of a wife doing housework was also granted by the Rabbis.[6]

In the traditional *ketubbah*, the groom pledges to provide his bride food, clothing, and sexual relations. He also designates a certain amount of income for the bride in case he dies or divorces her. Lastly, the *ketubbah* assures that the woman can leave the marriage with her dowry and its increment (*Shulḥan Arukh Even Ha'ezer* 1:126). Over time, the Rabbis expanded the range of a husband's duties (BT *Ketubbot* 51a-52b) so that he became obliged to provide his wife with medical care, to ransom her from captivity, and to bear the costs of her funeral. They also allowed for the addition of *tena'im*, which might add additional financial terms or protections for the woman agreed upon by the families of the bride and groom. A woman's obligations to her husband were not the focus of the *ketubbah* or *tena'im*, and were assumed.

Today, most Conservative and all Orthodox *ketubbot* use the traditional format, written in Aramaic (the everyday language of most Jews in antiquity). Some defend the traditional *ketubbah* by claiming that under modern civil governments which protect women's interests and have jurisdiction over marriage, "the only function of the *ketubbah* is to perpetuate an ancient tradition."[7] However, by accepting the traditional *ketubbah,* or slightly modifying it within the scope of traditional Jewish marriage law, one perforce is also accepting traditional gender role assumptions. This is demonstrated by the fact that the Conservative movement halakhic "egalitarian" *ketubbot* do not allow the bride to promise to support her groom, except in the event of his illness, nor to recite the same words to him that he says to her.[8]

Most Reform and Reconstructionist rabbis, as well as some Conservative rabbis, use egalitarian *ketubbot.* But these documents do not discuss such "mundane" aspects of a couple's life as finances, sex, or division of labor and assets. Thus, they fail to address the concerns that originally gave rise to the *ketubbah*: Naming responsibilities, protecting the woman, and anticipating problems, including the possibility that the marriage might end. *Halakhah* guides us to contemplate and devise respectful solutions for potential conflicts. By using only expressions of romantic love, egalitarian *ketubbot* ignore halakhic cautions to be realistic during the most dream-like moment of our lives.

Towards a Transformation of the *Ketubbah*

Arik and I felt that perpetuating—or eliminating—an ancient tradition without wrestling with its meaning would betray our own commitment to *halakhah*. We relied upon modern Jewish philosophy of *halakhah* to bridge the gap between ourselves and our tradition. We used interpretation as a means and standard by which to change observances and engage in the traditional halakhic process.

Two major Jewish thinkers set the methodological basis of our reinterpretation: Mordecai Kaplan and Abraham Joshua Heschel.

Kaplan's discussion of the principle of "reevaluation" presented a system of reinterpreting *halakhah* from a historic perspective.[9] The process of reevaluation requires first, a clarification of the values and the religious and psychological needs that a particular observance served in the past, and second, an adaptation of the observance and the creation of a modern *halakhah* that remains faithful to those needs and values, as well as to modern sensibilities. Heschel's views on the importance of *aggadah* (Jewish lore) in the determination of *halakhah* served as another guideline. He held that Jewish law only fleshed out the divine vision set forth by the *aggadah*.[10]

Following Kaplan, we tried to outline the original needs that the *ketubbah* served: To protect the wife and to regulate obligations that would lead to a dignified marriage and, if necessary, a dissolution of it. We therefore signed and notarized a prenuptial agreement mentioned in our *ketubbah*, an agreement that outlined the division of property in case of divorce.[11] To flesh out a renewed vision of the marital union, we established appropriate physical and financial duties for modern men and women. We felt that the modern *ketubbah* must spell out a broader range of obligations for both partners. Thus we incorporated a reference to mutual responsibility in all aspects of life, including housework. We also mentioned commitments to various educational, social, and national tasks that affect our relationship.

The idea of protecting the woman through the *ketubbah* presented a dilemma. On the one hand, holding on to this original purpose meant that we would perpetuate a non-egalitarian view of men and women. On the other hand, the *ketubbah* was instituted to mend a world that is not yet mended. Given that our society is still male-dominated, it would be hypocritical to pretend that men and women need equal protection. We resolved this tension by having Arik give me our new document and not vice versa. This one-sidedness symbolically stated that in a world where women still suffer discrimination, they need extra protection. At the same time, by making all of our pledges reciprocal we stressed that equality and mutuality are the best possible protections for women.

We attempted to preserve the language of the traditional *ketubbah* as much as possible. In addition, we incorporated expressions from an ancient *ketubbah* found in Assuan, Egypt, including the formula "Thou art my wife and I am thy husband forever." This phrase was disallowed by post-Talmudic rabbinical authorities because it implied that the groom consecrated himself to the bride as well.[12] We liked this phrase for precisely the same reason that the Rabbis decided to eliminate it.

Heschel's thought inspired us to develop non-halakhic statements that portray the essence of Jewish marriage. One was from the prophet Malachi: "God is a witness between you and the wife of your youth...she is your partner and covenanted spouse" (2:14). Another was from the Babylonian Talmud: "He who loves his wife as himself and respects her more than himself...about him Scripture says: 'You know that all is well in your tent'" (Job 5:24; BT *Yevamot* 62b). Maimonides turned this *aggadah* into *halakhah* by incorporating it as a law in *Mishneh Torah Hilkhot Ishut* 15:19. We followed his path by introducing this *halakhah* as an explicit mutual obligation.

The traditional concept of *kedushah* (holiness, with a connotation of exclusivity or being set apart) fashioned our understanding of the *ketubbah*: The word *"kedushah"* means holiness; the value concept *kedushah* means that we must embrace as holy every aspect of Jewish life, from praying to sexual relations. Maimonides invoked *kedushah* in his description of the appropriate sexual behavior for Jewish scholars and leaders of the community (*Mishneh Torah Hilkhot De'ot* 5:4-5). *Kedushah yeterah* (special holiness) is the way we think a husband and a wife should treat one another in all their speech and daily behavior.

It is interesting that Jewish tradition viewed sex as an obligation of the man toward the woman. This duty was explicitly mentioned in the traditional *ketubbah*. It ensured that moments of intimacy would not be pre-empted by the husband's potential involvement with other wives (at the time when polygamy was allowed) or by his work. We tried to address the issue of preserving time for intimacy by establishing priorities and principles of mutuality. Intimacy in this sense meant more to us than intercourse. However, we maintained the tradition of referring specifically in the *ketubbah* to sexual intercourse, using a phrase based on Maimonides (*Mishneh Torah Hilkhot De'ot* 5:4-5): "The bride and the groom agree to come to one another when they are both willing and happy," affirming that sexual expression takes place only under conditions of mutual desire and joy.

The following is a generic translation of our *ketubbah*:[13]

On the _____ day of the Hebrew month _____ in the year 57__ since the creation of the world, according to our way of reckoning here in _____,

The bridegroom, _____	The bride, _____
son of _____ and	daughter of _____ and
_____ said to the bride:	_____ said to the groom:
"Be my partner and	"Be my partner and
covenanted spouse,	covenanted spouse,
and I will be your man	and I will be your woman
forever and give you	forever, according to the
your *ketubbah*, according	law of Moses and Israel."
to the law of Moses	
and Israel."	
And _____ accepted.	And _____ accepted.

The bride and the groom took upon themselves to cherish, honor, support, and maintain each other; to come to one another when they are both willing and happy; to treat one another with special holiness, to respect each other more than themselves and to love one another as much as themselves; to nurture each other's growth, personal development, and joy of living.

In addition they pledged that their home will become their first priority / the fountainhead of their lives, that it will be established on mutual support, equality in responsibilities, and sharing of all aspects of life.

The bridegroom and the bride aspire to build a Zionist home in the Land of Israel which will reflect the striving toward and practice of mending the world and to raise children to do justly, love mercy, and walk humbly with their God.

As part of this *ketubbah*, the couple has signed a property agreement.

The authority and contents of this *ketubbah* they took upon themselves freely as is the custom of Jewish communities. This contract is not to be considered a non-serious obligation or as

mere form. And we have received a token of acquisition from
the groom _____ son of _____ and _____ to the bride
_____, and from the bride _____ daughter of _____ and
_____ to the groom _____, regarding all that has been
written and explained above.
  And all is valid and binding.

_____Witness   _____Witness

A major debate evolved between us concerning the pledge about
our home being a first priority in our lives. I wanted this condition
because the setting of priorities was (and is), to my mind, the most
important feminist issue facing middle-class Western families.
Arik, however, saw himself dedicated equally to family and to
tikkun olam. Clearly, our gender differences came up in this discussion. We finally agreed to use the expression *"berosh ma'ayanei-
hem,"* an idiom with a double meaning: "Their first priority" and
"their fountainhead." Thus, our home could be understood as our
first priority as well as the source from which our lives will flow.
  While the *ketubbah* outlined the basic principles of our marriage, the *tena'im* document fleshed out their daily implications.
We had a *tena'im* ceremony in New York for our friends who could
not attend the wedding in Jerusalem. We listed our own personal
terms for creating a home together. During the gathering we broke
a plate following the old practice of smashing a dish on this occasion. Afterwards all of our guests, not just two males, signed the
document as witnesses. We also asked guests to add suggestions
on a sheet of paper attached to the contract, so that we would
have not only their best wishes, but their best advice on staying
happily married. Our *tena'im* document reflects the conviction that
specific measures must be planned and taken if an egalitarian
vision of marriage is to become a reality. It addresses in detail such
issues as housekeeping, public service, private time (apart and as
a couple), Jewish study, childrearing, vacations, Sabbath observance, etc. We still find our *tena'im* so meaningful and practical
that I encourage couples whose weddings I perform to write their
own. To cite some representative clauses:

  1. We will clean our house thoroughly once a week for *Shabbat*.

2. We will study Jewish texts together at least two hours per week.

3. We will not continue to rehash unalterable decisions more than twenty-four hours after they are made.

4. We will coordinate a day off once a week where we will spend time doing something unconnected to either of our usual daily activities.

5. Hebrew and English will be the first two languages which we teach our children (should we be blessed with children). We will teach them Arabic at the earliest age healthy for a child to learn a third language.

6. We must compliment each other on something not superficial at least once a day.

7. We will live only in places where both of us have opportunities to engage in meaningful work.

8. Arik will consider going to the barber before the wedding.

We were not under the illusion that all marital issues could be decided in advance, but we believed that agreeing on a set of conditions would anticipate and resolve some of them. Moreover, by jointly writing the *tena'im*, we modeled, for our community and ourselves, both an egalitarian process and a method of negotiating the details and priorities of married life.

The Wedding: Spiritual Preparation

The nuptial festivities began with our signing papers at the offices of a justice of the peace in New York. Ironically, Arik and I, two rabbis, had to follow the procedure of civil marriage at New York's City Hall, because our religious wedding conducted six weeks later by two non-Orthodox rabbis would not be recognized by the State of Israel. While our situation reflected the predicament of non-Orthodox Judaism in Israel, it also indicated that there are ways to circumvent the restrictions of the Chief Rabbinate because any marriage that is recognized by international law must be recognized by Israeli civil law.[14]

The spiritual preparations that preceded the wedding followed traditional patterns. We went to my grandfather's grave to remember him and acknowledge that his spirit had inspired our union and would be with us under the *huppah* (wedding canopy). As is customary, we separated for a few days to give ourselves time alone, with our families, and with close friends. On the day of the wedding we both fasted. As on *Yom Kippur* (Day of Atonement), this is an act of purification and preparation for the new life that is about to begin. We each took time for writing, reflection, and prayer.

On the night before our wedding I went to the *mikveh* (ritual bath). Arik too immersed himself in a source of living water, the traditional requirement for ritual bathing, with his three brothers and two close male friends at the beach in Tel Aviv. This "bachelors' party" also fulfilled a spiritual purpose. The ancient observance of immersing in a source of living water was one that I very much wanted to keep, despite the popular Orthodox interpretation which I find offensive, that the immersion in the *mikveh* purifies women from the "pollution" of their menstruation. However, ritual immersion is also understood as symbolic of purification and rebirth, and it marks events in the spiritual lifecycle, as well as in the menstrual cycle.

My mother offered to accompany me to the *mikveh*. Her company was so important to me that it justified abandoning a standing rule in my life—to avoid any unnecessary contact with Orthodox religious institutions. As my mother watched me dip in the water, a peaceful holiness clothed the two of us. It seemed like we had suddenly shared a glimpse of the past thirty years of our lives: From the moment that I came out of the waters of her body, to this moment on the eve of another stage of separation.

Kiddushin (Holy Matrimony)

The wedding itself incorporated as many community and family members as possible. It began with a short prayer service that consisted of selected readings from the Bible, *Zohar* (premier Jewish mystical text), and modern Hebrew poetry. This service was modeled after similar ceremonies conducted in Israeli Reform *kibbutzim* (communes). The readings were aesthetic expressions that reflected our perceptions of the marital union and of God's presence in it. We read from the *Zohar* (II:85b) about God's formation of the souls as male and female. According to this passage, the male and female aspects separate from one another as they descend to earth. Only God, The-Holy-One-Of-Blessing, knows how to match them properly, and only those "who walk in the path of truth" find their original soul mate. We also read a passage about the rebellion of the labor Zionists against some of the traditional marriage customs, and two poems by Israeli poets Raḥel and Zelda. Between the readings, we sang Israeli love songs and we concluded with a selection from the Song of Songs, "My beloved is mine and I am his" (2:16). Before the procession, we had a private *badeken* (bridal veiling ceremony); only our parents and a few family members were present. In traditional settings, the men dance and sing before the bridegroom and follow him to the place where the bride is seated with all the women, waiting for him. There, the groom puts the veil over the bride's face, while rabbi, groom, and/or guests recite the blessing given to Rebecca before she married Isaac: "Our sister be thou the mother of thousands and myriads" (Genesis 24:60). We deviated from custom in this case because we preferred to keep this moment short and private in the midst of the public celebration. According to kabbalistic traditions, the veiled bride alludes to the concealed *Shekhinah* (close-dwelling presence of God, associated with the feminine), and we felt this awesome image and presence deserved a moment of silence.

The first blessing recited under the *ḥuppa* is that of *erusin* (betrothal), in which we mark the transition from forbidden to permissible sexual relations. We preserved the blessing's reference to the prohibition of incestuous sexual relations, but eliminated the reference to pre-marital sex, because we believe that a modern Jewish sexual ethic should prevail.[15] The traditional version of the betrothal blessing addresses the groom. We changed the language of that blessing so that it would refer both to bride and bridegroom. In general, however, we preferred to follow Kaplan and Heschel, and retain the basic structure and terminology of the ceremony while giving it new or renewed meaning. The Hebrew term *"kiddushin"* (holy matrimony) has accumulated layers of sexual discrimination over the years. In Rabbinic literature it defines the act of acquiring a wife by a ring or other property and a one-sided declaration. We chose not to select a new term because we thought that the Rabbinic use of *"kiddushin"* was a corruption of the word, which comes from the root k.d.sh., meaning set aside as sacred—the same root as *kedushah yeterah*. Implementing Heschel's call to find new relevance in religious ritual,[16] we restored the original meaning of the word *"kiddushin"* by modifying the ritual into one of mutual consecration of and by bride and groom. Arik and I exchanged rings and each of us recited the traditional phrase: "By this ring you are consecrated to me according to the laws of Moses and Israel." According to traditional Jewish law, it is forbidden for the bride to give a ring to the groom while reciting the same words that he said to her, since this act throws into question whether an acquisition of the woman has truly taken place.[17] By making the declaration of consecration a mutual one, Arik and I lifted it out of the Rabbinic interpretation of symbolic purchase of the wife.

A Note about the *Sheva Berakhot* (Seven Marital Blessings)

The seven blessings recited under the *ḥuppah* and during the first week of marriage celebrate the unity of masculine and feminine in God and in the world. The paradigm of male-female harmony is revealed in the blessing that honors the creation of humanity, male and female, in the image of God. It is present, too, in blessings that convey the prophetic, messianic vision of the unification of God, the Father of the people of Israel, with Mother Zion. The concluding blessings focus on the newly-wed couple, who manifest this metaphysical male-female harmony.

While male and female are invoked, God is described by the traditional text in exclusively male terms and images. *He* is the *King* of the universe. This undercuts the profound meaning of the liturgy. As long as the blessings include only male metaphors, they transmit an incomplete, broken image of God. Therefore, I substitute the word *"malkhut"* (sovereignty) for the word *"melekh"* (king). *"Malkhut"* is a feminine noun and yet not an anthropomorphic image. Nevertheless, it is not totally abstract because *Malkhut* is also the name of one of the feminine spheres of the Divine, according to Jewish mystical interpretation. In *kabbalah* (Jewish mysticism) *Malkhut* is another name for *Shekhinah,* Torah, Sabbath, Zion, and other manifestations of the Divine that are grammatically and metaphorically feminine.

The seven blessings can easily incorporate both male and female God-language, if they begin with masculine verbs and pronouns (*barukh attah adonai eloheinu*) and continue with feminine images and verbs (*malkhut ha'olam boret peri hagafen*). This combination embraces the harmony of masculinity and femininity within the Divine and in the world.

A Glimpse of a Mended World

By the time our wedding ceremony was over, evening had already fallen and a curtain of stars was spread over Jerusalem, a city that yearns for peace. Unfortunately, the joy of the day was marred by tragedy. A terrorist forced a bus going from Tel Aviv to Jerusalem off the road, causing the deaths of fourteen people. Arik and his brothers almost took that bus. When Arik and I broke a glass at the conclusion of our ceremony, we were reminded of the wider world yet to be mended, a world where the line between life and death is so narrow, and the boundaries between people, so wide. As is customary, before breaking the glass, we recited the verses that commemorate the destruction of ancient Jerusalem: "If I forget thee, O Jerusalem, let my right hand forget her cunning; let my tongue cleave to the roof of my mouth, if I do not remember thee, if I do not set Jerusalem above my highest joy" (Psalms 137:5-6).

Yet, with the breaking of the glass and the exclamations of *"mazal tov,"* we began a happy, life-affirming celebration that broke the unnecessary boundaries between people who came from different nations and ethnic groups. Christian, Moslem, and Jewish men and women of many backgrounds and orientations sang and celebrated with one another. This was perhaps a taste of the "world to come," a glimpse of the future Zion, the mountain of God's dwelling which "all the nations shall flow into" (Isaiah 2:2). For me, our wedding was a precious hint of *hit'allut haneshamah* (elevation of the soul), a sacred moment in which God and humanity found one another.

Uncharted Territory: Lesbian Commitment Ceremonies

LEILA GAL BERNER AND RENEE GAL PRIMACK

"The rules break like a thermometer,/quicksilver spills across the charted systems,/we're out in a country that has no language/no laws, we're chasing the raven and the wren/through gorges unexplored since dawn/whatever we do together is pure invention/the maps they gave us were out of date by years...."
—ADRIENNE RICH, *TWENTY-ONE LOVE POEMS: XIII*

When two women wish to proclaim their commitment to one another, they walk into uncharted territory. As we considered whether and how to sanctify our relationship through ritual, we explored the implications of our decision and questions abounded. Do we need a commitment ceremony at all? Since secular and religious law afford us no legal standing, what validity is there in a commitment ceremony? What power does communal affirmation have for us? Would we simply be mimicking heterosexual weddings by choosing to have a ritual of our own?[18] Each couple will answer these questions in its own way and we know that many more questions may arise.

As committed Jews who appreciate traditional ritual, we found that we needed a Jewish way of expressing our love and dedication to a life-partnership. In Judaism, lifecycle rituals are the mechanism by which individuals are embraced by the tradition. Though we know that traditional Judaism does not embrace us or our relationship, we believe that we have a right to avail ourselves of newly-created Jewish rituals, and thereby make room for ourselves within an evolving religious tradition. We chose to embrace the tradition, even if it recoiled from us, thereby contributing to what we hoped would be its transformation.

Rabbi Leila Gal Berner is a congregational rabbi, a historian of medieval Jewish history, a composer of Jewish music, a liturgist, a teacher of Judaism and feminism, and the life-partner of Renee Gal Primack.
Renee Gal Primack is a conference coordinator for a mental health organization in Pennsylvania, a Jewish craft artist, a sometime Jewish bookseller, a fan of feminist fiction/fantasy literature, and the life-partner of Leila Gal Berner.

Historically, Jewish custom and even law have changed as a result of communal recognition and tacit or explicit legitimation. Though at present, our marriage is not binding according to secular law or Jewish law, the community in which we live (and who witnessed our expression of commitment) *does* consider our relationship valid and binding. We believe that the more lesbian and gay people sanctify their relationships through lifecycle rituals, the sooner Jewish tradition will be compelled to acknowledge our status and recognize our commitment as legitimate. Since we and our community recognize the binding nature of our ceremony, we believe that a formal dissolution ritual would be necessary, should we decide to separate.

After much struggle over the question of whether to embrace traditional Jewish marriage rituals and symbols, we concluded that in order to truly "own" Jewish ritual tradition, and thereby be genuinely enfranchised, we did not need to "re-invent the wheel" by creating totally new and different rituals. Rather, our goal was, in Rav Kuk's words, to "make the old new and the new, holy."[19]

Ultimately, we incorporated many Jewish rituals into our ceremony, though some in uniquely adapted forms. The *huppah* (wedding canopy) was not a *tallit* (prayer shawl), as is traditional, but a beautiful cloth embroidered by women. The words we used to exchange rings were those spoken by Ruth to Naomi: "Wherever you go, I shall go, and where you lodge, I shall lodge. Your people shall be my people, and your God my God" (Ruth 1:16). Our *ketubbah* (marriage contract) was truly a document of commitment, outlining specifically what we were committing to, and stating explicitly the contribution our ceremony made to *tikkun olam* (repairing the world). Between paragraphs, we used appropriate quotes from the Jewish textual tradition to further root ourselves within it. Rather than feminizing the traditional *Sheva Berakhot* (seven marital blessings) and simply deleting references to a groom, our adaptations in both Hebrew and English addressed the themes of each blessing and linked them to us as Jewish lesbians. The blessings were recited in feminized Hebrew and egalitarian English. For example, the second blessing is rendered *at berukhah yah, eloheinu hei ha'olamim, yotzeret kol enosh*. Blessed are You, *Yah*, Eternal God of space and time, who creates all humans.[20]

Since we had privately expressed our commitment to one

another long before our decision to consecrate it with ritual, we chose to call our ceremony a *Brit Ahavah* (covenant of loving dedication), rather than a commitment ceremony. The Hebrew word *brit* holds much power for us. It is the word used to signify the special loving relationship and binding "contractual" connection between God and the Jewish people. And *ahavah* means love. Using a word that resonates so strongly in Jewish history and tradition, along with the simple word that expresses our deepest feelings for each other, seemed right to us. This phrase was certainly as powerful to us as "wedding." As a symbol of our covenant with each other, we chose a family name which each of us took on and which is explained in the *ketubbah* below.

In the year we spent preparing for our *Brit Ahavah*, we navigated the uncharted territory together, sometimes with trepidation, sometimes with exhilaration, and always with tender love.

Ketubbah

At Sabbath's wane, on the seventh day of the month of *Shevat*, in the year five thousand, seven hundred and fifty two, corresponding to the eleventh day of January, nineteen hundred and ninety-two, as we reckon time here in Philadelphia, Pennsylvania, joyfully *Leila bat Eliyahu ve Zina* and *Raḥel bat Eliezer Moshe ve Ḥannah Malkah* stood under the *ḥuppah* before family and friends to consecrate their covenant of loving dedication.

1. "Rise up my love, my fair one, and come away...the time of singing has come..." (Song of Songs 2:10-12).

   We make this commitment in expression of our deep love, affection, passion and caring for one another. We will continue to laugh and play together and gently support one another through life's sorrows and disappointments.

2. "Were our mouths filled with song as the sea, and our tongues with ringing praise as the roaring waves...still we could not sufficiently thank you, our God and God of our ancestors for even one minute portion of the good You have done us..." (BT *Pesaḥim* 118a, Passover *Haggadah*, and traditional liturgy).

In celebration of our new family unity, we have adopted a shared name—*Gal*—the Hebrew word for "wave." As the waters of a wave wash over the sand, so our love washes over us, sometimes overwhelming us, sometimes bathing us in softness, ebbing and flowing with our own passions. We choose a name that reminds us always of the power of our feelings for one another—lest we forget in the mundane flow of our ordinary lives.

3. "There is no person that does not have [her] hour, and no thing that does not have its place" (Mishnah *Avot* 4:3).

   We know that we each respond differently to what life brings us. Sometimes we need companionship and conversation and sometimes, quiet time and aloneness. We promise to build a home in which separateness and togetherness are equally valued and respected.

4. "Two are better than one; because they have a good reward for their labor" (Ecclesiastes 4:9).

   We have agreed upon a division of household duties that feels fair and equitable to us. We promise to fulfill this agreement as best we can and to reassess it periodically to ensure that it is still working well for us.

5. "If there is no flour [for food], there can be no Torah" (Mishnah *Avot* 3:21).

   We are committed to negotiating our common financial obligations fairly and to implementing these agreements in a manner that will prevent guilt or inappropriate dependence. We have established legal powers-of-attorney and wills in the event, God forbid, of severe illness or death.

6. "My God, the soul You have given me is pure"(BT *Berakhot* 60b and traditional morning liturgy).

   We recognize our individual struggles with our bodies and pledge to help each other to honor our individual needs for proper diet, exercise, and a positive body image.

7. "More counsel, more understanding" (Mishnah *Avot* 2:8).

   When we face disagreements we will each honor the other's perceptions. Should a problem become too difficult to solve ourselves, we will seek the wise counsel of friends and professionals. We will endeavor to be patient and kind with each other during these times.

8. "...The study of Torah surpasses all" (Mishnah *Pe'ah* 1:1, BT *Shabbat* 127a).

    We value and appreciate in each other our love of learning. We will encourage one another and share in the learning process as we continue the lively discussions that already characterize our relationship.

9. "And you shall teach them diligently unto your children" (Deuteronomy 6:7).

    Should we be blessed with children, we will raise them with love, gentleness and respect for their unique personalities. We will teach them the ethical principles that guide our own lives. We will help them to face with courage and pride the prejudice they may encounter due to the nature of our family.

10. "This is the day our Creator has made. Let us be happy and rejoice in it" (Psalms 118:24).

    We will build a home open to the spiritual potential in all life; a home wherein our family celebrates the flow of the seasons and the passages of life through the symbols of our Jewish tradition. In our home, we will cherish our people's ancient ways and enrich them with new rituals and traditions.

11. "A faithful friend is a source of strength; whoever finds one has found a treasure" (Wisdom of Sirach 6:14).

    We recognize our need for friends and family, both individually and as a couple—and we hope that we will share a lifetime of celebrations and life passages with them. We will continue to build a community that is supportive of our family, as we offer friendship and support in return.

12. "You are not required to finish the work; neither are you free to desist from it" (Mishnah *Avot* 2:21).

    We know, as lesbians, that the world does not always nurture or affirm us. We will support one another when outside prejudice hurts us and we will strengthen each other as we endeavor to live as openly as possible in a sometimes inhospitable society. The world is still an imperfect place, in need of mending. We affirm our commitment to the ongoing task of *tikkun olam* (repairing the world).

13. "If you will it, it is no dream" (Theodore Herzl, *Altneuland*).

We understand that we cannot anticipate all the changes that life will bring us. We each intend to fulfill these commitments with honesty, integrity, and trust. The length of our partnership will be for the time that we share this common vision. We hope it will last a lifetime.

And all is valid and binding (from the traditional *ketubbah*).

Yiḥud and the Holiness of Matrimony

DEBRA ORENSTEIN

"Therefore a man leaves his father and mother and cleaves to his wife, and they become one flesh."

—GENESIS 2:24

Yiḥud is the technical requirement that bride and groom spend several minutes alone immediately following the wedding ceremony in a room whose privacy is formally guarded. The couple's seclusion has been understood as a symbolic consummation of the marriage, as well as an occasion, in cases of arranged marriages or chaperoned courtships, for the bride and groom to meet privately for the first time. The privacy of a guarded *Yiḥud* room counterbalances the public nature of the day and the open-sided *ḥuppah* (wedding canopy). It implicitly asserts that one feature of marital status is being separated from others—from one's family of origin, from other potential partners—and joined, first and foremost, with

---

Rabbi Debra Orenstein, editor of *Lifecycles,* fellow of the Wilstein Institute of Jewish Policy Studies, and instructor at the University of Judaism in Los Angeles, regularly writes and speaks on Jewish spirituality and gender studies.

one's spouse. So important is the required seclusion under Jewish law, that Maimonides ruled it is *Yihud* which seals and validates the marriage ceremony (*Mishneh Torah Hilkhot Ishut* 10:1).

On a practical level, *Yihud* also provides the couple an opportunity to eat, since it is traditional for bride and groom to fast on their wedding day, and since there will be little time to sit, eat, or relax later, during the reception. It is customary for Ashkenazim to serve chicken soup, a food that builds strength and health and, by its golden color, augurs a prosperous marriage. Some Sephardim serve doves or foods molded in the shape of doves, to symbolize marital peace.[21] Just as the first act under the *huppah* is an act of sharing (in which groom and bride drink from a single cup of wine), so, too, the first act as a married couple is one of sharing; this time the partners share a private meal.

In some communities, *Yihud* has been replaced by the receiving line: A sad turn of events. The communal aspects of weddings are pressing and important, but it is wonderful, I think, to preserve a moment of privacy in the midst of a day devoted to being "on display."[22]

The following is a ritual intended to revitalize the practice of *Yihud* and to help couples mark the sanctity of the moment. It was written with heterosexual couples in mind but can easily be adapted for same-sex couples.

HOLINESS AND MATRIMONY
Order of the Ritual

Celebrating the Moment
and Putting Each Other First

Once in seclusion, the couple reads: Now, with friends and family outside celebrating, we take our private time: Time to drink each other in, to be alone together, to acknowledge that we are married! *Yihud* comes from a root that means both aloneness and togetherness. No matter how much we are partners in this new marriage, we will always be our individual selves. No matter how alone each of us may feel, we will always have each other.

These first few minutes of our marriage, we take for us—for *our* joy, *our* privacy, *our* chance to laugh or cry. There are many times and occasions when we serve the community, but sometimes, we as a couple come first. Sometimes, we close the door and say, "They will wait. I need you." Going to that place of love and need, we do not cheat or scorn the wider world. We strike a balance with it. We make ourselves ready for it. We learn to face and serve it together. We feed ourselves and each other, so that we may, in turn, as a family, nourish the world.

Eating, Drinking, and Nurturing

The newly-weds recite appropriate blessings over the food, and then alternately feed each other mouthfuls (three times). With each "feeding," one of the following lines is recited:

I will feed you forever.
I will feed you with righteousness.
I will feed you with justice.
I will feed you with love.
I will feed you with compassion.
I will feed you with faithfulness.

(AFTER HOSEA 2:21-22)

Before drinking a beverage, each partner says: "Many waters cannot quench love and no flood can sweep it away" (Song of Songs 8:7).

Declaring Love and Gratitude

Groom: And Isaac took Rebecca and made her his wife. And he loved her and found comfort[23] (after Genesis 24:67).

Bride: And Rebecca lifted her eyes and beheld Isaac and was jolted with the surprise of love. And she said, "That is my husband" (after Genesis 24:64-65).

The couple continues eating, drinking, and celebrating spontaneously together. Their final act in the Yiḥud room is to recite the Sheheḥeyanu *(blessing for reaching a new or momentous occasion):*

Blessed are You, *Adonai,* Our God, Ruler of the universe, who has kept us in life and sustained us and enabled us to reach this time.

On Being Married

DEBRA CANTOR

"God creates new worlds constantly. In what way? By causing marriages to take place."

—*ZOHAR* 1:89A.

Hanging on the wall above our bed are two framed documents. The first, hand-calligraphed and elaborately illuminated, is our *ketubbah,* the formal marriage contract which my husband, Jim, and I, along with two witnesses, signed on our wedding day. The other document, typed on a thin sheet of onionskin and stuck in a dime-store plastic frame, also relates to our marriage. It is a poem which Jim gave me on our fifth wedding anniversary. It is entitled *"Torat Ahavah"* ("Torah / Teaching of Love"):

(I) The first is longest:
Beginnings are the hardest and least predictable.
We made a kind of covenant,
Found a place and ways to live our love.

(II) Wherever we were, we were together.
Love had found place and person for direction.
Now you, then I, searched for the right work.

Rabbi Debra Cantor, spiritual leader of the Kane Street Synagogue in Brooklyn, New York, was a member of the first rabbinical school class at The Jewish Theological Seminary to include women.

(III) The third reminded us
With new rules and living spaces
That it, too, was special.

(IV) We wandered while waiting,
Our time replete with conflicts, hesitations,
Moments of insights.

(V) At last a stabler state,
Sometimes a repetition of all before,
As we poise before the new situation.

At the time Jim wrote this, I was about to enter my senior year of rabbinical school at The Jewish Theological Seminary and we looked forward with both eagerness and trepidation to the prospect of my (finally!) finishing school. We knew we were soon to venture out together into unexplored territory. Both of us view our marriage as a kind of journey, one in which we accompany and support each other as we move forward.

It is not surprising that Jim drew parallels between our personal odyssey and the one undertaken by the Israelites on their way to the Promised Land. After all, Torah brought the two of us together (we met as graduate students) and Jewish texts have remained tremendously important to us as a way of communicating with each other, sorting out difficult questions, and understanding the life's journey we are making together. We study Torah together regularly, and both of us teach Jewish texts (though Jim works as a bank analyst by day).

Our bond to and through Torah is particularly important to us on *Shabbat* (Sabbath), which is an *ot* (sign) of the covenant between God and Israel (Exodus 31:16-17). For Jim and me, *Shabbat* also symbolizes the covenant we have made with each other to build a Jewish home together. Though the rhythm of *Shabbat* has changed for us since I became a congregational rabbi, *Shabbat* remains the anchor of our week and of our relationship. We try to feed our senses—to eat especially tasty meals, to linger over coffee, to nap, to make love, to take leisurely walks together, and to talk to one another without schedules or agenda in mind.

It is not that we do not talk during the rest of the week. But we long ago agreed to exclude certain topics from our *Shabbat* conversation. For example, we do not argue over money or family matters on *Shabbat*, we do not complain about work, and are particularly careful to avoid engaging in *lashon harah* (idle talk and gossip). There are six other days of the week during which to debate and work out the logistics of our lives. On *Shabbat*, freed of that burden, we talk about ideas, about the week's Torah portion, about our dreams, about the things we value most.

When Jim gave me that poem, we were about to embark upon another venture as well; we wanted to have a child. This turned out to be fraught with obstacles. For five years, we rode an emotional roller-coaster as we endured countless trips to fertility specialists and suffered a series of miscarriages.

Before, our sex lives had been regulated by our desire for one another and by the teachings of Jewish law. Each month, with the onset of my period, we took a hiatus from sexual contact with each other. Then, after I visited the *mikveh* (ritual bath), we once again eagerly renewed our sexual connection. Both Jim and I felt strongly that our observance of the laws of *tohorat hamishpaḥah* (family purity) and my monthly immersion in the *mikveh* (ritual bath) added a measure of *kedushah* (holiness) to our marital relationship. Now, though, it was neither the demands of Torah nor personal proclivity which ordered our sexual lives, but the dictates of fertility doctors and fluctuating hormone levels.

Gradually, instead of associating sex with pleasure and *kedushah*, we associated our most intimate moments with tension and disappointment. We found ourselves identifying with the anguish and despair, as well as the faith, of Sarah and Abraham, Rebecca and Isaac, Hannah and Elkanah. Their stories gave us some solace during that very difficult time.

Two weeks before our tenth anniversary, our son, Max Raphael, was born. Since then, our journey as a couple has been totally transformed. Our marriage has been immeasurably enriched by the arrival of our long-awaited child. Our Jewish observance, especially, has been infused with a fresh excitement as we share holidays and *Shabbatot* with Max. When he was a week old, we brought Max to *shul* (synagogue) for the first time. Now, at thirteen months, he claps when the Torah is carried around, helps put coins in our *pushkeh* (charity collection box), "blows" the *shofar* (ram's horn), and delightedly slurps down grape juice from his lit-

tle silver *kiddush* cup (special goblet used when reciting the blessing over wine on sacred occasions). Our Jewish life right now is far
more experiential than cerebral; Max is not only our student, but
our teacher, and our partner in doing *mitzvot* (commandments).

This great blessing has brought with it a challenge as well. We
find we are often incredibly overtired. We have had to search for
ways to renew our private connection with one another as husband and wife. Our quiet moments—long talks, leisurely cud-
dling—must usually, these days, be scheduled and orchestrated.
And so we struggle to rearrange our lives and juggle our commitments in order to make time for each other. We do this because
each of us needs, and wants, to be with our partner in life; we also
do this because we believe our marriage is a covenant—demanding, obligating, and deeply enduring. We are bound together by a
Torat Ahavah, a Torah of love, and we pray to be able to continue
our journey side by side for many more years to come.

9

Divorce

ivorce is a passage that more and more Jews experience. This is a reflection of general cultural trends and especially of greater social freedom to seek personal happiness. Although divorce is no longer rare, it remains a source of tremendous individual and family pain.

The Jewish divorce ceremony is stark and bare; its text is legal, not liturgical. The ceremony takes place in relative privacy, and without special blessings, foods, clothing, candles, or other accoutrements of religious ritual. All this reasonably reflects the nature of divorce, which, even under the best of circumstances, is lonely and austere. No attempt is made by the tradition to obscure this reality or to "pretty it up."

For Jewish women, however, and especially for Jewish women who run their lives according to *halakhah* (Jewish law), the severity of the divorce ceremony goes beyond what is fitting to the occasion. For, under traditional Jewish law, the *get* (bill of divorce) is given by husbands and received by wives. Thus, a Jewish man who divorces may be in pain, but he remains in power; a Jewish woman who gets divorced is disempowered by the very structure of divorce law, even if her husband cooperates fully.

Rivka Haut, an Orthodox feminist, raises incisive questions about Jewish women who are trapped in marriages from which their husbands will not release them. She argues that Orthodox women must begin to challenge their rabbis' implementation and interpretation of Jewish law. Haut does not treat divorce in a vacuum, but considers it in light of the Jewish wedding ceremony. She finds that the most offensive and unequal aspects of undoing a marriage have their seeds in the "doing"—i.e. in the fact that women traditionally take a passive role and are "acquired" under the wedding canopy. Thus, her critique of traditional Judaism cuts deep. In the past, many Orthodox women, including Haut, would have been satisfied with a technical resolution of the problem of *agunot* (women chained to dead marriages), whereby (male) rabbis would somehow use their authority to protect women from recalcitrant or vindictive husbands. Now, Haut and others seek a correction of the balance of power in the law itself.

Haut's critique not only illuminates feminist concerns, it also serves as an example of how modern Jews may respond to texts or traditions they find outmoded, or even morally untenable. This example is especially important and controversial for Orthodox Jews, who do not ordain women as rabbis or admit women to positions of legal authority, who accept Jewish law as binding and change it slowly and reluctantly or, in some camps, not at all.

Rabbi Vicki Hollander recounts how she, a Reform Jew, incorporated and supplemented traditional Jewish practice at the time of her own divorce. The Reform movement does not require a *get* and instead regards civil divorce as sufficient to dissolve a Jewish marriage. But Rabbi Hollander wanted "a possibility without precedent": To make use of the traditional divorce ritual—so that she might participate fully in the ancient practices of our people and be recognized by every segment of the Jewish community as properly divorced—and, at the same time, to be an autonomous agent throughout the divorce process, so that her transition could be one of power, and not abdication. Her essay is a record of how she achieved this. It includes reflections on her own passage, a chronicle of her choices, and advice to the reader, along with a copy of the supplementary divorce document she created. Imitated exactly or used as a model, her practices and divorce document are an empowering addition to the *get*. They are also a fine example of how traditional symbols and texts can be used newly, creatively, and authentically to mark ritual occasions for which they were not originally intended.

While the Jewish tradition speaks explicitly to divorce (albeit in a language we may wish to modify) it does not speak at all to the modern phenomenon of marital separation. Rabbi Nina Beth Cardin has innovated a "ritual acknowledging separation." Like Rabbi Hollander, she draws on the practices and images of Jewish wedding and mourning to create a new ritual. Again like Rabbi Hollander, she takes account of the fact that every member of the family—not just the couple breaking up—is affected by separation and divorce. Rabbi Cardin also attempts to balance the "what is" of separation—anger, pain, loneliness, austerity—with the "what may be"—new avenues opened, hope, coming to peace, mutual well-wishing. Though the ritual was conceived for a Jewish woman who is leaving a marriage, it could apply to men who leave and to non-legal relationships, including lesbian and gay relationships.

The essays in this chapter do not offer a definitive solution to the essential imbalance in men's and women's positions when it comes to Jewish divorce. They do point to certain trends, however. In the Orthodox world, where divorce law is enforced most strictly, women's protest against their lack of power and recourse is providing a challenge to the nature, speed, and selectivity of the modern halakhic process. That challenge and its results have only just begun to unfold. Orthodox synagogues have increasingly adopted the practice of reading aloud the names of recalcitrant husbands, held in contempt of rabbinic courts for withholding a *get*.[1] In the more liberal Jewish movements, there is an attempt to redress disparities by adding new rituals and legal options, so that women have a more active and equal role in Jewish divorce.

Ultimately, these efforts could be combined, so that traditional divorce law would include a requirement for women, as well as men, to "grant" their spouse a divorce, and a viable, universal remedy when a spouse is unreasonably uncooperative. That would not decrease the incidence of divorce or make it a happy occasion, but it would insure that all parties are treated with respect.

The *Agunah* and Divorce

RIVKA HAUT

*"One who is half slave and half free works one day for his master
and one day for himself, according to the School of Hillel. The
School of Shammai says: You have repaired [taken care of] his master, but you have not repaired him; he cannot marry a slave
woman, for he is half free, he cannot marry a free woman, for he is
still half slave. Should he then desist [from procreation]? But the
world was created only for the sake of procreation, as it is said
(Isaiah 45:18) 'He did not create it [the earth] a waste, but formed
it for habitation,' therefore, because of tikkun ha'olam [repairing
the world], the master is compelled to free him, and write a contract for half his worth. And the School of Hillel changed their
view and taught [this law] according to the School of Shammai."*
—BT *PESAHIM 88*A-B

The shattering of a glass under the *huppah* (marriage canopy)
injects a note of sorrow into one of life's happiest events. When
my husband and I stood under the wedding canopy at our daughters' weddings, we were joined by the specter of divorce, an
unwelcome but real presence under every *huppah*. Today, one in
three Jewish marriages ends in divorce. For us, as Orthodox parents, the breaking of the glass under the groom's foot was symbolic not only of the destruction of the Temple, but also of the potential for break-up of the new marriage, and with it, the vulnerability of our daughters to becoming *agunot*, women whose present
pain we feel far more than we mourn for the ruined Temple.

An *agunah* (plural: *agunot*) is a married woman who is unable
to obtain a *get* (Jewish divorce). Under Jewish law, a marriage
ends only upon the death of a spouse or when a husband willingly gives his wife a *get* and the wife willingly accepts it.[2] If she
refuses acceptance, there are available remedies for the husband.[3]
For women whose husbands refuse to grant a *get*, however, no
widely accepted remedies exist; they may remain in this state of
limbo for the rest of their lives.

A woman needs to receive a *get* far more than a man needs to

---

Rivka Haut, co-editor of *Daughters of the King: Women and the Synagogue* (Jewish
Publication Society, 1992) is a director of Agunah, Inc.

grant it or have it accepted. If she remarries without it, even though she may have a civil divorce, she is considered an adulteress according to traditional Jewish law. He, on the other hand, is not an adulterer. Historically Jewish men sometimes married more than one wife, but Jewish women were never permitted to marry more than one husband. Children born to a married woman from a second union are considered *mamzerim* (bastards), forbidden to marry other Jews.[4]

Jewish marital law applies to all Jews in the state of Israel, where the Orthodox rabbinate controls marriage and divorce. Outside of Israel, it applies to Orthodox and Conservative Jews. The Conservative movement has addressed the problem of *agunot* by establishing a *beit din* (rabbinical court) to annul marriages. For Reform and Reconstructionist Jews, a civil divorce is sufficient.

The tragedy of the *agunah* is causing many in the Orthodox world to reevaluate Rabbinic constructs of marriage and divorce. Orthodox women, who in the past accepted the authority of their rabbis, are now questioning and rebelling. There is reason to hope that the rabbinate will be sufficiently motivated by the large number of women calling for change, sufficiently embarrassed by negative publicity, and sufficiently moved by the integrity of Torah, that they will soon devise means to free *agunot*. However, Jewish jurisprudence must undergo systemic changes. Not only must we explore and utilize all avenues available to free women within *halakhah* (Jewish law), but we must also reform the rabbinic court system, and, ultimately, re-interpret *halakhah* to reflect the dignity and equality of women as a basic assumption of modern life.

As one of the directors of Agunah, Inc., the only advocacy organization for *agunot* established and run by women, I have dealt with this problem for more than ten years. It has forced me to face facts, which, as an Orthodox, Torah feminist, I would rather avoid. It is more pleasant and spiritually satisfying to be involved with women's prayer groups, develop new liturgy, study Talmud, and write feminist-oriented bible commentaries. My work on behalf of *agunot* involves a painful confrontation with the tradition I love and from which I derive my sense of ethics. But the ongoing anguish of *agunot* threatens complacent acceptance of halakhic standards. To fully comprehend the *agunah* problem, we must first understand halakhic attitudes toward marriage and divorce.

Marriage: Creating the Sacred Circle

Jewish weddings, joyous occasions, traditionally require many ritual, as well as logistical, preparations.[5] The couple first see each
other, after a customary week's separation, at the *badeken* (bridal
veiling ceremony). Surrounded by dancing friends and accompanied by music, the groom approaches the bride and lowers her
veil over her face, often whispering private endearments. One reason for veiling the bride is that this enables her to pray, under the
huppah, in privacy, hidden from curious eyes. Another is that it
satisfies her sense of modesty.

Lately, as I attend weddings of relatives and friends, I feel
robbed of experiencing the beauty of the veiling ceremony. I cannot help but feel that the veiling itself, an act of concealment, actually reveals more than it conceals. It now represents to me the
blinding of the bride to her new legal status. She is about to be
sold by her father to another man. "A woman is acquired (*nikneit*;
literally, bought) in three ways...by money, deed or intercourse"
(Mishnah *Kiddushin* 1:1). The veiled bride enters new territory, one
whose laws she has not fully been taught. She will not be free to
leave without a *get*, and the power to grant her this passport lies
solely with her husband.

This cynical view of a beautiful ceremony is the heritage of
those who are knowledgeable about *agunot*. Our eyes have been
uncovered, the veil lifted. We see clearly that which has been concealed behind rabbinic declarations of honor and respect for
Jewish women.

After the *badeken*, the bride and groom are accompanied by
their parents down the aisle. The bride, in her only active role, circles the groom seven times.

After the blessings over the wine and for the betrothal are
recited, the bride stands silently and the groom recites the formula
"*Harei at mekuddeshet li....*" "Lo, you are consecrated to me, with
this ring, according to the laws of Moses and Israel," and places a
ring on the bride's finger. (This is the "money" referred to in the
Mishnah.) The *ketubbah* (marriage contract) is read. It contains the
bride's name and that of her father. In Orthodox documents, neither her mother's name nor the groom's mother's name is mentioned. The *ketubbah* spells out the groom's obligations to his bride

and specifies the amount of money she is to receive in the event of his death, or if he divorces her. The amount is a standard sum: Two hundred *zuzim* if she is a virgin at the time of the marriage, one hundred if she is not.[6] The *ketubbah*, after being solemnly read aloud, is handed to the bride, who keeps it with her for the duration of the marriage.

Seven blessings are recited by a man or men honored with that role. The groom steps on and breaks the glass. The couple retires for *Yihud* (brief seclusion of a couple immediately after the wedding ceremony) symbolically consummating the marriage. When they emerge, the Jewish community has been enriched by the addition of a new family unit.

Divorce: Undoing the Marriage

While marriage and the traditional family are the mainstay of Orthodox Judaism, divorce has always been an accepted practice. People make mistakes; the *halakhah* acknowledges this and provides redress. The problems that have arisen result from the Talmudic Rabbis' interpretation of Deuteronomy 24:1 as decreeing divorce to be the option of the husband alone.

Divorce is the dark mirror-image of the marriage ceremony. Just as the husband gives the wife a *ketubbah* and she accepts it, so, in the event of a divorce, it is he who grants the *get* and, again, she who accepts it. Unlike any other ceremony, divorce is the acting out of the undoing, the unraveling, of another sacred ritual.

The proceeding consists of one basic act. The husband gives, and the wife accepts, the *get*. There is now no sugar-coating of the man's ownership of the woman, no hiding behind gowns, food, music. All illusions are gone. Divorce is clearly *his* decision. If she withholds acceptance of the *get*, he has a number of options. Without his consent, she is forever imprisoned in the marriage.

In contrast to the wedding, there is no advance preparation for the *get*. Theoretically, it may be written immediately, as soon as the husband decides to divorce his wife. The community is not involved or represented. Usually, only the couple, the rabbi, a scribe, and two witnesses are present. There is no special dress or food. No wine is drunk. This parting is unaccompanied by any blessings. Interestingly, God is not mentioned at all.

Unlike the *ketubbah*, which may be a standard form with the names filled in, the entire *get* must be written anew for each divorce, and must be prepared at the actual *get* proceeding.[7] At the beginning of the proceeding, a scribe gives the husband writing implements, parchment, and ink. He intones that now these writing implements belong to the husband, who is instructed to lift them up as a sign of acquisition. This prescribed exchange stresses the fact that the *get* is the property of the husband.

The scribe and rabbi are most careful to write the names of the spouses correctly. Whereas a marriage may be validated in more ways than one, the *get* is the only means by which to confirm a divorce. If it is written in any way improperly, it may be challenged (*Shulḥan Arukh Even Ha'ezer* 127).

The husband is always asked if he is granting the *get* under any duress, since a "coerced *get*" is invalid. He is also asked if there are any conditions attached to the *get*, and instructed by the rabbi to respond in the negative. There was a time when rabbinical courts could "persuade" a husband into granting a *get* by using punitive measures. The courts no longer have such power, except in Israel, where it is rarely used. In contrast, rabbis often use their power as intermediaries to extort concessions from the wife, in order that the husband grant a *get*.

After the *get* is written, the wife is instructed to form a cup with her hands. The husband then drops the *get* into her open palms. She takes it, puts it under her arm, and walks away, leaving him in any direction, in no direction, without direction. So is the marriage dissolved. Walking away slashes the circle she wove around him at the wedding. Those invisible threads—like the connection between husband and wife—are now broken. The divorce ceremony, in its simplicity and without the veil of joy, unmistakably shows that the woman has now been released.

Ostensibly, the wife who emerged from under the *huppah* with her *ketubbah*, should now leave the shelter of the marriage with the monetary value named in the *ketubbah*. This protection is what the Rabbis intended. They set its value at an amount which enabled her to live off the *ketubbah* money for about a year.[8] Sadly, unjustifiably, the *ketubbah* money is almost never given. It is one of the many abuses of the rabbinical courts that, despite the solemn reading of the *ketubbah* under the *huppah*, complete with rabbinic instructions to the brides to keep the *ketubbah* with them always, the document is virtually useless. This is another instance of veiling, of covering up. In fact, today's rabbis are not even sure of the modern equivalent to the monetary value named in a standard *ketubbah*.[9]

At the conclusion of the proceeding, the *mesadder haget* (supervising rabbi at a divorce) says to the woman "*Harei at mutteret lekhol adam*"—"Lo, you are permitted to any man." This statement, contained in the *get* itself, is harsh and shocking as well as untrue. For example, a divorced woman is prohibited from marrying a *kohen* (member of the priestly tribe) (Leviticus 21:14). This phrase is particularly insulting since it is said to the woman alone.

Yet it tells us about the nature of marriage, as well as divorce. It echoes the groom's declaration under the *ḥuppah*: "*Harei at mekuddeshet li....*" "Behold, you are consecrated [only] to me...." The statement at the giving of the *get* illuminates and uncovers the meaning of the groom's words. Despite assertions that *mekuddeshet* means holy or special, we see now that its meaning is confined to a sexual connotation. If "permitted to any man" is what divorce means, then "*mekuddeshet*" means set aside sexually for only one man. Marriage means that *her* sexual function is reserved for *him*. Divorce means that he no longer owns her sexuality, she is now available to anyone. Nothing similar is said to him. He is not "released" at the time of the *get*, for *he* has never been forbidden to others.

Unlike the wedding, where joy is intentionally mixed with an element of sadness in the breaking of the glass, here sadness is not at all interlaced with joy. The grim and bleak *get* proceeding demonstrates the power of Jewish ceremony. All aspects of the event coalesce to give a sense of finality, of closure. Many women who have obtained civil divorces say that they did not feel truly divorced until they received the *get*, not so much for religious reasons as because of the ritual's power. The starkness of the ceremony underscores a sense of failure, the death of a once beautiful dream, and the loss to the Jewish community of what was once a family.

Agunot and the Culpability of Rabbis

Were it not for the *agunah* problem, Orthodox feminists would probably never have begun to question the institution of marriage, nor the wedding ceremony. We would accept the passivity of the woman and the fact that the male "buys" her as archaic but somewhat charming artifacts, as harmless as retaining Aramaic as the language of the *ketubbah*. However, the growing presence of *agunot* forces us to tear the veil from our eyes, and see what transpires under the *ḥuppah*, along with its potentially tragic consequences.

Never in history have there been as many *agunot* as today, and the rising numbers are having a radical impact on Orthodox women.[10] The anguish of *agunot* belies the veneer of Torah justice. It presents the greatest challenge to Orthodox feminists—and Orthodoxy—today.

The *agunah* was, classically, a woman whose husband disappeared without a trace and without a witness that he had died. After the Holocaust, there were many cases of wives who were "chained" to missing husbands. Orthodox rabbis utilized various halakhic approaches to permit these women to remarry. Today, however, the term is generally used for a woman whose husband is available but unwilling to grant a *get*.

The disparity of power between men and women under the current system has resulted in an untold number of abusive practices. When a man wishes to divorce his wife, the rabbinical courts make perfunctory efforts to convince him not to. However, when the husband wants *"shelom bayit"* (harmony in the household), rabbis counsel women to stay in the marriage, knowing that she may be unable to obtain a *get*. Many women return repeatedly to abusive husbands because of rabbinical advice.

Extortion by husbands is prevalent, with large sums of money demanded by unscrupulous men who use the *get* as a bargaining chip. Instead of combatting this base extortion, many in the rabbinic world capitulate to it. Rabbis often collect money from the community in order to pay off a reluctant husband, piously declaring that they are thus helping an *agunah*. Some men demand child custody or increased visitation in addition to money. The worst scenarios are those in which the men refuse to grant the *get* out of hatred and spite. Often, their wives remain life-long *agunot*.

Ironically, many marriages themselves are victims of this problem. Men feel they can get away with a degree of abuse, secure in the knowledge that their wives will be unable to leave them and remarry. In the right-wing Orthodox world, where many *agunot* come from, women do not normally leave marriages unless conditions have become completely intolerable. Some leave only when the children are at risk. The social pressures to remain married are enormous. In fact, parents often encourage daughters to endure, because divorce is still viewed as a stain on the family.

Obtaining a *get* entails becoming involved with a rabbinical court system that is in a terrible state of disrepair. Since any three rabbis can constitute themselves as a *beit din* (rabbinical court), many courts are private enterprises. Corruption is rife. There is no monitoring of the system and no appeal from its decisions. The Jewish community has turned a blind eye to the functioning of these courts, which wield tremendous power, often deciding child custody and division of marital assets. Of course, the courts rule on women as well as men; however, Conservative and Orthodox courts officiating over divorces are composed exclusively of men.

Many judges have received no education outside of *yeshivot* (traditional academies of Jewish learning). Sometimes, decisions are based solely on halakhic criteria. Often, the parent judged to be the most "religious" is given custody.[11] Reasons for not granting custody can be unpredictable, and mental health specialists are rarely consulted.

According to *halakhah*, if mother and father are "equally fit" parents, then children under age six remain with their mothers. After age six, boys are awarded to fathers, girls to mothers (BT *Ketubbot* 102b-103a, *Shulḥan Arukh Even Ha'ezer* 82:7). This fact keeps many mothers of sons afraid to appeal to rabbinical courts, choosing to spend their lives without a partner, rather than lose their sons.

Under Jewish law all marital assets, except those the wife brings into the marriage, belong to the husband (*Shulḥan Arukh Even Ha'ezer* 115:5). Upon divorce, she receives no ongoing maintenance even if the couple has been married long and accumulated much. (The law assumes she will receive the value of the *ketubbah*.)

Rabbinical courts usually take into account whose side paid for the wedding, the furniture, etc., and attempt to mediate fair settlements. But the bottom line is that assets belong to the man, and if he demands his "rights" before granting a *get*, he can often get them through a *beit din*.

Because they do not generally receive the Jewish education

their brothers do, most Orthodox women have little knowledge of rabbinical courts until they must resort to one. Often, they are talked into signing a *shetar berurin*, a legal document renouncing all settlements in civil court and agreeing to re-litigate *everything* in the rabbinical courts. Signing this document means that the spouses have accepted the authority of the rabbinical court, and that the court's decision is regarded civilly as legal arbitration.

Efforts to Aid *Agunot*

Current efforts to end the deplorable situation are four-pronged: To pressure the Orthodox rabbinate into action, to reform the Jewish court system, to utilize halakhic solutions in the freeing of *agunot*, and to appeal to secular institutions for redress. After years of work, more Jews have become sensitized to the problem. Two volunteer organizations whose sole purpose is to deal with this issue, Agunah, Inc. and Get, recently joined with others to form an umbrella organization for all parties concerned with *agunot*, the International Coalition for Agunah Rights (ICAR).[12] Members of ICAR include major Jewish women's organizations, such as Hadassah and B'nai B'rith Women. ICAR's primary goal is to influence the Israeli rabbinate to enact rabbinic legislation that will impact Jews all over the world.

The plight of individual *agunot* has been publicized by demonstrations, including the picketing of homes and businesses owned by recalcitrant husbands. Agunah, Inc. has led two demonstrations at annual conventions of Agudath Israel, a large and powerful right-wing rabbinic organization. Despite efforts by security guards to throw them out, several *agunot* stood silently during a major address by a respected rabbi and held up large posters demanding help. They collected hundreds of signatures on petitions circulated throughout the hall. When the daughter of the owner of the *Jewish Press*, an Orthodox weekly, became an *agunah*, that paper embarked on a crusade, going so far as to print the names of recalcitrants and urge community response against them.

Jews outside of Orthodoxy are beginning to see the *agunah* problem as a major Jewish issue. While some secular feminists look upon *agunot* with disdain, unsympathetic to their religious affiliation, most non-Orthodox women understand the nobility and strength that *agunot* exercise everyday, upholding their religious values in the face of an unresponsive system. Feminist theologian Judith Plaskow has called the situation of *agunot* "a crime against women."

Halakhah has always managed to keep up with the times. In the area of finance, for example, nobody is disadvantaged because s/he is Orthodox. Despite the clear Toraitic prohibition against taking interest from fellow Jews (Exodus 22:24), the banking system in Israel works smoothly. Halakhic technicalities have been worked out in a manner acceptable even to the most punctiliously observant. The same creative halakhic thinking must be applied to help Jewish women. The organized Orthodox rabbinate is able to resolve the problem of *agunot*; it simply has not chosen to do so. The only viable solution is creative systemic change.

The first step is to overhaul the *beit din* system. Agunah, Inc. has outlined how this can be done, calling for the creation of rabbinical courts in major metropolitan areas that would be monitored by community groups and financed by community funds. Such courts would adhere to strict standards of Torah justice and provide grievance committees made up of rabbis and lay leaders, including women. This, together with courts of appeal, would provide Orthodox Jews with a viable alternative to civil courts.

Even if the rabbinical court system were to become a place in which women could receive justice, halakhic difficulties would remain, most notably the imbalance of women's rights under Jewish law. Halakhic solutions, many with historical precedents, exist. Marriage contracts are extant from the fifth century B.C.E., in the Jewish community of Elephantine, enabling a wife to divorce her husband. Likewise, in the early Middle Ages, women could appeal to *batei din* to force recalcitrant spouses to grant a *get*, under certain conditions. This practice was officially terminated in the twelfth century by Rabbenu Tam, who felt that it was becoming too easy for women to end their marriages.

One possibility to free *agunot* is for a *beit din* to annul the marriage. In the Orthodox world, the late revered Rabbi Moshe Feinstein freed individual *agunot* by annulment. Today, there are rabbis and scholars, such as Rabbi Emanuel Rackman and Israeli Supreme Court Justice Menachem Elon, who suggest annulment when husbands refuse to grant a *get*. Few rabbis have acted on their recommendation. In the Conservative movement, extortion for a *get* is not permitted and when all else fails, the marriage is annulled by a special *beit din* set up for that purpose. Yet, even in the Conservative movement, the *get* is still granted by the husband to the wife, and there has been no effort to equalize the power of the spouses.

Rabbi Marvin Antelman has freed twenty women in Israel, utilizing a different remedy. It is technically complicated but, he insists, equally within the bounds of Jewish law. His *beit din* issues a *get* to an *agunah* when her husband has been ordered by a *beit din* to divorce his wife and has refused. This is done on the grounds that the man himself will benefit if the sin of defying rabbinic authority is "removed from him."

Another approach is to turn to the civil courts or legislatures for redress. A number of women have civilly sued rabbinical courts for unjust decisions. They have been winning, but such litigation takes time and money. Women have also had monies they paid for the *get* returned to them by judges sympathetic to their plight. In 1992, the New York State Legislature, in response to requests by a number of Orthodox groups, enacted a bill (the Amendment to the Equitable Distribution Act), permitting judges of the civil courts to take into consideration refusal to grant a *get* when deciding distribution of marital assets. While technically not coercion to grant a *get*, the bill provides financial motivation for a husband to grant one.[13]

In another response, prenuptial agreements have been developed that are acceptable according to both Jewish and civil law. The Conservative movement has added a clause in its official *ketubbah*, known after its author as the Lieberman clause, stating the agreement to obtain a *get* if a secular divorce ensues. Orthodox agreements provide that, in cases of civil divorce, there will be serious monetary penalties if a *get* has not been given or accepted. Such agreements have been in use for years.

The history and availability of prenuptial agreements provide clear proof that rabbis are not providing leadership in this area. Rather, they were the last to endorse the agreements. As more couples utilized them, and encouraged their friends to use them, more rabbis began to accept them. Yet, it was not until 1992 that the Rabbinical Council of America finally approved the concept of prenuptials, and began to endorse specific agreements. They now recommend that all rabbis use them.

These agreements have no effect on marriages already entered into without them, nor are they a guarantee against becoming an *agunah*. They do, however, motivate husbands to grant a *get*.

Resorting to secular law to resolve halakhic issues is a tactic preferred by many rabbis, for it enables them to leave the halakhic status quo intact. Torah feminists find these efforts insufficient. We view them as a *hillul hashem* (desecration of God's name), for they imply that Jewish law, on its own, is incapable of providing justice to Jewish women. The spirit of justice that is inherent to *halakhah* is violated by the continued existence of *agunot* and should be remedied by halakhic solutions.

Everywhere I go I encounter the bewilderment of religious women: Does our Torah, which legislates compassion for the stranger, widow, and orphan, really sanction such injustice? How can the Torah, "whose ways are ways of pleasantness," cause such suffering? Nobody but the rabbis doubts that it is within the rabbinic powers to provide remedies. The question is: Will rabbis regard the *agunah* problem as urgent enough to merit Jewish legal interpretation? Rabbis seem "unable" to deal with *agunot* because it is women who suffer, and women are powerless in the Orthodox world. It is the rabbinic refusal to tamper with halakhically legislated male control over women in marriage which perpetuates the horrors of *agunah* status.

One could ponder endlessly why Orthodox rabbis fear permitting women to exit marriage at will. Preservation of family life is an important value, but imprisoning women in dead marriages is not the way to strengthen Jewish families. The system harms the family since the threat of becoming an *agunah* can create suspicion between men and women. Moreover, the *agunah* problem denies large numbers of Jewish women the opportunity to remarry or bring Jewish children into the world. In the post-Holocaust era, in an age of intermarriage and of low Jewish birthrate, it is unforgivable to prevent even one *agunah* from remarrying and bearing children.

Everywhere Orthodox women gather, they are beginning to speak the previously unspeakable, condemning rabbinic authorities for not providing leadership, expressing anger at a tradition that permits men such absolute power, challenging halakhic justice. They have been raised to revere rabbis, but know in their hearts that their rabbis do not deserve respect. This creates tremendous conflict.

As Jews who suffer because of their commitment to *halakhah*, *agunot* should receive the same attention and respect that Russian *refusniks* (dissidents) received. They should get at least some of the attention Jonathan Pollard has gotten, for they too are prisoners. Yet, they are largely ignored and betrayed by the Jewish world.

I have always looked upon *halakhah* as being capable of great flexibility. In my work with women's prayer groups including Women at the Wall, I never challenged *halakhah*, choosing to work within its confines. I always found its boundaries afforded me great freedom; I welcomed the limitations it set. I never challenged the primacy or authority of *halakhah*. But the existence of *agunot* is a blot upon Judaism and the entire halakhic system, as well as on current rabbinic structures and practices.

I find myself face to face with an uncomfortable yet undeniable reality: I must painfully acknowledge that the *halakhah*, or at least the rabbinic interpretation of it by which we live, has given Jewish men unfair advantage over women, spawning unbelievable suffering. Only when this imbalance is corrected will both men and women be truly equal partners in marriage.

As a student of Talmud, I know that if the ancient Rabbis were alive today they would never permit this injustice to continue. They would find, or create, halakhic solutions to this problem as they did with other problems. They found a way to free a non-Jewish slave who was only half-free, arguing that he must be able to marry and procreate, for that is God's will. Jewish women are as deserving of rabbinic compassion as were those half-enslaved Canaanites. Clearly, we are living in an era of unworthy rabbinic authorities. We should not abdicate the tradition we love because of their weakness.

The Talmud teaches that when a man divorces his first wife, the altar sheds tears (BT *Gittin* 90b and Malachi 2:14-16). The altar must be drowning by now in a river of tears, shed in sorrow because of those men who refuse to divorce their wives, chaining them to dead marriages. May the day soon arrive when "God will dry the tears from every face," when halakhic Judaism will truly be a system of justice for every Jew.

Weathering the Passage: Jewish Divorce[14]

VICKI HOLLANDER

"Blessed are You, Shaper of the universe, who forms light and creates darkness, makes shalom *(peace), and creates the whole."*

—AFTER THE MORNING LITURGY,
WHICH IS ADAPTED FROM ISAIAH 45:7

The Passage of Divorce: Paving One's Way

To what does this compare?
To the earth
when it moves and quakes
and shifts beneath one's feet.
And when the movement stops,
one walks away.

I am a woman, mother, rabbi. I was a wife.

Eight years have passed, enabling me to look at my divorce with hindsight and keener vision. What follows are tools to help others travel the craggy pass of divorce.

For one must actively navigate this most crucial passage, this time of death, of leave-taking, of crisis, of potential cleansing, of unprecedented possibility for deepening and growth.

I wanted roots at a time when I had none. I wanted a time-bound ceremony that reached into the past, connecting with others of my people who had traversed the same straits through which I was moving. I wanted recognition from the entire Jewish community that I had journeyed this way.[15]

I wanted clarity, at a time when nothing else was clear. I chose to have a traditional Jewish divorce with an Orthodox *beit din* (rabbinical court).

But I wanted a possibility without precedent—to stand as an equal participant. Rather than having the ceremony "happen" to me, I wished to sculpt the ritual of my passage. Thus, I shaped

---

Rabbi Vicki Hollander weaves together the creation of ritual and poetry with rabbinic work at Congregation Eitz Or, hospice work, and single parenting.

new forms to dance with the old, new forms drawn from the wells of rituals around death and around marriage.

Divorce is like rewinding a tape, going backwards to the marriage ceremony. We unwrap the bonds that bind and relinquish vows of holiness. Yet, at the divorce, unlike the wedding, there are no special foods prepared, no distinct garments worn, no guests waiting. Unlike mourners of a physical death, one who mourns the end of a marriage digs no grave, and has no *shiv'ah* (formal period of mourning). No one brings food, stays to offer comfort, nor holds one's hand.

I sought ritual, enactment, to break through the numbness of this passage. I knew, with the shattering of my world, feeling could emerge; feeling, the crucial prerequisite for healing.

Rituals of Passage: A Mini-*Yom Kippur* (Day of Atonement)

The time before the wedding is as *Yom Kippur*, a time to come before God, to review one's life, to fast, to do *teshuvah* (to repent or return), to be reborn.

The evening before the divorce, I began my fast. In the morning, wrapped in my *tallit* (prayer shawl), I recited the *Viddui* (confessional, said before one's marriage, on *Yom Kippur*, and on one's death bed) acknowledging my part in the undoing of the marriage.

As on *Yom Kippur*, I wore no jewelry, no make-up. I dressed in white, the color of the *kittel*, the garment that traditionally shrouds Jewish men on their wedding day, on various Jewish holidays, and at their burial.

Divorce and *Yom Kippur*: Loss. Death. Straying from the path. Rebirth. Freedom.

Aloneness and Companionship: Pain and Comfort

The morning: Time to review and reflect, to be by myself, to be alone with God.

The rest of the day: *Shomerot* (female guardians; shifts of women friends) drove me, stayed with me through the traditional ceremony as my witnesses, shared my evening meal. Like the *shomerim* (guardians) who accompany a body before it is buried, like the *edim* (witnesses) who guard the couple's privacy immediately after a wedding ceremony, like the visitors who sit silently and supportively at a mourner's home or a convalescent's bedside, they sustained me.

Tradition and Innovation: An Orthodox Ceremony and My Document

Special paper, ink-dipped quill, a letter of release to my husband. Writing the letter, I recalled the *ketubbah* (marriage contract), and anticipated the traditional *get* (divorce document).

At the Orthodox ceremony, a declaration: "No party is here under duress." As the scribe labored over the *get*—special paper, ink-dipped quill—my husband and I were dismissed to wander, neither married nor yet divorced.

A friend greeted me in this twilight time. I read aloud the document I had written, and listened in turn, as she read it to me. Both the reading and the listening concretized what was happening that day, made it more real, made it witnessed.

Back to the *beit din*: The traditional *get*, my husband's release of me. The document was handed to me and, following tradition, I walked with it, signifying acceptance. As we rose to leave, I silently dropped my own "document of release" into my ex-husband's hands, completing, for me, the ceremony.

After the Ceremony: Endings and Beginnings

Returning home, I washed, as is customary to do when leaving a graveside. Water: Symbol of life, purification, and renewal. I changed from my white burial garment into garments of color.

A meal of consolation, of transition, prepared by women friends. As at *shiv'ah*, we ate hard-boiled eggs—a "comfort food" and symbol of renewal. Lighting colored candles, we spoke of the end of paths of white, death, blankness, and of the beginning of roads of color. We sang the blessings over the food and I recited the *Sheheheyanu* (blessing for reaching a new or momentous occasion), thanking God for having brought me to and through this moment. As we ate and prayed, we asked ourselves and each other what we wanted in order to live full lives as women.

In the evening, a walk around the block, as is traditional at the conclusion of *shiv'ah*. Creating, by our steps, a circle, embodying life's continuity. We watched the cars pass, witnessing that life goes on.

Words of Advice to Those Weathering the Passage

Some members of the *beit din* may seek to squelch or have you repress sadness and tears. Hang on tenaciously to your emotions, for it is *your* passage; it is not a time to take care of others.

Divorce is a journey, as well, for one's immediate and extended family. They, too, have residues of pain, anger, hurt, sorrow, and perhaps fewer condoned routes through which these can be expressed. They may be more helpless than we.

How to instruct those who love us about how to help? "Please just listen, without attempting to cheer me up, assure me of better days, or relate stories of others who have it worse. I need to express my pain, so as to lift it from body, heart, and soul. I need loving presence and recognition that what I am going through is hard."

Divorce is a time of change and loss and an opportunity to learn to ask for help. Divorce teaches one to accept assistance graciously, to say thank you from the heart. It invites one to plumb and work through layers of feelings; provides an opening to break through to new levels of being for oneself, and if a parent, for one's children.

The Opportunity

Divorce is a true passage. If we do our work, nothing remains the same. Our traditions are resources, enabling us to break through the numbness; to travel, across the painful transition, safely to the other side. In following the flow and merging into crisis, potential is released for the refining of one's spirit, the stretching of one's soul, the realigning of one's life.

> To what does this compare?
> To the earth
> when it moves and quakes
> and shifts beneath one's feet.

And when the movement stops,
one walks away shaken,
touched,
transformed.

Form of release based on the language of the traditional Jewish marriage and divorce documents

On the _____ day of the week, the _____ day of _____
57__since the creation of the world, the _____ day of
_____ 19__ as we reckon time here in _____, I, _____
daughter of _____ and _____ (Hebrew names), do depart
from the bindings and vows of *kiddushin* (holy matrimony)
that took place _____ years ago on _____ in _____, ____.
To _____, son of _____ & _____, I declare: This day I am
no longer bound to the task and commitment to cherish and
honor you in faithfulness and in integrity as my husband. This
day I am no longer bound to stand as wife, companion, and
partner. This day I am no longer bound by honor or law to
affirm and maintain *kedushah* (holiness and exclusivity) within
our relationship. This day I am no longer set aside, special to
only you. This day the *kiddushin* vows become null and void.
Hereby, I am no longer *mekuddeshet* to you, no longer your
wife, and you are no longer *mekuddash* to me, no longer my
husband.

   On this day according to our tradition I depart as a free
woman. I stand as a free agent in the Jewish community, in the
world, before God, and before myself. I stand, having completed our people's traditional way of unbinding a marital relationship. I stand as a Jewish woman with dignity and with
strength. I stand restored to a single unit as a whole and complete person. This document shall stand as a release and a letter of freedom in accordance with the values of our people,
Israel.

_____Witness   _____Witness

A Ritual Acknowledging Separation

NINA BETH CARDIN

"Let there be no quarrel between us, for we were once family."
　　　　　　　　　　　　　　　　　　　　　　　—GENESIS 13:8

The following ritual was designed to be performed by a woman surrounded and supported by her friends and family. The setting should be familiar, comfortable, and comforting. It should be performed as soon as possible after the parting. Particularly appropriate would be the Saturday night after the actual separation, following *Havdalah* (distinction-making ritual that separates Sabbath or holiday from weekday). Both marital separation and *Havdalah* mark the crossing of a threshold from one state and time into another.

Through the use of a cloth—specifically a portion of a pillowcase or sheet—and its act of tearing, this separation ceremony is meant to evoke images of marriage and divorce. In addition to the image of sexual intimacy, the cloth and its tearing also allude to the cloth of the *huppah* (wedding canopy) and the cutting of the *get* (bill of divorce) when divorce is final. The act of tearing may also summon associations with *keri'ah* (rending a garment in mourning). Indeed, the act of separation does signify the death of a couple, a family, and some of their feelings, particularly intimacy, love, and security.

Following the traditional rituals of loss and mourning in Judaism, this one uses symbols and acts to express our most profound pain. At the same time, it offers images and sentiments that, if received and believed, can lift us out of despair and past hurt, anger, and loss. Contemporary ritual and prayer should not limit themselves to the role of ratifying and affirming what we feel and believe right now; like the most powerful traditional liturgies, they should also provide the comfort, the vision, and the belief that the best can yet come to be.

There is no specific mention of children in this ritual, and no recommendation is made one way or another about their partici-

---

Rabbi Nina Beth Cardin is the advisor to students in the Rabbinical School of The Jewish Theological Seminary and editor of *Sh'ma* magazine.

pation. While the family is also rent, separation essentially occurs between wife and husband. The recitation from Genesis includes words like "family" and "house" to allow the images of family with children to be introduced. Participants are encouraged to determine the extent to which they wish to involve and reference children in the ritual beyond the modest inclusion already offered.

The cloth should have a slight cut mid-point along the upper edge, to facilitate tearing.

The ritual, designed to be simple and short, begins with lighting a candle and should be concluded with a meal of comfort. As at a mourner's home, such a repast can be composed of round foods (such as bagels, lentils, cheeses, etc.) to represent the continuity of life's cycle, despite the breach of sorrow.

A TIME TO CUT
AND A TIME TO HEAL
Order of the Ritual

Welcoming and Setting the Tone

Gathered among family and friends, the woman lights a candle and says:

יי אוֹרִי וְיִשְׁעִי, מִמִּי אִירָא.
יי מָעוֹז-חַיַּי, מִמִּי אֶפְחָד.
אַל-תִּטְּשֵׁנִי וְאַל-תַּעַזְבֵנִי אֱלֹהֵי יִשְׁעִי.
אַחַת שָׁאַלְתִּי מֵאֵת יי אוֹתָהּ אֲבַקֵּשׁ,
שִׁבְתִּי בְּבֵית-יי כָּל-יְמֵי חַיָּי.

Adonai ori veyishi mimmi ira. Adonai ma'oz-ḥayyai mimmi efḥad. Al-titteshemi ve'al-ta'azveni elohei yishi. Aḥat sha'alti me'et adonai otah avakkesh, shivti beveit-adonai kol-yemei ḥayyai.

God is my light and my help; whom shall I fear? God is the stronghold of my life; whom shall I dread? God will not forsake me, the Merciful One will not abandon me, God, my Deliverer. One thing I ask You God, only that do I seek; to live in the house of my God forever (after selections from Psalms 27:1,9,4).

Tearing and Building

*A friend or family member gives the woman the cloth or sheet
which has been prepared for the ceremony. The woman takes
the cloth, holds it at mid-point along the upper edge and
recites:*

אַל-נָא תְהִי מְרִיבָה בֵּינִי וּבֵינֶךָ . . . כִּי-אֲנָשִׁים אַחִים אֲנַחְנוּ וְאִישׁ
וְאִשָּׁה הָיִינוּ . . . הִפָּרֶד נָא מֵעָלַי, אִם-הַשְּׂמֹאל וְאֵימִנָה וְאִם
הַיָּמִין וְאַשְׂמְאִילָה.

*Al-na tehi merivah beini uveinekha...ki-anashim ahim anahnu [ish
ve'isha hayinu]....Hippared na me'alai, im-hasemol ve'eiminah ve'im
hayamin ve'asme'ilah.*

Let there be no quarrel between us, for we were once family;
let us separate gently; if one goes north, may the other go
south; if one goes east, may the other go west. May your house
be your house and my house be my house, and may strife and
contentions not rule our hearts (interpretive translation of
Genesis 13:8-9).

*The woman recites the following verse and then tears the gar-
ment:*

קִרְעוּ בִגְדֵיכֶם וְאַל לְבַבְכֶם . . . כִּי יי חַנּוּן וְרַחוּם, אֶרֶךְ אַפַּיִם
וְרַב-חֶסֶד.

*Kiru igdeikhem ve'al levavkhem . . . ki adonai hannun verahum erekh
appayim verav-hesed.*

Rend your garments and not your heart..., for God offers compassion and comfort (after Joel 2:13).

She tears the cloth and continues:

הַכְנִיסִינִי תַּחַת כְּנָפֵךְ
וַהֲיִי לִי אֵם וְאָחוֹת.
יְהִי חֵיקֵךְ מִקְלַט רֹאשִׁי
קַן תְּפִלּוֹתַי הַנִּדָּחוֹת.

*Hakhnisini tahat kenafekh/vahayi li em ve'ahot/yehi heikekh miklat
roshi/kan tefillotai haniddahot.*

O God, gather me gently under Your wing, / Be my mother, my sister. / Let my head find shelter in Your embrace / the nesting place for my homeless prayers (translation of "*Hakhnisini Taḥat Kenafekh*" by Chaim Naḥman Bialik).

Communal Support and Blessing

Family members and friends form a circle with the separated woman and say:

Wherever you go, we are there with you. Whatever your need, we are beside you.

The participants step forward each in turn speaking the name of the woman for whom they have gathered, declaring their presence and support, as follows:

הִנְנִי _____ , בַּת _____ וְ_____ -וְ_____ , כִּי קָרָאת לִי, וְאֶהְיֶה עִמָּךְ עוֹד.

Hineni _____ *bat* _____ *ve* _____, *ki karat li, ve'ehyeh immakh od.*

I am here, _____ daughter of _____ and _____, for you called me, and I will be with you throughout your journey.

Then all the participants bless the woman: May your way be illumined by the face of God, as it is said:

בְּאוֹר-פְּנֵי-מֶלֶךְ חַיִּים.

Be'or-penei-melekh ḥayyim.

For the radiance of God's face grants life (Proverbs 16:15).

And may you dwell in the house of God forever (after Psalms 27:4).

Other spontaneous blessings may be offered. A friend takes the cloth to be discarded or saved as a memento of this time.

Closing

The woman says: May the setting aside of this cloth help me to set aside a completed portion of my life, and to weave new and beautiful times and garments.

The group may recite a traditional Sheheḥeyanu *(blessing for reaching a new or momentous occasion) in closing:*

בָּרוּךְ אַתָּה יי אֱלֹהֵינוּ מֶלֶךְ הָעוֹלָם, שֶׁהֶחֱיָנוּ וְקִיְּמָנוּ וְהִגִּיעָנוּ לַזְּמַן הַזֶּה.

Barukh attah adonai eloheinu melekh ha'olam, sheheḥeyanu vekiyye-manu vehiggi'anu lazeman hazzeh.

Blessed are You, God, Ruler of the Universe, who has given us life and sustained us and enabled us to reach this time.

10

Intermarriage

"Continuity" has been the Jewish buzzword of the 90s. Communal concern with Jewish survival, dismissed by many just a decade ago as hyperbolic or manipulative, is now recognized as a function of plain realism. Intermarriage is the subject of countless communal deliberations, as well as increasing numbers of private—and painful—family discussions. I still rebel against the "Jewish numbers game," preferring to focus on the quality of Jewish programs, prayer services, and schools (over which, as a rabbi, I presumably have some control), rather than the quantity of Jews who attend them. However, the rising rates of Jewish assimilation and intermarriage documented by the *Council of Jewish Federations 1990 National Jewish Population Survey* demand serious and focused attention.

Not so long ago, even non-Orthodox Jewish families mourned children or siblings who intermarried as if they were dead. Setting aside the compelling moral and religious objections to this practice, it is now simply untenable. Intermarriage is too prevalent a phenomenon, with roughly one-half of the American Jewish population marrying non-Jews. Today, interfaith marriages are enough of a threat—and a commonality—that an anthology on Jewish lifecycle would be incomplete without a chapter on the subject.

Determined to stem the tide of intermarriage, some segments of the Jewish community have resisted dealing with this topic, arguing that any form of engagement condones the decision to intermarry. Increasingly, however, Jews and Jewish communal organizations advocate outreach, i.e. reaching out to the intermarried and affording them every possible opportunity to learn about Judaism and become active in the Jewish community. In a departure from the classical Rabbinic stance towards conversion, the Reform movement actively and publicly encourages the gentile spouses of Jews to convert. Debate continues over how to deal with intermarriage before (in terms of prevention), during (in terms of interfaith ceremonies), and after (once a couple is already married).

The term "intermarriage" raises many interrelated questions: How and why do we choose our mates and raise our children? What is the most effective Jewish response—and prophylactic—to intermarriage, by family members, rabbis, the intermarried themselves, the "marriageable" who are in search of a mate, and the community at large? What are our commitments and responsibilities to Jewish survival, as individuals, as a community, and as a nation? How do we define Jewish identity and membership in the peoplehood of Israel, and how do we pass it on? How and when do we include or exclude gentiles (especially those married to Jews) from synagogue worship, honors, Jewish communal life? How do we cultivate and communicate the value of having a Jewish home in the present, as well as that of having Jewish grandchildren sometime in the future?

Rabbi Eleanor Smith addresses many such questions in "The Price of Modernity and the Power of Choice." She deals with intermarriage on the most personal level—responding with love to her two Jewish parents and their respective gentile partners who became her stepparents, but struggling with the realities and conflicts of intermarriage. She also discusses intermarriage on the broadest possible scale—in terms of national statistics, historical background, prevention via education, and gender and family issues.

The other authors in this chapter also speak of intermarriage from personal experience. The daughter of a Jewish father and non-Jewish mother, Jane Baron Rechtman always thought of herself as Jewish, yet conflicts existed in the household and among extended family. Her self-understanding and identity led her to convert formally and to marry a Jew and raise her children in a Jewishly active and identified home. Yet she views intermarriage as a simple fact and viable option of Jewish life—including her own children's lives.

Elizabeth Warner Frank offers a perspective we hear too rarely—that of an intermarried Jew. Like most intermarried Jews today, her decision to marry a non-Jew was not a conscious rejection of Judaism, but a consequence of meeting a person with whom she wanted to spend the rest of her life. In relation to this, Rabbi Smith points out the contrast between "falling in love" and actively choosing a mate. She urges Jews to take responsibility for their love choices, and to follow through on the criterion of Jewishness in decisions to date or marry, with the same kind of dedication they evince to such considerations as educational status or common values and interests. Notwithstanding this good advice, Jews like Frank do come to love and marry gentiles, and yet sustain their commitment to Judaism and raise their children to be Jews. Not every intermarried Jew studies or observes the tradition as Frank does, nor is every gentile spouse interested in cooperating and participating in that process. But she provides us with one example of negotiating Jewish living within an intermarriage.

Mordecai Kaplan, founder of the Reconstructionist movement, taught that Jewish survival is the byproduct of the relevance of the tradition and the consequent desire of Jews to choose Judaism. This view could be a source of anxiety or even fatalism, in that it accepts the disappearance of the Jewish people as an evolutionary possibility. It could also be a source of comfort and renewed dedication, in that it sets in the foreground the relevance of the tradition and the strength of Jewish commitment, rather than intermarriage or other threats to Jewish survival. The authors in this chapter acknowledge the threats, but focus on the foreground, where our power lies.

Intermarriage: The Price of Modernity and the Power of Choice

ELEANOR SMITH

"Fair encounter of two most rare affections! Heavens rain grace on that which breeds between 'em!"
                                        —WILLIAM SHAKESPEARE, *THE TEMPEST*

Intermarriage in the lifecycle of the Jew is like a spider's web, laying a delicate tendril on every aspect of an individual's life and thereby, on the life of our community. This essay attempts to shed light on the web of intermarriage, if not unravel it, with a review of salient history and statistics, recommendations for communal action, a summary of gender and family considerations, and a personal response as a rabbi, daughter, and sister.

A Personal Preface

I was raised by Jewish parents in what our increasingly secular world might call a fairly observant Reform home. With mandatory weekly *Shabbat* (Sabbath) dinners, occasional synagogue attendance (for *yartzeits* [anniversaries of death], holidays, and *Shabbat*), and a formal Jewish education that continued through the tenth grade, we could not forget that we were Jews.

The summer before my brother's Bar Mitzvah (coming of age ceremony for boys), when I was ten, my parents divorced. Within three years both had remarried. Despite the bumpy transition, my parents chose wonderful new partners, both non-Jews. With dual creeds of maturity and flexibility as the new extended-family faith, much love and good will were salvaged, and we all made the best of the occasional religious awkwardness. Given all that went right in this exceptionally successful reorganization of the Smith family, we could not but count our blessings. Many years later, my brother also married a non-Jew.

As I grew into adulthood and religious maturity and began

Rabbi Eleanor Smith is a Reform rabbi practicing at Beth Emet, The Free Synagogue, in Evanston, Illinois.

thinking about marriage myself, the complexities of my family's interreligious mosaic increasingly occupied and pained me. At twenty-five, I found myself in the odd and lonely position of being a third-year rabbinic student, and the only person in my family married to a Jew. In what seemed like a betrayal of this family history, full of gratitude and love, I became urgently concerned with the personal implications of intermarriage: Would there ever be any more Jewish Smiths (we knew of at least four generations of Jewish Smiths before us)? What sort of Jewish identity would my half-brothers have with a Jewish father and a Catholic mother? Would my parents be buried together with their spouses in Jewish cemeteries like the pretty sculpted Midwestern hillside where my grandparents lay? While this introduction recounts *my* family's story, it raises larger concerns: How shall we formulate personal and communal responses to intermarriage? What do we do when the people we love do things which, religiously or ideologically, we oppose? Is a stance against intermarriage one of religious courage and conviction or familial betrayal?

Intermarriage: Where We Are and How We Got Here

The latest statistics on intermarriage are shocking because they belie the American Jewish myth of integration without assimilation, without disappearance. Nothing exposes the myth like the numbers themselves. Before 1965, 93 percent of Jews chose Jewish spouses whereas since 1985, only 48 percent of Jews have married other Jews, 5 percent of whom are Jews by choice. As a result, since 1985, twice as many mixed couples (born Jew with gentile spouse) have been created as Jewish couples.[1]

The roots of today's intermarriage trend go deep into the soil of modern Jewish history. Emancipation came incrementally to the Jews of Europe beginning in the late eighteenth century and signalled a more radical and far-reaching encounter with the non-Jewish world than ever before. Where once communal authority had determined all matters of lifestyle and Jewish observance, now the individual Jew emerged as an autonomous entity. For the first time, Jews could *choose*: University or *yeshivah* (traditional academy of Jewish learning), concert hall (even church) or synagogue, secular or religious. Emancipated Jews struggled to refashion their Judaism in a way that would balance their sacred tradition and their precious new inheritance of autonomy, individualism, freedom, and equality.

While freedom from a ghettoized life brought many blessings, it could neither define nor conceal the difference between integration (finding an authentic Jewish way to be modern) and assimilation (forsaking Judaism in the full embrace of another faith or culture). For many, this double bind of freedom is even more intense in our own day.

Distinguishing Approaches and Responding to the Intermarried

Age, gender, sexual orientation, geography, family history, movement affiliation, and current marital status all affect the context and realities of intermarriage. A couple beyond their childbearing years, for example, faces quite different issues than does a young, newly married couple looking forward to having children, while a gay or lesbian couple faces still different realities, whether or not they want children. Different positions on the arc of the lifecycle will affect one's interests and concerns regarding religious affiliation, identity, dating, marriage, commitment, and childrearing. Ultimately, the most obvious distinction to be made is between those who already have non-Jewish spouses and those who are unmarried, being single, widowed, or divorced.

As urgently as I assess the threat of intermarriage to the longevity and vigor of non-Orthodox Jewish life, condemnation or exclusion of those who have already chosen non-Jewish partners will only exacerbate the fraying of our community, not to mention that the intermarried are so often our siblings, parents, cousins, friends, and children.[2]

To illustrate this dilemma, we might borrow from the Rabbinic dialectic between *lekhathillah* and *bedi'avad*. *Lekhathillah* is the *a priori* law or expectation and *bedi'avad* is the *a posteriori* reality of a situation that has already taken place. In other words, *lekhathillah*, intermarriage is forbidden. However, a Jew who is already intermarried, *bedi'avad*, must be dealt with, not ignored, censured, or shunned. A positive *bedi'avad* stance ensures that participation in the Jewish community and conversion will remain viable options throughout the life of an interfaith marriage. This is especially important in light of declining rates of conversion of the non-Jewish spouse.

Nurturing Jewish Identity

Creating a positive Jewish identity can be compared to providing good health care. Research shows that preventive/family care or a holistic "wellness" approach are most effective. The ideal, for good health and positive Jewish identity, is proactive, routine, vigilant, and sensitive attention, birth to grave. In practice, however, we often take a reactive approach both with our health care and with Jewish identity formation, mobilizing only in times of crisis or trauma.

At the most basic level, "proactive identity formation" means exposing the Jewish child to the myriad dimensions of Jewish life as they are appropriate to age and development. It means collaboration among the partners in identity formation: Educators, families, rabbis, counselors, and whoever else has a direct impact on our children. Though education is not a panacea, quality, consistent Jewish education beginning in early childhood and continuing through adolescence into adulthood seems to be the most effective prescription for lasting identity.[3] According to the *CJF 1990 National Jewish Population Survey*, American Jews with higher levels of Jewish education are far more likely to marry other Jews and to observe Jewish rituals than those who have little or no education. Beyond the classroom and the foundation of a richly textured Jewish home, the two most formative and galvanizing experiences for young Jews are study/travel opportunities in Israel and Jewish summer camps. These proactive opportunities are ripe with potential for self-discovery and independence within the framework of a *comprehensive* model of Jewish life, where Judaism is revealed in the daily bread and inhaled with every breath.

For many non-Orthodox Jews, identity founders, given the paucity of resources and instruction. Few, if any, road signs on the path toward young adulthood point the way to Jewish belonging, knowledge, and commitment. Jewish memories, if we have them at all, typically have feeling as their primary content: A joyous Passover *seder* (ordered readings and meal), a scary Holocaust lesson, fun carnivals for *Purim* (Festival of Lots), etc. If we lack a more substantive grounding in Judaism, emotional and nostalgic associations may not by themselves be sufficiently compelling to influence our choice of a life partner. In so many cases, the issue of religion surfaces at the penultimate moment, when a young couple enters a rabbi's (or minister's) study, or breaks the news of their engagement to their parents.

Strangely, the crisis of climbing intermarriage rates has spawned more reactive approaches to Jewish identity than proactive. Outreach in the Reform movement, for example, primarily serves people seriously involved in an interfaith relationship, i.e. those well beyond the proactive stage of Jewish identity development. We must right this imbalance, and begin our outreach/"inreach" in the formative years of a Jewish life rather than on the eve or in the wake of our most important choices.

The Centrality of the Jewish Family and the Question of Gender Roles

Even under the best of circumstances, where Jewish education is proactive, meaningful and regular, there is no rival to the Jewish family in its capacity to create and nurture Jewish identity; even in nontraditional configurations, it remains the primary vehicle for transmission of Judaism from generation to generation.[4]

While the centrality of the Jewish family has remained constant, its makeup certainly has not. The prevalence of divorce and single parenting, and the increasing openness and acceptance of gay and lesbian families all exert a legitimate pressure for re-examination of the Jewish family and its role as a conduit for Jewish love and learning. Our generation has been challenged in a historically unique way to refashion traditional parental roles without sacrificing the profoundly wise and rich traditions of Judaism.

Naive or oppressive as they may seem today, there was a time in Jewish family life when the roles of men and women were more clearly delineable than they are today. Women, whether or not they worked outside the home, had primary responsibility for many of the Jewish rituals practiced at home and a profound influence on the moral development of their children. Our foremothers were primary bearers of the cultural mantle of Judaism, with all its attendant artifacts. Men, according to traditional dictates, were in charge of formal education, public ritual, and synagogue life.

Despite the changing face of the Jewish family, many of these traditional Jewish parenting roles retain some influence. There remain distinct areas in Jewish life where women and men fulfill different roles. Carol Gilligan, writing on gender differences in moral and psychological development, says that "the life cycle itself arises from an alternation between the world of women and that of men."[5] Today's call for equality is complicated by the fact that many women are reclaiming the legitimacy and the practice of their mother's religious expression. Even in the liberal Jewish movements, women express a comfort and territorialism in tasks of our inherited domestic domain, whether that means baking *ḥahllah* (braided egg bread), lighting Sabbath candles, reciting *tkhines* (petitionary prayers for and/or by women, traditionally written in Yiddish), or generally taking it as our charge to shape the character of home and family.

However we may now wish to recategorize, reassign, or integrate historically distinct parental roles (male and female, public and private), what seems very clear is the deeply complementary nature of these roles, regardless of who fills them. Whatever the social, cultural, and historical reasons that Jewish women and men have generally filled different roles, we have relied equally on private and public domains for the richness and longevity of Jewish life. Ultimately, the goal is not to assign people by gender to one domain or the other, but to see that all bases are covered. And, of course, these "classic domains" intersect. To make a Jewish home is to understand its place in the larger constellation of Jewish community and history and to follow the public and private rhythms of its calendar.

This challenge to honor and, one hopes, to integrate all dimensions of Jewish life reveals how great the burden of Jewish parenting can be, especially when the parents themselves may not have been provided with broad education and exposure to a variety of Jewish roles. And the challenge is even greater for the single Jewish parent raising children. Still and all, the probability of nurturing a full Jewish identity would seem greater in any Jewish family constellation than in a family situation where two faiths compete, where statistically Judaism takes precedence only twenty-eight percent of the time. With intermarriage, achieving Jewish "holism" becomes exponentially more difficult.

Jewish women married to non-Jewish men face slightly different issues than Jewish men married to non-Jewish women. Jewish women marrying gentiles often hear "Well, at least the kids will be Jewish," but the issue of establishing a household religion persists regardless of whether or not the children are Jewish according to *halakhah* (Jewish law). Also, children will likely bear their father's last name, so if it is distinctively "non-Jewish" (e.g. O'Reilly or Takasaki) it will stand out and may raise questions in Jewish settings. If neither the intermarried gentile mother nor the children convert, the Conservative and Orthodox movements will not consider the children Jewish regardless of how the household is run. While the Reform movement has officially approved patrilineal descent with certain caveats, its acceptance on the grassroots level is less clear.

So Why Do People Intermarry?

In a culture where the autonomy of the self is nearly unassailable, we find an irony when it comes to marriage. If choosing a life partner is the most awesome decision we autonomous selves make, it is often the decision made in the least deliberate or critical way. With divorce rates upward of fifty percent and even higher among the intermarried, we clearly need to emphasize the need for informed and deliberate marriage choices.

Most often we simply, accidentally, "fall" in love. In fact, one who admits to looking for love will be subject to a brief lesson on the folly of such a notion, since it contradicts the reigning mythology of romance. Even post-feminism, the prevailing culture teaches that you must "wait" for Prince Charming (or Ms. Right); you must trust in fate that you will lock eyes with your intended across a crowded room; you must believe that the one "perfect" person is out there somewhere, awaiting you. For many committed Jews, allegiance to Judaism seems to go hand in hand with the unhappy and untenable prospect of foregoing companionship for faith.

Prevalent Jewish stereotypes, particularly about Jewish

women, may be barriers to intrafaith romance. Who wants, after all, to marry a "JAP" or a "mama's boy"? For many years, it was the case that Jewish men married "out" more frequently than Jewish women. As those percentages have evened out, another statistic has emerged showing that when Jewish women marry non-Jews, they do so at a later age, 26 on average, as opposed to 23.2 for Jewish men.[6] Feminist exegesis as well as anecdotal experience interpret this discrepancy as a greater reluctance on the part of Jewish women to intermarry, or conversely a greater willingness or even eagerness on the part of Jewish men to marry the exotic "other." This is fertile ground for sociological analysis of the self-hatred which seems to plague modern Jews, but stands beyond the purview of this chapter.

So, if one is lucky enough to fall in love with a decent person with whom a life together shows promise, religious differences are often quickly set aside or negotiated for fear of losing that "once-in-a-lifetime" chance (note the mythology again).

Romantic idealism leaves us ill-equipped to make wise marriage decisions. To illustrate this it is helpful to contrast choices made in pursuit of a profession with those made about marriage. Increasingly in the working world, one needs a bachelor's or advanced degree, large sums of tuition money (or willingness to go into debt), readiness to move around the country plus years of hard work—in other words, total commitment and accommodation of one's life to the realization of the professional goal. Despite the challenges, many pursue this difficult course to its end. And if a person sets out to be a lawyer, rarely does s/he find her or himself in medical school by mistake. The process of choosing a career is endowed with deliberate choices and intense commitment.

With marriage, on the other hand, one rarely sees such intentionality at play. Regardless of Jewish identity and connectedness, relatively few contemporary Jews have and carry out an articulated, conscious commitment to basic religious requirements for a potential spouse.

But once such priorities are on the table, the illogic of dating someone who does not or will not someday match them becomes evident. If we think that establishing criteria for the ideal spouse is somehow old-fashioned, undemocratic, or even tribalistic, we must acknowledge that many other types of "preselective" criteria abound in human relationships, from the ridiculous to the sublime. Education, physical appearance, previous marriage(s), financial status, race, and cultural background are just a few such considerations.

In a world where thoughtful choice is both a privilege and a responsibility, we must challenge our culture's thesis of "lucky love" and ask ourselves some searching questions: What does being Jewish mean to me? (Why) should I/might I restrict myself to dating Jews? What is Jewish about me? What are the implications of my marrying a non-Jew? In my generation? For my children's and grandchildren's generation (if I should have children and grandchildren)? Would I ask the person I love to convert? What are the concrete implications of raising children with a dual religious heritage? How do I envision holiday and lifecycle celebrations with my spouse and family? (How) do I want to celebrate the birth of children? Their coming of age? Their weddings?

The real problem here, or so it seems to me, is not that most individuals do not care about these questions on some level, but that they are unschooled in exploring them for themselves, much less with a prospective partner. Truth be told, many liberal Jews have only the vaguest notion about their beliefs or the Jewish philosophy which might underlie them, and so their commitment is shaky. Others relate to their Judaism in so primitive or childlike a fashion that they dare not claim fidelity to it for fear of having to describe or defend it, especially its non-rational elements. Many of us live with the irony of being intelligent and articulate about our professions and other secular matters, but undereducated about our tradition and unpracticed in exploring religious beliefs. Rather than confront our sense of Jewish inadequacy, we put religion aside, tuck it away, turning to it only on rare occasions. After all, contemporary American culture has long since sanctioned the peripheralization of religion.

Furthermore, many of us have never been taught positive reasons to commit ourselves to the perpetuation of Judaism. The most common incentives offered extend a few generations in either direction: There is guilt over the past (the Holocaust, giving Hitler "a posthumous victory," breaking the chain of Jewish tradition) or guilt over the future (within a few generations the Jews of America will disappear), and too little that applies in the here and now.

So Why Marry a Jew?

The religious character and consistency of the home play a critical role in shaping solid Jewish identities for adults and children. Where a religious mix prevails, a more eclectic identity generally evolves.

Even if they are unaffiliated and uninterested Jewishly, the union of two Jewish adults contains an ember which may someday light a Jewish fire in their hearts and their home. If I myself had not many times witnessed the faintest breath required to ignite such an ember into a passion for Judaism, I would be suspicious of such a facile metaphor. But examples abound. Learning the meaning and habit of just one simple ritual which sanctifies time, connects us to other Jews past and present, or brings the spirit of blessing into a home often has a contagious effect, setting something like a brushfire in the soul. Where Jewish involvement follows, the question "Why marry a Jew?" becomes rhetorical. The answer lies in the intrinsic rewards and fulfillment of building a Jewish home. People regularly come into my office after two, six, fifteen years of marriage to mourn the sense of spiritual loss they have belatedly discovered in taking a life partner who does not share their religious identity, an identity they often did not know was precious until a twist in life's journey revealed it as such.

In Conclusion

The Jewish community's confrontation with intermarriage has forced not only investigations of demographic trends and cultural patterns, but an internal investigation as well, a search of our communal soul. The soul, like the body, requires constant tending and nurturing. This fact has forced us to reexamine Jewish education in all its phases and venues and to reinvigorate the partnership behind effective Jewish identity formation. It also encourages each of us to examine our personal choices and beliefs. As a modern, emancipated people still anchored to its tradition, we are struggling to define Jewish choices, name Jewish priorities and forge a solid Jewish community. The many quandaries of intermarriage offer us, at bottom, just three choices: (1) Ignore the problem, (2) condemn or write off the intermarried, or (3) commit ourselves to "creative cartography," mapping out a rich Jewish future, against unfriendly odds, with concrete personal and communal decisions.

A Personal Afterword

During the time in which I was working on this project, I received a remarkable gift. One spring evening, my mother and stepfather called with surprising news: My stepfather was converting to Judaism. His reasons for doing so, after fifteen years of marriage to my mother, belong to him alone. I can only share my own reaction: A burst of feeling whole and at peace in that most intimate and central place, my family. Our relationship, which has always known so much love and harmony, became complete in the split second it took the news to travel the internal network from my mind to my heart.

Children of Intermarriage

JANE BARON RECHTMAN

"The Edge of the Sea is a strange and beautiful place."
—RACHEL CARSON, *THE EDGE OF THE SEA*

When I was a young adult, I took a few classes at The Jewish Theological Seminary. There I met a number of rabbinical students who would ask me out for an enjoyable evening, perhaps twice, and then never contact me again. Frustrated and saddened by this rebuff from people with whom I thought I had so much in common, I asked a friend who worked at the Seminary why I was striking out so often. She confided to me that the reason, according to one young fellow, was that I was not Jewish. This greatly surprised me. For, naive as it may sound, although I was born of a Christian mother and a Jewish father, although I had not had a religious upbringing of any sort, and although I was studying at the Protestant seminary across the street, I always thought of myself as Jewish. It was at that moment, standing in my friend's kitchen that I decided to seek official designation as a Jew. Not because it would make me feel any different, but because it would make me appear differently to others.

I am one of the many converts for whom conversion meant not a change in cultural and religious affiliation, but rather a confirmation of my Jewish roots and attachments. We are the children of mixed marriages: Children who have a Jewish father and a Jewish family, children who perhaps even celebrate Jewish customs and holidays, but are not considered Jewish by many segments of the community because our mothers are not Jewish.

We grew up feeling at home with both Jews and Christians. We see the world as larger and perhaps more complex because we are able to see "both sides." Many of us, like myself, have chosen to live on the Jewish side of the fence, but we still understand and feel at home with the other, and that makes us different from those who have grown up in a completely Jewish household.

Jane Baron Rechtman is a mother, wife, director of a nursery school, and adjunct professor of religion at Mercy College. She has a master's degree in divinity from Union Theological Seminary in New York.

Family Background

My father is the son of Russian Jews who immigrated to the Lower East Side. Although they were not religious, their lives revolved around Jewish culture. I was very close to my paternal grandparents, aunts, uncles, and cousins. There was no better way to spend a weekend than to drive to the house in Far Rockaway Queens, run into the arms of loving grandparents, munch humongous amounts of lox and bagels at the heavy, oversized European dining table (which now graces my home), spend the day playing with cousins and listening to grownups argue, laugh, and play cards. During vacations I would sometimes get to spend time there by myself, and my grandmother would regale me with stories about the family. Like a polished gem, each story became more beautiful and lustrous with retelling.

My mother, a first generation immigrant of the Stewart-McFall clan from Northern Ireland and Scotland, was raised High Church of England, attended a Catholic school, and has her own pantheistic/Quaker outlook. Her father, who wore a kilt until the age of twelve, died many years before I was born. Her mother, Granny England, lived with us for one year when I was a child, but then returned to Northern Ireland. We kept in touch by letter until she died.

My family celebrated Christmas and Passover. Both holidays were times of family, food, and excitement. The story of promise, hope, and a baby's miraculous birth in the winter did not seem to conflict with the story of promise, hope, and a people's rebirth in the spring. The joy of getting together with loved ones to celebrate year after year in the same ways did not seem problematic, nor did the magic of Santa or the *Afikomen* (*matzah* eaten for dessert at a Passover *seder* [ordered readings and meal]). Other than observing these holidays and occasionally attending synagogue or a Quaker meeting, we had no religious training at all. We were strictly lox-and-bagel-Christmas-Passover-Christian/Jews.

The first time I recognized that others considered this upbringing to be a problem was when my parents' marriage ended. Although the dissolution of their marriage did not relate to religion, it was then I was told that my father's parents had been so incensed at his marrying a non-Jew that they did not speak to him until six months after I was born. When my parents divorced, my grandfather sat my brothers and me down on a bench at his Long Island Beach Club. "You see," he proclaimed to us as we obediently listened and ate ice cream, "this is what happens with a mixed marriage. It shouldn't happen, it's not good for the children. I told them, but Achh," he said with a dismissive swat of his hand, "they didn't listen. What can you do?" Indulging him, I sat and listened to him rant and rave. But I felt as I did about Santa Claus.

Let me explain: My father tells a story about me as a little girl. Apparently I asked him one day, "Dad, do you believe in Santa Claus?" I knew my father was a grownup, and I knew he was Jewish. Not wanting to lie, my father replied, "Well, many people believe in Santa Claus." "Yes, Daddy, but do *you* believe in Santa?" "No," he admitted, and then felt badly for the rest of the day that he had spoiled my innocence. Later on he was comforted when he heard me tell a neighbor, "Some people don't believe in Santa, but I do."

Childhood and Adult Philosophies of Religion

Although I have long since stopped believing in Santa Claus, I have never stopped believing in that approach to faith. Many people may believe differently than I do, but I still believe. I recognize that there are different paths—sometimes conflicting, sometimes not—and that is all right. This acceptance, I believe, comes in part from growing up in a mixed marriage. And so, when my grandfather said mixed marriages were no good, my attitude was, and still is, well, maybe not for some people, but for this child of a mixed marriage it was a gift of openness. I made the conscious choice to marry a Jewish spouse and to raise and educate my children as Jews. But if my children decided to intermarry, my reaction would not be that of my grandfather but that of the child I was.

So why did I take a stand and declare myself, officially and with a *mikveh* (ritual immersion), a Jew? Partly it was to strengthen ties to the family I knew and grew up with. Also, I had a strong desire for community, to belong to a group of humans bound together by a shared perspective on matters spiritual and meaningful. Becoming a Christian was out of the question because, for all the beauty I see in the idea of God becoming human, it is not an idea that speaks to me. Although I find Christianity quite meaningful and relevant ("Some people believe in it, but I don't"), and have studied Christian ideas, I have always known that I am not Christian. Furthermore, in my mind, negating my Jewish roots would diminish the historical continuity of my people. While the same could be said of negating Christian roots, it never felt like the same magnitude of loss—either to Christian demographics or in my life.

My decision to affiliate with the Jewish community stemmed from a theological affinity, as well. The humanity of the biblical characters, the strength and vision of the prophetic voices, the relationship between people and God expressed in the Talmud and prayerbook are dear to me. More than that, they are my life's grounding. I like a community where I, like my heroes Abraham and Job, can argue with God; a community where learning is valued and questioning is essential; a community where there is a reverence for the people who came before and a cherishing of those we raise; a community where family, with all its *meshugas* (craziness), is central to religious celebrations. And yes, I like a community where even food, the sustenance of life, is made holy and central. It is within the Jewish context that I am nurtured, that I grow. I am "like a tree planted by water, that sends out its roots by the stream" (Jeremiah 17:8).

It will be interesting to see how the Jewish community deals with people like me, the more there are people like me. Many in the Jewish community are afraid that intermarriage will dilute and change Judaism. But Judaism has always changed and adapted and that is part of the reason that it has survived. Some are afraid that Judaism will cease to exist. Perhaps there will be fewer Jews. But the idea of a holy, potentially redemptive remnant is biblical—and valid for renewal. Only two of my father's four grandchildren are Jewish. But they are confident, proud Jews who understand, respect, and are not afraid of the views of others. As an American Jew, that is what I want to pass on.

On Being Intermarried

ELIZABETH WARNER FRANK

*"You can build a Jewish identity, and the road to building identifi-
cation and emotional commitment begins with learning."*
— LYDIA KUKOFF, *CHOOSING JUDAISM*

When I received the call from Rabbi Debra Orenstein, asking me if
I would participate in this book, I was moved to tears by the
implied message: My husband Richard and I were accepted in the
Jewish community in a warm and respectful fashion. Rabbi
Orenstein was referred to me by Rabbi Neal Weinberg, the director
of the Introduction to Judaism program at the University of
Judaism. He taught Richard and me when we were engaged.
Richard and I have been married for three and a half years. He is
not Jewish.

Growing up in a Reform home in West Los Angeles, in an
environment more culturally Jewish than religious, one of my criteria for a mate was that he be Jewish. But life had other plans for
me. Richard comes from a large German/Polish Catholic family
(he has seven brothers and sisters) and grew up in upstate New
York. He also came from a culturally-identified home. Shortly
after we started dating, I stressed to Richard the importance of my
Jewish identity and my desire to have a Jewish home. When we
decided to get married, we agreed to take the Introduction to
Judaism class so we could both learn about what, in fact, it means
to have a Jewish home. My mother also took the class with us, and
this created a wonderful bond between her and Richard.

Richard and I met privately with the rabbi at the Temple
where I grew up, as well. Rabbi Finley, Richard, and I had many
conversations about Jewish values, spirituality, and daily living.
Richard did not wish to convert. Although he was willing to have
a Jewish home and raise Jewish children, he was and remains
unready to give up his own cultural identity. After several sessions, Rabbi Finley offered to marry us because he felt comfortable
with Richard's quest for Jewish knowledge and our commitment

Elizabeth Warner Frank is a talent coordinator for FOX Television. She lives in
Burbank, California with her husband, Richard, and son, Aaron.

to establishing a Jewish home and family. We were married by Rabbi Finley in 1990 with our immediate and extended families present. In 1992, I gave birth to our beautiful son, Aaron.

We have had a relatively easy time in our intermarriage. Richard's parents and siblings have totally accepted our choice to have a Jewish home and his mother sends us *Rosh Hashanah* (New Year) and *Ḥanukkah* (Festival of the Lights) cards. She went to Israel last year and brought us back a lovely gift from Jerusalem. My mom and sisters love Richard and my mom has even taught him to make marvelous chicken soup and potato *latkes* (pancakes). We keep a kosher home, and *Shabbat* (Sabbath) dinner is a celebrated event in our house. Aaron loves to see his mommy light the Sabbath candles and he wears his *kippah* (skullcap) on Friday nights. On most Friday nights we walk to Temple for services.

Though Richard has given up all other aspects of his Christian observance, we still contend with the issue of Christmas. He misses having a Christmas tree. For him, it symbolizes family and togetherness, rather than the religious meaning of the holiday. It reminds him of his childhood and the excitement and warmth he experienced. I understand his feelings. I would certainly miss the Jewish holiday symbols if we did not have them in our home. Still, Richard recognizes the importance of having one religion in our home. We both agree that Aaron needs to be exposed to a consistent set of practices and beliefs. We continue to work on the issue of Christmas by talking about our feelings and not holding back about December being a difficult month. We strive to make the season a fun and especially festive one, with lots of *Ḥanukkah* decorations around the house. We also decorate our *sukkah* (hut for the Festival of Tabernacles) each year.

Intermarriage can work. If there is a commitment to Jewish life in the home and continued acceptance from the community, then Judaism will be the path taken in the marriage. My hope is that Richard will convert someday, but even if he does not, he is still a "fellow traveler" and a righteous one at that.

11

Choosing Judaism

O f all life passages, conversion is perhaps the most deliberate and the most dramatic. Milestones like Bat
Mitzvah (coming of age ceremony for girls), pregnancy,
menopause, aging, and death can arrive with or without planning. But choosing Judaism is just that—a choice.
Moreover, even the major transformations in status incurred as
part of such life choices as marriage or parenthood pale in comparison to the shift in community and identity that comes with
choosing Judaism. There is an aura of bravery and destiny around
this passage.

There is also a pull of identities. After conversion, one is forever
a Jew. But, in many cases, one remains a "convert" or "Jew by
choice" as well, at least for a time—both in one's own eyes and in
the eyes of family and community. Two of the authors in this chapter—Antonia M. Bookbinder and Catherine Hall Myrowitz—raise

the question of whether one ever really stops being a convert. In addition to being both "Jew" and "convert," one remains attached to a non-Jewish family of origin and a non-Jewish childhood.

For the female convert to Judaism, identity is still further complicated and enriched. To cite just one example, most female converts have a burden that neither male Jews by choice nor female Jews by birth share: i.e., the pressure to be one hundred percent "kosher" in their status, so that all segments of the community will regard any children they may have as Jewish.

The placement of this chapter after the chapter on intermarriage should in no way imply that conversion is the consequence of intermarriage—or the "solution" to it. Conversion sometimes results when a gentile marries a Jew and learns about his or her heritage, but the motivations for choosing Judaism are varied and usually quite complex.

Several of the authors in this chapter found in Judaism not a *new* culture, religion, or family, but an identity and affiliation that they felt, in some mystical sense, to have been theirs already. It is partly for that reason that the term "choosing Judaism" is generally preferred over "conversion." One has not, as the dictionary definition of conversion states, "changed from one use, function, or purpose to another," but rather made a choice which supports and furthers one's essential "use, function, and purpose."

In the Introduction to Judaism courses that I teach, I am regularly impressed by the seriousness and spiritual maturity of prospective converts, as well as their internal sense of "coming home." Many students have told me that they did not just "empathize" with Jewish suffering; they felt as if they had borne it. The strength of their anger or despair over the Holocaust startled family, friends, and even themselves. Often, it was the impetus for them to study Judaism. Many Jews by choice feel themselves to have been Jews, somehow, all along—whether through a forgotten Jewish ancestor, the recycling of a Jewish soul in their body, or some other unnameable connection. This complements the tradition that the souls of all future converts to Judaism received the Torah at Mt. Sinai with the rest of the Israelites (BT *Shavu'ot* 39a).

The Rabbis do not dwell on the convert's motivations, except to be cautious of turncoats and spies (a legitimate fear in earlier times), to warn the potential convert of the difficulties associated with being Jewish, and to winnow out the insincere or merely curious by demanding significant study and commitment to *mitzvot* (commandments). With rare exception, the Rabbis held an extremely positive view of converts, who, since the days of the Talmud, have been among our religious and intellectual leaders. According to one tradition, Jews by choice are especially loved by God (*Mekhilta Nezikin [Mishpatim]* 18). In the Rabbinic understanding, converts are considered members of the Israelite tribe (*Tosefta Nedarim* 2:4; JT *Kiddushin* 4:1), and are equal to born Jews liturgically and ritually. Even the most negative Talmudic characterization of the convert, Rabbi Helbo's statement that "Proselytes are as hard for Israel [to endure] as a sore" (BT *Yevamot* 47b; see also BT *Ketubbot* 70b) is commonly interpreted to mean that converts to Judaism are a constant "irritant," in that they remind Jews by birth that they do not have the merit of having chosen Judaism. This reminder becomes a goad to better and more consistent Jewish observance. The Rabbinic view of converts is a far cry from a racial or ethnic understanding of what it means to be Jewish, on which anti-Semitism often thrives.

The first three authors in this chapter are Jews by choice. The Jewish community has heard too little from these Jews about their lives and decisions, and this chapter represents a small step toward remedying this deficiency.

In her letter to a hypothetical prospective convert, Shoshana Brown-Gutoff communicates some of the salient factors to consider if one is thinking of conversion. The essay has tremendous practical value, as a summary of the basic elements in conversion, as a reflection of traditional attitudes toward the prospective convert, and as a missive to those who may, in fact, be interested in exploring Judaism.

It is striking that so much of Brown-Gutoff's discussion of converts and conversion applies to all Jews, throughout their lives. Her advice on finding a synagogue and choosing a rabbi will speak to anyone who has searched or is searching for a niche in the Jewish community. The four traditional components of conversion which she outlines extend beyond the conversion ritual. They remain relevant in dedication to and celebration of covenant; in lifelong Jewish study; in acceptance of Jewish law and rabbinic authority, as a guiding principle if not a binding code; and in the perennial return to the *mikveh* (ritual bath) on holidays, special occasions, and, for many women, on a monthly basis.

Similarly, Antonia M. Bookbinder regards conversion as a process that continues well past the moment of immersion in the *mikveh* and, ideally, throughout one's lifetime. Clearly, this notion of "becoming Jewish" as a continual choice and task applies to Jews by birth, as well as Jews by choice. The applicability of the convert's dilemmas and process to all Jews is evident, also, in Bookbinder's struggle to honor her parents—a commandment with whose awesome dimensions we must all wrestle. The place of women in Judaism was a persuasive factor in Bookbinder's conversion, and the narrative of her journey to Judaism reveals aspects of the internal experience of conversion, notably the bridging of old and new family patterns.

Catherine Hall Myrowitz reverses some usual roles and overturns expectations. Instead of instructing converts in what they need to know about the Jewish community, she tells the community what we need to know about Jews by choice. Myrowitz writes of the attractions Judaism holds for converts, especially women, of the problems they face, and of the responses—useful and harmful—that the community offers.

A Jew by birth, Rabbi Jane Litman brings the chapter to a close, providing thought- and spirit-provoking meditations for immersion in the *mikveh* at the moment of conversion. These can be adapted both to subsequent occasions for immersion and to prayerful reflection on conversion outside the ritual bath.

"Ruth," to whom Brown-Gutoff directs her letter refers to the biblical Ruth, a strong and independent female character, our first convert, and the foremother of the messiah. Such is the esteem we have for Jews by choice.

Dear Ruth: Letter to an Aspiring Convert [1]

SHOSHANA BROWN-GUTOFF

"'To love the Lord your God' (Deuteronomy 11:13): [This means] all that you do, do it only out of love."

—*SIFRE* DEUTERONOMY 41

Introductory Note

The following is a pastiche of excerpts from a journal kept during the time I was at Episcopal Divinity School, conducting a project entitled "A Personal/Experiential Exploration of Judaism."

What my eyes have seen, and ears heard, have hardly ever entered the heart of a Christian. Yesterday at 4:59 PM I found myself in a plain room with a divider down the middle—men on one side, women on the other—with an open "cabinet" in the front, its contents veiled by some kind of canvas. A man began a prayer in Hebrew. Others joined in, each at his own pace, mumbling, humming, swaying, bowing....Songs broke out, mysterious, joyful. "*Lekhah Dodi*...." We welcomed the Sabbath bride. An Orthodox Jewish Sabbath Eve service, at Harvard Hillel.

Most of the time I stood, or sat, depending on the mood of the group of women I had joined, not knowing where we were in the prayerbook, or what any of the words meant....I closed my eyes and felt tears welling up beneath the lids. "Yes," my gut said. "This is authentic. There is something here, a rejoicing, a calm recognition of one's identity, of history, of tradition, of one's people....

I am truly not trying to "prove" anything. I am just drawn to it, like a moth to the lamp. Perhaps I shall flutter my wings and bash my head against its bright light, while it ignores me. But I must fly there.

Shoshana Brown-Gutoff, a Ph.D. candidate in *midrash* at The Jewish Theological Seminary, teaches adult Jewish education in St. Paul, Minnesota, where she lives with her husband Rabbi Joshua Gutoff and their daughter, Mira Abigail. She converted to Judaism in 1987.

The full story of my attraction to, falling-in-love with, wooing, and finally, "consummating" my love for Judaism is too long to tell here in full. I do, however, want to say a word about the letter-format of this essay. In 1984, while still in my first year of study at Episcopal Divinity School, I attended a lecture by Jakob Petuchowski, a professor of liturgy at Hebrew Union College in Cincinnati. He was a mesmerizing bundle of stories, wit, erudite scholarship, and *mentschlikhkeit* (essence of being a good person). He was also a doorway for me to something that was calling me, as I described above, with an almost eerie power.

When I decided to study in Jerusalem for a year, I began a correspondence with Jakob and his wife Elizabeth that was to be one of the most important factors in my becoming a Jew. The day that I received Jakob's letter welcoming me with open arms into the "tribe," I was ecstatic. I had been accepted and thus "brought back" into the fold of what I somehow felt was my long-lost family.

Conversion is not just an intellectual process. It has everything to do with relationships. So I cast this essay in the form of a letter to a young woman I have never met, referred to me by a mutual acquaintance. I hope it will prove useful to many "Ruths" and to the Jewish families and communities that will ultimately welcome them.

Dear Ruth,

I received your note from our mutual friend, Sarah, asking me to explain the process of conversion. The crucial question you must ask yourself is not "How do I become a Jew?" but rather, "What does it mean to *be* a Jew?" Your vision of what being Jewish means will determine, more than any other factor, what kind of Jew you will become.

Identity and Choice

The convert lives with a double standard. According to the Rabbis, a convert is every bit as Jewish as a born Jew (BT *Yevamot* 47b)—and yet...things are different. The born Jew may take no interest in his/her Jewishness, or even try to hide it. S/he may exist as a "negative" Jew. But this option makes no sense for a convert: If you had no interest in Judaism, nor any intention of living a positively-identified Jewish life, you would not become Jewish. Because your Jewishness comes by an intellectual and spiritual choice, and not by simply being born, you are compelled to an intense self-scrutiny. This self-consciousness parallels that of Jews throughout the millennia who were constantly reminded of their Jewishness in Christian and Muslim lands. Converts are thus different from other Jews and also, paradoxically, the most "Jewish" of the Jews.

By converting, you are not joining a club or culture or even an ideology—you are becoming a member of a people, taking on a new identity. You will begin to experience *history* differently, and to take part in it differently. If you read a book or see a film that deals with the Holocaust, for example, you will say "These are *my* people," and when you hear news of Israel on the radio, you might stop whatever you are doing and listen, for it is *your* news. You will experience your *present* differently. Your relationship with your family will change: No more helping Mom trim the tree or going with her to midnight Mass. These are just the obvious examples—there will be many subtle changes as well. You will have to explain yourself to family or friends, who may be mystified at why you are "rejecting" them by becoming Jewish, and you may be surprised at the odd notions new friends or neighbors harbor about you on account of your Jewishness. Your decision will affect the *future*, as well. By raising Jewish children, becoming involved in the Jewish social action projects, or simply bringing a Jewish perspective to whatever you do in the world, you will be woven into the great tapestry of Jewish destiny. That tapestry will look different on account of you.

When I became a Jew, I emerged out of what had been for me (until that point) a life-long identity crisis. I was never at ease in my native white Southern culture, and even in the more intellectual and free-thinking culture of New England, where I moved, I still felt lonely. I was in search of community, which I tried to find in the Episcopal Church. You may know that I was in seminary, on my way to becoming a priest, living and studying in an intensely questioning intellectual and spiritual community, when I began to delve into Judaism. As wonderful as that community was, I still felt my kinship lay elsewhere...with Abraham who argued with God, with Jacob who wrestled the angel, with the myriad of Jewish intellectuals, political dissidents, and comedians who never could or would confine their conversations to "polite" subjects. It is hard to convey what it feels like to "find your people," but for me it was like discovering a dinner table full of friends and strangers with whom I could, completely, be myself.

The Place of Law in Jewish Conversion, and of Conversion in Jewish Law

Not all Jews identify as religious or practice their faith within the framework of *halakhah* (Jewish law). That is, we do not all keep the traditional laws of the Sabbath, festivals, *kashrut* (keeping kosher), family purity, *tzedakah* (sacred practice of charity), etc. I am an "observant" Jew, having embraced the halakhic framework for my life and faith, and my views of Judaism are prejudiced toward that perspective. Personally, I do not understand what becoming a Jew can mean if your Sabbath differs in no way from your pre-Jewish Saturday, if your charitable practices are no different after becoming Jewish than they were before, if the study of Torah does not assume a central place in your life.

I urge you in the strongest terms to try any and all observances before rejecting them. Traditionally, a convert to Judaism is asked if s/he is prepared to take on the "yoke of the commandments." Whatever this might mean for you, understand that the community and God will have claims on you when and if you become Jewish.

If I sound a bit gruff, I am only doing my duty. The tradition enjoins Jews to turn away the prospective convert three times; if s/he still seeks to convert despite this discouragement, then s/he should be received. But even then, one should "Push away with the left hand while drawing near with the right" (Ruth *Rabbah* 2:1). Further, we are to say: "What has made you want to convert? Don't you know that the people of Israel at this time are persecuted and oppressed, despised, harassed, and overcome with sufferings" (BT *Yevamot* 47a)? While it is not the case at this time (at least, not in the United States) that we Jews are persecuted, conversion will make your life harder in many ways. I have already mentioned how it will change your relationship with your family and friends. If you choose an observant lifestyle, know that keeping the Sabbath and *kashrut* in a world where these practices are wholly alien is difficult indeed. Some converts also encounter difficulty from the Jewish community itself. Personally, I have never had a negative reaction from any Jew with whom I shared my story. (Rather, I have received respect and admiration.) But there are Jews who do not accept converts as "true Jews." These are generally not religious Jews, but those whose concept of Judaism is wholly ethnic.

If you are converting for the sake of marriage—or "for the children's sake" (which is frequently another way of saying for the in-laws' sake)—I have another "sermon of discouragement" for you. Many converts come to their decision because they have fallen in love with a Jew and want to marry. They may be every bit as sincere as those who convert with no romantic interest. Perhaps for many of them it is no accident that they fall in love with a Jew— perhaps that Jew's Jewishness is part of what attracts them to their intended in the first place. But if your motivation is to please your (future) spouse or in-laws, or to have a shared religion for children, I urge you to wait. If you convert and Judaism means little to you, it will probably likewise mean little to your children. But if your children see you as a person of integrity, who is learning about a prospective religion and whose deeds are in harmony with her words; if you tell them about their dual heritage without trying to force them or yourself into an identity you do not yet inhabit, they—and you—will stand a better chance of becoming Jewish in a meaningful way.

And to those grandparents who are anxious about the next generation's religious status, I urge, "Don't work out any guilt you may feel by demanding that your future son- or daughter-in-law convert. Instead, take a more active interest in Jewish life yourselves—and perhaps you will thereby instill a love of Judaism in your grandchildren. One day they, and your son- or daughter-in-law, may joyfully make the decision to convert."[2] This last missive is directed more at potential in-laws than at you. If it is applicable to your situation, you may pass it along in my name.

Finding a Community

You have asked me what kind of conversion you should pursue. "What kind of conversion?" is another way of asking what rabbi and movement you should choose. Our movements are not rigidly divided denominations; there is much commonality and fluidity among them. Still, you must educate yourself about the differences among Orthodox, Conservative, Reform, and Reconstructionist Judaism. Your studies toward conversion and your conversion ritual itself will differ, depending on which movement sponsors you.[3] Your task is to decide which community practices the kind of Jewish life you want to live, and by whom it is important to you to be accepted.

While your life as a Jew may offer you opportunities to learn from many teachers and to pray with various communities, your choice about "what kind" of conversion to undergo will have lasting consequences. Since not all conversions are accepted by all stripes of Jews, you might want to select an Orthodox rabbi to sponsor you so that your conversion will be accepted as "valid" by the greatest number of Jews possible. This would also alleviate problems of status if you marry an Orthodox Jew, and prevent any questioning of your children's status as Jews, should they want to marry someone from a halakhically-oriented community. Of course you should not seek a conversion you do not feel comfortable with, and whose requirements you cannot honestly promise to meet. If, like me, you want to be observant and egalitarian,[4] you will probably feel more comfortable with a conversion under Conservative auspices. As I am committed to living my Jewish life within the framework of *halakhah*, I cannot be a spokesperson for the Reform or Reconstructionist movements, but I encourage you to explore all your options.

A community may be chosen after "shopping around," but sometimes would-be converts find a spiritual home while still relatively ignorant of denominational differences. Many converts choose their rabbi and synagogue largely because they feel comfortable with them. You may agree with the Conservative movement's ideology, but be unable to find a Conservative congregation in your area that actually lives by it. Thus, you may be more fulfilled in a modern Orthodox congregation. You might find that the

Reform temple in your town, despite the movement's liberal ideology, is too rigid about liturgy, or unwelcoming of women in leadership roles, and thus turn to the Reconstructionist synagogue. You might find a home in an unaffiliated *havurah* (Jewish worship/study fellowship), eclectic and undogmatic in its ideology. *Havurot* often have no rabbi, and so you would need to weigh various factors in choosing a rabbi outside your own praying community.

Ideology, politics, comfort. You have to do your homework. Find out what "they" believe (Is this what you believe? Are you willing to take it on?), and find a community with whom you feel comfortable and joyful. All this returns me—and you—to my original question: What does it mean to be a Jew—for you?

The Conversion Process

Now, let's take a look at the formal elements of a halakhic conversion:[5]

Hattafat Dam/Brit Milah: **Drawing a Drop of Blood from the Penile Area or the Covenant of Circumcision** Since you are a woman, you do not have to deal directly with circumcision, a requirement for male converts. (A man already circumcised would undergo a *Hattafat Dam*.) You should study this aspect of conversion nonetheless, for it raises several important issues: It introduces you to the centrality of covenant in Judaism, circumcision being its bodily sign; it emphasizes physicality and sexuality in Judaism; and it reminds you that the convert becomes a child of Abraham's covenant with God. Finally, the very fact that this bodily mark of the covenant is not one that girls or women wear should give you pause to notice that there are areas of disparity if not inequity for women under Jewish law. Certainly, you will have to wrestle with that.[6]

Talmud Torah: **Jewish Learning** No amount of education can make up for lack of commitment—but commitment can make up for incompleteness of education. None of us can ever learn "enough." We spend our entire life learning Bible, Talmud, *halakhah*, liturgy, the Jewish calendar, history, philosophy, literature, etc. Still, we can never exhaust all there is to know about being a Jew.

There are three kinds of Jewish education: The book kind, the people kind, and the practicing kind. There are many wonderful books, and any list I might give you would commit terrible sins of omission. You and your rabbi ought to compile a list together. In the meantime, consult Barry Holtz, ed., *The Schocken Guide to Jewish Books* (Schocken, 1992). The book consists of bibliographical essays which point you to a variety of other books, and includes a chapter on Jewish women's studies.

Then there is the long road to learning Hebrew. Hebrew literacy and fluency are not legal requirements for conversion; however, they will help you feel more at home with the *siddur* (prayerbook) and in the synagogue, and will generally enable you to better appreciate and enjoy Jewish ritual life.

You cannot study in a vacuum; you have to mingle with Jews. Get involved in a study group or adult education program, or if you can afford the time and money, go study in Israel. Volunteer for Jewish social action projects, attend Jewish conventions and concerts, find a Jewish mentor, get involved with Jews! Invite friends over for Sabbath meals. Eat Jewish foods, sing Jewish songs, and discuss Jewish issues (and any issue can be Jewish, when discussed from a Jewish perspective). This method may be the most important way to learn.

Finally, practice, practice, practice. This word has a double meaning: First you must "practice"—prepare—to become Jewish; then you must put *into* practice the Jewish life you have chosen. Jews who are born into the faith may have decades of practice under their belt. They may have experienced the High Holidays and Passover *seder* (ordered readings and meal) dozens of times. You will need to make a concerted effort to master and feel at home with this experiential part of the heritage. And it will take time.

***Beit Din*: The Rabbinical Court** After you have prepared through study and before your immersion, you will meet with your *beit din*. Three rabbis/judges will ask you questions, to ascertain that you have studied and mastered a basic body of knowledge, that you know what you are "getting yourself into," and that you are doing this with a sound mind and without coercion. They will also give you an opportunity to explore the spiritual meaning of your transition. The questioning is friendly, but solemn.

What I remember from my own *beit din*, however, is a moment of laughter. One of the judges asked me if I was aware that I did not need to convert to merit redemption and reward in the world-to-come.[7] I said, "Yes, but I don't want to wait for the world-to-come to receive my 'reward.' I want to be happy *now*!" My sponsoring rabbi let out a guffaw, "She sounds like a *Lubavitcher*!" (The *Lubavitch* branch of Ḥasidism is famous for their chant, "We want *mashiaḥ* [messiah] now!")

Mikveh: **Ritual Bath** Immersion in a *mikveh* is mandatory, according to traditional Jewish law. The rules require that you be either naked or in some very loose-fitting garment, so that the water touches all parts of your body. In accordance with the Talmud (BT *Yevamot* 47a), you may be instructed in "some of the lighter and some of the heavier" of the commandments while you are standing in the water. You will immerse a total of three times, and recite the appropriate blessings. When you come out of the water for the third time, you come out Jewish!

Although traditionally converts are not supposed to draw attention to their status, some "newly born" Jews (yes, the *mikveh* does both feel and function like a "womb") like to celebrate their "birth" with their praying community. I had been learning how to chant a Torah portion for months before my conversion, so that I could read from a Torah scroll in synagogue on the *Shabbat* immediately following my conversion. The awe I felt at being able to participate fully and chant words of Torah publicly for the first time is something I will never forget.

Conversion is an astounding opportunity rarely met with in life—an opportunity to make yourself anew, and at the same time, to come into your own most profoundly true identity. You gain a new people, a new community, a new name (some use this name only for ritual purposes; others, like me, in the secular world as well), and although not a "new" God, a new way to love the God you already knew with all your heart, soul, and might—by living a Jewish life.

Ruth, you need no more words from me. Get yourself a rabbi, a community, some good books, and get going. May God be with you.

Coming Home

ANTONIA M. BOOKBINDER

"Indeed You desire truth about that which is hidden; teach me wisdom about secret things."

—PSALMS 51:8

My conversion began in childhood, probably before I had ever met a Jew.

When I was growing up, my family neither belonged to a church nor celebrated most holidays. We did not often eat meals together. My family was violent, chaotic, and isolated.

At fourteen, I was baptized and sent to a Catholic girls' boarding school. I studied Church teachings and history and participated enthusiastically in religious activities. I continued to participate in Catholic worship throughout college and law school, but slowly realized that my religion did not address some of my spiritual needs. It seemed to me that worship occurred in church rather than in the daily activities of life, and in church I felt like a bystander at rituals performed only by men. In addition, some priests emphasized the importance of forgiveness in such a way as to dismiss my suffering. By my mid-twenties, I no longer went to church and did not call myself a Christian.

Earlier, as a young adult, I read an eclectic assortment of Jewish writers: Anzia Yezierska, Elie Wiesel, Shalom Aleikhem, Emma Goldman, and Golda Meir. I listened to Yiddish folk music and read translations of Yiddish folk tales. My undergraduate thesis at a Catholic women's college focused on the role of religious education of Jewish women in the acculturation of Jewish immigrant families in the United States. I was fascinated by Jewish culture and inspired by the courage I saw in Jewish role models.

Two facets of Judaism particularly attracted me: Jewish religious feminism and responses to loss and mourning. I needed a religion to recognize my female body and life. The Jewish calendar follows the earth's cyclical changes and helps connect me to

---

Antonia M. Bookbinder is a former lawyer and a doctoral candidate in clinical psychology at Boston University. She is currently writing a dissertation on religious development among converts to Judaism.

tides and seasons. However one evaluates the interaction between feminism and the Jewish tradition, Judaism imbues women's roles as wives and mothers with explicit, central religious meaning. The daily tasks required to maintain a home and family are ritualized in a religious context, complete with appropriate blessings. They reflect aspects of God that one may not experience in public religious services. I feel the divine presence as I prepare for *Shabbat* (Sabbath)—cooking a meal, baking *ḥallah* (braided egg bread), cleaning my home, and later, welcoming and feeding friends and family.

In synagogue, the presence of women rabbis and inclusion of women in the *minyan* (prayer quorum) makes me more than an audience for men's worship. In public and private life, I am a central actor rather than an onlooker.

Jewish women strengthened my decision to convert. They encouraged me to do what I felt was right and did not laugh when I wondered about becoming a Jew. One said that I had a Jewish soul and that conversion would simply rectify my having been born into the wrong family.

Having experienced significant losses in childhood, I was also attracted by Jewish efforts to understand loss and mourning. I learned about a people who resisted despair and were not destroyed by suffering. When I visited Jerusalem, I was moved by the Jews' most sacred place—the Western Wall—which represents a space left by destruction. The bombed synagogues in the Jewish Quarter are preserved as ruins; we remember but do not try to recreate the destroyed past. Jews allow these spaces to remain empty, and have days and seasons for remembering personal and communal losses. Mourning is both encouraged and limited by ritual. Grief has its place, but does not destroy occasions for celebration and joy.

As I prepared for formal conversion, I imagined that my interview with the *beit din* (rabbinical court) and immersion in the *mikveh* (ritual bath) would mark the end of my conversion. I expected that I would feel transformed. Actually, I was disappointed by the ordinariness of my conversion day. I walked to the *mikveh* alone. The *"mikveh* lady" (attendant at the ritual bath) led me to a room where I bathed, and then sat naked and bored on the edge of the tub. One of the rabbis was stuck in traffic. As I waited to be led from the mundane to the ritual bath, I lectured myself on how solemn this change was. The *mikveh* lady came back when the rabbi arrived, checked my fingers and toes for nail polish and led me to the *mikveh*.

As I stood in the warm water up to my shoulders, she opened the door a crack and I could hear my teacher's voice on the other side. "Are you okay?" is all I remember him saying. Then I dunked and said the blessings. The attendant yelled *"Kosher"* (signifying a ritually fit immersion), and I came out and took the towel she gave me. It was gentle and undramatic. Yet the very "ordinariness" of the *mikveh* testifies to how I became a Jew: Through a gradual process of changing attitudes and practices—a process that will last a lifetime.

Because I learned as a child to blend into my surroundings, I studied Judaism initially as if to camouflage myself, to be indistinguishable from "real" Jews. I thought that learning facts and skills and "making it legal" via conversion would make me feel like a "real" Jew. But I felt unchanged by the conversion ritual. I was disappointed to learn that I still had to work to create each celebration. Jewish study and observance had not brought instant religious bliss, and initially I thought that this was because I was a "convert" rather than a "real" Jew. Jewish ritual became more meaningful only when I began to abandon my identity as convert and outsider. Shortly before my formal conversion, I heard and took to heart a *derash* (Torah explanation) given by a convert. He discussed the injunction not to remind converts of their gentile origins in order not to embarrass them, and said that he tried to apply this even to himself.

At the outset, I converted partly to gain a new past and forget my own history. I embraced the tradition that a convert's Jewish parents are Abraham and Sarah, and not her biological parents. This is reflected in the Hebrew name I chose: *Alonah* (oak tree); only after the fact did I realize that in English my name was Alone.

Ironically, the conversion that I hoped would shut the door on my past has done the opposite. As I began to see myself as a Jew and not primarily a convert, I was surprised to find that Judaism helped me reclaim my pre-Jewish past. The commandment "Honor your father and mother" instructs us to remain connected to and respectful of our personal past. There is no exception for converts. Although I tried to ignore this *mitzvah* (commandment), I have come to see it as central to my ongoing conversion. My connection to my new community has allowed me to remember and mourn my past in new ways. I have confronted some family members and established new, more honest connections with others. I have apologized to those whom I have hurt, particularly by my attempt to renounce my past. Far from severing family ties, Judaism permits and encourages me to integrate them into my present life.

In turn, my family has begun relating to me as a Jew and thus strengthened my Jewish identity, sometimes in surprising ways. Last winter my husband and I visited the Alabama town where my mother's family has lived for six generations. We were the only Jews many of my relatives had ever met, and they received us with grace and interest. They asked about *kashrut* (kosher laws), branches of American Judaism, Israeli politics. We made *latkes* (potato pancakes) for a family dinner and surprised everyone by telling them that blackeyed peas and cornbread were kosher and frequently eaten in our home. The centrality of memory and community in Jewish thought gave me the willingness and strength to reclaim these relationships, and thus my own memory.

Conversion has transformed my whole life, although not in the dramatic way I originally expected. "Conversion" no longer means that now faraway ritual. Instead, it signifies the continual process of striving to live a more authentic Jewish life. I have learned that many Jews, not just converts, must work at that process. My husband was raised with a Jewish identity but no religious practices. We have studied together, and his overcoming a fierce resistance to Judaism was as much a conversion as my own. Recently, I complained to a friend, a rabbi's daughter, that I was not sure what I should do next to grow as a Jew; she responded that she too was wondering what to do next. No matter what our religious backgrounds, we all work to weave Judaism into our lives. As a Jew, my conversion continues for a lifetime.

Who We Are and What We Need: An Open Letter to the Jewish Community from a Jew by Choice

CATHERINE HALL MYROWITZ

"One thing have I asked of the Lord, this do I desire: That I may dwell in the house of the Lord all the days of my life, to behold the graciousness of the Lord, and to enter into God's sanctuary."
—PSALMS 27:4

Being a Jew feels to me as if I am wrapped in a garment—a luminous prayer shawl—an extra layer to protect me from this sometimes mad world and a boost in appreciating all the goodness that life makes possible. I have never wondered why anyone would become Jewish. If anything, I wonder why more people do not choose this way of life. Yet born Jews often ask me, in amazement, what attracted me to Judaism. This "open letter to the Jewish community" is really a love letter—an opportunity to let you know what attracts me, and the fifty or so converts I have interviewed, to the Jewish tradition. It is also a chance to register a few hints and instructions on how the established Jewish community might love us in turn, and make us even more welcome.

One of the great draws to Jews by choice is that Judaism is so life-affirming. Every Jew begins on an even footing, and in a state of possibility. In the Jewish tradition, there is no original sin or fire and brimstone. Born Jews may not realize how welcome such an outlook is.

Another appealing aspect of Judaism is that participation in the Jewish religion is in the hands of each individual. This responsibility is a welcome gift for many converts. A direct relationship with God, with no need for an intermediary, is compelling. The possibility to argue with God, or even to doubt the existence of God, and yet remain within the fold is most comforting, especially during times of spiritual crisis.

Catherine Hall Myrowitz, M.S.W., a Jew by choice, is a mother, wife, and, in between, a writer, farmer, and psychotherapist. She is the editor of *Finding A Home For the Soul: The Stories of Jews by Choice* (Jason Aronson, 1995), a collection of interviews.

I find the fact that God is not given human form enormously liberating, both from the standpoint of appreciating God's limitlessness and also because I need not envision God as gendered. All nouns in the Hebrew language are either male or female, and God is "linguistically" male. But in the case of Judaism, that has not been codified in an irrevocably male personage, as have Jesus, the "only son" and God, his Father.

Although women's position in traditional Judaism can be severely circumscribed, it carries relatively little of the baggage of the historical view of women in Christianity—either pure and virginal or lower in spiritual status and corruptive of men.

The *ketubbah* (marriage contract) with its protection and guarantees for women and the *Eshet Ḥayil* (poem about a valiant woman found in Proverbs 31, which is sung on Friday nights), though seen by some as quaint or sexist, can also be read as tender and loving. That Jewish law affirms a woman's right to sexual satisfaction in marriage is a subject that gets a lot of approving whoops and hollers at mixed Jewish/non-Jewish women's gatherings, as well as sober reflection on how such a positive view of female sexuality might affect a woman's spirit. For many converts, it was especially gratifying that Jewish culture accommodates and honors strong, vibrant female personalities. That these qualities are seen by most Jews as assets and not liabilities is quite remarkable to many formerly non-Jewish women.

Some women have found a comfortable and satisfying place for themselves in a traditional life with its firmly separate roles for men and women and strict observance of religious law. These women are focused on leading a God-centered life through Orthodoxy, and any dissonance they may feel between their identity as women and Jews is dispelled by their firm conviction that it is all part of God's plan for their lives.

Some converts face problems with observance not in terms of their own comfort or feminist philosophies, but because of their mates. Rabbis often ask potential converts whose mates are Jewish, "What will happen if, God forbid, your spouse dies or you get a divorce?" More rabbis should also ask, "What will happen if your spouse does not want to lead a Jewish life?" This, unfortunately, is not so rare an occurrence. The Jewish spouse may want a Jewish wedding, but not a Jewish marriage. Part of the problem may lie in the fact that a born Jew feels, rightly or wrongly, that he or she can just "be" Jewish. For the convert almost the only way to be Jewish is to "do" Jewish.

Ironically, a convert's loyalty to Judaism is often questioned because of the stereotype that we convert only to marry. As with many stereotypes, it contains a kernel of truth. But applied indiscriminately it causes hurt, misunderstanding, and, most significantly, masks a greater truth: Judaism is an all-encompassing value system and way of life that many people long for. Many converts searched for a faith-based lifestyle but never thought of choosing Judaism because of its seemingly inextricable link to culture and ancestry. Only when they met, fell in love with, and decided to marry a Jew were they exposed to the possibility of becoming Jewish themselves.

Since Jewish identity is traced matrilineally by Orthodox and Conservative Jews, as well as by the State of Israel, a woman must be Jewish in order for her children to be acknowledged as Jews by these segments of the community. This can put tremendous pressure to convert on a non-Jewish woman about to marry a Jewish man or to have a child.

Yet, the community has historically looked askance at "conversion for marriage." Since women are most often the ones seeking to convert they are exposed to a certain suspicion of the non-Jewish female. I have heard remarks that the non-Jewish woman or convert is somehow taking an available man from women who were born Jewish—a position not likely to engender feelings of sisterhood. Other biases: The woman, if she converts, is not really Jewish or does not have a Jewish "feeling" about her. She may not "look" Jewish. There is a supposition she will not be able to run a Jewish household or raise Jewish children. (A recent demographic study showed, however, that conversion of a non-Jewish spouse virtually guarantees that children will be raised as Jews.)[8]

One of the most appealing aspects of Judaism, the home-based nature of most ritual, can also be one of its biggest obstacles for the new Jew. Clearly, the home focus puts in the hands of each individual Jew the power to sanctify everyday life, as well as all the holidays and lifecycle events, and it helps to solidify and enrich family relationships. But just how do you go about it? Despite our positive efforts, many of us feel "culturally vulnerable." We are in need of guidance from Jews with more experience, but are sometimes too shy, embarrassed, or proud to ask.

Given the great gift we perceive Judaism to be and our efforts to embrace it fully, it is especially disconcerting to hear, as most of us have, that we should not become "too Jewish," or that we know more than a "real" Jew. Perhaps the Jewish community would do well to treat converts in keeping with the model offered by adoption: Just as adopted children are the *real* sons and daughters of their *real* (adoptive) parents, so are converts *real* Jews. Most of us are proud or at least do not mind others knowing of our "adoptive" status. But we do not tell our stories glibly or indiscriminately. If you are really interested to learn about us, ask—gently—and be prepared to sit a spell; there are no short or easy answers.

Genuine interest goes a long way toward making us feel welcome—both before and after conversion. Over and over again, my interviewees named the warmth and acceptance they experienced from Jewish people as the deciding factor in their conversion. Carrying the "adoption" analogy one step further, I cannot imagine a greater *mitzvah* (sacred obligation) than a Jewish family's adoption of someone newly Jewish. Of all the Jews by choice I interviewed, those who had the most positive view of Judaism and their own Jewish identity had all found a niche within the Jewish community where they felt a sense of belonging. Becoming part of a community gives the Jew by choice a sense of acceptance and a home-base from which to explore the many ways there are to be authentically Jewish.

Another aid in developing our Jewish lives is the discovery that many of the born Jews around us also have insecurities, doubts, and questions about how to be Jewish. It comes as a welcome realization that we have time—our whole lives, really—to develop into the Jews we want to be. It was also a relief to find that whether or not another Jew was willing to see me as part of *kelal yisra'el* (totality of the Jewish people) had more to do with that individual's personality, philosophy, and experience, than with any "official" position—traditional or modern—on converts or conversion.

I have used the terms "convert" and "Jew by choice" interchangeably. "Jew by choice" was an innovation, and ostensibly an improvement, over "convert." It implies a positive assertion of identity on the part of the new Jew, whereas "convert" implies passivity. Most converts/Jews by choice feel that those labels are transitional in any case. Once the transitional period is over, we generally identify ourselves and prefer to be identified simply as "Jews." The Jewish community has an important role to play in helping us make this transition. By welcoming us, seeing us as full and "normal" Jews, helping us to fill in any educational or experiential gaps, and being sensitive to the newness, and sometimes rawness, of our status, each individual Jew and the community as a whole can fulfill the commandment of loving the *ger* (stranger or convert). And you shall love the *ger*, "And you shall know the soul of the *ger*" (Exodus 23:9).

Meditation for the *Mikveh*

JANE LITMAN

"It is a fountain in the gardens, a well of living waters."
—SONG OF SONGS 4:15

Each of the following meditations can be recited, in turn, before the traditional three immersions in the ritual bath.

Letting Go of the Past (Gently)

Take a breath. Feel the water around you. Let it wash and cleanse every part of you. Think of things in your past that you need to let go. Let the water gently wash them away. Let the tender waves of the *mikveh* (ritual bath) carry off your hurts, let it cleanse your sore spots. Think of things in the past—finished relationships, negative behaviors, violations, and losses. Let this womb hold you. Feel its strength and purity. Let it wash away the pain and sadness. Think of things which will not be part of your life as a Jew. Allow yourself a moment of parting from these things. It is time to say goodbye to these pieces of your past. Watch them float away. Feel the warm water surround you, comfort you, bathe you. This is the womb of the Jewish people. Let it rebirth you as a Jew.

בָּרוּךְ אַתָּה יי אֱלֹהֵינוּ מֶלֶךְ הָעוֹלָם, אֲשֶׁר קִדְּשָׁנוּ בְּמִצְוֹתָיו וְצִוָּנוּ עַל הַטְּבִילָה.

Barukh attah adonai eloheinu melekh ha'olam, asher kiddeshanu bemitzvotav vetzivvanu al hatevilah.

Blessed are You *Adonai* Ruler of the Universe, who has sanctified us with the *mitzvot* (commandments) and commanded us concerning immersion.

Immerse.

Rabbi Jane Litman is on the faculty of California State University at Northridge and is the rabbi of Congregation Kol Simcha of Orange County.

Welcoming the Future (Slowly, Slowly)

Stretch your body. Breathe. Think of your future. Let the
water's spiritual tide bring your desire. What do you
want as a Jewish person? Feel the water wash you with
love, with contentment, with the joy of life, with the
presence of God. Imagine all the possibilities which
await you. Envision your Jewish self celebrating your
new identity. Bathe yourself in the promise of fulfillment
which your choices will bring.

בָּרוּךְ אַתָּה יי אֱלֹהֵינוּ מֶלֶךְ הָעוֹלָם, שֶׁהֶחֱיָנוּ וְקִיְּמָנוּ וְהִגִּיעָנוּ לַזְּמַן
הַזֶּה.

*Barukh attah adonai eloheinu melekh ha'olam, sheheheyanu vekiyye-
manu vehiggi'anu lazeman hazeh.*

Blessed are You *Adonai* Ruler of the Universe, who has kept us
alive and sustained us and enabled us to reach this time.

Immerse.

Feeling the Present (Keep It Slow)

Breathe. Feel the sense of your own well-being. Where
are you this moment? Feel your body...your toes, your
legs, your buttocks, your genitals, your belly. Feel the
water soothe your back; feel the wetness on your shoulders, your neck, your face, in your hair. Feel this
moment. Feel the life force in your body. Float in the
warm liquid, in the sacredness of this event. Feel the
mayim hayyim (living waters) merge with you. Feel your
connection to this place, to this moment, to the Jewish
people, the universe, and eternity.

שְׁמַע יִשְׂרָאֵל יי אֱלֹהֵינוּ יי אֶחָד.

Shema yisra'el adonai eloheinu adonai ehad.

Hear O Israel, *Adonai* Our God, *Adonai* is one.

Immerse.

12

Parenting

P arenting has certain unique features as a life passage. Having been married, one can be divorced; having taken part in a superficial Bat Mitzvah (coming of age ceremony for girls) as a twelve year old, one can decide to renew one's commitment as an Adult Bat Mitzvah. But parenting can be neither undone nor done over. My mother is fond of saying that there are only three irrevocable decisions: Parenthood, murder, and suicide. Everything else—joyful or tragic—is negotiable.

Not only does becoming a parent change forever and profoundly the course of one's life, it affects parents' perceptions of most other life passages. Various events and passages are filtered through the question: "What will this mean for the children?" In addition, children's passages reflect back on and can addend the meaning of a parent's own childhood experiences. It is common for parents to re-live and re-examine childhood issues through

255

their children, and the experience of parenthood depends in many ways on the meaning one ascribes to one's own childhood.

In the Rabbinic understanding, honoring parents is comparable to honoring God (BT *Kiddushin* 30b; JT *Kiddushin* 1:7). We generally focus on what this means for children, rather than what it means for parents to command such respect and wield such power. Being entrusted with the care of a soul—raising children to love others and themselves, to be good people and good Jews—has always been an awesome responsibility. Moreover, while there is an explicit biblical duty to honor parents (and not children), the Rabbis generally agree that our primary obligation is toward the generation that follows us, rather than the one which precedes us (BT *Sotah* 49a).

From a Jewish perspective, parenting may be the most important life passage. The commandment to have children is the very first commandment in the Bible (Genesis 1:28), and the commandment to teach one's children is an essential Jewish value, expressed in the *Shema* and *Ve'ahavta* (central prayer that declares God's oneness and the paragraph following, taken from Deuteronomy 6:4-9) three to five times daily, and on every Jewish doorpost. The place of children in Jewish life, and especially in home-centered ritual, is so central that those who do not have children often feel excluded or, at least, marginal. (See Chapters Two and Five.)

Parenting is not a quantifiable endeavor, but the tradition does specify certain responsibilities. For the father, these include circumcising sons, arranging for children's marriages, teaching sons to swim, and providing sons with training in a trade. Primarily, a father is obligated to teach or hire someone to teach his sons Torah and to provide financial maintenance for the needs of all his children, regardless of whether or not he is married to their mother (BT *Kiddushin* 29b–30b; *Shulḥan Arukh Yoreh De'ah* 245:1,4; *Even Ha'ezer* 58:1; 73:6, 7; 82:7). Mothers are obligated to care for young children (*Shulḥan Arukh Even Ha'ezer* 80:6-8) and traditionally teach daughters modesty and housekeeping skills. Custody generally goes to mothers for minor girls and for boys under age six, and to fathers for boys six and over, according to tradition (BT *Ketubbot* 102b-103a, *Shulḥan Arukh Even Ha'ezer* 82:7). However, custody, visitation, and any other agreements between parents are always negotiable, as long as the criterion for negotiations is the welfare of the children, and not the convenience or preference of the parents.

Over the years, these laws have been supplemented and reinterpreted. In our own day, most liberal Jews apply any and all parental requirements to both mother and father, and all benefits of such requirements to sons and daughters equally.

Although parenting is a highly personal passage and responsibility, it also has a communal and political dimension. According to Jewish law, parenting is a Jewish corporate charge, as well as an individual one. Traditionally, the entire Jewish population of a town can be excommunicated if they have twenty-five children (some say even fewer) and fail to provide a teacher for them, on the grounds that "the world is sustained only by the breath of children in the schoolhouse" (*Shulḥan Arukh Yoreh De'ah* 245:7f citing BT *Shabbat* 119b). In addition, the community as a whole is obligated to raise, educate, and provide dowries for orphans.

A major feminist critique of "the Jewish family" is precisely that the community has abdicated its responsibility for the next generation, and made of childrearing a privatized, domestic (read: women's) responsibility. Nessa Rapaport has noted that for all our professions of concern for Jewish continuity and Jewish family, the Jewish community has failed to provide Jewish childcare, day schools, and camps that are both excellent and affordable. She writes of the "unborn third child" that committed Jewish parents do not have, due largely to the high cost of Jewish living.[1]

Synagogues all support the Jewish family, of course, but how many have childcare during services and board meetings, and how many rabbis have had strained negotiations over maternity or paternity leave? The cry "I support the Jewish family, but I don't want *my* rabbi getting pregnant" is not so much an argument against women in the rabbinate, as it is a demonstration of the expectation that our male religious leaders and role models will not actively parent their children. Historian Dr. Paula Hyman has noted that, in the century before World War I and even until today, "the failings of Jewish mothers as transmitters of Jewish culture" were blamed for increasing rates of assimilation, as communal leaders "transformed assimilation from an individual to a familial act, from activity in the public (masculine) sphere to inactivity in the domestic (feminine) sphere."[2] Feminist Jews oppose such a stance by urging both sexes to participate in the domestic project of building a Jewish household and by charging Jewish public institutions to support parents actively and play their own roles in rearing the next generation.

Jewish parenting is more challenging than ever, not only due to inadequate community support, but because of such growing and various factors as street crime, gangs, divorce, drugs, cutbacks on afterschool activities, distance from extended family, and the need for many primary caretakers (usually mothers) to work full-time outside the home, as well. Today, we rear children with a more sophisticated awareness of self-esteem[3] and gender issues, yet parents themselves have little or no training in these areas. Feminist Jews attempt to offer our children something that we ourselves have never known: A milieu in which gender does not determine roles. And however far we may have come in creating non-sexist households, social messages and popular sex-role stereotypes seep in early and powerfully. Sex-role stereotypes are entrenched, even in homes that seek to eliminate them, and even, already, in the minds and behavior of preschoolers from feminist homes.[4] When feminist parents discover that boys make cannons of their baby carriages and girls make dollhouses of their fire trucks—a common anecdotal finding—they ask if some portion of gendered behavior may be genetically or developmentally programmed. This is a valid question to which we have, as yet, no answer. As long as there are so many social factors encouraging sex-role distinctions, it will be impossible to isolate biological vs. psychological vs. cultural variables.

In contemplating the creation of a Jewish feminist theory and practice of parenting, questions abound. For example, how do the traditional sex-differentiated laws affect us on practical or psychic levels? What does it mean to be a Jewish mother vs. a Jewish father vs. a Jewish parent? "Mothering" elicits associations that "parenting" does not, including the myth of the ideal mother and negative stereotypes of the passively aggressive or domineering Jewish mother. As women dismiss the need to be "perfect" and seek to reclaim the positive aspects of negative stereotypes (e.g. the investment and caring of the Jewish mother), they are not necessarily willing to give up positive associations, or to agree that mothers and fathers should ideally have the same styles, play the same roles, or make the same contributions. Are there things that fathers generally do better for sons, and mothers for daughters, or vice versa? Is it possible that the bonding which occurs with birth and/or the identification that children have with a parent of the same sex means that certain tasks are carried out more effectively, or simply differently, by one parent or the other? If so, what does that mean for single and gay or lesbian parents? How much are the ingrained images and roles of parents related to gender, and how much are they a function of the differences between primary and non-primary caregivers? Do boys and girls, especially given the differing social messages they continue to receive, require different messages or lessons at home? If so, what should these be? And is it even possible to generalize about these issues?

Considering the centrality of parenting in Jewish self-understanding and its importance for the Jewish future, it is shocking to realize that there is no comprehensive philosophy of Jewish parenting—feminist or otherwise—and little treatment of parenting as a religious enterprise. This chapter takes a significant step toward developing a religious Jewish feminist parenting ethic by identifying what we do that is sexist, and/or contravenes Jewish values (see Dr. Clara Frances Zilberstein's essay), as well as articulating affirmatively what Jewish feminist parenting should look like (see, for example, that same essay or those by Treasure Cohen and Dr. Ellen M. Umansky).

Treasure Cohen explores the entire parenting cycle as a series of occasions for holding on and letting go. She traces the image of the laying on and removal of hands from the time of infancy to, in the normal turn of events, a final reversal of roles in which children must let go of their parents, and let them die. While parenting an infant has little or nothing obvious in common with parenting a teenager, Cohen shows that the discontinuities in daily tasks may be balanced by consistent love for the child, an abiding identity and mission as a parent, and the continuing challenge to hold on or let go in the proper time. My grandmother used to say that the hardest thing about parenthood was getting your children through their mid-fifties. Cohen would add that even after that, challenges persist.

Dr. Clara Frances Zilberstein takes on several of the feminist issues cited earlier. Drawing on her experience as a family psychologist, she considers the narcissistic and destructive ways that parents relate to their children and impose their values. She also explores the tension between parenting as the custodianship of a child's individuality and parenting as the shaping of a child's mind and morals. This tension is expressed in the differing interpretations of Proverbs 22:6, depending on which word in the verse is emphasized: "Teach a child in the way *he* [sic] should go" supports the child's individuality and "teach a child in the way he *should* go" stresses the importance of moral instruction. In the end, Dr. Zilberstein cites the parent's ultimate motivation—whether self-gratification or care of the child—as the key to their quality as a parent, both in feminist and in Jewish terms.

The remaining essays in the parenting chapter cover a range of issues, and appear in chronological order, based on the ages of the children in focus. The contributors, all mothers, speak from their personal experience. Rabbi Debra Newman Kamin, echoing Cohen, mentions holding on and letting go—this time specifically in relation to weaning her son. She discusses her physical and emotional attachment to him, her needs as a mother, and her wish that a popular Jewish weaning ritual had been available to her. As it was not, she created one and shares it here.

Dr. Ellen M. Umansky addresses the question of how a feminist raises and relates to boys. While feminist childrearing offers an obviously positive message to daughters (it is OK to be strong and assertive; you can do anything you want—including become a cantor or the president of IBM), its message to boys has sometimes been interpreted as negative.[5] Boys may understand themselves to be identified with the "oppressor group." In addition, the positive messages that boys receive freeing them from stereotypical roles (it is OK to be gentle and empathic; you can do anything you want—including stay at home and raise children) are supported even less by the general society than are feminist messages to girls. Thus, adopting feminist values can mean pain for boys.

Dr. Umansky, the mother of three sons, offers a heartening perspective on these issues. She consciously forges connections with her sons in Jewish settings where there are traditionally distinctions—and sometimes a physical partition—between men and women. She also asserts that, for all the surface differences, she would treat daughters no differently than her boys, and would wish for them exactly the same freedoms, insights, and blessings.

In the final piece, Rabbi Sue Levi Elwell explores the theme of struggle and potential heartbreak in the teen years. She talks of a family Sabbath that does not fit the storybooks: The traditional foods are store-bought, the parents are divorced, the children rebel against enforced family time and traditional rituals, and the mother, a rabbi, is oftentimes away, helping other families to have a peaceful *Shabbat* (Sabbath). Yet, come Friday night, everyone sits down at a table with a clean cloth, the candles are lit, special foods are laid out, prayers are said, and *Shabbat* in this single-parent household is not only good enough, it is good.

There is a dark side to parenting—in terms of parental self-doubts, child abuse, children acting out with painful or even dangerous forms of rebellion, painful pulls that parents experience between their children's needs and their own or between their home life and their work life. Many parents resist letting go of their children or even accepting their children for and as who they are. Much of this is acknowledged by the authors in this chapter. In the end, though, they stress the other side: The love in healthy parent-child relationships that makes sacrifices worthwhile.

Between Parent and Child:
Holding On and Letting Go

TREASURE COHEN

"Barukh shepetarani me'onsho shel zeh. *Blessed is God who
has released me from responsibilities for this child.*"
—GENESIS *RABBAH* 63:10

Our eyes were fixed on her every movement, our mouths lipsync-
ing the notes of trope we had memorized over the past several
months. She was no longer a child and not yet a woman, but a
graceful hologram of the two. Although we sat in the congregation
and she stood before us on the *bimah* (pulpit), our hearts were
invisibly tethered to hers, as our daughter Esther presented herself
as a *bat mitzvah* (juridical Jewish adult). We who had given her life
and supported her over the past twelve years, held our breath as
she made her passage to Jewish adulthood alone. Witnessing our
daughter lead the congregation in prayer, chant the Torah and
Haftarah (prophetic reading), and teach a community of adults, we
saw her as a separate and successful individual who stood and
would be able to stand without us.

And Esther saw it too—a vision of her own independence and
competence. After sharing her personal thank-yous before the congregation, she addressed us with her own plea: "Mom and Dad,
please understand that I am getting older and at times want my
space. So here's my deal—let me have my space, and most likely
when I get older, I might not want it so much." Her gentle cries for
independence echoed the blessing which parents traditionally
recite at Bnei Mitzvah (coming of age ceremonies), signalling a
shift in their parental role: "*Barukh shepetarani me'onsho shel zeh.*"
Blessed is God who has released me from responsibilities for this
child.

Treasure Cohen is a Jewish family educator, teacher of young children, and
mother of four.

Holding On and Letting Go

At such a pivotal moment in the child's life, it is not easy for parents to offer "space" or "release," when up to this point, good parenting has largely meant holding on. In Hebrew, the word for "hand" (*yad*) and the word for "loving" (*yedid*) both derive from the same uniconsonantal root d.[6] Any parent knows that this is no coincidence, since loving our young is a hands-on process. At the moment of birth we are handed a squirming infant and taught to hold her closely and securely to ensure lasting bonds. From that point on, we nurse, embrace, and support the child emotionally as well as physically. Every *Shabbat* (Sabbath) we bless her with our hands, and we pull her close to us when she needs assurance and security. Our instincts teach us that holding on to our children is a way of showing love.

But even young children push our hands away. They do not always want the protection we can offer them. No matter how loving our intentions or how effective our help, we often hear our little ones protest, "I can do it myself!" Their instincts tell them there are times when we have done enough, when our involvement keeps them from growing.

Interestingly, the Hebrew word for "enough" (*dai*) also derives from the same root as "hand" (*yad*) and "loving" (*yedid*). There is a visual connection between *yad* and *dai*, for hands that are filled to overflowing contain "enough." And there are times in every relationship between parent and child when we have given enough. At that point, we must show our love to our children by taking our hands away and releasing our children to themselves. Parenting is largely a matter of finding *yedid* between *yad* and *dai*.

Yad and *dai* are good images for setting limits on parental control, since hands that parent are not always loving and gentle. Hands used to nurture can also be misused to hurt or hit or restrain a child from growing. And *dai* may be an especially important word for women who have been taught that a good (Jewish) mother does "everything" for her children. For such women, learning to say "enough" is important for their sanity, their children's growth, their own self-esteem, and the example they provide to their children.

Being a Child—Being a Parent

Remember the ritual of learning to ride a two-wheeler? We clutched the handlebars as our parents held the seat behind us. We begged and pleaded, "Don't let go!" Yet we knew that if they did not, we would never learn to ride. Our parents ran along behind us, pushing the bike forward, and then suddenly released. Although we sometimes fell, at one magic moment we were able to sail along without the hands that held us. To re-experience this ritual as a parent can be powerful, since we can see ourselves in our children, even as we play a new role.

No matter how old we become, memories of our own childhoods frame our perspectives. Most of our parents worked hard to give us security and support, but sometimes we had to challenge their judgment simply to prove that we could take care of ourselves. Despite their desire to protect us from pain and sorrow, they could and would not quell the life force that drove us to make mistakes and take risks as we asserted our independence. Whether by peaceful means or volatile struggle, we all have to free ourselves from our parents' hands to prove to ourselves and to them that we can stand alone.

Our own children may not perceive that we too needed—and perhaps still need—to separate ourselves from our parents' hands in order to become ourselves. If fifty year olds sometimes take parental advice to "Take it easy," "Drive carefully!" or "Stay home after dark!" as fighting words, it is because they still struggle to establish their autonomy in relation to their parents.

Esther might not believe it, but as a thirteen year old, I too wanted my space and autonomy. Most of the time my parents gave me leeway, but every now and then they set a standard that gave me no options. Despite my heated protests, I was forced to attend and graduate from Hebrew High School. Although I begged to be allowed to attend fancy Bar Mitzvah parties on Friday nights, my mother refused, explaining that one does not teach a child to exalt *Shabbat* one week and ignore it the next. Now I am middle-aged and my parents are no longer alive, and still their voices and values reverberate in my head. These messages influence me, especially when I deal with setting limits for my own children, and have to decide when to use a "heavy hand" and when a "light touch."

Our sixteen-year-old daughter jumps back and forth between wanting our hands off and expecting our hands to catch her when she teeters or falls. On *Shabbat*, she vigorously shakes her father's hands from her head, but graciously accepts his blessing when he offers it from six inches above. She is teaching us the equivocal nature of nurturing her, and we have learned that it is a fine art to know when to reach out and when to allow her to find her own balance.

When our son left for college two years ago, we sought a ritual to mark this passage which would quite literally take him "out of our hands." His leave-taking coincided with the Torah portion *Ki Tavo* (Deuteronomy 26:1-11) about the ritual surrounding the giving up of first fruits in the sanctuary. The Torah details how we are supposed to present our offering, look back over our history, release the offering, and celebrate. We saw a parallel between that ceremony for giving up first fruits and our own passage of giving up our firstborn to a world outside our own. We marked the occasion by remembering and reviewing the past and then releasing our son with celebration and wistful joy. We recalled selections from the same formula said by the Israelite pilgrims:

אֲרַמִּי אֹבֵד אָבִי, וַיֵּרֶד מִצְרַיְמָה, וַיָּגָר שָׁם בִּמְתֵי מְעָט, וַיְהִי־שָׁם לְגוֹי גָּדוֹל עָצוּם וָרָב. וְעַתָּה הִנֵּה הֵבֵאתִי אֶת־רֵאשִׁית פְּרִי הָאֲדָמָה אֲשֶׁר־נָתַתָּה לִי יי . . . .

Arammi oved avi, vayered mitzraymah, vayagor sham bimtei me'at, vayhi-sham legoy gadol atzum varav. Ve'attah hinneh heveti et-reshit peri ha'adamah asher-natattah li adonai.

My ancestor was a nomadic Aramean, who went down to Egypt and sojourned there with few in number, but became there a nation great, mighty, and populous. And now behold I have brought the first fruits which You have given me, O God...(Deuteronomy 26:5, 10).

When he first came home from college, our son was determined not to re-fill the empty space he had left in our home and heart. He held fiercely to his independence. Initially, there was a strained impasse: We wanted to embrace him; he feared that we would engulf him. It once again became clear that we had to be willing to let go.

While all parents know that they will eventually have to release their children, it is more difficult for children to accept that they will someday lose their parents. As I thought, in writing this essay, about my children asking me to let go of them, I was jolted by a powerful memory I had buried. I remembered standing at my mother's death bed after months of watching her gradually lose her grip on life. In an unexpected burst of clarity, she turned to me and pleaded, "Treasure, let go of me!" Much to my surprise, she was asking me to relinquish control that I did not know I had, and to give her permission to leave me. In the merging voices of my dying mother and my growing children, I now understand that holding on and letting go are part of a continuous life dynamic in which parent and child may someday find their roles reversed.

Children may grow, change, separate, and individuate, but parents remain parents. No matter how old and independent our children become, we as parents still worry about them, endure their pain, try to protect them from sadness and disappointment, and rejoice in their achievements. They are our precious creations and we are intimately and infinitely bound to them. Yet we must accept that they are not our possessions—that we must gradually give up control and let them take it. And this is not a rite that can be experienced in a day—at a Bat Mitzvah or other ceremony of passage. Rather it happens in a dance that is choreographed over many years and through many experiences.

At our synagogue, the choreography of the Bar or Bat Mitzvah ceremony represents this in miniature: First we see a child standing before the congregation embracing and cradling the Torah, just as her/his parents once held her/him. Then s/he walks around the sanctuary supporting the Torah, and the parents follow, supporting their child, in turn. The youngster leads the congregation in prayer, chants from the Torah, and shares her/his learning. Now as s/he returns the Torah to the ark, s/he marches around the sanctuary without parents behind. Thus, we symbolize a young Jew's achievement of separation and success.

Sometimes in joy and sometimes in pain, we gradually let go of our children and let them support themselves completely. To achieve this, we must have faith in them and they must have faith in themselves. Thus, together we will find the loving balance between *yad* and *dai*.

Of *Naḥas* and Narcissism

CLARA FRANCES ZILBERSTEIN

"Only a person who lives in a way which is compatible with the mystery of human existence is capable of evoking reverence in a child. The basic problem is the parent, not the child."
—ABRAHAM JOSHUA HESCHEL, *THE WISDOM OF HESCHEL*

The Challenge

Raising children is said to be the most challenging of tasks; raising happy and fulfilled children more difficult yet. Imparting Jewish values that children truly integrate adds to the task. The goal of raising children with feminist sensibilities who truly integrate Jewish values into lives that are happy and fulfilled is monumental.

Is it possible? Most parents have their hands full just getting their children through a day of carpool, dentist appointments, homework, as well as endless enrichment activities, including sports, tutoring, computers, and the creative arts. What most complicates childrearing, however, and keeps it from being simple rests in the parent. Parents are full of expectations. From the moment of conception, they begin to develop images of who and what they want their child to be. Hopes, dreams, and aspirations are fine as long as they do not cloud the parent's perception of who their child actually is, and becomes. Unfortunately, parents often have difficulty distinguishing what they want for their child from what their child wants; who they think their child should be, from who their child actually is. Most parents think that if they are the kind of parents they wish they had, they are seeing and hearing their children. They tend to guess or assume they know their children instead of developing a healthy curiosity about them.

Narcissism and *Naḥas* (Joy)

The formidable problem of parenting takes on a particular color in the Jewish family. We have a concept in Jewish life called *naḥas*.

Dr. Clara Frances Zilberstein is a clinical psychologist in private practice and serves on the clinical faculty of the University of California, Los Angeles School of Medicine as trainer/supervisor of psychology interns.

This Yiddishism comes from the Hebrew word *"naḥat"* meaning ease or pleasure. *"Naḥas"* is popularly understood as pleasure and pride derived from the success of children.

Many jokes reflect this concept of *naḥas*. "When is a fetus considered viable according to Jewish law?" asks one. Answer: "When it graduates from medical school." Being a doctor means prestige, money, and respect—but for whom? "Yes, of course, I enjoy the praise and recognition," a parent might answer, "but the desire is for the child's good, not mine. This is what would make my child happy."

The assumption is that if children are a source of *naḥas* to their parents, they will automatically be a source of *naḥas* to themselves. There is nothing wrong with parents wanting their children to be successful and productive people. The question is, at what cost? *Naḥas*-laden careers meet the narcissistic needs of parents. "I have a child who is a doctor, a lawyer, a rich businessperson. I must be very good. And I sacrificed everything to assure my child's future."

Asked if they want their children to be happy and fulfilled, any parent would answer in the affirmative. However, many parents would also convince themselves that the well-being of their children actually matches their own desires. And if this means a little less fulfillment to the children, if this means sacrificing a bit of the child's spirit, creativity, or freedom, then so be it. "They will thank me later," parents tell themselves, as they guide their children to choose the path of *naḥas*.

Almost all parents have a degree of narcissism. Narcissism is often present when the parent feels most sacrificed or sacrificing. On a deep level, parents want to lovingly meet every need of their children. When the needs become overwhelming, the parent often rejects the child's right to have needs. At bottom, parents may be angry at their children for having needs they cannot fill. In that moment when love is frustrated and parents lash out in anger, they are more in tune with their own need to fulfill the child's need, than with the child's right to have a need, whether or not it can be met.

Naḥas, Narcissism, and Gender

Generally, *naḥas* tends to be gender related. Parents have different expectations for their sons than for their daughters. Until the present generation, and still to some extent today, most parents expect domestic success from their daughters and worldly success from their sons. If parents are narcissistic and have preconceived notions about "feminine" behavior and women's life goals, they will subtly coerce their daughters into conforming to their expectations, with little regard for who their daughters actually are or what they want and need. Often these expectations get lodged in the daughter's psyche at such an early stage, that by the time she is in a position to choose for herself what she wants to do in life, she has fully absorbed her parents' expectations and thinks they are her own. Her own ability to want, strive, or fantasize in a direction different from the one foisted on her becomes stunted and stifled.

The narcissistic parent does the same thing to boys. The results of the dynamic are generally less stifling to boys because the roles ascribed to them are more expansive. Nevertheless, similar problems emerge. If the parent has a need for a son to be a doctor, and that son desires another professional expression, he will suffer the same consequences and pain as an unseen daughter.

If children make their parents' expectation their own, even when it is antithetical to their nature and spirit, there will be a price to pay internally, intrapsychically, and ultimately, in the parent-child relationship. In the meantime, however, that child can feel love and acceptance—gifts which narcissistic parents often withhold if their expectations are not met.

Clearly, the ideal is for parents to rise above their discomfort and be willing to see children for who they are. This means creating a safe and contained environment in which they can explore their many curiosities and interests, and stepping back and allowing them to grow according to their own destiny and destination.

Narcissism and the Jewish Question

How then does one impart Jewish values and observance—systems that are binding and certainly restricting—and still allow children to grow according to their own spirits? Surely parents must have a vehicle for teaching values in which they are allowed to shape and mold their children—truly for their children's good.

As Jews, we believe that following Torah, in its varied interpretations, is the best way of life, and essential to a fulfilled life. Both the narcissistic parent and the developed parent may feel an obligation to teach Judaism to their children. Unfortunately, for the narcissistic parent, the content of Judaism becomes just like any other content—another opportunity to collect *naḥas*.

It is the obligation of Jewish parents to impart a serious sense of self while transmitting Jewish values to both sons and daughters. To do that effectively, parents must take their children seriously and model an attitude of individual personhood, entitlement, and self-acceptance. This can only be done by parents who are "clean," whose focus is on the needs of the child. These healthy parents are capable of imparting Judaism for its own sake, because it is a parent's obligation, because it is essential to the child—not because of the *naḥas* value.

Accepting a child, taking a child seriously, hearing and seeing a child, does not mean that parents place no demands on children, nor does it mean that children alone set the pace and tempo of their lives. Parents have a right to have children make their beds, conduct themselves politely, finish tasks, and keep promises, whether or not the child "wants to." The place from which parents make their demands, however, is essential in preserving the spirit of the child. Too many parents are motivated by their need for control or power.

Parents have a right to instill a Jewish way of life. However, the model for listening to children must be adhered to even in this important area. Often, I see children "act out" in religious contexts because that is the most devastating way to retaliate against a parent who refuses to see them. The intensity of the parent's response when stirred to fury feels like a connection to the child and actually reinforces the acting out. When children rebel against going to Hebrew school or synagogue, parents tend to extremes, either ignoring the child's feelings and forcing attendance, or giving up and allowing the child to drop out. Judaism itself provides a model for how to deal with this. The phrase uttered by the Jewish people in response to being offered the Torah—*na'aseh venishma* (we will do and then we will understand)—is a refreshing model for approaching a child's doubts. Parents can help children continue Jewish practice (*na'aseh*—insisting on attendance) while children pursue answers to a search for meaning that is deemed legitimate by parents (*venishma*—keeping dialogue open). There is so much to find out about and discuss when a child wishes to quit religious education. The healthy parent welcomes expressions of autonomy and wonders how best to facilitate the child's journey into a more resilient and meaningful relationship to Judaism. The narcissistic parent is threatened by a child's autonomy and worries about what the neighbors will think.

The *Amidah* (series of blessing which is the centerpiece of every prayer service) begins, "Blessed are You, our God, the God of our forbears: The God of Abraham, the God of Isaac, the God of Jacob." This seemingly cumbersome form is used to indicate that each had to seek and come to God in his own way. This is a magnificent model for raising Jewish children, the understanding that each child must be free to seek and explore an individual relationship with God, in the context of knowledge, ritual, and a model of belief and practice provided by their parents.

As Jews committed to the perpetuation of Judaism, the challenge is to impart Judaism without imposing it. The more self-aware a parent is, the more that parent can see the child. Seeing a child is the antidote to forcing on the child what does not and should not belong to the child. Moreover, seeing a child will enhance the possibility for Judaism to take root and become a lasting way of life. It is the parent's obligation to recognize his or her own narcissism and to reject the "*nahas*" method of parenting. Parents who have boundaries and relate to the child as another help to nourish and nurture a true other in their children. It is the less manipulative, more difficult, self-sacrificing, and fulfilling way to raise children. Too few parents actually choose it.

A Jewish Weaning Ritual

DEBRA NEWMAN KAMIN

"What will your meals be? Bread, rice, and halvah,
and manna sprinkled over."
                              —KURDISTANI JEWISH FEEDING RHYME

My father-in-law was excited by a sermon he heard in synagogue one *Shabbat* (Sabbath) morning. He told me it was all about appreciating the little things in life, "small events" that sometimes go unnoticed. He asked me if I was aware that when Sarah weaned Isaac, Abraham had thrown a party. The rabbi used this event to illustrate the point that our ancestors paid attention to something as "unimportant" as weaning a child.

My interpretation of the biblical source is much different. The weaning of my first son was neither "an event" nor was it "small." It was a process that lasted for several months and was full of mixed emotions.

After nine months of pregnancy and six months of nursing, there was a part of me that longed to have my body back and no longer be physically tied to the needs of another. I wanted to lose the weight I had gained during pregnancy so that I might feel attractive in a non-maternal way. Yet I had other feelings looking at my beautiful son, bone of my bone, flesh of my flesh. How could I want to separate from this creature? Part of me still wanted him in my womb. Breastfeeding was the one thing only I could do for him. After he was weaned anyone could care for him; he would no longer need me. A bit melodramatic to be sure, but then again who called this process easy? A small thing? Perhaps for the father, perhaps for other mothers. I found it confusing and difficult.

My oldest son is now two years old. I weaned him at nine and a half months. The physical cessation happened quickly, over just a few days. To my dismay after three days of refusing to let him nurse he totally forgot about it and happily took a bottle instead. It hurt to be replaced so easily.

Rabbi Debra Newman Kamin is the associate rabbi at Am Yisrael Congregation in Northfield, Illinois. She was the Conservative movement's first female rabbi in the Chicago area.

I now have a second son, at the time of this writing just two months old. I vowed that with this baby I would be more relaxed. I would give him a bottle once a day right from the beginning. I have not been able to bring myself to do it. People told me that my older son might start asking to nurse again when he saw his little brother doing so. For weeks nothing happened. Oddly enough, I found myself saddened. I realized that I wanted to hold this big boy, my first-born, and once again lift him to my breast.

After a few weeks, when I least expected it, he came to me and pointed to my breast. "Shai eat?" he asked. Following the advice in all the baby books, I blandly offered him my breast. He took a look, then glanced up at me with an uninterested expression as if to say "What's the big deal?" and walked away.

There is no going backwards with my older son; his days of babyhood are over. But I do try to learn to pay attention. In that respect my father-in-law's rabbi was right: This time goes by so quickly, and each moment is so precious. And Abraham and Sarah were right also. The weaning of a child, their first real step towards independence, deserves a party.

Unfortunately Judaism has no ritual to mark this event in a woman's and baby's life. When thinking about rituals for weaning it is important to remember that it is a process, not a one-time event. Therefore we need markers that can be done over time. I developed the following ritual framework for weaning.

Declaring the Intention

הִנְנִי מוּכָנָה וּמְזֻמֶּנֶת . . .

Hineni mukhanah umezummenet

I am prepared and ready to hold on and to let go—to fulfill the *mitzvah* (commandment) of rearing this child.

Offering Blessings

I then included the beautiful blessings written by Marcia Falk:

נְבָרֵךְ אֶת עֵין הַחַיִּים, וְנִשְׁזוֹר אֶת סְרִיגֵי חַיֵּינוּ בְּמָסֹרֶת הָעָם.

Nevarekh et ein haḥayyim, venishzor et serigei ḥayyeinu bemasoret ha'am.

Let us bless the Source of life as we weave the branches of our lives into the tradition.

נְבָרֵךְ אֶת מַעְיַן חַיֵּינוּ, שֶׁהֶחֱיֵנוּ וְקִיְּמֵנוּ וְהִגִּיעֵנוּ לַזְּמַן הַזֶּה.

Nevarekh et ma'yan ḥayyeinu sheheḥeyanu vekiyyemanu vehig-gi'anu lazeman hazeh.

Let us bless the Flow of life that revives us, sustains us, and brings us to this time.

As an alternative to this second blessing, one could recite the traditional Sheheḥeyanu *(blessing for reaching a new or momentous occasion).*

בָּרוּךְ אַתָּה יי אֱלֹהֵינוּ מֶלֶךְ הָעוֹלָם, שֶׁהֶחֱיֵנוּ וְקִיְּמֵנוּ וְהִגִּיעֵנוּ לַזְּמַן הַזֶּה.

Barukh attah adonai, eloheinu melekh ha'olam, sheheḥeyanu vekiyye-manu vehiggi'anu lazeman hazeh.

Blessed are You, God, Ruler of the Universe, who has kept us in life and sustained us and enabled us to reach this time.

You can repeat the statement of intention and the blessings daily, weekly or monthly from the beginning of the weaning process.

Celebrating Completion

At the end of weaning I repeated the statement of intention and the blessings and concluded with Genesis 21:6-8. "Sarah said 'God has brought me laughter, everyone who hears will laugh with me....' The child grew up and was weaned, and Abraham held a great feast on the day Isaac was weaned."

One could also personalize a modern naming blessing, adapt-ed from the liturgy of *Brit Milah* (covenant of circumcision ritual) by phrasing parts of it in the first person.[7] While the duty to raise the child falls on both parents, this is a very special moment for the mother.

> "My God and God of my ancestors, I thank you for the precious gift of life and for the blessing of parenthood which has allowed me to share in the miracle of creation. Grant this child length of days and vigor of body and mind. Endow me with love and understanding that my partner and I may raise this child imbued with love of Torah and the performance of good deeds. May we be privileged to bring (her/him) to the wedding canopy."

In the tradition of Abraham, your partner, friend, or other relative could make you a special dinner following the completion of the weaning process.

It is important to stress that the mother is still vitally important to the child and his/her nurturance, even though the child is weaned. This may sound obvious, but a mother may want reassurance.

I wish I had had personal reassurance and religious acknowledgement when I was going through this passage with my first son. Although I was stimulated by having to create a weaning ritual, I wish that my tradition had provided it, that this lifecycle event could have been part of my Jewish heritage. Let's hope that it will for our daughters.

On Being the Mother of Sons

ELLEN M. UMANSKY

"The angel of God said to her further,'Behold you are with child and shall bear a son....'"
—GENESIS 16:11

Several months ago, my cousin, who is the mother of two sons, told me about a women's group of which she is a member. All of the members have sons, but no daughters. Their purpose in getting together is simply to talk about their experiences as women raising sons in households where they are the only woman.

I often find myself feeling a special bond to women who, like my cousin and me, have sons and no daughters. I feel this bond particularly with other American, middle-class women who have young sons, as I do. Chances are, we will have many of the same toys strewn throughout our homes, will know the same TV shows, will tell similar potty-training stories, and wash pint-sized superhero underpants of identical designs.

Women who have both sons and daughters may also share the above, but those of us who have only sons are more inundated with male activity and possessions. This intensifies as our sons get older and become more involved in sports, collecting and trading baseball cards, playing after school only with other boys, inviting only boys to their birthday parties, etc. Male-identification also intensifies periodically as a part of boys' development and generally increases when boys are exposed to sex-role stereotypes at their schools and clubs.

As much as I would love to have a daughter, for me, as a feminist, the prospect of watching my three sons grow into manhood does not fill me with a feeling of aloneness. I do not see their immersion in traditionally male activities as excluding me, nor do I see their growing up, leaving home, and embarking on a career as signalling their entering into a man's world from which I, as a woman, will necessarily feel excluded. The truth is, my hopes and

---

Dr. Ellen M. Umansky is the author of numerous essays and books on women and Judaism, including the co-edited *Four Centuries of Jewish Women's Spirituality: A Sourcebook* (Beacon Press, 1992).

dreams for my sons are the same as those I would have for a daughter. If I have succeeded in conveying anything to my sons in relation to gender it is that there *are* differences between men and women, both biological and cultural, but that these differences should in no way predetermine their lives and choices.

As a liberal Jew, I am not part of a Jewish community in which men and women take on (or are taught to assume) sex-differentiated roles. My sons already take for granted the fact that men and women can be, and are, rabbis, cantors, and temple educators. At home, we recite, as a family, the blessings over the kindling of Sabbath lights as well as the *Kiddush* and *Motzi* (blessings recited over wine and bread, respectively).[8] The Jewish community of which my sons and I are a part is one in which men and women sit together in worship, can be called to the Torah together, and count equally as members of the congregation. I in no way mean to denigrate Orthodoxy, and I believe that Orthodox women who are the mothers of sons develop different channels through which they and their sons can feel close to one another as Jews. For me, however, it is essential that my participation in the Jewish community does not physically, ritually, or emotionally pull me away from my sons, but rather draws me closer to them.

On the other hand, I recognize that choosing to have a traditional *Brit Milah* (covenant of circumcision ritual) for all three of my sons meant participating in what is in many ways a male bonding ritual. Some have claimed that *Brit Milah* symbolically represents a replacing of the primal mother-son bond with a culturally created physical and emotional bond between son and father. In any case, *Brit Milah* remains for many liberal Jews, including me, the exception to the claim that our Jewish community is not sex-differentiated. Nonetheless, by framing the traditional ceremony of *Brit Milah* within a naming ceremony that I had created for each birth, the occasion of *Brit Milah* became not an occasion of emotional separation, but rather an intimate celebration which my husband and I chose to share with family and friends.

Eleven days before the birth of my second son, Ezra, I wrote a prayer expressing both my feelings about the anticipated birth and my hopes for my second son-to-be. It still conveys my hopes not only for Ezra but also for Abraham and Seth, his brothers. I include it here as a personal record of what motherhood has meant, and continues to mean, to me.

Dear God,

I have been blessed with the greatest gift that any human being can have: The ability to create a new life. The life that now stirs inside me, getting ready to free himself from my womb, is entering a private world of love amidst a public world of fear and hate, poverty and illness—a world that may self-destruct before he reaches adulthood. Help me to teach him that both of these worlds are real, to make him understand that believing things will inevitably turn out all right or that people always get what they deserve is naive, to show him that life without love is empty, that one must learn how to love in order to be loved by others. Guide me to teach him the importance of self-respect and of personal integrity, the necessity of taking risks though not blindly, the nobility of striving to do well, the value of rest and relaxation. Help him gain the wisdom to know which of his parents' attributes are worthy of emulation. And help him to view Judaism lovingly yet critically, teaching him, as you have taught me, that Judaism is not just a pre-established set of laws or customs that one inherits, but a four-thousand-year-old spiritual journey to which we have been born to participate, help navigate, and claim as our own. Amen.

A Family Sabbath: Dreams and Reality

SUE LEVI ELWELL

"Come in peace, angelic messengers of peace."
— *"SHALOM ALEIKHEM,"* SABBATH SONG
BASED ON BT *SHABBAT* 119B

I long for a Friday when I rise, help my children off to school, shop, cook, and ready myself and my house for *Shabbat* (Sabbath). In my dreams, I pick up one daughter from school and welcome her home to a house filled with the smells of carrots, onions, and fresh noodle pudding. She sets the table, running her hand lovingly over my grandmother's embroidered cloth, humming to herself as she sets out the *kiddush* cup (special cup or goblet used when reciting the blessing over wine on sacred occasions), the *hallah* (braided egg bread), the candlesticks. She remembers that once as a small child, she chided me for setting the *Shabbat* table in the kitchen instead of the dining room. "The angels need to see the white tablecloth and the candles burning," she warned. "They won't come if we sit in the kitchen." She laughs, the twelve year old delighting in her five-year-old self.

As the day wanes, my older daughter comes home from the bakery where she works after school, carrying *hallot* under her arm. The girls tease one another, arguing about who will take the first shower. One lingers in the kitchen while I stir the soup, and we talk about the friends who are about to arrive, as the *matzah* balls nod to one another in the steaming broth. In my dreams, this happens every week.

In real life, *Shabbat* with my daughters is a rare pleasure. When we are together, our dance is one of approach and retreat. My *Shabbat* is not theirs. We do not agree on who should share our table, on what to eat, on which tunes to sing or prayers to say. Each daughter has her own complaints: "I already made *Shabbat* in school today" or: "If you think that this is going to ensure that I'll be Jewish when I can choose for myself, you're wrong." I try to remember: How was this different before I became a rabbi and

Rabbi Sue Levi Elwell, Ph.D., is the founding director of the American Jewish Congress Feminist Center, in Los Angeles.

had to work on too many *Shabbatot*? I am now absent on many
Friday nights, making *Shabbat* for other families while longing for
my own home, my own table, my own children at my side. How
was this different before the divorce? We were more careful then,
more afraid of loud voices and disagreements, always aware of
the delicate balance we maintained. They were smaller then, more
compliant, less opinionated, and less bruised by the world.

Our lives, our *Shabbatot*, have changed. And as I sit at the head
of our table, I think of the women throughout Jewish history who
have presided at *Shabbat* tables by default or by design, women
who have guided children as contentious as mine into a *Shabbat* of
nourishing food and healing song. I think of the many women
who juggle their passion for teaching Judaism with their love for
their families. I think of women like me who have realized our
dreams in *Shabbatot* that exist in real time, with real families.

Even without freshly-baked *kugel* (noodle pudding) or guests
we all agree upon, *Shabbat* arrives. The table is set with a white
cloth, and the candles are placed in their holders. She *does* remember the *ḥallah*, and we begin to sing. And then, between the
Kiddush and *Motzi* (blessings recited over wine and bread, respectively), each of my daughters grudgingly grants me a moment,
and I whisper my blessing into their ears. Then, the angels once
again surround our table.

13

Midlife

Our experience of midlife is quite different from that of even a few generations ago. On the most basic demographic level, we live longer, and midlife lasts longer. At the turn of the century in the United States, life expectancy was forty-seven years, and only four percent of the population passed their sixty-fifth birthday. Women, who were subject to repeated pregnancies and complications of pregnancy and childbirth, had a shorter life expectancy than men.[1] Today, women live longer than men—on average, to age eighty in Western countries.

In addition to "real time" gained, especially by women, medical progress and new approaches to aging have delayed the perceived onset of "old age" and thus further extended midlife. Extended, too, is the phenomenon of a "sandwich generation," who because of their parents' increased life span and their tendency to delay childbirth, may bear responsibility for growing children and elderly parents simultaneously, and for decades at a time. Since it is still mostly women who care for both children and the elderly, this dual midlife responsibility devolves primarily on women. The protracted period of caretaking reverses a century-long, steady decline in the time American women spend tending to others. Thus, especially for women, midlife has become a longer and more demanding passage than ever before.

The last few years have brought an explosion of books and rituals dealing with midlife, especially menopause. Many of these uncover and criticize the popular cultural understanding of menopause and post-menopausal women. Women in and after midlife are, in a variety of subtle and not-so-subtle ways, deemed inadequate or superannuated. As they are infertile, they cannot fulfill what many still consider their "truest" function. Even with careful attention to diet and exercise, it becomes increasingly difficult, if not impossible, to meet this society's criteria for (youthful) beauty. In some cultures, women gain status after menopause, because they are no longer subject to a blood taboo and/or because they join the ranks of male leaders.[2] In our society, however, menopausal women cannot easily step into leadership roles that have generally been filled by men. Feminists who study menopause and midlife debunk rigid stereotypes, seek to free women and men from sex-role division, and oppose the characterization of menopause as a disease. Cross-cultural studies have shown that women experience dis-ease during menopause in direct proportion to the degree of their decline in social possibilities and prestige at midlife.[3]

There is contention among women over the new focus on menopause and its ritual celebration. Some caution that this focus may return us to an identification of women primarily or exclusively with their biological functioning. Others see the focus on menopause as a reflection of the fact that the women's movement and its leaders have come of (middle) age, and of their determination to explore and celebrate every aspect of women's lives. This means reclaiming and honoring biology and embodiment as important aspects of our experience, though not the whole of it. It also means acknowledging the connections among body, mind, and spirit, and naming what we gain with midlife, as well as what we lose.

The losses are well-rehearsed: Fertility ends; menopausal symptoms such as vaginal dryness, mood swings, and hot flashes may ensue; women are faced with an array of unappealing medical options in response to symptoms and as preventatives; adult children leave home; parents get sick and die; divorce and illness often occur at this time; and one's own mortality looms undeniably closer.

But there are gains as well. One essential benefit is a sense of freedom, in not having, or even being able, to be the "perfect little girl" anymore.[4] There is increased freedom, too, for the many women whose children are grown or nearly grown by this time. Research shows that in the long term the "empty nest syndrome" affects men more, and more negatively, than women. Statistically, midlife is the time when women are least likely to become depressed.[5]

The dramatic physical and social changes that we undergo at midlife generally leave little room for denial, and encourage women to find non-biological, non-youthful means of being fertile, productive, and generative.[6] This is not to say that women are sublimating a "natural" procreative drive, but that the possibility of women being creative in non-biological ways becomes unmistakably apparent at midlife. Thus, midlife represents an opportunity for self- and societal recognition of women's creative powers. Even the distress and crisis that many women and men experience at midlife may become an impetus for setting new priorities and finding purpose and fulfillment in the second half of life.

Rabbinic notions of midlife are limited. The Rabbis have no developmental concept of "middle years," and it is hard to determine when they use numbers literally, and when symbolically. Nor is it clear where they would draw the line between middle and old age. Still, Rabbinic examples and dicta can illuminate our understanding of midlife. That the great sage Rabbi Akiva started learning at forty is an example of continuing possibility in midlife (and, considering the average lifespan in the first century CE, in old age, as well). The saying "forty is the age of wisdom, fifty is the age of giving advice, sixty is the age of eldership" (Mishnah *Avot* 5:25) re-enforces the Rabbinic notion that one is ready for true understanding and mystical wisdom only at age forty, if then (Shaḥ on *Shulḥan Arukh Yoreh De'ah* 246:4). The designation of fifty as the age of giving advice implies respect for knowledge gained by experience, as well as a humbling caution to younger people.

In "The *Amidah* and Midlife," Rabbi Sheila Peltz Weinberg weaves together Rabbinic ideals with modern midlife themes. She explores the *Amidah* (series of blessings which is the centerpiece of every prayer service), and finds, particularly in its three introductory blessings, a fountain of wisdom and guidance for the Jew in midlife. She highlights the pattern of first identifying issues, then struggling with them, and finally coming to acceptance—a pattern played out in themes common to midlife and the *Amidah*: Mortality; fear of loss; being part of a larger whole; the passage of time; the limits of our control over events, people, energy, and health; reliance on the divine; willingness to see our many strengths and weaknesses; and the search for ultimate meaning and inner peace.

Rabbi Weinberg demonstrates how the *Amidah* is structured, and introduces the insight that its first three blessings are echoed throughout. Her list of all the daily *Amidah* blessings will be particularly helpful for those who are not familiar with the prayer. This essay is as useful a tool for understanding *Amidah* and prayer in general as it is for understanding midlife. Rabbi Weinberg's approach and dual agenda are in concert with the general Jewish interpretive enterprise. The Rabbinic method uncovers many layers of meaning in any text, and the *Amidah* is a particularly rich resource, since it is meant to be inclusive and broad.

Dr. Mary Gendler uses the term "spiritual menopause" to describe the changes in self and focus that commonly occur at midlife. Just as the body takes on new rhythms, so does the spirit: "Achieving" and "doing" are balanced, more and more, by "appreciating" and "being." "What to discard?" becomes as important a question as "What to pursue and keep?" (These are shifts which Rabbi Weinberg notes, as well.) At midlife, we may be more likely to leave open any "extra" time gained from the cessation of childcare or other duties, than to fill it up immediately. The ancient image of the tree, the model of our matriarch Sarah, and Dr. Gendler's own story exemplify the spirit of midlife, and remind us of its fruitfulness.

Two poems by Merle Feld form "Standing Between Generations." In "And Then There's My Father," Feld expresses the deep sadness that many of us feel at midlife as our parents decline in health and vitality, and we reverse roles with them, becoming their caretakers, often by proxy and across great distances. "Though I Stared Earnestly At My Fingernail" describes the blurring of boundaries of time and generations. Memory, vision, empathy, and shared destiny allow Feld to conjure her father, young and healthy, and to merge with her daughter's girlhood.

In sum, the authors in this chapter do not shy away from the burdens of midlife, but they also celebrate its blessings.

The *Amidah* and Midlife

SHEILA PELTZ WEINBERG

"...[W]e can discover the greater fertility."
      —GAIL SHEEHY, *THE SILENT PASSAGE: MENOPAUSE*

I am writing this article a few months before my forty-seventh birthday. A hundred years ago, I would have reached the life span for women by now. If I reflected average statistics, I would have borne eight children and my adult life would have been filled with nursing children almost up to menopause.

In the past century, we have been pushing the boundaries of evolution. I started to menstruate when I was ten, nearly thirty-seven years ago. In another thirty-seven years I will be eighty-four, one year younger than my very vigorous mother, and close to the current female life span. It is apparent that I am in midlife, although women ten years on either side of me could qualify also. Midlife now occupies almost two-thirds of life's span, and, for women especially, this period holds more freedom and a greater variety of possibilities than ever before. As a Jewish woman, rabbi, feminist, and single parent whose youngest is ready to leave home, I face the autumn of my adulthood. How do I use my remaining time to actualize to the fullest the purpose of my existence? Six interrelated demons stalk my progress toward God and wholeness. They probably bedevil many others at this stage of life. They survive from childhood, resilient and embarrassing to recount.

My need and desire for things to go my way The older I get the more I realize how little control I have over the awesome facts of life, especially the losses. Youth is convinced of infinite possibility. Midlife turns to see the undone, the disappointments, the limitations.

Self negation The voices that tell me I am not good enough, not worth love or success, echo in my ears still from childhood, passed down from generation to generation and reinforced as a

---

Sheila Peltz Weinberg is a Reconstructionist rabbi of an unaffiliated liberal synagogue, The Jewish Community of Amherst, Massachusetts.

woman and as a Jew by sexism and anti-Semitism. They sneak silently into my brain, their noise often deafening.

Fear of change Aging smells of death. Who will I be when I am no longer what I am now? Fear of loss, sagging, wrinkles, illness, memory gone, helplessness, the unknown. Terror at loneliness.[7]

Residual dependencies Some have been broken—cigarettes, alcohol, caffeine. But others remain, such as ongoing anxieties about having enough money and the most sinister need—for approval. My greatest dependency is for external validation.

Resistance to meaning and connectedness Isolated in my own uniqueness, no one can understand me. Poor me. Help is not available, and besides—I am uniquely unhelpable.

Lack of balance Incapacity or unwillingness to cope with stress leads me full circle to the first barrier and my persistent failure when I try to be superwoman, serving all, handling all.

I turn to the *siddur* (prayerbook). Is there, perhaps, a way that I can relate my struggle for understanding and perspective in these transitional years to the words of my ancestors?

In the daily prayerbook I find a complex and concentrated prayer which is recited three times a day and forms the core of one's formal communication with the divine. Variously known as the *Amidah* (Standing [prayer]), or *Tefillah* (Prayer), or *Shemoneh Esreh* (Eighteen [blessings]), the words of this prayer proffer the essence of a spiritual approach to Jewish living. I remember feeling lifted aloft by the *Amidah* as a teenager. Its words can touch and connect a person to the Source of existence at many points along the lifecycle, and I return to it whenever I want to measure my growth and the tradition's wisdom. Its essential power is its capacity to link us to a loving Force, greater than ourselves. Here is guidance and inspiration for Jews in every time and place, and for the particular issues of midlife.

The *Amidah* is a symphony of prayer. It begins with three introductory blessings of affirmation and connection, *Avot* (Ancestors), *Gevurot* (Vast Power), *Kedushat Hashem* (Holiness of God's Name), which locate us in the presence of the divine and call to mind the power of prayer in Jewish history. Our varied metaphors for God are unified in the qualities of love, vast power, and holiness. In my middle years, these blessings offer gifts of serenity, power, responsibility, and connectedness.

The body of the weekday *Amidah* is composed of thirteen blessings. These are divided into two sets of six each, the thirteenth blessing functioning like a seal, an amen. The first six are petitions regarding one's personal life and the last six are petitions regarding the national and political state of the Jewish people. The *Amidah* closes with three standard blessings, which, together with the first three, frame weekday, Sabbath, and festival *Amidot* alike.

The themes of the *Amidah's* first three blessings weave through the entire prayer like a golden thread. Each subsequent petitionary blessing is yet another opening to receive one of these great gifts of spirit, since the themes of *Avot*, *Gevurot*, and *Kidushat Hashem* are echoed and enhanced throughout the *Amidah* prayer.

Avot

The *Avot* prayer moves me from selfish preoccupations to a theater of more vast dimensions. I call upon *el elyon*, the Higher Being, the God of Abraham, the God of Isaac, and the God of Jacob. I remember that my ancestors were engaged in a direct relationship with Spirit. Along with other feminists, I add the four matriarchs to the first blessing: God of Sarah, God of Rebecca, God of Leah, God of Rachel. Any cursory glance at Genesis reveals that women were addressed by God.

With the strengthening awareness of my own mortality, it becomes increasingly urgent for me to purify and strengthen my direct relationship with Spirit, in the tradition of these first Jews. I acknowledge these four mothers and three fathers as seven archetypes of prayer, applicable to different personalities, moods, circumstances, and choices.

The *Avot* blessing also tells us that God bestows kindness, creates everything and brings, with love, a Redeemer to our parents' children (namely, us). In the *Amidah* I attest to the kinds of help available from a Higher Power and the enormous relief in knowing, as Abraham and Sarah knew, that I am never alone. *Magen avraham vesarah*, the Shield of Abraham and Sarah, will guard me against the great unknown that looms ahead.

For many of us, it is only at midlife that such a relationship with a care-taking God becomes possible, because only now, finally, do we believe that we are worthy of a loving God. By forty or fifty, if we are lucky, we have accepted our own humanity. Perhaps now, facing so much real and potential loss, the impetus to self-acceptance and surrender to divine care becomes, paradoxically, both easier and more pressing.

This is the time when, in different ways, we commonly lose our parents, our children, sometimes our lovers and friends. I have, to some degree, lost youthful looks, health, energy, and eyesight. Most of all, at midlife we are losing our belief in our own immortality, and, one hopes, our need to control the results of our efforts. But, as Germaine Greer writes, "As you grow older, and are pushed to the margins, you begin to realize that everything is not about you, and that is the beginning of freedom."[8] This attitude toward loss allows me to shift from possessing center stage and to cast myself in a less grandiose role in life's drama. If I am able to accept divine love in the universe, it is because I am learning to wear my life more loosely.

The themes of the *Avot* prayer are confirmed in a variety of later blessings that emphasize the possibility of a direct relationship with a loving, caring God. This relationship can annul the narrow perspective of low self-esteem. Once open to a primal source of love in my life, I am naturally filled with gratitude, another theme that flows from *Avot*.

Ge'ullah (Redemption), a plea for triumph over adversity, is the seventh blessing. In this outpouring of the heart I express my emotional exhaustion. I am sick of the internal judgments and cruelty. I become willing to call upon the power and strength of God (*go'el ḥazak*). I recall in a flashing instant that there is a Source of help in the universe waiting for me to call upon it, anytime, now. This Source resides within me. The present tense is used. At any moment I can wake up to the Redeemer, ever-present Source of help, who is wishing me well, urging me to be gentle and kind to myself.

Still later, the sixteenth *Amidah* blessing *Shome'a Tefillah* (Plea for Divine Acceptance of Prayer) echoes the theme of relating to a loving God. It opens with the words *shema kolenu*, hear our voices, and continues with multiple references to God's grace and compassion. The words are less important than the sound of voices, the urgency and intensity with which we can experience the truth of divine love in our hearts. I stand before God as a member of the people Israel and as an individual human being. In both capacities I rely on the mercy of forces beyond my control. The youthful illusion of immortality and control has given way through the process of maturity to an acceptance of fragility and emptiness. Yet it is when we are empty that we can be filled with spirit (*reikam al tashivenu*, do not leave us empty).

Gail Sheehy writes of this exact metaphor in relation to menopause: "Each major life passage entails emptying and refilling. It is particularly poignant, during menopause....If we hold fast through the dark night of unknowing, we can discover the greater fertility."[9]

The eighteenth blessing is *Hoda'ah* (Thanksgiving). This blessing is a summary of concepts we have already encountered. The security I received from our God and the God of *avoteinu*, our ancestors, is invoked; I remember the free gift of love present on a daily basis; I focus on the continuity from generation to generation and the timelessness of God's compassion; I affirm that my life is in God's hands and I exult in the gifts of my life and in the pleasure of praising the Source of all life.

A primary spiritual and midlife task is to make gratitude the centerpiece of our lives. This task is made difficult because many of us have been taught to notice primarily what is lacking. I need to train myself to see the fullness of my life, to resist with my whole being (and for this I need a community of support, the "we" of the prayer) the tendency to allow storm clouds to overwhelm the horizon of my life.

It is customary to bow twice in this blessing as a physical gesture of gratitude. In this bow of acknowledgment, I recognize that I have been carried by a loving Friend through it all. I open my eyes, too, to the daily miracles (*al nissekha shebekhol yom imanu*) with which God graces me.

Gevurot

The second blessing of the *Amidah*, *Gevurot*, acknowledges God's vast and eternal might in contrast with our own limited power. This orientation, born out of our vulnerability and fear of death, leads to the awareness that life and death are indivisible. As with *Avot*, the themes of *Gevurot* reverberate through the *berakhot* of the *Amidah* that follow.

Daniel Levenson, the pioneer researcher on male lifecycle, explains why midlife conjures up a confrontation with death: "Our profound anxiety at passing forty reflects the ancient experience of the species. We still fear that life ends at forty. The threat is based on the equating of youth with strength and vitality, and of age—even middle age—with weakness, vulnerability and death."[10]

Gevurot offers a response to this fear. It tells us that the process of renewal is built into the universe. Nothing dies or is diminished in nature without life coming forth, perhaps in another form, space, or time. Traditionally, Jews have understood this to mean a literal resurrection of the dead. For me this means that we swim in an ocean of endless time. The only certainty is, in fact, that all will pass—except the Force that underlies all arising and passing.

In *Gevurot*, I address that force when I say: "*Attah gibbor*—You, Power!" Then I name the manifestations of change in nature and humanity: The blowing wind and the falling rain, those who fall and receive support, the sick who are becoming well, the bound who become free. The *Gevurot* blessing helps me see renewal of the whole cycle, rather than focus on what is lost, dry, closed, hidden. We call the power of *Gevurot* "flowering of salvation," (*matzmiah yeshu'ah*). When I feel threatened by the relentless progression of the calendar, the message of *Gevurot* reminds me that death is never final.

At bottom, the problem is less the losing (of life, health, employment) than the *fear* of losing. As Greer writes:

> ...Most of what we are afraid of losing is already gone and we have survived. Our illusions of omnipotence and perfectibility were never anything but illusions. That is the dreadful thing that has already happened. Now we can relax and let things slip through our fingers.[11]

The blessings in the body of the *Amidah* that reflect the themes of *Gevurot* all relate to the process of setting limits. The awareness of change and the contrast between the infinite/eternal and the fleeting provides guidance and balance: I am a player in a setting of vast proportions, yet I have a channel to the Power that under-lies all of creation.

In the fourth blessing, *Da'at* (Intellect), I struggle with human limits and divine inspiration. I acknowledge God as the source of my wisdom. I ask that my intellect (*da'at*), understanding (*binah*), and wisdom (*haskel*) continue to flow into me from their divine root. I ask that they reflect the highest possible perspective, that of our Creator.

We have quick and easy access to mountains of research and information in our time. In this blessing, I ask for and open myself to the wisdom to know the difference between what knowledge I must seek and what arenas must be surrendered to unknowing. I ask for deep understanding, to make the crucial decisions affect-ing the lives of my children, my mother, and myself.

A better perspective on my own powers is both challenging and liberating. As long as my expectations of myself are unbound-ed I can crouch on the sidelines, where I dream of perfection and rest in inaction. As I let go of these fantasies and have a correct appraisal of my true capacities, I am less grandiose and more responsible. I realize that I alone am accountable for my life and growth.

As women age, we generally become more willing to say and defend what we believe and to share our knowledge and insight with the young. We delight in this precious gift of intellect and in its gentle ripening, and learn not to be intimidated by those who use the mind as a weapon.

Intellectual honesty leads inexorably to a confrontation with our own failings. Two *Amidah* blessings offer a context for this struggle. They are *Teshuvah* (Returning), the fifth blessing; and *Seliḥah* (Forgiveness), the sixth. They point us toward daily self-reflection, reviewing wrongs and making amends. In midlife, this effort may assume daunting dimensions, especially if it has been neglected until now.

While these blessings remind us of the need to better our-selves, they also remind us that we are fundamentally good. Notwithstanding doubts and failings, God wishes us (*harotzeh biteshuvah*) to return to our true nature. Loving intimacy is possi-ble with One who is a divine and perfect Parent (*avinu*), as well as the Power of the universe.

Even if I have changed, I can be burdened with guilt and remorse. Change is necessary, but not always sufficient, for forgiveness. In the *Seliḥah* blessing, I address the Source of Abounding Forgiveness (*hamarbeh lislo'aḥ*), unlimited by the pettiness of humans who sometimes clutch their resentments.

The eighth blessing is *Refu'ah* (Healing), a wonderful acknowledgment of the interconnection between body and spirit. The changes in our bodies sometimes make us feel helpless and remind us of the Power named in *Gevurot*. Our tradition teaches that God participates in every successful healing procedure and that the *Shekhinah* (close-dwelling presence of God, associated with the feminine) rests at the head of every sick person. I believe, too, that praising God is good for the health.

Bodily health and spiritual well-being feed each other. While this truth is evident along the life path, it is particularly significant during midlife. Tragically and ironically, it often takes severe illness to recognize the subtle balance between flesh and spirit. In midlife we learn that healing may not always mean returning to a former state of health, but rather achieving new balance, serenity, and peace. Recently, an ancient silence has been broken and menopause has become the subject of important discussions. This is a relief for us all. Meanwhile, childless women may experience especially poignant grief during this stage. The ending of fertility often demands a radical facing of loss of dreams and hopes. In these difficult times, the blessing for *refu'ah* also reminds us to direct our gaze beyond the narrow, temporary images of self toward the compassionate and faithful Healing Power present within all life.

The ninth blessing, *Birkat Hashanim* (Blessing of the Yearly Seasons), also hearkens back to the themes of power and limits found in the *Gevurot* prayer. Financial insecurity may beset us at any time in the lifecycle, but at midlife we are especially vulnerable as we face a future of reduced earning potential, fewer opportunities to begin again, and ageist hiring practices. On the other hand, we may have attained wealth and are questioning its capacity to satisfy our cravings. I ask to be filled with divine goodness (*sabbe'enu mituvekha*). Midlife is an opportunity to move beyond the materialism of our culture and recognize that true prosperity is a matter of attitude as well as substance.

Kedushat Hashem

The third introductory blessing, following *Avot* and *Gevurot*, is *Kedushat Hashem*, which names the holy and the holiness of God's name. The term *kedushah* is inextricably linked with the Jewish spiritual path. God is *kadosh* (holy) and God's name is *kadosh*, and we are repeatedly directed to become holy and practice holiness (e.g. Leviticus 19:1f). The *mitzvot* (commandments), ethical and ritual, are intended to support the emergence of holiness on earth, the permeation of human life with the presence of the divine.

Kedushat Hashem deals with the issue of ultimate meaning that we often face in midlife. One notices, with grief and disappointment, how much energy one has invested into the passing features of our lives, be they relationships, careers, material things, or self-images. Perhaps now is the time to assert priorities—not necessarily to discard the old, but to reconsider what is important. The *Kedushat Hashem* blessing instills an attitude toward life of spiritual awareness and search, an effort to manifest God's will through individual choices, moving from "having more" to "being more." Part of "being more" is connecting to something larger than oneself by moving beyond personal goals and petitions to communal concerns, as the later blessings of the *Amidah* do.

Midlife generally finds women facing outward and becoming more involved with politics and society, assuming leadership and responsibility. While this may seem to be the reverse of the male journey, the truth is that both genders are becoming more centered, seeking a new, more authentic and sustaining balance between self and society. This goal is reflected in the *Kedushah* (Holiness) prayer that is recited during the *Amidah*, when praying with a *minyan* (prayer quorum). All aspects of my world are permeated with greater sanctity (*melo khol ha'aretz kevodo*, the *entire* earth is filled with God's glory). I am freer to see life in the fullness of its connection to past and future and to timeless holiness. This empowers me to enter into areas I feared or disdained before, to try new things—some small, some large.

One of the ways holiness permeates the daily interactions of our life is through a concern with justice and right action. Women have accrued greater power and responsibility both as a group in this century and over the course of our individual lives. Thus we have special concerns in grappling with the social questions raised in the eleventh *Amidah* blessing, *Din* (Restoration of Justice). How can we assure the high moral standards of our leaders without sabotaging them? How do we understand the primary functions of Jewish leaders and their relationship with community? How do we avoid polarizing our communities because of different political visions? How do we integrate the classic ideas of justice identified with male authority and women's traditional expertise at connection, intimacy, and compassion?

Defining what is holy implicitly requires that we define what is unholy. *Birkat Haminim* (blessing against sectarians), the twelfth blessing, was included in the *Amidah*, it is believed, as a response to threats of sectarians: Essenes, early Christians, and heretics (BT *Berakhot* 28b). Today, it challenges us to name who and what we believe to be the true enemies of the Jewish people, worthy of destruction.

As I move into midlife, I am more apt to see the world in shades of gray, to embrace my own shadow rather than projecting it outward. Nonetheless, there is, I believe, real evil in the world: Cruelty, hatred, bigotry, violence. We need to acknowledge this, and it is fitting to pray and act for the destruction of evil.

In *Boneh Yerushalayim* (Rebuilding Jerusalem), the fourteenth *Amidah* blessing, I pray for the rebuilding of the holy city and the flowering of the House of David. While some Jews take this text as a literal wish for Messianic rule, I see it as our yearning for the rule of righteousness, holiness, and wisdom in Jewish communities and among all people. This may not be realized in our time, but I uphold its possibility as the birthright of our people and all humanity. It is a flowering (*tzemah david*), an organic process with its own rhythm and timing. Nonetheless I wish it to happen speedily (*bimeherah*), and I commit to do my part to bring it about.

My identification with communal pain and yearning, as well as hopes for a just and peaceful future, drive me out of my self-centeredness and dovetail well with the midlife turn toward generativity and continuity. Also, the ability to wait, to receive things in their proper time, even when I am impatient, is a lesson of midlife.

The last blessing of the *Amidah* is *Shalom* (Peace). It refers to integrity of character and peace of mind, qualities that we especially aspire to in midlife, after so much effort and struggle. Now is the time to balance, integrate, and bring to peace all the polarities of life: Mind and body, self and society, giving and receiving. This harmony is not dull or static; it is fruitful and vital and holy.

Shalom integrates serenity and power, themes of the *Amidah* and of midlife spirituality. The prayer for *shalom* is highly personal, but inner peace leads to harmony in the family, among Jews and between nations in the world.

In attempting to use the *Amidah* as a text for midlife, I am painfully aware of the inadequacy of even the *Amidah*'s seasoned and inspired letters to reflect and address the turmoil of a human being struggling with the life issues of loss, control, forgiveness, and meaning. Our ancestors gave us many words. The Jewish obsession with words and their power to create and destroy is seen in the *Amidah*'s extraordinary outpouring of words, words seeking to touch, even break open, the heart; words designed to tear away the masks of avoidance and numbness which mark our lives; words which are subject to distortion before they leave the mouth.

Sometimes I need fewer words and more silence to feel truth resonate in my blood and bones. Then, I balk at the discipline of saying so many words three times daily. We live in a world on "word overload," and often I feel the work of transformation is better accomplished in the spaces between the words. The traditional *Amidah* includes a pause for silent personal prayer and quiet openness to God's voice. I feel a great need to recover and probe that silence, still acknowledging the words that reverberate in the text and in my soul.

The gates of midlife are opening. I pray for the willingness to seek a closer relationship with Spirit. I pray for a willingness to let go of my need to always feel in control of my life. I pray for the ability to appreciate the daily miracles that are with us. I pray for my people and for all people. May we be granted peace.

ORDER OF *BERAKHOT*

אָבוֹת

Avot (Ancestors)

Patriarchs and matriarchs model a direct relationship with a loving and caring God/Spirit, and God's greatness and protection are invoked.

גְּבוּרוֹת

Gevurot (Vast Power)

God's power is manifest in our awareness of limits and in the contrast between the fleeting and the eternal.

קְדֻשַּׁת הַשֵּׁם

Kedushat Hashem (Holiness of God's Name)

We seek to expand our awareness of holiness in the world, and to recognize the holiness of God and the divine name.

דַּעַת

Da'at (Intellect)

Receiving wisdom as a gift and reflection of God. Pursuing keener self-understanding and the insight to know what to accept and when to act.

תְּשׁוּבָה

Teshuvah (Returning)

That is, returning to our true nature through repentance.

סְלִיחָה

Selihah (Forgiveness)

Cultivating compassion for myself for not being perfect and, in turn, compassion for all others.

גְּאֻלָּה

Ge'ullah (Redemption)

Finding personal salvation by facing internal and external
obstacles to wellbeing.

רְפוּאָה

Refu'ah (Healing)

Praying for health and healing as we refine our understanding
of the connection between body and spirit.

בִּרְכַּת הַשָּׁנִים

Birkat Hashanim (Blessing of the Yearly Seasons)

Asking for a year of prosperity and financial security, and the
capacity to enjoy what we have.

קִבּוּץ גָּלֻיּוֹת

Kibbutz Galuyyot (Ingathering of Exiles)

Bringing home the hidden, the secret, the broken, and the
lost—in ourselves and in the community.

דִּין

Din (Restoration of Justice)

Applying justice in all relations, and praying for God's rule in
our lives.

בִּרְכַּת הַמִּינִים

Birkat Haminim (Blessing Against Sectarians)

Acknowledging enemies and dangers along the path.

צַדִּיקִים

Tzaddikim (The Righteous)

Basking in, and learning from, the splendor of good people.

בּוֹנֵה יְרוּשָׁלַיִם

Boneh Yerushalayim (Rebuilding Jerusalem)

Yearning for the rule of righteousness, for national security, and for peace.

מַלְכוּת בֵּית דָּוִד

Malkhut Beit David (Davidic Reign)

A looking to the future with hope for salvation.

שׁוֹמֵעַ תְּפִלָּה

Shome'a Tefillah (Plea for Divine Acceptance of Prayer)

Developing our awareness of divine love and acceptance.

עֲבוֹדָה

Avodah (Temple Service)

Touching the remembered intensity of authentic devotion. Learning to perceive God's presence in Zion and elsewhere.

הוֹדָאָה

Hoda'ah (Thanksgiving)

Fostering gratitude as a vital spiritual practice.

שָׁלוֹם

Shalom (Peace)

Integrating serenity and power, thus establishing peace on all levels.

Spiritual Menopause

MARY GENDLER

"...They are always green and full of sap...."

—PSALMS 92:15

The day of my fortieth birthday I woke up with chest pains. Instead of heading to the airport for my eagerly awaited weekend away, I went to the hospital where an EKG revealed that all was well. I was both relieved and embarrassed to discover that my "heart attack" was caused by gas. I spent much of that year uncharacteristically in and out of the doctor's office with a variety of other minor problems. That same year I went back to school to begin work on my doctorate in psychology, a program that involved five years of nonstop work and left me gasping but degreed somewhere into my forty-fifth year. It seemed, for the time being, I had warded off growing old.

My fiftieth birthday was quite a different experience. Notwithstanding the cast firmly supporting the ankle I had broken in Bali that summer, I jitterbugged and had a wonderful time at my "50s" party. I had gotten over the shock of realizing that I was old enough to join AARP (American Association of Retired Persons) and the psychosomatic illnesses had disappeared. So, also, had my serious ambitions. Gone was that compelling drive which had enabled me to pull "all-nighters" with my adolescent daughters and fueled my capacity to run seven children's groups a week while taking four graduate courses. My need to prove myself seemingly accomplished, something else was stirring in me.

As the decade progresses, this feeling of well-being remains, as does my urge to make time for myself and the small pleasures of life. While I still wish to work and be productive, I am increasingly resistant to "busy-ness," and more interested in sorting out what really matters. The balance between "being" and "doing" is shifting. What is going on?

Dr. Mary Gendler is a psychologist and clinical director of the Jewish Family Service of Merrimack Valley, Massachusetts.

Changes in Midlife

Menopause marks the end of a woman's ability to reproduce, a finality which can bring twinges of regret even to those who are longing only for the limited responsibilities of grandparenthood or those who have chosen not to have children. Yet, for some this is a time of opening, of moving beyond gender definition, of surging energy and a sense of liberation. Like menstruation, menopause is a time of emptying and refilling, a cycle familiar to women. Now that the womb is destined to remain empty of blood, the "refilling" must come in a different mode.

This can be confusing, leaving us lost and floundering, filled with fears of emptiness. Indeed, the "empty womb" syndrome may be even more of a problem than the "empty nest." Although we are no longer physically tied to the moon-cycle, our deepest rhythms are still intimately connected with the rhythms of the Mother, moon, sea, and tides, granting us a kind of knowing, a "womb wisdom" that is precious. The key question is how to cultivate and remain connected to this wisdom.

Certainly, worldly activities in and outside the home can be fulfilling, but too often they run the risk of being purely linear, outward, filling the empty space with too much doing, pulling us away from our centers. How to satisfy the archaic rhythms? How to open to the larger questions, our purpose? I suggest we call these aspects of the passage "spiritual menopause."

Spiritual menopause challenges us to make deep changes in our souls, just as physical menopause engenders deep changes in our bodies. It leads us to move beyond old definitions of ourselves, our roles, and our ways of being.

How can the Jewish tradition help in this passage? Is there a Jewish way to celebrate the changes occurring in our bodies, to acknowledge that a new space is opening, a new rhythm developing, a new energy flowing, new aspirations and needs emerging? Is there a symbol with which we can reconnect to help us in this passage?

Jewish Images and Models

The tree represents our desires to stay rooted in our lives and yet let our spirits soar. According to Mircea Eliade, the tree in ancient times represented the "living cosmos endlessly renewing itself."[12] Throughout Scripture the image of the tree is that of wisdom (Proverbs 3:13-18), vitality (Jeremiah 17:8; Psalms 1:3), righteousness (Proverbs 11:30), and fruitfulness (Ezekiel 17:23). The *Zohar* (premiere Jewish mystical text) invokes the "tree of life" (5:38), an image applied to Torah itself (Proverbs 3:18). Cedars in particular are traditionally associated with miraculous and mysterious renewal.[13]

Evoking reverence for the "Great Mother" in the form of a tree,[14] the words of Psalms 92:13-14 are especially relevant to menopause:

> The righteous flourish like the palm tree,
> and grow like a cedar in Lebanon.
> They are planted in the house of *Adonai*;
> They flourish in the courts of our God.
> In old age they still produce fruit,
> They are always green and full of sap....

So what might bearing fruit mean for us in our advancing years? How can we, post-menopausal women, be "always green and full of sap" even though our monthly blood cycle has come to an end? How can we renew our strength and generativity, beyond the time of youth and fertility, beyond all "rational" limits and expectations? Meditating on these questions, I thought of Sarah, our mother.

Sarah, whose menopause is clearly long past, laughs when God tells her that she will bear a child in her old age. This is commonly interpreted as a sign of Sarah's cynicism, but it can also be read as a sign of her righteousness, which lies in a laughing acceptance of God's gift which flows through her, ultimately yielding fine fruit. Sarah is able to conceive Isaac in her old age because her sap is still flowing even if her menstrual blood is not. Her milk also flows so plentifully that she not only nurses Isaac (Genesis 21:7), but, according to the *midrash* (Rabbinic legend), many gentile infants as well. Converts to Judaism are said to descend from her sucklings (*Pesikta Rabbati* 180a). We have much to learn from Sarah, our spiritual as well as biological mother. Through her we learn not to be too hasty in declaring ourselves or others "barren." A wizened old woman in her nineties, Sarah is "up" for anything. Although she was not actively seeking when God came to call, she was available and ready, and this is why she both flourishes and nourishes.

May we have the courage to follow Sarah's example, to be open to new challenges, new opportunities, new paths and voices, never to forget that despite the changes in our bodies, the sap continues to flow. May the blood of our wombs be replaced by the milk of Righteousness, the sap of Age and Spirit. May Wisdom cycle through our "womb knowing," our understanding of the cycles of birth and death, emptying and filling, ebbing and flowing. As we move into the later decades of life, let us not forget to make space and time for the sap of the Source to flow; let us be careful that we do not plug up the sources with too much activity; let us find ways to be deeply rooted in our Mother even as we stretch our hearts and spirits as far as they will reach; and, finally, let us trust in and begin to share our wisdom with others. In uniting our spirits with earth(l)iness, we will reconnect to the divine in Earth our Mother and to the cosmic tree of life, and like Sarah and all the righteous, produce much fruit in our old age.

Standing Between Generations:
Two Poems

MERLE FELD

"In these middle years, I find it hard to cry."
                              —MERLE FELD, "I STAYED HOME THIS YEAR
                              FOR THE REJOICING OF THE LAW"

And Then There's My Father[15]

> when it seems as though
> there's nothing left
> to be depressed about
> I can always get depressed
> about my father
>
> living alone in Florida
> eating out of cans
>
> he no longer goes out after dark
> he no longer drives a car
> no longer speaks on the phone in a storm
> or watches while the TV is playing
> he no longer reads a book or a newspaper
> or goes swimming in the pool
> he no longer invites a woman out to dinner
> or gets a homecooked meal
> no longer sends anybody a birthday card
> or goes to temple on the holidays
> he no longer walks alone on the beach collecting shells
>
> at four in the morning
> in my bed in New Jersey
> I lie awake and
> think about my father.

Merle Feld is an award-winning playwright, a poet, a political activist, and a long-time Jewish feminist.

Though I Stared Earnestly at My Fingernail[16]

Yesterday when I was on the #7 bus
I happened to look at the cuticle on my right forefinger
and for a moment I thought not that it was mine
but that it was my father's—

the same small confusion I have from time to time
when I catch sight of my daughter
in her denim skirt, size 3
and I feel lean, willowy, in her clothes.

So there I was on the #7 bus
overtaken by a longing very close to love
staring at the cuticle of my right forefinger.

I remembered how clean and short he kept his nails
and suddenly there was the whole man
reconstituted from a fingernail
standing before me, smiling broadly
his face flushed with pleasure.

But then just as suddenly he was gone
and though I stared earnestly at my fingernail
I failed to bring him back.

14

Aging

J ewish law and lore teach respect for the elderly as a key
value. The very word *"zaken"*—elder—is creatively interpreted as an acronym for *zeh shekanah ḥokhmah,* the one who has
attained wisdom (BT *Kiddushin* 32b). However, this ideal is not
always actualized. We often mock or infantilize our
elders, and perpetuate negative stereotypes of elderly Jews that
would be considered anti-Semitic if they were ascribed to younger
generations. Following general American demographic trends, we
increasingly move away from our parents and grandparents.

Still, the sins of the Jewish community against elders pale by
comparison with those on the general American scene. The elderly
are seen so little in the mass media and, often, heard so little by
their own doctors and families that psychologist Ellen McGrath
coined the term "age rage" to name the source of their situational
depression. The way we treat the aged in this country testifies to

our immense capacity for denial. For, no matter how far we push the boundaries of old age, we will, if we are lucky, get there.

Sociologists and gerontologists are finding that the decline commonly associated with old age is not a necessary function of the aging process. Ironically, we define people who age happily and successfully as "youthful"—which keeps us locked into the association of aging with deterioration and loss. According to sociological studies, three key factors influence both psychic well-being in the aging process and actual longevity: Control over one's decisions, continuing engagement with new challenges, and bonds of intimacy.[1] One recent study identified seven common factors among centenarians who remain active and retain all their faculties: Some form of daily movement or exercise; adaptability to loss; sense of humor; adventurousness and willingness to try new things; flexibility; engagement with an outside interest, work- or non-work-related; and optimism. Diet and heredity were not statistically significant.

Old age, like midlife, can be understood and experienced as a time of new possibilities, even though, again like midlife, it is commonly perceived as a time of loss. It is during old age that men and women can most easily escape the tyranny of the macho image or the "beauty myth."[2] With age, the possibility of meeting the standards for rigid sex-role stereotypes and youthful vigor and beauty becomes more and more remote. Paradoxically, this "decline" frees the elderly to embrace qualities that are generally attributed to the "opposite" sex. This type of crossover is seen cross-culturally among the aged.[3] Retirement presents opportunities to pursue new fields of interest and, for those who have the money, to travel. Not surprisingly, those who have successfully negotiated the challenges of earlier life stages are most likely to adapt successfully to the aging process, and find ways to grow in their later years.

Remembering is a central task in old age. This means recalling the past for oneself and passing it on to the next generations. (Dr. Dena Shenk, writing in this chapter, names "family historian" as one role that grandmothers play.) It also means literally re-membering one's life, piecing and knitting it together to make of it a whole, with all parts and all one's history, honored and integrated.[4] In so doing, the elder also re-members the family, sewing together relationships. The pain of the elder's eventual death is mitigated for the next generation, because the tear and dismemberment that the family will suffer as a result has been anticipated and healed, to a degree, in advance. Moreover, the wholeness of the deceased becomes a comfort.

For all the considerable opportunities for growth, real losses do accrue with age: Serious health problems, the death of loved ones, decreased mobility and autonomy. The tradition, while venerating the elderly, also acknowledges the pain and frailty that often come with age (Psalms 71:9). Harriet M. Perl's contribution to this chapter disabuses us of the illusion that any part of aging is easy, and provides an antidote for saccharine or glib cheerfulness.

Dr. Shenk analyses aging as it occurs between generations, in the relationship between adult daughters and their aging mothers, in Jewish teachings about intergenerational behavior, and in the gradual process by which the middle generation becomes the elder. She examines the aging process of Jewish women within the family, in terms of peculiarly Jewish factors, gender differences, and various roles. As a gerontologist and a woman in her middle years, Dr. Shenk draws on both scholarship and personal experience to trace continuity and change from one generation to the next. Along the way, she supplies a survey of traditional Jewish attitudes and sources on honoring one's parents and on aging.

Dr. Mildred Seltzer, a retired gerontologist of Dr. Shenk's mother's generation, responds to Dr. Shenk's essay in both a personal and a professional capacity. Dr. Seltzer sees significant continuity between generations even in times of drastic change and areas of great contention. Criticizing negative stereotypes of the older generation, especially women, she takes pride in the adaptability of her and her mother's generations in the face of social upheaval. She makes a moving plea not to be abandoned in old age, an appeal to the agelessness of wisdom and common sense, and a realistic assessment of the losses and joys of elderhood.

Perl, mentioned above, minces no words about the difficulties and fears associated with aging. She refers to what "they"—the experts, gerontologists, doctors, younger generation—deem appropriate, and implicates the hubris involved in young people presuming to know what old age is like or requires. She confronts the possibility of infirmity and loss of independence, the certainty of death, and the fact most of us ultimately face these alone.

In "Widowhood After A Long Marriage: Two Poems," Barbara D. Holender presents two powerful images of the grief and adjustment to life without a mate that so many women experience as they age. Her "A Ceremony of Passage on My Sixty-Fifth Birthday" is all the more moving, since we have some notion of the sorrow she has overcome, and the strength on which she has drawn, in order to come to the point of celebrating her elderhood. The ceremony itself is completely original, but draws on Jewish symbols and on the relatively new practice of Jewish "croning" or eldering rituals, specifically the *Simḥot Ḥokhmah* (celebrations of elder wisdom) developed by Dr. Savina Teubal and Marcia Cohen Spiegel.[5] Such ceremonies offer elders the opportunity to acknowledge a new stage in their lives, and the community, the opportunity to honor and learn from them.

The essays in this chapter are useful as a guide to understanding the elderly; relating to them with respect, according to tradition; and consciously preparing for the continual aging process—whatever one's age.

Honor Thy Mother:
Continuity and Change in the Lives
of Aging Jewish Women

DENA SHENK

"There are three partners in the creation of every human being:
The Holy One, blessed be God, the father, and the mother. When a
person honors his/her father and mother, God says, 'It is as though
I had dwelt among them and they had honored Me.'"

—AFTER BT *KIDDUSHIN* 30B

Americans tend to view aging as a social problem, focusing on the decline and discontinuities that are part of the aging experience in twentieth century America. Old age generally augurs lessened prestige, and a decline in physical health. Those who retire from work outside the home face the loss of regular interactions with colleagues, of structured responsibilities, of income, and of the identity accorded by their job. The aging individual may also be "at a loss" for role models of how to age successfully, because the experiences of earlier generations may seem irrelevant.

In *Of Woman Born*, Adrienne Rich defines "matrophobia" as the "fear not of one's mother or of motherhood but of *becoming* one's mother."[6] In many ways we are *expected* to become our mothers, to take on their roles and responsibilities within the family and Jewish community. In this sense, Jewish traditions, religion, and ethnicity provide continuity in the aging experience.[7]

At the same time, however, the historical and cultural changes of the last fifty years have created a gulf between generations and led to differing roles and attitudes among grandmothers, mothers, and daughters. We may be both pleased *and* dismayed to recognize character traits and deeply-held values within ourselves as "inherited" from our mothers. Such traits and values may not fully resonate with our images of who we are and want to be.

I recently compared two visits with my mother: The first was a relaxed visit to my parents' home without children or responsibili-

---

Dr. Dena Shenk is professor of anthropology and coordinator of The Gerontology Program, University of North Carolina at Charlotte.

ty; the second, a stressful time at my home with my family preparing to move and my parents there to help. While we were all glad to be together, I found myself struggling to maintain my patience and enjoy this second occasion.

The stress stemmed from our conflicting roles. As I rushed around the house before and after my work outside the home, my mother watched, asked questions, tried not to interfere, and waited for specific requests for help. At times, I felt that she was evaluating my performance, occasionally wanting to intercede and make suggestions.

In a private moment, I asked her, "Doesn't it feel funny to have me tell you what to do?" She responded warmly, and we talked briefly about the dilemma: I was mother, daughter, teacher, and host; she was mother, grandmother, helper, and guest. I—not she—was in charge of the household. We found ourselves in a situation where the rules and roles were new, confusing, and contradictory, and we felt closer for having acknowledged this.

Such situations are of particular importance to Jewish women because of the centrality of their family roles. Generally, Jewish men age within formal religious institutions and the larger community, while Jewish women age within the family system and home. Though this is also true for many non-Jewish families, the way gender roles are cast in the Jewish tradition serves to strengthen this tendency and, generally, to define the Jewish experience.

What does it mean to age as a Jewish woman within the family? This is actually two questions. First, what is *Jewish* about aging as experienced by Jewish women? Second, what are the specific *gender* differences in the experience of the aging process? Aging within the *tradition* is characterized by an extreme sense of responsibility of adults for their aging parents, along with parental responsibility for children, and limitations in regard to all responsibilities. A Jewish *woman* relates to the traditional role of family caregiver.

Continuity through Jewish identity on the one hand, and generational differences due to social change on the other, are key to understanding the aging experience of Jewish women in the United States. Jewish traditions and values taught within the family offer a strong thread of continuity to aging Jewish women. At the same time, there is tension and ambivalence in the mother-daughter relationship, especially relating to the interpretation of traditional values. Generational tensions have always framed the experience of American Jewish women, and this is strongly the case today because of rapid changes in the role of women in American society.

Relationships between adult Jewish women and their aging mothers often evolve through two stages. In the first, we feel ambivalence as we compare ourselves to our mothers, sometimes wishing they were more like us and sometimes wishing we were more like them. This can lead to matrophobia and a denial of resemblances.

In the second stage, we view the differences between ourselves and our mothers through a lens of appreciation of the different adjustments we have had to make and the different social climates in which we were raised. At the same time, we value our similarities and use the skills and lessons learned from our mothers and grandmothers to cope with our own lives and aging process. For myself, the progression to this second stage did not occur until several years after the birth of my first child.

In this essay, I examine a number of related issues: (1) The view of aging within the Jewish tradition, (2) religious/ethnic identity as a source of continuity in the lives of aging Jewish women, (3) generational tensions and changes among Jewish women in the United States, and (4) the central role of motherhood in old age.

Jewish Adaptation to Lifecycle Issues of Old Age

"Harken unto thy father that begot thee, and despise not thy mother when she is old."
—PROVERBS 23:22

The unifying force in the aging experience of Jewish older women and their daughters derives from traditional Jewish values, beliefs, and sources. While most American Jews are not learned in the Scriptures, many have an understanding of the essence and import of Jewish texts and ethics—an understanding often informally transmitted by mothers and grandmothers.

Mutual Responsibilities within the Family The Jewish family ideally rests on interdependency and mutual responsibility. The Book of Ruth exemplifies this in its portrait of Naomi and Ruth who support and nurture each other. The ideal dynamic among family members is summarized by sociologist and biblicist Rachel Dulin who explains, "Just as the old nurtured and cared for the young, so were the young expected to support and provide a dignified life for the old."[8] Parents had to provide for, protect, and teach their children (e.g. Deuteronomy 6:20-25, 8:5, 11:19-21). Children were required to respect and obey their parents (e.g. Exodus 20:21, 21:15-17; Leviticus 20:9; Deuteronomy 5:16, 21:18-20; Proverbs 23:22), and to help them in the family work (e.g. Genesis 24:15, 29:6, 37:12; I Samuel 9:11, 17:15).

Children's Treatment of Aging Mothers and Fathers The first duty children have to their parents derives from the fifth commandment to "honor thy father and thy mother" (Exodus 20:12 and Deuteronomy 5:16). A few Talmudic tracts refer specifically to a son's treatment of his mother. For example, Rabbi Tarfon reportedly bent down when his elderly mother wanted to get into bed, so she could climb on his back (BT *Kiddushin* 31b). He told this to his colleagues in the House of Study and they responded: "You have not yet reached one half of the duty of honoring your mother. Has she thrown a purse of gold into the sea in your presence and have you refrained from rebuking her?"[9]

The relative importance of honoring one's mother is explained in the *Mekhilta* of Rabbi Ishmael (Pisḥa 1).

> "Honor your father and your mother." I might understand that because the father precedes in the text, he should actually take precedence over the mother. But in another passage, "You shall each fear/revere his mother and his father" (Leviticus 19:3), the mother precedes. Scripture thus declares that both are equal.

The Rabbis teach another lesson with respect to these same two verses. They assume we would "naturally" honor our mothers and fear and revere our fathers, not expecting us automatically to fear and revere our mothers or honor our fathers. It is as a corrective, therefore, that mothers are mentioned first where fear and reverence are concerned, and fathers are mentioned first where honor is concerned. This division between mother/honor and father/awe is typical in American society due to the way we stereotype men and women. Fathers are more often the disciplinarians to be feared and respected, and mothers the nurturers, whom we honor more but listen to less.[10]

Respect comprises psychological and symbolic elements (which the tradition identifies as *yir'ah*/reverence), as well as physical and caretaking needs (which the tradition identifies as *kavod*/honor) (BT *Kiddushin* 31b). Researcher Natalie Joffe quotes an Eastern European immigrant who expresses how this ideal was interpreted and experienced:

> You cannot imagine the respect I felt for my parents....There is a Jewish expression for it which explains it so well, *derekh eretz* (lit. "way of the land," but meaning respectful demeanor)....It is not fear. If it were fear, then the respect would be asked of the child, and my parents never asked for anything.[11]

Limits of Children's Responsibilities Within a system of respect and responsibilities, the Jewish tradition defines the limits of children's responsibilities. It was considered allowable under certain circumstances to have someone else fulfill the child's duties of respect to a parent. According to Maimonides:

> If the mind of his father or his mother is affected, the son should make every effort to indulge the vagaries of the stricken parent until God will have mercy on the afflicted. But if the condition of the parent has grown worse, and the son is no longer able to endure the strain, he may leave his father or mother, go elsewhere, and delegate to others to give the parent proper care (*Mishneh Torah Hilkhot Mamrim* 6:10).

In terms of economic support, too, children are required to offer respect and support, but not at the cost of self-preservation (*Shulḥan Arukh Yoreh De'ah* 197).

Part of the reason for the limitations on children's responsibility is the valuation of the next generation. It was understood as the way of the world that "A father's love is for his children; the children's love is for their own children" (BT *Sotah* 49a). That

Talmudic insight is validated by Glueckel of Hameln, whose *Memoirs* offer insights into German-Jewish life and thought during the seventeenth century. She wrote about a father bird struggling to transport his three fledglings across a windy sea. He asked each bird in turn if they would do as much for him and provide for his old age. The first two replied that they would and, as liars, were dropped into the sea. The third fledgling replied: "My dear father, I shall be wrong not to repay you when you are old, but I cannot bind myself. This, though, I can promise: When I am grown up and have children of my own, I shall do as much for them as you have done for me."[12]

Wisdom of Elders A traditional value which persists in the American Jewish context is the veneration of knowledge and education. The respect accorded to elders in the Jewish tradition reflects, at least in part, the belief that wisdom comes with age. As the Rabbis teach, "One who takes counsel with the old will not falter" (Exodus *Rabbah* 3). It was primarily old men who are assumed to have attained wisdom, as it was men, overwhelmingly, who studied Jewish texts. Accordingly, the Talmud teaches: "We must be careful with an old man who has forgotten his learning...so as not to shame him....For were not the broken tablets placed side by side with the whole ones in the Ark [of the Covenant]?" (BT *Berakhot* 8b)

Aging Women in the Jewish Tradition Although biblical and Talmudic traditions clearly urge respect for the aged and particularly one's parents, there is both a relative dearth of references to aging women and evidence of unequal treatment accorded elderly men and women. Old women are assumed to possess the same infirmities as old men. Less often, in traditional sources, do women share the respect and wisdom accorded to men in old age. As it is stated: "Thou shalt rise up before the hoary head, and honor the face of the *old man*..." (Leviticus 19:32). Women certainly did not generally win respect by an accumulation of public or scholarly activities.

Losses with Aging Although the tradition's view of age and aging is positive, there is also a recognition of the losses that can accompany old age. The frailty and physical decline of old age were always feared, as evident in the plea: "Do not cast me off in old age; when my strength fails, do not forsake me" (Psalms 71:9).[13]

Domestic Religion and Ethnic Identity as a Source of Continuity

"These things were injected into you in childhood and chained together with that beautiful grandmother, so ever since infancy you can't know life without it....When it goes in this way I describe, Jewish comes up in you from the roots and it stays with you all your life."
—BASHA IN BARBARA MYERHOFF'S *NUMBER OUR DAYS*[14]

Ethnicity often resurges in late life, and people rework the "themes" of their lives around their ethnicity.[15] Ethnicity is also used to cope with specific incidents, transitions, and changes in people's lives, such as surgeries, decreased mobility, or a move to a retirement home. In these ways, Jewish religion as ethnic heritage provides continuity in the lives of aging Jewish women through domestic religion.

Traditionally taught within the home and family, more closely associated with feelings than with understanding, domestic religion was the realm of Jewish women.[16] In her study of Jewish women who immigrated to the United States between 1898 and 1925, Sydney Stahl Weinberg summarizes both sex-role division and women's domestic religion in the patriarchal society of Jewish immigrants. Except for earning money during extreme times of need, collecting money for charity, and caring for the sick, women had "no accepted public role outside the home...." On the home front,

> the God the women prayed to in the kitchen seemed to have a more personal nature than the deity the men invoked in *shul* [synagogue]. Because their religious concepts were minimally related to a body of dogma, a place or worship or even a religious leader...the essence of their faith might be retained regardless of the degree of conscious religiosity.[17]

The boundaries between men's and women's roles no longer define so rigidly the choices available to younger generations of

Jewish women in America. They do, however, continue to affect the aging experience of widows who, for example, are less likely than widowers to seek support through formal religious institutions during a time of difficult transition. When a man's wife dies, he can find a community of support in the daily *minyan* (prayer quorum), as he says *Kaddish* (mourner's prayer). While widows are not necessarily barred, they are not encouraged to attend and are more likely to frequent the socially-based Sisterhood. This is likely to change for future generations with increased involvement of Jewish women in public ritual and religious observance.

The passing on of women's domestic religion can lead to the recognition, in families with daughters, that the daughter is becoming her mother. For myself, recognition of this cycle comes when I sit at the Passover *seder* (ordered readings and meal), as the parental generation, with my own children engaging in the ritual questioning. There are elements of both continuity and discontinuity. While I fulfill my mother's Passover roles, I am also a more active leader of the ritual than she was, and my husband helps to cook and serve the ritual meal more than my father did.

It is not only from the immediate family that we learn—and eventually take over—the practice of being a Jewish woman. We may take our examples from friends, contemporary leaders, and history. This is evident in the very title of Letty Cottin Pogrebin's book *Deborah, Golda, and Me* (Crown Publishing Group, 1991). The feminist critique that the tradition offers us too few role models is valid. Still, at different points in our lives we may identify with Sarah, Rebecca, Rachel, Leah, Miriam, or Ruth. Women today are increasingly reading our selves and our foremothers back into traditional texts.

Generational Tensions and Change

Mom agonized when welfare workers/uncovered the cooking pots,
searched the refrigerator./As the much younger "baby,"/I could
stand aside,/they protected me, played with me,/looked to me to
become all they could not be....Poverty faded in gathering of the
clan, breaking the fast./Blessing the matzah,[18] sipping sacramental
wine./Recalling pains of heritage in bitter herbs,/ chanting, 'Let my
people go.'"
                    —RUTH WEG, "I KNEW THE GREAT DEPRESSION"

For all that we have in common, there will be obvious differences and discontinuities between my old age and that of my mother and her generation. Moreover, the same sort of contrast can be drawn between my mother's and grandmothers' generations. My image of my maternal grandmother is of a gray-haired old woman, cooking and caring for her family, wearing an apron over her housedress, and handling hot pots without a potholder. My children see their grandmother in a running suit as well as a housedress. Their memories will include lessons learned and values taught, as well as visits to Disney World and swimming pools. The changing historical context has been especially pronounced among immigrant families, affecting both the aging experience and the relationships between Jewish women and their daughters.

One major area of tension is the pull between the value of family closeness and the values of education and "success." In the United States, education became increasingly available to girls. Initially however, gender, age at immigration, and the financial status of the family determined whether a young woman was able to attend school or was required to work or be married off. Educational and career possibilities have expanded beyond many of our grandmothers' imaginations. These new opportunities have often led to conflicting needs and goals. Higher education and occupational success often necessitate geographic mobility which complicates the maintenance of close family relationships. Aging mothers have had to adjust to this situation, which may mean that adult children are not available to provide necessary care. This reality is increasingly accommodated by formal programming and elder-care providers. Because education and knowledge are venerated in the Jewish tradition, the adaptations required along with success in America have generally been accepted by aging Jewish parents. In many cases, however, there is significant discontinuity and discomfort due to the abandonment of direct care. The subjects most adult children study are not necessarily subjects valued by parents, and education "for girls"—particularly higher education—may seem like an extravagance to the elder generation. Disruption and discontinuity can also occur as mothers realize that what they did for their mothers, their daughters may not do for them. They may not be invited to live with their children or provided with the *naḥas* (joy) of Jewish grandchildren, for example.

With the changing rules and possibilities for women of middle age and younger, older mothers may feel remorse that they did not have the opportunities and choices now available. Also, they may want to relate to their daughters' experience but find themselves unable to do so because they inhabit such a different world. Though we have stressed the continuity provided by Jewish identity in the lives of the elderly, identity can also be a source of discontinuity. As Allen Glicksman points out in a report for the American Jewish Committee, "A strong Jewish identity...is not always a buttress against the problems of old age. If children and grandchildren are highly assimilated or intermarried, a strong sense of Jewish identity can cause pain and rifts among the three generations."[19]

From the point of view of the younger generation, stepping into our mother's shoes can be difficult to imagine. How will today's Jewish daughters fill the role of aging Jewish mother? I can only speculate that we will continue to juggle roles as we have throughout our lives—adapting what we have learned from our mothers and drawing on our own experiences.

Motherhood in Old Age

*"My husband died, my daughter left for medical school, and my
son had just gotten married. And I was left alone. And my first
reaction was, 'For whom will I do anything?'"*

—DORA W. IN SYDNEY STAHL WEINBERG'S
WORLD OF OUR MOTHERS

The aging Jewish mother has generally performed a range of roles throughout her life, but the role that ultimately counted for the elderly Jews Barbara Myerhoff studied was that of parenting.

> Above all [was] the rearing of children who were well-educated, well-married, good citizens, good parents in their own right, children who considered themselves Jews and raised their children as Jews, and who respected their elderly parents....The old women had the deck stacked in their favor. Nearly always they had maintained closer ties with their children than the men, and fairly or not, it was they who were considered most responsible for "how the children turned out."[20]

Responsibility to "turn the children out well" reflects and feeds stereotypes of the over-involved, excessively giving, and/or martyred Jewish mother. Ironically, as Susan Weidman Schneider points out, this *Yiddishe* (Jewish) Mama is alleged to raise nothing but over-indulged, ungiving Jewish American Princesses who are eventually supposed to become *Yiddishe* Mama's themselves.[21]

The role of Jewish mothers in America should be viewed in terms of the adaptations required by changing expectations after immigration to this country. Once in America, many women had less power and involvement in the economic life of the family than they had had in Europe. The stereotypical Jewish mother seems to be exaggerated because she has lost most of her social functions, and because her behavior "does not fit in with American notions about mothers."[22] Putting the same energies into the raising of children that previously had gone into home labor plus additional responsibilities, this mother overdoes her job. The Jewish mother stereotype is less likely to be applicable to the present generation whose lives have expanded beyond the boundaries of family and home, although the value of commitment to one's children remains strong.

Mother-Son and Mother-Daughter Relationships The proverb "A son's a son till he takes him a wife. A daughter's a daughter the rest of her life" suggests different expectations of male and female children. Feminist psychoanalytic theory suggests that girls identify with their mother for a longer time than boys. Girls also differentiate differently—not just more slowly— because boys can more clearly distinguish themselves from their mothers, while girls know that, in a sense, they will become their mothers. This brings us back to Rich's conception of matrophobia. In addition, mothers may be more interested in seeing daughters, rather than sons, as reflections of themselves.

Susan Starr Sered studied the attitudes of Kurdistani Jewish women in Jerusalem. They felt: "It is better to have daughters because daughters have more mercy and compassion than do sons, and daughters care if their elderly mothers are sick or unhappy."[23] Jewish women have traditionally been the caregivers, the nurturers, the keepers of the home, and the ones responsible for passing on family tradition. If mothers are caregivers and nurturers, daughters often share and, in later life, exchange those roles with them.

According to E.M. Bromberg, "mutuality, interdependence and positive connection" are reported to characterize the Jewish mother-daughter relationship in later life. This emotional closeness was also found in the family structures of Slavic and Italian women in a comparative study, but the Jewish women tended to seek geographic separation, living in a different household or neighborhood than their mothers. There is "constant tension between obligation and independence....The conflict between the desire for individuality and the obligation to family is not easily resolved."[24]

Care for Aging Mothers It is a common concern of elders in our society "not to be a burden." Sociologist Pauline Bart discusses the phenomenon of older Jewish parents who live frugally in order to save money to use if they should become ill or disabled. These parents are reluctant to ask for help from their children for fear of putting the relationship "to the test which it may not survive."[25] As I have noted, daughters or daughters-in-law have typically been the ones responsible for care of their aging parents in our society. Adult daughters who have had children later in life than their mothers, are likely to find themselves caught between the pressures of caring for children and those of caring for aging parents. In a reflection of the traditional guidelines outlined above, Bart and other researchers suggest that Jewish women are more devoted to their children than to their parents. Yet, as much as aging Jewish mothers may agree in principle that "the children" should take first priority, they may also have urgent needs.

Grandmotherhood Grandparents are usually "peripheral to the day-to-day business of living" as Abraham Monk has written. Yet, the relationship is often an important one to Jewish grandmothers and their grandchildren, being based not so much on discipline as on unconditional love.[26]

The role of Jewish grandmother can be pivotal to the teaching of domestic religion and to a sense of continuity. Grandmothers are often the family historians, and remain in touch with surviving members of the extended family. Moreover, "In addition to radiating and receiving unconditional love, grandparents often provide a 'safety net'—not to mention a babysitting service—during times of family transition or stress."²⁷ *Bubbe Meisehs By Shayneh Maidelehs*, written by Jewish granddaughters about their grandmothers, uncovers several themes: Storytelling, family history and roots, food, love, trust, and warm relationships. *My Grandmother's Stories: A Collection of Jewish Folk Tales* uses a girl's visit to her grandmother as an occasion for telling stories rooted in the grandmother's Russian Jewish heritage.²⁸ Reading these books with my children, I pass on important lessons which I learned informally from my own grandmother.

Conclusions

The domestic religion taught to us by our grandmothers and mothers provides a link to the traditional biblical and Talmudic teachings about age and aging. It also serves as a potentially important source of continuity in the aging process of Jewish women. At the same time, the rapid changes which characterize our lives typically complicate the picture. We are left with some answers and many more questions about how to fulfill our roles as adult daughters to aging mothers, and as aging women ourselves.

Researching and writing this chapter has been a personal, as well as a professional, quest. Looking back, I see that my decision to become a gerontologist was shaped by my view of aging, based on my Jewish ethnic tradition and my early positive experiences with my own grandparents. My choice to continue my education was fostered by the traditional respect for education I learned from my grandmother and mother, and made possible for me as a woman by the cultural context of American society. My relationship to my own mother is now filled with a greater respect for the legacy of attitudes, stories, and tools she has imparted to me. Writing this article has helped me mature into a deeper acceptance of my mother—a well-rooted version of the "second stage" described earlier which follows our initial attempts to distance ourselves from mother. Perhaps we can better prepare ourselves for our own aging experience—the later stages of our journey as Jewish women—by viewing ourselves as the adult daughters of Jewish mothers and embracing the resemblances we bear to them.

Responsum: A Voice from the Older Generation

MILDRED SELTZER

"What the daughter does, the mother did."
            —LEO ROSTEN, *TREASURY OF JEWISH QUOTATIONS*

I write this response to Dr. Dena Shenk's essay as her friend and as a member of her mother's generation. Dena and I represent two generations of gerontologists, as well as two generations of Jewish women.

Dear Dena,

In this space, I can respond to only a few of the many issues you raise, most importantly those relating to continuity and change between generations; between you and me. You make the familiar complaint that most daughters make: As you age you hear me in yourself. Yet the tune of continuity counterpoints with the chant of change. The singular theme of *Yiddishkeit* (Jewishness) is expressed in many voices. But remember: Just as daughters are not all one, so too mothers provide many role models. Your generation's process of interpreting traditions for these times is not unlike previous efforts to interpret, modify, and live out traditions. My generation, too, observed, discarded, adapted—just as centuries of women have done before.

You note an unusual degree of generational tension and change among Jews today. But when and for what people have there been no generational tensions and changes? In what ethnic group do mothers and daughters see eye to eye? The chasm between you and me is probably no greater than the one between my mother and me or my mother and her mother.

Barbara Myerhoff named four kinds of continuity: Social, per-

---

Dr. Mildred M. Seltzer is senior fellow of the Scripps Gerontology Center and professor emerita, Department of Sociology and Anthropology, Miami University, Oxford, Ohio.

sonal life-historical, cultural, and spiritual.[29] Being a Jew involves all four although, perhaps, the spiritual is less alive for me than it was to my mother or grandmother. Myerhoff also writes of the importance of ritual as "an assertion of continuity."[30] Ritual ties past, present, and future; the old with the new. Home ritual, and, increasingly, synagogue rituals in which women participate, help mothers and daughters to connect. Tools of home ritual become part of family history handed down from mother to daughter. Many of us have Sabbath candlesticks, mortar and pestle sets that have traveled across time, as well as space. Using them, we are tied to our foremothers in age-old behaviors. And even if we own, but do not use them, they represent, in a material way, our continuity with the past.

Mutual Responsibilities and Intergenerational Relations

The continued existence of our people rests upon the strength of the family. We care for one another out of the need to survive, as much for altruistic reasons or to follow biblical injunctions. The injunctions teach and reinforce an ideal; they do not necessarily describe historical reality. Indeed, they can be read as exhortations in reaction to the inadequacy of care provided to the elderly.

Current literature portrays a view of parent-child relationships in marked contrast with traditional descriptions. When I read some of the contemporary American-Jewish literature and see some of the films purporting to be descriptive of American-Jewish family life, I almost weep at the caricature of Jewish mothers and daughters. The strengths and capabilities of Jewish women are absurdly minimized. Writers and filmmakers have transformed strength into masochism and love into guilt. Anti-Semites could not have done a better job than some of the home-grown creators of the stereotypical American-Jewish Mother and American-Jewish Princess.

Lest you think this is an expression of hostility toward males, I would point out that literature, including some "scientific" articles written by women, do similar damage. Feminists, Jewish or otherwise, who view their mothers as devalued victims may overlook their strengths and ignore their experiences. They forget the women who worked outside the home so that their husbands might study. They overlook the competence of immigrant women who adapted to a new world. They ignore the research that Eva and Boaz Kahana cite, which indicates that Jewish immigrant women were expected to help in earning income.[31]

Opportunities, Losses, and Lessons

It is a challenge to be a Jew, a woman, and specifically an *old* Jewish woman—none are easy roles. Given our increased life expectancy, we experience new roles, more transitions, greater opportunities, more flexibility in defining ourselves. We also experience loss of friends, spouses, and other family members, as well as chronic illness. In a tradition for which the physical seems less important than the intellectual, deterioration of the body may be less feared than that of the mind. Increased life expectancy and duration itself can constitute a problem.

My generation may not have had role models to provide us with ways to handle some of these specific developments, but we learned from our mothers to adapt to the new without discarding what is valuable in the old. For example, we saw our mothers' involvement in Sisterhood and other synagogue activities and learned the importance of volunteer work in all arenas. We observed them holding offices in such organizations, and learned about leadership roles. We saw our mothers relating to new family members (e.g. sons-in-law, immigrants from Europe who came and stayed with us), and learned how to adapt to our children's reconstituted families.

Children's Treatment of Aging Parents

Ideally we honor, respect, and care for our aged parents within limits, as you point out. I am intrigued that the illustrations about caring for children and parents are mostly drawn from stories told by men, those who are usually not the caregivers. All the research shows that the bulk of care provided to aging people is provided within the family, usually by wives and daughters. It is not easy to provide nor to receive that care.

I ask that you forsake me not in my old age. I say to you and all the daughters of the next generation: "If I enter a retirement community or nursing home, let it be my choice. Let my wishes guide decisions about my care. When the time comes, let me die with dignity." The words sound trite as I write, perhaps because of their familiarity. I heard similar words from my mother and she, no doubt, from hers.

The Wisdom of Old Age

I do not believe that one necessarily becomes wise with age any more than one becomes patient, understanding, or kind. There is significant continuity to personality; kindness, patience, nastiness, and hostility are usually life-long characteristics, and not likely to spring forth full-blown in old age. One tradition teaches "At seventy, a man is as he was at seven."[32] Whether this refers to the continuity of personality, to senility, or to both is left unspoken. With luck, perspective may come with age, but I have never seen data to suggest that good sense is age or gender-related. If the sacred literature venerates age, folk proverbs reflect an everyday understanding: We are reminded that "Gray hair is a sign of age, not wisdom."[33]

Grandmotherhood

Being a grandmother is a *meḥayyeh* (pleasure; literally, enlivener)—I can personally assure you. It provides biological immortality. It ties us to the future. We become the bridge over which continuity and change occur, on which past, present, and future meet. We provide roots and resources—both familial and ethnic. We sing songs and tell stories we learned from *our* grandparents. The words to lullabies such as "Under Gitteleh's Cradle" change to reflect current times and changing roles; instead of marrying a student, Gitteleh may become one. Family stories tell of heroic deeds, teach values, and provide role models for children.

Conclusions

As life's circumstances continue to change, as you age, certain things remain immutable: You are woman, anthropologist, gerontologist, wife, daughter, mother, and fundamentally Jew. You may

not be a Jew in the way your ancestors were—I certainly am not—
but we are born, age, and die as Jews whether we embrace that
fact or reject it.

Like your generation, mine has struggled with beliefs, responsibilities, and our mothers. We survive—physically and vicariously through you, the next link in the chain—and look toward the
future. That is not too shabby an accomplishment—or legacy.

Leḥayyim (to life),
Your Mother's Voice

Growing Old—My View

HARRIET M. PERL

"Growing old is hell, but it does beat the alternative."
—*SOMEBODY* SAID IT FOR THE FIRST TIME

It is not news that our culture worships youth—I have always
known that. But it did not begin to infuriate me until my friends
started praising me for appearing or acting younger than my sev-
enty-three years. I do not want to be younger; I am not, as "they"
say, into denial.

Yes, I do have a part-time job, and yes, I am fairly energetic,
and yes, I have pretty good stamina—all of this attributable to a
lucky combination of genes, circumstances, and—believe it or
not—loneliness.

I am a single woman with no siblings and very few blood relatives, none in my city. I live alone, by preference, and I cherish my
independence. But, as the shrinks would say, my dependency
needs are seldom met.

Therefore, if I do not want to spend all of my time in solitude,
it is important to be what "they" call active: Belong, participate,
reach out, give, smile. No one (including me) likes a *kvetch* (whin-
er) nor a health wailer nor a pessimist.

I take seriously my duties as a member of the board of direc-

---

Harriet M. Perl, a secondary teacher for thirty-five years, is a feminist and pioneer in consciousness raising, a political liberal, a part-time worker for the teachers' union, and a very Reform Jew.

tors of Beth Chayim Chadashim, the world's first gay/lesbian religious entity fully accepted by its parent organization—in this case the Union of American Hebrew Congregations. Our meetings can make me cry or laugh or worry or go wild with anger, often all at one sitting. I drag myself to services when I must, but my atheism refuses to bow to my love of being Jewish. I have learned to live with the contradiction, and I now even *bentsch likht* (light Sabbath and holiday candles) in honor and memory of my grandmother.

My job is also both stressful and wonderful—I help produce the prize-winning newspaper of UTLA (United Teachers Los Angeles). I was a teacher for thirty-five years, a union member for all of them. The money I earn from my union, along with my pension, helps me eke out a living.

So I do what "they" say to do: I even exercise, though I am cheerfully and irrevocably overweight and a chocoholic. One of these days the doctors will find that enjoying food is better for health than worrying over cholesterol. Then I will have pleased all of "them".

What "they" do not talk about and pretend does not exist is the knowledge I gained on my own, as I suspect every old person does: I must live in the present because I have no future. The statistics and my personal experience with parents and others tell me that I am close to the time when I will lose my independence—when I will not be able to drive a car or manage my home alone or see my doctor just for semi-annual checkups. The frailty awaiting me casts a dark shadow over the future, because it means no job and no usefulness; it means having to buy services I now perform for myself; it means the terrifying possibility of outliving my money. The worst fear of all is that my mind will go before my body. I saw it happen to my mother—and she had me to help. I have friends, but there are limits to friendship.

So I put the fear away, keeping it private. Friends my age do not need to be told, and the younger ones do not want to know. I do not blame them; I do not want to know, either. My memories also belong to me alone, since the young are not generally interested in the past. But the rest of me is up and going, eager to see what will happen today—and furious because I know that there will be a day when I will not be here and the world will go on without me—intolerable thought.

I demand immortality.

Widowhood after a Long Marriage: Two Poems

BARBARA D. HOLENDER

"Our dead reach out to us in mysterious ways."
                                        —BARBARA HOLENDER, "LIFELINE"

Killing the Fish

> I'm killing the fish
> the way you used to—
> overfeeding, undercleaning—
>
> When you, who never asked for anything—
> and let me know
> you never asked for anything—
> asked for fish,
> I brought you angels, black and silver,
> fiery platys, golden swords,
> instead of the little goldfish
> you said you expected.
> Deprived of grace,
> you watched from your wheelchair
> their delicate passes.
>
> And we, who never bickered,
> bickered. *You're killing the fish*,
> I said three times a day,
> and you said, *Look, they're hungry*,
> and you said, *Either feed them yourself*
> *or get out of here while I do.*
>
> Then one fish died.
> Then another fish died.
> Then I fed them myself because
> you could no longer raise your arm.

Barbara D. Holender is the author of *Shivah Poems: Poems of Mourning* (Andrew Mountain Press, 1992) and *Ladies of Genesis* (Jewish Women's Resource Center, 1991) and is represented in numerous anthologies.

The fish were dying
and you were dying,
and then you really did it—
died—and left me
with eight fish and a deep desire
never to care for anything again.

On the Other Hand

Our friends remark how well I have adjusted
to this year of widowhood.
Yesterday I pried off the wedding band
restricting my circulation.

Make it fit, I told the jeweler, *either hand.*
Left or right? he said. *They're different.*
What do widows do?
They do what they want to do.

All my fingers clenched.
Not one would choose.

I could put on a guard, he said.
You'd have a nice pinky ring
till you made up your mind.

I'm wearing it fifth finger
left hand, the heart side.
I have adjusted to everything
but the facts.

A Ceremony of Passage
on My Sixty-Fifth Birthday

BARBARA D. HOLENDER

*"...A time to plant and a time to uproot that
which has been planted."*

—ECCLESIASTES 3:2

The following is adapted from a ceremony of Simḥat Ḥokhmah *(celebration of elder wisdom) written for and shared with my Bible study group, a* minyan *(quorum) of women friends who have studied together for over thirty years. Only the ten of us were present on March 15, 1992, my sixty-fifth birthday. After the ceremony, each of my friends shared her perceptions of me—a surprising conclusion, this bonding of women in one of our rare celebratory rites of passage.*

Although it can be said that life begins anew at seventy (Psalms 90:10), my rite of passage coincides with my sixty-fifth year, because it is the end of a ten-year period of change and growth. I want to celebrate with my *minyan* of scholars because you have kept me alive and warm at a time when I needed you, and I love you for that.

In these ten years, I have lost my husband, my father, my mother—my most intimate connections. I have lived through fear, loneliness, pain, and the most fundamental upheaval, and gained confidence, independence, a whole exciting new life.

These past few months I have sensed a sea-change, something new developing that I could not identify, but I acted on it by finishing and sending off my collected poems because I do not write the same way any more. Words kept recurring in my mind: Divest, accept, cleanse, plant. A ceremonial mood took hold, and I decided to see where it would take me, to define the implications of those words.

Divest Divest of old guilts, false obligations, ills and evils long since lived through and resolved. Of petty distractions and unwelcome intrusions. Travel light, because I feel mortality breathing down my neck.

Accept Accept time, its ravages, brevity, unpredictability.

Accept my body, its aging, its demands, the awkward and ludicrous. Accept the possibility that my loved ones, spirit, mind, comfort, and health could be swept away in a breath. Relish what I have. But *never* allow myself to accept my limitations, nor even to ask what they are.

Cleanse Water is important in my life. I go to the ocean for comfort and healing. The *mikveh* (ritual bath) seemed the right place—to enter naked, to say the *berakhot* (blessings), to immerse and emerge purified in an ancient ritual, a link with Eden, according to Aryeh Kaplan.[34] It was my first time.

Plant I wanted to plant seeds, real, living seeds, not the seeds of poems and ideas I deal with all the time. I chose sage, which represents longevity, wisdom, and sagacity.

Although I am a very celebratory person, I am not usually ceremonious. But I felt the need to mark this transition. I modeled my ceremony on the archetypal Jewish rite of passage: That of Abraham. It consists of a naming and a covenant.

A CEREMONY OF PASSAGE ON MY SIXTY-FIFTH BIRTHDAY

Naming and Renaming

My parents gave me a beautiful name, Bluma Ḥaya,
which translates as "living flower." To that I add
Beruriah from the root meaning clear, a scholar's name.
Beruriah was the wife of the second century scholar
Rabbi Meir and a famous scholar in her own right.[35] I
hope for a flowering of wisdom in my old age.

My renaming renews my life as a Jewish woman and
poet trying to reach out to others, perhaps giving them
the words they need. The taking of a new Hebrew name
also marks my commitment to begin at long last the serious study of Hebrew.

Immersing Myself in Covenant

Symbols are part of every ritual. Mine are water, a ring,
an apple. Water—the water of the *mikveh* for spiritual
cleansing. A ring—the cycle and binding of generations.

I wear my grandmother's wedding ring; one day my daughter will wear it.

Abraham concluded a covenant with God by cutting an animal in two (Genesis 15:10). I cut an apple, Eve's fruit.[36] In choosing knowledge, we are her heirs.

Words of Song and Blessing

Of course, we must have a poem:

Song for Her Next Age

> Ride, ride, old woman
> ride down your days, hound them to heel
> wind in your teeth, ride to the sea
> salt on your tongue, brine in your blood
> naked and nerved, sing down your days.
>
> Howl down the sea, old woman
> into its mouth cry out your name
> into its wake cast off your bones
> into its womb bury your own.
>
> Old woman, rise from the sea undone—
> you have won, you have won.

Blessed are You *Shekhinah* (close-dwelling presence of God, associated with the feminine), in whose name we come into our own.

As we planted the sage, we recited: Praised be You, Holy One of Blessing, giver of life and wisdom. May these seeds take root to remind us that we have it within us to gain *hokhmah* (wisdom), and may we be granted long life for our purpose.[37]

בָּרוּךְ אַתָּה יי אֱלֹהֵינוּ מֶלֶךְ הָעוֹלָם, שֶׁהֶחֱיָנוּ וְקִיְּמָנוּ וְהִגִּיעָנוּ לַזְּמַן הַזֶּה.

Barukh attah adonai eloheinu melekh ha'olam, sheheheyanu vekiyyemanu vehiggi'anu lazeman hazeh.

Praised are You Ruler of the world who has kept us in life, sustained us, and brought us to this day.

15

Death and Mourning

The death of a loved one usually means chaos for the survivors. The ordered world we know will never be the same, and in the new landscape of a universe without that loved one, we are lost. Implicitly and explicitly, Jewish mourning practices address the chaos and unstable ground, and help in finding, we hope, a surer footing and a new order.

Traditionally, we acknowledge losses by ripping our clothes, just as the fabric of life has been torn. In addition, Jewish law designates discrete periods in the mourning process, through which mourners are meant gradually to mend their private universe and re-enter the world of shared community. During *aninut* (period between death and burial) no expectations are placed on the mourner, who may be in shock, enraged, or in denial. After the burial, the first three days of *shiv'ah* (formal period of mourning) are set aside for the most intense bereavement and restrictions from normal activity. Over the next four days of *shiv'ah*, mourners take a few tiny steps toward restoring a degree of normalcy. For example, after day three, but not earlier, mourners are allowed to respond to the greetings of those who may not realize that they are in mourning (BT *Mo'ed Katan* 15a, *Shulḥan Arukh Yoreh De'ah* 385:1). Yet for the entire seven days mourners eschew "normal" daily tasks and ablutions, for life is not yet, or again, normal. Not working (except when there is extreme financial need, and then only during the latter four days and usually at home); not going to synagogue (except on Sabbaths and holidays); not (with the above exceptions) leaving home; not, by custom, looking in mirrors; not bathing; not having sex; not sitting on normal chairs—these and other traditional prohibitions give mourners the time and impetus to face their grief, rather than burying it along with the dead.[1] At the end of *shiv'ah*, a walk around the block symbolizes re-entry into the world and reminds us of the indifference of nature, which has gone on as before, which encompasses death and is therefore not, as we are, rent by it.

After *shiv'ah*, mourners return to most regular daily activities, but do not immediately buy or wear new clothes, cut their hair or beards, give nor receive gifts, listen to music, or attend celebrations, feasts, or parties—even those associated with lifecycle rituals.[2] For mourners of siblings, spouses, and children, these traditional restrictions are lifted at *sheloshim* (thirty days after death or sooner if a festival intervenes).[3] Those mourning a parent continue to avoid listening to music and attending celebrations for a full year. A mourner generally says *Kaddish* (mourner's prayer) for thirty days after the death of a spouse, sibling, or child, and for eleven months after the death of a parent. The unveiling of a tombstone usually takes place around the time of the first *yartzeit* (anniversary of a death). Thereafter, mourning and remembrance become part of a yearly rhythm. *Kaddish* is recited on each *yartzeit* and four times a year at a communal *Yizkor* (memorial service). In addition, it is customary to visit the graves of loved ones during the High Holiday season.

Rabbi Harlan Wexler once remarked that no one approaches a rabbi and says, "Rabbi, I'm in love! What should I do?" whereas even Jews who know mourning law thoroughly will ask, "Rabbi, s/he is dead. What should I do?" This is not to denigrate the importance of a Jewish sex ethic or of marital law. Rather, it stresses the tremendous need we have for ritual and structure at the time of death, in the face of chaos. We seek ultimate meaning and correctness at a time of ultimate uncertainty. If ritual generally helps us to traverse life's bumpy and sometimes frightening thresholds, then this final passage, this room with no apparent exit, requires ritual all the more. Jews find some measure of solace and stability in rites and customs observed in their proper sequence.

Often, mourners find great comfort, as well, in talking and hearing about the one who has died. The tradition wisely advises *menaḥamei avelim* (comforters of those who mourn) to allow the bereaved to assume the lead in all discussions during *shiv'ah* (BT *Mo'ed Katan* 28b). Unfortunately, visitors to a house of mourning sometimes hesitate to discuss the deceased for fear of upsetting the mourners, even though recalling the life that was, is almost invariably exactly what mourners want and need. Officiating at weddings is my favorite duty as a rabbi, but I never feel more useful than at a funeral when I offer the *hesped* (eulogy)—a careful and truthful summing up of a life and its gifts. Somehow, at least in part, the cosmic order is restored by story.

The finality of death raises two kinds of questions: Whys and whats. Whys are cries of pain masquerading as theological or moral questions: "Why me?" "Why her?" "Why so young?" "Why so much suffering, Rabbi, if God is good?" These are worthy and fair questions, which legitimately occupy all thoughtful people, at one time or another. We could talk of the randomness of nature, of the appreciation for the preciousness of life that comes with the awareness of death, of faith as a choice made in the face of uncertainty, of theodicy and theology and love. No tidy answers are possible, and, at the time of grief, answers are not even really desired. What people really want is to cry and be angry and have their loved ones back. If they desire answers at all, it is to the "what" questions, which come to the fore as grief begins to recede. "Whats" are the result of living life within the boundaries of certain death, and the consequent necessity of setting priorities: "What did I learn from him/her?" "What can I do to honor the memory?" "What meaning and purpose can I find in life, circumscribed and imperfect as it is?" "Having witnessed this death, what sort of a death do I want?" And, therefore, "Having witnessed this life, what sort of life do I want?" Relating to this, Rabbi Eliezer taught, "Repent one day before your death" (Mishnah *Avot* 2:15), which is another way of saying live each day in the integrity you would choose if you knew it to be your last. It may be.

Theorizing on what exists after death, the Rabbis postulate two main ideas: Resurrection of the dead and immortality of the soul. Whether souls are quiescent or active between the time of death and resurrection is open to Rabbinic dispute and interpretation. The ancient Rabbis also have differing criteria and visions of reward and punishment in the next life, and there is no uniform doctrine of *gan eden, geihinnom,* and *she'ol* (loosely, heaven, hell, and purgatory). Equally diverse and contradictory are Rabbinic views of the timing of the messianic era and the events leading to and following its inauguration.

Of all the conceptions of afterlife, the most consistent and doctrinal is the resurrection of the dead. The Rabbis traced this view to the Bible and, in contrast to the Sadducees, staunchly supported it (Mishnah *Sanhedrin* 10:1, BT *Sanhedrin* 91a-b, 99b, 105a). Many modern Jews reject the belief in resurrection or at least interpret it on a symbolic, rather than a literal, physical level. The Reform and Reconstructionist prayerbooks have changed the traditional language of the *Amidah* (series of blessings which is the centerpiece of every prayer service) to distance themselves from the assertion of a physical resurrection. Contemporary Jews tend to be more comfortable with a non-literal belief in the immortality of the soul— via lasting contributions, progeny, students, and human memory—than with the concept that souls are stored in heaven and eventually reunited with their bodies, now healed and in the land of Israel (*Tanḥuma Buber, Vayiggash* 104b, BT *Ketubbot* 111a-b).

The generalizations that Judaism measures its adherents more by behavior than by belief and is more this-worldly than other-worldly find their best support in the conflicting Rabbinic images, teachings, and predictions of the afterlife. This world may be just "a vestibule to the world to come" (Mishnah *Avot* 4:21), but even so, we emphasize what is here rather than what is hereafter. Rabbi Jacob, author of the above quotation, spells out the Rabbinic paradox: "Better one hour of repentance and good deeds in this world than the whole of the world to come. Yet better one hour of bliss in the world to come than the whole of this life" (Mishnah *Avot* 4:17). The next world has a sort of bliss we cannot know, but that is precisely the point: We cannot know it, just as we cannot know the answers to our "why" questions. We can only fulfill our highest purpose in this life. As Rabbi Yokhanan taught: "...As for the world to come, no eye has seen what God has prepared for those who wait for [the divine]" (after BT *Berakhot* 34b). Thus, "We Jews take our worlds one at a time."

Rabbi Margaret Holub writes of death from the point of view of the mourner, the dying person, and, impressively, of the soul itself. There are fine books and articles, to which she refers the reader, outlining the correlation between Jewish mourning rituals and the psychological process of grief and healing. It has been widely argued that laws around death and mourning both respect the various psychological stages of mourning—including denial, anger, bargaining with God, depression, and acceptance—and help the bereaved to pass through them successfully. Rabbi Holub argues for a correlation between mourning law and cosmology, finding in the traditional observances not only a potential source of spiritual and psychological strength for the bereaved, but a key to the Rabbinic understanding of how our very existence is structured. In particular, she characterizes life as the union of body and soul, death as their separation, and mourning as the process by which those who have been close to the deceased repair the degree of separation caused in them, by the full separation which their loved one has undergone. Her point of view leads to innovative and persuasive interpretations of everything from the *Kaddish* to *aninut* to the tradition of opening windows after a death. In addition to enriching and providing alternatives to traditional explanations of the law, Rabbi Holub also critiques the limits set by Jewish law, particularly in prescribing whom we may and must mourn formally.

Anne Brener's essay could be cited as a prooftext for Rabbi Holub's, in that Brener went through a spiritual "coming apart" after her mother's suicide. Her returning to wholeness was a gradual process, achieved in community—first among women and later among Jewish men and women. Brener made use of "why" questions, free self-expression, journal writing, group support, prayer, and the Jewish legal attitude toward suicide, to help her separate herself from her mother's separation and connect with her mother's humanity. The official repeal of several burial and mourning rituals in the case of suicide, together with women's traditional exclusion from reciting *Kaddish*, gave her a sense of "open-ness" and helped her to find healing, compassion, and, in her words, a "holy place of comfort." Her "Dream *Kaddish*" uses the image of an umbilical cord to describe the powerful and lasting connection between mother and daughter.

Rabbi Vicki Hollander offers a modern version of the traditional confessional before dying, selecting and paraphrasing from the original. The words of the confessional are powerful not only in bringing a life to closure, but also in inspiring the living to live more nobly and to value the gift of life.

Carol V. Davis' poems on her mother's death capture the terrible pain of loss, the different reactions it evokes at different stages, and the different colors it takes on. The final poem, "The Seventh Year," indicts the cruelty of death and of God, as its apparent orchestrator. The overriding impression in these poems, however, is of love and of the pain of losing a mother whose memory is clearly for a blessing.

In the end, that last phrase is the point of this chapter—and even of life itself. We live and ritualize each stage of our lives that our existence may be, ultimately, for a blessing.

A Cosmology of Mourning

MARGARET HOLUB

"Return unto thy rest, O my soul, for the Lord hath dealt bounti-
fully with thee."

—PSALMS 116:7

"I've been with many people whose grief has been beyond bearing. And in some ways it has been the best thing that ever happened to them,"[4] writes Stephen Levine in a popular book that I
turned to when I was in mourning. People flock to Levine's semi-
nars—people with cancer, people who have lost children, people
who are reckoning with death. He, Elisabeth Kübler-Ross, and
others have brought death front and center on the American
stage.[5]

When the man I loved died, I read Levine and Kübler-Ross
and gratefully accepted their adjurations not to stifle my grief, to
welcome and feel fully each of its inevitable stages. I wept every
day for two years. This new psychological perspective on grief
probably saved my life, and I am thankful that a "stiff upper lip"
is no longer considered a virtue. But for all my willingness to face
and express my feelings, something was missing for me at the
time of my grieving. I needed a deeper understanding of death
and of my own heartbreak.

Grief is not only a psychological response to a mystery. It is
part of the mystery itself. Mourning is an essential process of
tikkun (repair) by which the world can continue to function.
Jewish tradition is rich in ritual which helps people survive the
death of a loved one. And this ritual is grounded in a particular
cosmology, without which the ritual may be comforting, but does
not make philosophical sense.

What Is Death?

At the last moment of Moses' life, say the Rabbis, Moses' soul
protests being compelled, even by the kiss of God, to leave his

---

Rabbi Margaret Holub is the spiritual leader of a rural, alternative *"shtetl"* on the
North Coast of California.

pure and beautiful body. "Never a fly rested upon [Moses' body], never did leprosy show itself upon it," says the voice of the soul, which is described in the feminine. "Therefore do I love it and do not wish to leave it." And God, Godself, addresses Moses' soul: "Hesitate not, my daughter...I myself will take you to the highest heavens and let you dwell under the throne of My Glory, like the Seraphim, Ofannim, Cherubim and other angels." In the end, Moses himself must dismiss her. "Return unto Thy rest, O my soul, for the Lord has dealt bountifully with me," he quotes from Psalms 116:7; and at that moment God kisses Moses upon the lips in a sublime coupling that allows the soul to return to its Source.[6]

At the moment of a person's death, it is customary for people standing nearby to open the windows, as though literally to let the soul escape and ascend.[7] And at the graveside we pray, "May the God of mercy bring the soul of [so-and-so] under the cover of God's wings, and may his/her soul be bound up in the bond of eternal life." Thus, for Moses and for us all, the soul leaves the body at the time of death and is bound up in the limitless being of God.

Though the final moment of death is specific and instantaneous, the separation of body and soul may occur over time. Jewish law recognizes an interval during which death is in process. This does not refer to a decline in health or a diagnosis of terminal illness, but to the final moments when one is lingering between this world and the next. During this interval a person is called a *goses/goseset* (dying person), technically alive, yet with the quality of a dead body. A *kohen* (member of the priestly class) is not permitted to enter the resting place of a *goses/goseset*, just as a *kohen* may not go near a dead body. Yet a doctor, even a *kohen*, must endeavor fully to preserve the life even for another moment.

I was a *goseset* once. I took my kayak from the mouth of a local river into a swirl of riptides and was washed out of the boat into the ocean, where I was pounded against rocks for a full hour. I remember the progression of my thoughts exactly, from certainty that I would survive to the encroaching realization that I would not, could not, that I had a minute left; one more washing wave and I would inhale the water and drown. Like Moses in the *midrash* (Rabbinic legend), I saw the future. I saw my husband bereft, witnessed my mother hearing the news of my death, watched my funeral in detail. And I remember shouting, "No! No!" against death, over and over into the waves and rocks, though no one was nearby and the pounding water obliterated any sound I could make.

Somehow, unlike Moses, I was successful in my appeal. I was finally seen thrashing in the water and rescued by the fire department. Depressed and confused for the next six weeks, I visited a friend who told me, "You are still out of your body." I realized that she was exactly, literally right.

Neither the body nor the soul on its own is a human life. Human life is a meeting, a miracle, a volatile, unstable coupling of elements. We understand that the body will return to dust and the soul to the one great, undifferentiated breath. At the moment of death, we are taught that it is meritorious to say, "I hereby accept my actual death joyfully and wholeheartedly....I transmit my body, life, soul, and spirit for the unification of God's great Name."[8] It is also customary to say the *Shema* (central prayer that declares God's oneness). When the breath leaves a body and returns to its Source, God's name is unified. And the individuality of that person is no more.

After death, one is no longer woman or man, adult or child, ignorant or learned, good or evil. It is striking that a baby girl is welcomed to the world very differently than a baby boy; a young woman enters puberty differently than a young man; at a wedding, the separate roles of *kallah* and *ḥatan* (bride and groom) are clearly delineated; a scholar is treated differently than a rogue. Yet the guarding, washing, burial, eulogizing, and mourning of every Jew is essentially identical, whomever the person may have been in life.

Life in its specificity, when we exist with our individual attributes—gender, family and lineage, talents and deficits, body and soul, accrued experiences—is an explosion in time, a fusion, a bit of luck or grace in a vast, tumbling universe of which we are a minute part. From our own embodied, ensouled perspective, this momentary coupling is of overriding importance. The fact that our own soul will unwrap from our body, the fact that the same will happen to all those whom we love, the fact that forces of illness, violence, and accident are agents of this uncoupling—at times these facts intrude on us with terrible force. One can see in our spiritual tradition a guide towards gratitude for the fusion of body and soul into life, a blueprint for squandering as little precious presence as we can, and a prescription for mourning the inevitable detachment of body from soul.

The Metaphysics of Mourning

How can we tell where one person ends and another begins? The material finitude of our bodies is evident, but the borders of the soul are less definite. We merge as we learn from one another, live together and accrue common experiences, take on each other's projects, and enter into shared fates. Love blurs the boundaries between one soul and another. In fact, love might be defined as that very erosion, absorption, commingling.

When the tenuous coupling of a person's body and soul is undone by death, the bond of body and soul within each person who has been close to the *met/metah* is also weakened. The breath of God within all who were bound up with that person wishes, as it were, to leave the bodies of its temporary residence and to flee to the one great Source. And so it is that a survivor must mourn, to heal and repair the bond between his or her own body and soul—literally, in some measure, to stay alive.

Anthropologist Victor Turner speaks of liminality, of a time when everything is changing, when a person is especially vulnerable, almost as though his or her skin were missing. At such a time, Turner says, the community comes together, the tradition steps in, and together we walk the person through the tunnel of liminality to a new place in a world reconnected.[9]

Mourning is perhaps the ultimate liminal, or disconnected, state. Outside us, the web of life has been torn. Within us, body and soul are wrestling apart. Our tradition recognizes that, while body and soul may have been severed almost instantaneously for the loved one who died, the reweaving of body and soul in the survivors—the agenda of mourning—happens in stages over weeks, months, years, and generations. No wonder, then, that the reuniting of the bodies and souls of all people for the great messianic resurrection is imagined to require millennia of preparation.

A Few Holy Tools

The task of mourning is to re-cement the bond between body and soul in people facing the internal rift left by the death of their loved one. Jewish tradition offers a set of finely crafted tools for reviving the union that makes for life in survivors. These rituals have a metaphysical as well as a psychological dimension.[10]

As a rabbi with a non-halakhic (non-legal) orientation, who considers Jewish law instructive rather than binding, I often find myself in the ironic position of—for want of a better word—negotiating with mourners to observe traditional mourning rituals: "Maybe you would consider three days of *shiv'ah* (formal period of mourning, usually seven days) and a *minyan* (prayer quorum) on the thirtieth day after the death? No? How about just one *minyan* to say *Kaddish* (mourner's prayer) and, later, an unveiling?" In almost every other aspect of Jewish practice, I think that people should do what they want to do, what coheres with their vision of life. But I sense that the task of mourning may demand something different than what people want in the moment, may in fact be exactly the opposite of what they want. And there may be more at stake than they can possibly know in those early days of grief.

Below are a few examples of Jewish mourning practices and the cosmological concerns that I believe they address:

Aninut **(Period between Death and Burial)** Jewish law exempts *kerovim* (close relatives obligated to mourn) from normal religious requirements during the period between the death and the burial of their beloved. The usual reason given is that *onenim* (the bereft during *aninut*) are engaged in one commandment—i.e. preparing for the funeral—and are therefore exempt from others (*Shulḥan Arukh Yoreh De'ah* 341:1). However, we can also read the *halakhah* (Jewish law) according to a cosmological construct. *Onenim* are exempt, from this point of view, because only the fully living must perform *mitzvot* (commandments), and, following the death of a beloved, survivors border on death themselves. This cosmological perspective is re-enforced by the striking, halakhic exemption of the community from caring for mourners in those first hours or days. The community is not expected to visit, bring food, or even extend words of comfort. It is as though the angel of death were still in the house, stalking with sword raised. Until the burial, the death is still happening, body and soul are shaking apart throughout the household. The community stays away, as rebuilding cannot begin until the earthquake is over.

I well remember a moment, immediately after the death of the man I loved, when I was at the home of friends. It was a grey afternoon, and I sat outside on a log, weeping. As I sat there, it began to rain. And I recall vividly that, at that moment, the decision to stand up and walk into the house was simply beyond me, and I sat outside until I was soaked. Right then I was like a *metah*, unable to carry on even the simplest functions of life. It was too soon to comfort me, too soon to feed me, too soon to reason with me.

During the time of *aninut*, the *kerovim* are not traditionally involved with caring for the dead body, which has its own needs. This work is done by others, either at a funeral home or, more traditionally, by a *hevrah kaddishah* (burial society). Members of the burial society wash and dress the body and accompany it until the moment of burial. When our community's *hevrah kaddishah* arrives to do its holy work, a family member or close friend of the one who died will sometimes ask to help. We discourage it, but once or twice relatives of the deceased have joined in. It takes great strength of soul, and a certain amount of bodily strength as well, to do *levayat hamet* (caring for/accompanying the dead). Close family and friends, we have learned, are invariably too broken to do this work. At the moment when death is so fresh, when it may still be invisibly in process, the work of the *kerovim* is to survive.

Hespedim **(Eulogies)**   At the funeral at least one eulogy is usually given. In my community, often everyone present will offer a memory, teaching, or observation about the person who has died. And these narratives fix, like fixer in a darkroom, an image of the life which blew through the universe like a comet.

We have all had the experience of coming home after a vacation. Someone asks us, "How was your trip?" And to answer, we condense days or weeks into a narrative. After we have told a few people about our vacation, we may notice that the actual memory of the trip begins to fade. What remains is the story we have been telling. So, too, at the moment when we bury the body, when we pray for the ascension of the soul, we hold onto the story.

Kevurah **(Burial)** People who attend a Jewish funeral for the first time often remark on the beautiful, brutal custom of having family members pitch shovelsful of dirt into the grave. "It makes death real," they say. What resounds in my recollection of burials is the sound of clods of soil hitting the wooden coffin, the hollow thud. This is something you would never do to any living being, much less to a person you loved. And so it hits you as you hold the shovel: Whatever is in that hole in the ground is not that person. Their existence is over; body and soul are wholly separated. Any ambivalence, lingering question or hope ends with that hollow sound.

Kaddish **(Mourner's Prayer)** Rabbi Billy Berkowitz conceived the exercise of giving his congregants a prayerbook and a red pencil and challenging them to edit out anything they found to be untrue. I asked Billy what, if anything, he would retain. "Only a fragment of one line," he said, "from the *Kaddish*: '[God is] far beyond any blessings, songs, praises, and consolations that can be expressed in the world.'" There are many forms of the *Kaddish* recited in prayer services and study halls, but mourners stand and recite a special *Kaddish*. Their *Kaddish* echoes what appears eminently true for mourners, that God is far away, "far beyond," that the words of most prayers may not even come close to the feelings in the speaker's heart. We tend to think of the *Kaddish* as a brave or comforting affirmation of God's glory, but from the perspective of the mourner, it may just as well be an acknowledgement of God's apparent distance.

Reintroducing Festivity Gradually For the first seven days following the funeral, body and soul are minimally tended. Most conspicuously, any element of the erotic, of the life-force, is muted. One does not have sex (BT *Mo'ed Katan* 21a, *Shulḥan Arukh Yoreh De'ah* 383:1). Mourners do not even wash or dress attractively (*Shulḥan Arukh Yoreh De'ah* 389:1, BT *Mo'ed Katan* 17b, *Sede Ḥemed, Avelut* 40). Sitting at normal height, wearing leather, shaving (for men), and wearing shoes are likewise prohibited (*Shulḥan Arukh Yoreh De'ah* 387:1-2, 380:1, 382:1, 390:1), and it is customary not to look in the mirror.

After seven days (sometimes fewer if the death happens shortly before a festival) mourners clean up, dress in fresh clothing, and go back to work. But festivity is not permitted for three more weeks, or for a full year if it is a parent who died (Shaḥ on *Shulḥan Arukh Yoreh De'ah* 344:9). While it is permitted to attend lifecycle rituals, the festivities afterwards are to be avoided. Festivity is the linking of body and soul. While their bond is fragile, one does not stretch it by trying to be merry.

Finally, after thirty days or one year has ended, one may again dance, listen to music, attend parties, throw oneself into the happiness of the community. The *tikkun* is thereby considered to be more or less complete.

Elleh Ezkerah (These Do I Remember): Ongoing Markers

One never finishes mourning. Body and soul are rejoined, but with a scar at the bond. And so it is that two sorts of ritual mourning continue for the life of the mourner. On anniversaries of the death, the mourners are singled out. They light a *yartzeit* candle (candle burned on the anniversary of a family member's death) and stand in the congregation to say *Kaddish*. In addition, four times a year there is a moment of collective mourning. The *Yizkor* (memorial service) is essentially identical to the funeral service for an individual, but here the names of all the loved ones of the entire community are read and/or recorded. Everyone mourns together, publicly. How different it is to mark the *yartzeit* of a family member than it is to memorialize all the deaths in a community. The former custom makes a private, cosmological point: You, and not your loved one, are alive to stand and stand out, in the community. The latter makes a communal point about shared destiny; everyone sustains loss and everyone is part of the community of comforters. In many synagogues, these ideas are physicalized in the choreography of the prayer services: Only those who are in mourning or observing a *yartzeit* stand when the *Kaddish* is said, but the entire community stands during *Yizkor*.

How To Find Latitude in a System of Obligations and Proscriptions?

The line between the desirable and the mandatory is often blurred in Jewish practice. For example: One might reasonably wish to mourn the death of a parent. Therefore *halakhah* dictates that one must. So too the negative; what one is exempt from, one is often prohibited from doing. Because a woman is not required to pray three times a day, traditional Judaism holds that she is not permitted to be counted in a *minyan*. *Halakhah* does not have many optional categories, and this is a problem.

What if you want to go to a party three weeks after a death? What if you do not wish to mourn the death of a sister from whom you were estranged? What if four days of *shiv'ah* are enough? What if you still cannot stomach a happy occasion six months after the death of your child?

Halakhah prescribes for whom one should mourn. One is a *karov* (close relative obligated to mourn) to one's mother, father, spouse, sister, brother, son, or daughter. One is required to mourn for all of them. And, consequently, in most traditional settings, one is prohibited from officially mourning anyone else.

These days, and probably to some extent always, "family" may include people other than the seven traditional *kerovim*. Your lesbian partner, your godchild, your beloved neighbor, the elder who became like a grandparent to you, your non-Jewish spouse— all of these and more are *kerovim*, close to our hearts. Communities must make room for us to mourn those we love.

Conversely, Jewish communities must understand if we choose to mourn less, or differently, those whom we did not love. The question has been raised in more than one forum as to whether one is obligated to mourn an abusive parent. Benay Lappe cites halakhic precedents and principles, by which individuals may be exempted from saying *Kaddish* for parents who sexually abused them.[11] She favors providing a range of options from doing nothing at all when that abusive parent dies to taking on the full obligation of traditional mourning. Lappe also suggests that this is one instance in which some new sort of ritual would be useful.[12] There may be other such instances, and these may be particular to individual constellations of *kerovim*.

Under traditional law, the mourning of women and children is not honored.[13] This is a cruel variant of the permitted/required and exempt/proscribed problem mentioned earlier. In Orthodox settings, women and children are often told that a man must do the public mourning for family members. If a woman is not required to mourn publicly, and if her public mourning is halakhically inadequate or unacceptable, then it is a short jump to barring the door to her altogether.[14]

Children sometimes get completely forgotten in a house of mourning. In a class I once taught, a young girl said that when her grandfather died, everyone came to the house and comforted her mother, but no one extended any words of comfort to her. She was offered no role in the process of mourning, and she felt terribly alone. The gifts of our tradition should be extended to children in every way possible to heal the rift in their hearts.

In sum, there is a balance to be struck between submitting to a brilliant system of healing developed over millennia and trusting the wisdom of your own heart, which may have needs different than the tradition anticipated. We would do well to substitute the notion of "permitted" where tradition says "required" and "exempt" where it says "forbidden." Perhaps this will give some necessary latitude for the heart's voice as well as that of the tradition. What I am suggesting is in keeping with my Reform background. But even strictly halakhic Jews may be able to accommodate the heart's vicissitudes in trying times.

To What End?

There is no teacher like mourning. Now that death has come close to me, both by taking the man I once loved and then by almost taking me, I am not the person I was before. I can only describe the change in the most personal terms. I am so glad to be alive, so grateful that my parents are alive and healthy, so thankful that I went on to love another man and make such an interesting and enjoyable life with him. I am richly blessed to live in a loving community in a beautiful place.

Yet, it could all go in a minute. It *will* all go in a minute. This life is a brief stop, whether I die tomorrow or in fifty years. I would love not to know this, to have the innocent certainty that, when loved ones set out on a journey, they will return unharmed, that I can go out to sea in my boat, play in the waves and not be swallowed up. But I am more grateful now than I ever was in my innocence.

In the end it is all a gift, is it not? The brief entwinement of body and soul, the breath of God that gives and sustains human life, creates such a colorful, sparkling trail as it arcs through time. It is so ephemeral, and yet it affects everything. As we say when we open our eyes every morning: "I give thanks to You, God of life who is eternal, for returning my soul to me this morning. Great is Your faithfulness."

Mourning a Suicide

ANNE BRENER

"May God [literally, the Place] comfort you among the mourners of Zion and Jerusalem."

—BLESSING FOR MOURNERS, BASED ON
BT *SHABBAT* 12B AND *KETUBBOT* 8B

When we console mourners, we wish for them a Holy Place of Comfort. That "Place," another name for God, is hard to come by when grieving a natural death, but it is exponentially harder to find when mourning a suicide.

A healthy mourning process raises all kinds of questions about the relationship with the deceased and the nature of God and the universe. Suicide raises other questions in addition, including, "Does a person have the right to take his or her own life?"

The Rabbis say no. Suicide was considered a grievous sin—a sin for which atonement is, by definition, no longer possible. Mystics believe that mourners can help effect atonement for loved ones through their *Kaddish* (mourner's prayer). In the case of a suicide, *Kaddish* is recited for the maximum period of time: A full year, as opposed to eleven months (*Shulḥan Arukh Yoreh De'ah* 376:4). Despite this sympathy, *halakhah* (Jewish law) discriminates, at least officially, against suicides. Suicides may not be buried with their families, but rather on the outskirts of the cemetery. Many of the mourning laws and customs are suspended in the case of sui-

Anne Brener, LCSW, author of *Mourning & Mitzvah: A Guided Journal for Walking the Mourner's Path Through Grief to Healing* (Jewish Lights Publishing, 1993), is a Los Angeles based psychotherapist and teacher. She regularly leads workshops exploring the connection between spirituality and psychology, particularly as they relate to healing and bereavement.

cide; there is no tearing of garments, for example, and no eulogy (*Shulḥan Arukh Yoreh De'ah* 345:1). These *halakhot* are balanced by the Rabbinic presumption that no one of right mind would take their own life. Therefore, with rare exception, rabbis rule that the act of suicide was the result of mental illness, and the deceased is neither responsible for his or her actions, nor subject to the laws of suicide. Almost no deaths are considered deliberate suicides. Thus, suicide is both harshly condemned and sympathetically defined.

Although this compassionate application of the laws of mourning means that virtually no mourners are actually excluded from the healing tools of the mourning practices, the message implied by the *halakhah* is that grieving a suicide is going to be different: If suicide is an unnatural act, then mourning a suicide cannot follow the natural path.

I first learned of the Rabbinic attitude toward suicide in a phone call following my mother's death from Dr. Shlomo Bardin, a Jewish educator who had been a teacher to both my mother and me. He did not sound bereaved. He was angry. "She had no right to do that," he said. "God gave her life. It is up to God to take it." His tone gave communal sanction to my internal voice of anger and outrage—essential in the healing process and often hard to find in the early days of mourning. When the death of a loved one was their willing choice, the voice of rage is often drowned out by that of guilt, as survivors search their souls and try to rearrange history—looking for something that might have made a difference.

Perhaps it was easier for me to mourn my mother's suicide because I am a woman. According to traditional law, I was not bound by the obligation to say *Kaddish*, nor even counted in a prayer quorum. The exclusion of women from mourning practices is not unlike the formal exclusion of suicide survivors. In mourning, women must find or create their own forms, just like those who mourn one not to be mourned. They must retreat to a private place and create new paths for healing. They must mourn on the outskirts of the community, just as suicides are officially buried on the outskirts of the cemetery.

With no obligation under traditional law to say *Kaddish*, and with the subtle message that survivors of suicide must find their own way, I had a double-need to forge a new path to my own Holy Place of Comfort. Where did I go for healing? Not to *shul* (synagogue)—but to Breakaway, a feminist alternative school in the Berkeley of the 70s. There I took a writing class that encouraged me to tell my story and gave me a space to ask the mourner's questions: Where might I have made a difference? How can I cope with my pain? Why does God allow such suffering? My voice joined those of other women who, in 1972, were mourning not only loved ones but also the expectations and assumptions that made *Kaddish* unavailable to Jewish women, and open self-expression difficult for any woman. Questions filled our journals as we explored what it meant to be daughters at a time of such transition. Our losses, and particularly the example of my mother's suicide, impelled the group to look back on our mothers' lives and find the strength to separate ourselves from the past and yet build on it to create new lives.

With these women, I found a healing voice. I wrote and wrote, venting my angst, guilt, and anger. Through pen and ink I found a way to keep the conversation with my mother going until we could heal the pain of our relationship. I unloaded my feelings onto the Bosom of the Universe (a name for God implied in the Hebrew "*Shaddai*"). I learned about the biblical Hannah who poured out her grief at Shiloh with a fervency and outrageousness which the Talmud declares to be the model for prayer (BT *Berakhot* 30b-31a). In my fervent and outrageous expression of the mourner's questions I began to learn how to pray.

While the answers to the mourner's questions may ultimately be unknowable, they must be asked in order to transform the frozen emotions of early mourning and the chaotic ones which follow, into new relationships with the deceased, God, and the universe. Energetic expressions of the feelings that accompany these questions break through the denial of death and open our lives to the fertile possibilities of growth and change.

In retrospect, I am glad that I did not have access to the usual markers and comforts of mourning. The empty space left by non-practice was a gift. Moreover, in telling me that suicide is not normal or acceptable, the Jewish tradition gave me permission to uncover my feelings and discover my voice. It thus led me to what all mourners must have in order to heal: Community.

Ultimately, I had to bring the voice I found at Breakaway back to the Jewish community in order to complete my mourning. In studying Jewish mourning practices, I came to appreciate the Rabbinic compassion that gives special treatment to suicides and those who mourn them. The Rabbis knew that suicide is an act of insanity. In her right mind, my mother would not have chosen to leave me such a legacy. Rabbinic compassion allowed me the extra time and space I needed to find my own compassion, and to forgive my mother for the often unbearable pain that accompanies this kind of loss. It allowed my relationship with my mother to heal...and her memory, finally, to be for a blessing.

Dream-Kaddish: *A Meditation from Breakaway*

My mother was calling from far, far away,
perhaps another world.

The telephone was a model from the time of my birth:
Black, heavy, with a rotary dial.

But its cord was shimmering:
Translucent, somewhat metallic and pulsating
—filled with veins and blood
—connecting us after her death.

It is the silver cord that links the worlds,
before and after we take our human breaths.

The cycle, like the circular dial, rotates,
yet the connection remains.

The *Kaddish* is the silver cord.

A Modern Version of the Confessional Before Dying

VICKI HOLLANDER

"I am sending an angel before you to guard you on the way and to bring you to the place I have made ready."

—EXODUS 23:20

The viddui *(confessional) is traditionally recited when a person is at the point of death. It is important to stress that the* viddui *in no way requires or encourages the loss of hope or of the will to live* (Shulḥan Arukh Yoreh De'ah 338:1). *It is intended to comfort the* goses/goseset *(dying person), and lovingly address and ease any fears, guilt, or anxiety. The* viddui *offers an opportunity to say goodbye, and according to traditional Rabbinic understanding, to make of one's death a holy moment and a* kapparah *(atonement for one's sins).*

My Source, God of those who came before me: I know that my cure and my death are in Your hands. May You heal me completely, move me to wholeness. But if death is nearing, I am ready to receive it from Your hand.

May all the wrongdoings I have done in my life—those things I have done unwittingly, those things I have done knowingly; acts I have done to myself, to others, to You—may they all be forgiven.

Allow the hidden goodness stored for *tzaddikim* (the righteous) to flow over me. Help me to understand the path of life. Gift me continuing life in the hidden world yet to come.

As I come close to You now, Your face bathes me with light. Being at Your right hand fills me deeply.

One who watches over the vulnerable and needy, take care of my close ones, those precious ones with whom my soul is intertwined.

שְׁמַע יִשְׂרָאֵל יי אֱלֹהֵינוּ יי אֶחָד.

Shema yisra'el adonai eloheinu adonai eḥad.

Listen, Israel, our God, our Source, is one.

———

Rabbi Vicki Hollander weaves together the creation of ritual and poetry with rabbinic work at Congregation Eitz Or, hospice work, and single parenting.

Suite On My Mother's Death

CAROL V. DAVIS

"The journey back should be easy; if this reaches you,
wait for me."
> —LISEL MUELLER, "LETTER FROM THE END OF THE WORLD"

Packing Up the Clothes

First the sweaters go in piles:
burnt orange, a brown wool so deep
and rich, surely it was pulled from
the very center of the earth.
I can fold these easily—the body
knows when to obey, even in grief.
Then I cross the hall to her closet,
pass the mirror where she checked herself
each morning, refusing the illness
which burrowed in, then crawled
its way out.

Each year I grow more and more like my mother.
Her words tumble out of my mouth—
the desperation of love.
Those same hands, thin and distracted,
the gray hair surfacing.
I remember her eating with such concentration—
delicate as a small bird—as if each mouthful
mattered, and it did, so little flesh on
her to sustain life.

Now I inch my way to the silks and cottons.
The dress she wore to my wedding,
its black spots spread like ink in water.
The other clothes, each retaining shape
and smell. And when I come home, open
my front door, I still anticipate her voice
on my machine, ever surprised when there is
no message.

Carol V. Davis is a widely published poet and the author of a chapbook, *Letters From Prague* (Paper Bag Press, 1991).

My Daughter Was Born on My Mother's **Yartzeit**[15]

All morning I thought of my mother,
how often we waited for her to die
and then the affront of it

when she finally did, as if it were
up to her family to tell her
when she could let go,

as if by holding her tired fingers
we could drag her forcibly back
to this life, when only weeks

before she announced
*I'm tired; I don't want
to fight anymore* and I began

to tell her then I would have another
child, maybe a girl, with dark curls

and a smart tongue, hoping
to entice her with promises unfair
to make, as if I could really deliver
or even had the right to try.

The Seventh Year

My mother died a week before
the Jewish New Year and I have been
different ever since, my husband says.
Could it be the sucking of the tide
or the wrinkles on the yellowed moon?

Nightly waking to a flooded pillow.
Something of you held back at the funeral,
and has retreated ever since, he said.

My middle child, who never met her,
says his grandmother died because
her body didn't work.

That *Rosh Hashanah*[16], I sat in synagogue,
while all around, people pressed hands

in greeting. And on that day, it seemed
to me some strange ritual, as if the men
and women were desperate to seal in
the life left in them.

As if one of them might know
what is written in the book.
Who would be next and after that.

Now, approaching the seventh year
since her death, I look out at the
end-of-summer garden and see,
in gritty photos, the mothers parted
from their children, healthy to the right,
condemned to the left.
She always thrust to one side,
I to the other.

Afterword: How to Create a Ritual

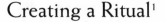

Creating a Ritual[1]

DEBRA ORENSTEIN

"Turn [the tradition] over and over again, [to study and review it].
Everything is in it."

—MISHNAH *AVOT* 5:24

While some people have a natural talent for authoring new rituals, the art of creating rituals can also be taught. Like other forms of creative expression, ritual-writing has a body of rules and skills, gleaned from both the theory of the discipline and the trial-and-error of its practitioners.

What follows is a seven-stage process toward the creation of rituals. It reflects the lessons of master liturgists and anthropologists; my observations of the, usually unconscious, steps in formulating a ritual; and the ritual theory I have developed. It is meant to make the endeavor of creating a ritual more accessible and, at the same time, more predictable, in terms of quality and outcome.

Rabbi Debra Orenstein, editor of *Lifecycles*, fellow of the Wilstein Institute of Jewish Policy Studies, and instructor at the University of Judaism in Los Angeles, regularly writes and speaks on Jewish spirituality and gender studies.

Do not feel wedded to this structure, however. You are engaging in a creative process and must do what it takes for *your* creative juices to flow.

Sometimes, rituals, like poetry or melodies, come suddenly and easily, by inspiration. If you wake up in the middle of the night and rush to your desk to write out a ritual you literally dreamed up, chances are it is an excellent one. You may then want to use some of my questions and suggestions as a check, but you will not need them to *create* a ritual. When the muse does not strike immediately, however, it may be useful to have a system for organizing your thinking.

Step One: What Is a Ritual—And Do I Need One?

The terms blessing, prayer, ceremony, and ritual are generally used loosely, if not interchangeably. Technically, however, they refer to different genres, one of which is probably more suitable than the others for marking a particular passage or milestone.

Blessings in the Jewish tradition follow a strict formula, beginning with the words *barukh attah adonai* (blessed are You, *Adonai*) and often continuing with *eloheinu melekh ha'olam* (our God, Ruler/King of the universe) and still further with *asher kiddeshanu bemitzvotav vetzivvanu* (who has sanctified us with Your commandments and commanded us...). There are a variety of modern adaptations to the traditional formulation, most of which use either gender neutral or feminine God language, and many of which eliminate the notion of sovereignty altogether, in favor of the image of God as creator. Whatever formulation is used, blessings usually consist of just one line. They can accompany a specific behavior (e.g. ritual washing of the hands), occasion (e.g. wearing a suit for the first time), time (e.g. beginning of Sabbath), or natural phenomenon (e.g. rainbow or earthquake). They may also serve as the *petiḥah* (opening) or *ḥatimah* (seal or closure) of a prayer. Prayers, longer liturgical expressions with a still wider array of applications, may or may not include a *berakhah* (blessing). Both blessings and prayers feature prominently in rituals and ceremonies. They are fitting for these public, communal occasions, but may also (or instead) be said privately.

In recent years, the terms "ritual" and "ceremony" have been applied increasingly broadly. Psychologists Evan Imber-Black and Janine Roberts name five purposes of rituals: (1) To shape, express and maintain relationships; (2) to make and mark transitions; (3) to heal from betrayal, trauma, or loss; (4) to voice beliefs and create meaning; and (5) to honor and celebrate individuals and life, generally.[2] In classical anthropological understanding, the second task named is highly emphasized, and is divided between ritual, which makes the transitions, and ceremony, which marks them. Ceremonies are said to celebrate an existing status, while rituals ideally help to effect a transition and transformation from one status to another. Thus, miscarriage "rituals" are technically ceremonies because they mark a status already established, but the circumcision "ceremony" is actually a ritual, because it changes the child's status, physically, spiritually, and socially. Even according to these strict (and admittedly artificial) definitions, the line between ritual and ceremony is not always so clearly drawn. In the days of arranged marriages, weddings were pure ritual, transforming single persons into married ones. Today, they are also part ceremony, acknowledging and celebrating a change that has already taken place in the status of a couple's relationship and commitment.

Ceremonies and rituals both make use of symbols and physical behaviors to concretize their messages. However, rituals need and tend to do this more strongly and reliably, since they endeavor to create a noticeable change, a "before-and-after" picture, that will be meaningful to both individual and community. Along the way, between "before" and "after," there is a transitional, liminal state, discussed in this volume by Rabbis Geller and Holub. At that point, one is, to return to our wedding example, neither married nor unmarried, but somewhere in an ambiguous, even dangerous interim. It is dangerous because the end result has not yet been established, but the status quo has already been abandoned. Yet this volatility offers the opportunity for identification with both past and future, and the benefit of encouraging keen and inquisitive focus on the actors in the ritual drama. The "after" stage does not usher in an utterly new status, unconnected with the old, but rather represents a re-embodiment and a re-incorporation of a transformed self.

Many anthropologists and liturgists now reject strict divisions between ritual and ceremony and argue that there has been an over-emphasis on the liminal—as if becoming were somehow more important than being. I like to stress the liminal, however, and believe that what is over-stressed, especially in the Jewish context, is the "after" stage, the reaggregation and coming to a new status quo. Liminality, which is sometimes called the threshold stage, is especially important for women, who as Marge Piercy writes in *The Sabbath of Mutual Respect* are "the doorways of life." The body of a woman was a physical threshold that each of us crossed in entering the world.[3] Traditionally, women have spent a great deal of their lives standing on thresholds and helping children and men across—by preparing children for rites of passage, orchestrating other lifecycle and holiday celebrations, and serving as the women "behind" men's transformations in status.

Victor Turner associated liminality with a time of intense egalitarianism and comradeship, as well as minimized sex role distinctions, due to the shared experience of *communitas* and the lack of structure and hierarchy during transition.[4] One of the reasons that feminists have taken so to ritual and seek out liminality is that these are precisely the qualities that we value. From a social activist point of view, it is in leaving behind our structured, hierarchical society and entering a fluid, inchoate state that we allow for the possibility of transforming gender roles.

If it is clear to you that you want to create for yourself or someone else a transformation in status, witnessed and honored in community, then it is probably indeed a ritual that is required. In any case, many of the "how-to" steps which follow will apply to all forms of liturgical expression.

Step Two: What Resources Are Already Available? (or, Avoid Reinventing the Wheel)

You will want to ascertain what other rituals and liturgies already exist. Consult traditional Jewish sources, either directly or via secondary readings. You can begin with those listed in the bibliography and/or ask your local rabbi and Judaica librarian for suggestions. Organizations and resource centers that deal with women and Jewish lifecycle can be helpful, as well.[5] Be sure to investigate aspects of the tradition with which you may be unfamiliar, including Sephardic, Ethiopian, Ḥasidic, and mystical texts and customs.

If relevant traditional or modern rituals are available, you will want to trace these to their most original source and adapt them, as necessary, in line with the suggestions on creating ritual, below.

Step Three: Creating a Ritual from the Ground Up

If you have few or no models and wish to create an entirely new ritual, I recommend that you ask and answer two questions to clarify your purpose in preparation for writing. First, what is the transformation you wish to effect? Second, if you conceive of your ritual in three stages—(1) before/status quo, (2) during/liminality, and (3) after/new state—what are the main characteristics of each stage, in your particular case? Once you have addressed these questions, engage in a "Jewish brainstorming" session. What are your Jewish associations to the transformation and to each stage? What Jewish heroes, texts, historical movements, symbols, ritual objects, songs, do they call to mind? Do not hesitate to ask rabbis and other Jewishly knowledgeable friends for their input.

As in any brainstorming session, simply let the ideas flow without judging them. You will be able to reject, use, alter, or combine them later on. First, just get them on paper. You will also generate associations from other sources and disciplines, such as women's studies, ethnography, and your own life story and imagination. This is all to the good. The list you create will contain within it the raw materials of a ritual.

If you wanted to create a ritual for taking on a new name, for example, you might end up with these lists—or something like them—before you:

Transformation I wish to effect: I wish to change my name and my spirit.

Associations: Abram becomes Abraham; Sarai becomes Sarah; Jacob becomes Israel; Asher Zvi Ginsberg becomes the Zionist thinker *Aḥad Ha'am* (literally, one of the people); a good name is a significant acquisition in this life (Mishnah *Avot* 2:8); the crown of a good name is superior to the crowns of Torah, priesthood, and royalty (Mishnah *Avot* 4:17); to gossip is to be *motzi shem ra* (giving out a bad name); God's name can be desecrated or honored; God has many names, including The

Name; the blessing for doing anything new (including taking a new name) is *Sheheheyanu;* there is a folk custom to change the names of sick people, so the angel of death will not know where to find them.

Before: I am attached to my old name, which represents my way of life before I was clean and sober...my ex-husband's family...my abusive father...my life before I was an observant Jew...the "old me" in some other respect.

Associations to "before": _____ (This will depend significantly on the nature of the "before.")

During: I release my old name and stand without a new one.

Associations to "during": I am like a baby boy who has already been circumcised, but not yet been named; I am like the woman in the Jewish feminist short story "The Woman Who Lost Her Names;"[6] I am like Abraham after he left Haran and before he understood where he was going.

After: I choose my identity and have come into my own.

Associations to "after": I am like the double-named Hadassah/Esther when she reveals her true self; I am like David following his pretense of having been crazy; I am like Jacob who emerged wounded, but with a blessing, a new relationship with God, and a new name, after battling with forces of the night.

Next, associate to the items on each list. As before, research them in your Judaica library and/or with experts. It is extremely helpful to look up the key words on your lists in a biblical and/or a Talmudic concordance. Many libraries also have Rabbinic literature on CD-ROMs. These sources will lead you to verses containing the same key words, which may be of use in fashioning prayers, or in choosing holy figures to "join you" at your ritual. It is common for lifecycle rituals to include Jewish heroes of the past as "special guests." For example, Elijah, who accused the Israelites of neglecting *brit* (covenant), is said to join participants at every *Brit Milah* (covenant of circumcision ritual), and a special chair is reserved for him at circumcisions. Likewise, Adam and Eve, the first human couple, and Isaac and Rebecca, the first Jewish couple whose meeting and love story are recorded, are implicitly invoked as guests at every Jewish wedding, when they are referred to in the *Sheva Berakhot* (seven marital blessings) and the *badeken* (bridal veiling ceremony), respectively.[7]

At this stage and with your ritual in mind, read through the Book of Psalms. Psalms are the source of a significant portion of our traditional liturgy. Since psalms speak of and from a personal relationship with God and reflect a wide range of emotions, the Book of Psalms is a likely source of liturgy for a variety of personal passages.

Look through the traditional prayerbook, as well, and especially at blessings we say on uncommon and/or special occasions. Many prayers and blessings may have open or double meanings that make them appropriate for use with ritual innovations. For example, the blessing traditionally said upon seeing wonders of nature, such as lightning, shooting stars, and sunrises, can be loosely translated as "Blessed are You, God, Ruler of the universe, continual Source of creation." Treasure Cohen uses this blessing as a *ḥatimah* for her tree-planting ceremony in honor of newborns. Similarly, Rabbi Sandy Eisenberg Sasso uses a *ḥatimah* from the High Holiday *Amidah* (series of blessing which is the centerpiece of every prayer service) for a blessing of healing after miscarriage. Of course, from an Orthodox point of view it is forbidden to offer blessings which are not required, as they are therefore considered to be recited in vain.[8] To use an old text in a new way, however, is in keeping with Rabbinic sensibilities and hermeneutics. New rituals, ceremonies, blessings, and prayers that incorporate ancient ones tend to ring right and true not only because the words are authentic, but because the method is as well.

Repetition of a "tag line" you find in the prayer services or through concordance work can be a powerful liturgical tool. "Tag lines" and refrains function both to reinforce an idea and, by the context and placement of the repetition, to show its various meanings. They also function as a mantra. They may appear at the beginning of a line, phrase, or paragraph (as does the phrase *ḥayim shel* [a life of] in the Prayer for the New Month and New Year and in Rabbi Pam Hoffman's birthday prayer in Chapter Five) or at the end of same (as does *ki le'olam ḥasdo* [for God's lovingkindness endures forever] in Psalm 118 and the *Hallel* [Psalms of praise]).

Now, review your lists: The list of associations to the topic, the list of associations to its stages, the sacred guest list, the list of concordance verses, and the lists of relevant Psalms, prayers, blessings, and possible tag lines/refrains. Reflect on any patterns you may see, and on how you might weave different elements together. Remember that while I have delineated three stages, and will, for purposes of clarity, continue to address them each in turn, your ritual is a whole. Try to avoid gaps or seams between stages, but do not become over-occupied with the stages, or push to make them all "come out even." Even anthropologists who distinguish rigidly between different stages, point out that the stages in a particular ritual are not necessarily of equal weight. The best themes, heroes, verses, etc. are those that speak to every aspect and stage of the ritual—wherever they appear—and resonate on many levels, not just one.

Step Four: Distinguishing the Stages of Ritual Jewishly, and Incorporating Them in Deed as Well as Word

I have been referring to the three stages of ritual as "before, during, and after," but actually the process is more complex. By the time you have gathered a group for a communal ritual, you are no longer really in the status quo. You have already begun to separate from it. Thus, the "before" stage is not so much the stage of one's previous status, as the stage of separation from one's previous status.[9]

The anthropologists' before, during, and after have their Jewish equivalent in creation, revelation, and redemption. During creation, God was *mavdil* (separator). God separated Godself from the totality of all existence, as well as day from night, sea from land, the earth from the human, etc. Thus, separation enables creation and establishes our initial status. Moreover, this remains our contemporary reality: Birth is creation by separation, just as psychological health is characterized, in part, by individuation.

Revelation corresponds to the "during" stage. It represents transition—from a gang of slaves to a people with a purpose, from lawlessness to holiness. Revelation, the receiving of Torah, is the mid-way point between being born and being reborn. At this limi-

nal stage of the ritual, Torah—the essential teaching of the ritual—
must be given.

Redemption is, obviously, "after." It comes after the end of
time and the world as we know it. It includes, whether physically
or metaphorically, the ultimate re-embodiment and re-incorporation: The resurrection of the dead. It brings creation full circle, just
as the new status achieved by a ritual is a completion, rather than
a contradiction, of one's "before" state.

Traditional Jewish historiography recognizes creation, revelation, and redemption as *the* indispensable stages of development,
to which everything else is commentary. Many Jewish liturgies—
from the blessings before and after the *Shema* prayer to the seven
marital blessings—make use of the three themes. You should certainly consider incorporating the themes into the stages of your
ritual.

You will want not only to bear in mind the anthropological
stages and their Jewish equivalents, but somehow to move the
participants from one stage to the next. This is *not* accomplished
by an announcement: "Now we are entering the transitional
stage." In general, the less your ritual explains itself, the better.
Rituals are not primarily teaching opportunities, though we sometimes use them that way; they are meant to be lived, not learned.
Ritual, like liturgy, is more dramatic than scholastic.

Thus, the best way to effect stages is by affect. For example, to
begin separating from your existing status in the "before" stage,
create a sense—literally via the senses—that a dramatic change is
coming. Depending on what is appropriate to the context, you
might gather in a special place, cast a sacred circle, use chanting,
prayer, spices, or a *kavvanah* (intentional meditation) to carry the
community to a new place. The traditional formulation *hineni
mukhan/mukhanah umezumman/umezummenet lekayyem mitz-
vat*...(Behold, I am prepared and ready to fulfill the *mitzvah* [com-
mandment] of...) is a "before/creation" prayer. By devotion and
assertion, by saying "Let there be readiness," it creates readiness,
and begins to separate participants from the status quo.

Of all three stages, the during/revelation stage most requires a
physical act. The communal response in ritual, as at the Sinaitic
revelation, is *na'aseh venishma*: We will act and thereby we will
understand. The fact that we have not yet found or agreed upon a

physical act for girls' naming ceremonies accounts, in my opinion, for their being less viscerally powerful than *Brit Milah* (covenant of circumcision ritual). As you look over your list of associations, see if there is a behavior that grows naturally from the tradition which you can incorporate into this stage. The behavior must resonate with the ritual occasion, as well as with the tradition. (The rituals in this book provide a variety of examples of how this can be done. See the index to rituals and blessings.)

The after/redemption stage requires affect to effect closure. Again, the use of symbols, ritual objects, and concrete behaviors will be helpful. Remember, as in all the stages, to appeal to all the senses. Where appropriate, use traditional or innovative music, chanting, *niggunim* (wordless melodies), scents, candles, foods, wine, dance/choreography (including hand motions, bowing, etc.). In the course of your ritual, you may don a *tallit* (prayer shawl), use a washing cup, hold a Torah, immerse in the *mikveh* (ritual bath), drink from a *kiddush* cup (special cup or goblet used when reciting the blessing over wine on sacred occasions), etc.

Before/creation, during/revelation, and after/redemption are equivalent to tonic-dominant-tonic in the world of music. Just as the first stage geared participants up, the last stage should in some measure "gear them down." Ideally, we end, as we began, with a sense of safety and familiarity, however great the transformation. In fact, the greater the transformation, the greater the need for group safety. The more the individual has changed, the more we need to connect this new self with the old, to see that the new is ultimately a fulfillment, not a subversion of the old. Many third stages involve blessing the new state, to confirm and grow comfortable with it. Invocations of peace and peacefulness are common. It is appropriate for these after/redemption blessings to anticipate and address the future, as well. They may offer a charge, as well as a blessing, to participants, so that participants emerge with purpose and energy, as well as serenity.

Step Five: Putting It All Together
(And Some Pitfalls to Avoid)

You now have the raw materials to create both the words and the actions of your ritual. Next comes the part that cannot really be taught. Sit down and have a quiet moment. Reflect on what you have learned, and on the passage you seek to mark. Ask yourself, "What do I *most* need to say and to do for this ritual?" and see what answer comes.

At this stage, you mostly need to select. By now, you have done significant research and have, we hope, found a variety of moving and effective associations, quotations, behaviors, heroes, and symbols. Resist the temptation to somehow incorporate all of them into your ritual. If you pick two themes/strands that run throughout the ritual, justify to yourself why they work together. If you have three or more separate themes, you are almost certainly mixing too many ingredients into the stew. Remember, too, that, when it comes to ritual, shorter is always better.

Ideally, you will be able to use one theme, object, hero, etc. in more than one context *and* to have its meaning operate on more than one level. In the example of the naming ritual, you might incorporate or refer to the presence of Jacob in all three ritual stages, since Jacob went from being a young man who did not know himself; to becoming the Jacob whose self-consciously constructed self caused grief and chaos, even as it contained great potential; to emerging as the wounded but brave *Yisra'el* (literally, one who wrestles with God), after his battle with forces in and outside himself. This might be done by referring explicitly to Jacob's story, by quoting or playing on some of his words, and/or by offering to the newly-named person some of the blessings given to and/or by Jacob in the Bible. If the naming ritual in question is meant specifically for a convert to take on her Hebrew name, a blessing in which she is declared *"bat yisra'el"* (daughter of *yisra'el*), refers both to her joining the tribe of the "children of Israel" and to the Godwrestling to which she, like the newly-named *Yisra'el*, stands committed.

If you find yourself unable to choose among the array of options you have generated, the following questions may help to get you "unstuck": What would a Martian think of the passage you are seeking to mark? What is Jewish about the passage? What is male about it? What is female about it? What identities does it (and do *you* wish to) promote and deny? What are its worldview and message? If you made this passage the center of your life, how would it affect your beliefs and behavior? If it could talk, what would it be saying? What possible meanings do you find in it, when you look at it—insofar as possible—with fresh eyes, naively, and without preconception? These questions, intended to help you set priorities, can be asked of existing rituals and passages, as well.

Along with including everything-plus-the-kitchen-sink, another temptation is to explain your ritual act, heroes, liturgy, etc. and your reason for choosing them. However, your task is to choose ritual acts, heroes, and liturgies that are rich in and of themselves, that require, as it were, little or no introduction. You may wish to write an essay on how and why you came to choose the elements you did, but that is a separate matter for liturgists and other interested parties.[10] In a community that gathers to witness and experience transformation, those kinds of explanations take away from the ritual, rather than add to it.

Another word of caution: The best innovative rituals, ceremonies, prayers, and blessings come from the heart *and* are grounded in Jewish sources and ritual theory. If you are missing either the personal or the scholarly component, or if the balance between them is grossly uneven, your innovation will suffer. A scholarly approach that discusses symbols and events "objectively" is unengaged and unengaging.[11] No matter how carefully researched and how resonant the Jewish connections included in such a ritual, it tends to become a laundry list of associations. Personal perspectives are the passion that drives ritual innovations; they not only deserve to be honored, they are essential to the creative process.

On the other hand, a personal perspective without a thoroughgoing basis in theory, methodology, and traditional sources can degenerate into autobiographical indulgence. New rituals created in and for a particular community may be profound religious experiences for the people involved, but the recording of these experiences will not, by itself, necessarily make them accessible or meaningful to others. A chronicling is not grounded, and will often float away when the effort is made to apply it in other situations or settings. Of course, if you are aiming to do something completely idiosyncratic, this is irrelevant. However, my experience is that most ritual innovators create the ritual because they sense that others also need it, or something very like it, and they want to make a contribution to the Jewish community. Lack of grounding can make a ritual seem unweighty even for the first, and perhaps only, generation of celebrants.

Another potential pitfall is to undervalue the role of community in ritual. Most people creating rituals today are creating them for personal life passages; thus, the focus is on the individual. But if our focus on the individual takes the personal out of the communal context, we have gone too far. It is as if we have declared that our individual lives are personal and our communal lives, impersonal, and that the two are unconnected. In fact, lifecycle ritual transforms personal *and* communal status, and can be seen as the nexus of the personal and the communal. What event is more private *and* more public than a wedding—unless it is a circumcision or a funeral? What is more an issue of family than a Passover *seder* (ordered readings and meal), and, at the same time, what is more an issue of peoplehood?"

It was the feminist movement, following Virginia Woolf, that declared the personal to be political. To so declare is to acknowledge the connection between our corporate and private lives. The most compelling personal lifecycle rituals are those that draw the community in, as witnesses and as participants. As in a good theatrical performance, the fourth wall of the proscenium stage collapses, the boundary between performer and audience disappears, and all are drawn into the drama.[12] A good personal ritual is felt vicariously by everyone present, and carries the feeling and the message that the Jewish people will be just a little bit different and more complete because the ritual took place. Ritual not only requires community, it can re-enforce and even create it.

Finally, consider the ethical import of your ritual. What do you endorse, deny, or denounce—implicitly and explicitly? Anticipate some likely effects on the individuals involved and on the larger community. Is the ritual blaming? Healing? When you contemplate creating a ritual, imagine first preparing for it, then performing it, and later reflecting back on it.[13] Will you be satisfied with the ritual's moral message and communal impact at each stage, or, in a worst case scenario, will you be sorry you undertook it, because you have ended up hurting people and misrepresenting your own values? Some good questions to ask in advance: Are there people whom the ritual affects directly who should be in on the planning, or see the text beforehand? Would the full gamut of the Jewish community—including converts, young children, single people, infertile couples, the disabled, gay men and lesbians, men and women generally, the Orthodox—feel welcome at the ritual, based on its language and messages? If not, can you live with that—and potentially with their hurt? On a microcosmic level, is there a group of friends or a side of your family that you are excluding and/or making uncomfortable—and, again, can you live with that? A week after the ritual is over, how do you want people to summarize its tenor, meaning, and mood? How do you want it remembered ten or twenty years from now?

Bearing all this in mind, write a draft of the ritual, including "stage directions" for when cups are lifted, a *kittel* (garment traditionally worn on one's wedding day, various Jewish holidays, and for burial) is donned, spices are smelled or passed in a circle, etc.

Step Six: Critiquing Your Own Ritual—A Checklist

Now that your ritual is before you, ask yourself some review questions:

- Does the ritual have three stages?
- Do they merge naturally and seamlessly, one into another?
- Does any part read awkwardly, "explain itself to death," or force an image or association?
- Are some parts of the text so general they could be about anything? Are others so specific to your experience that someone has to know your history to find meaning in them?
- Do the behaviors flow from the words and vice versa?
- Are there stray images that do not seem connected to anything else?
- Does the ritual move you?
- Will the person undergoing the ritual emerge differently than s/he entered it?
- Will the observing/participating community likewise feel transformed?

- How is the community addressed, implicitly and explicitly?
- How does this lifecycle ritual relate across time, forward and backward, to other passages and rituals? What liturgical and symbolic vocabulary, if any, does it share with them?
- Are both women and men addressed in and by this ritual?
- Is the ritual practical as well

as symbolic? Can it be reproduced in a variety of settings and communities, without extraordinary expense or special equipment?

- Will many, if not all, segments of the community feel included and welcome to participate?
- Is there a richness and a layering to the ritual, such that it resonates with Jewish tradition and personal experience on a number of levels?

Make revisions based on your answers to these questions, if you find your ritual lacking.

Step Seven: Enacting and Sharing the Ritual

Many Jews, and especially women, who create new liturgies or rituals feel hesitant about performing them in their own prayer community, much less disseminating them to strangers.

Every prayer was new at one time. Some new rituals and prayers will "take" immediately and have the feel of having been around forever. These will likely spread quickly and be with us for a long time. It will be clear with other rituals, on first performance, that the text and behaviors feel forced, and that the current form needs to be revised or abandoned. Still other rituals may serve an immediate, idiosyncratic purpose, but not transfer, travel, or keep well. Only time will tell.

Barbara Myerhoff notes that all ritual is effective to some degree simply by virtue of bringing people together.[14] At the very least, you will have investigated a passage and attempted to tie it to the tradition. You will have learned some *torah lishmah* (Torah for its own sake). You will have gathered a community together to share and celebrate those efforts. And you will have honored our ancient tradition by expecting and seeking within it the answers to every life passage and life question.

Honoring Your Efforts in Prayer

"Sing unto Adonai *a new song."*

—PSALMS 96:1

Working on this book and teaching liturgy-writing workshops, I have had numerous occasions to witness ritual and liturgical inno-vations. When a ritual is used for the first time, especially when it is used for a joyous occasion, there is a tremendous sense of excite-ment. Participants feel joy and relief, not only around the passage being traversed and marked, but around the (we hope, successful) debut of a new prayer or ceremony. When a liturgical or ritual innovation feels immediately "right," the author and community often have the impulse to celebrate the creative process itself, as well as the life passage it honors.

The following prayer may be said on the occasion of creating liturgy, or at the time of the first liturgical use of a prayer, ritual, blessing, or meditation. It is meant to be read responsively, and thus to allude to the silent (and sometimes verbal and explicit) conversations that transpire between liturgists and the communi-ties they serve. In the case of a "liturgy committee" or a creative prayer group, the group can divide itself in two, and recite the prayer twice, so that each half of the group speaks the words of the creator(s) and of the community. A lone author of private prayer might recite both halves on her/his own. The prayer should be followed by a traditional *Sheheheyanu* (blessing for reaching a new or momentous occasion).

The creator(s) of the prayer say(s):

אַטֶּה לְמָשָׁל אָזְנִי, אֶפְתַּח בְּכִנּוֹר חִידָתִי.

Atteh lemashal ozni, eftah bekhinnor ḥidati

I will incline my ear to a parable; I will lay open[15] my mys-tery[16] to the music of a lyre (Psalms 49:5).

The community answers:

כִּי הִנְנִי־בָא וְשָׁכַנְתִּי בְתוֹכֵךְ, נְאֻם־יי.

Ki hineni-va veshakhanti vetokhekh, ne'um-adonai

"For, here I am, I come, and I will dwell inside you," says *Adonai* (Zachariah 2:14).

The words recited by the liturgist(s) are meant to evoke the experience of creating prayer. *Atteh,* translated here as "incline," comes from the verbal root n.t.h, which variously connotes stretch out, spread out, extend, lean, or bend. It thus suggests the physical/spiritual action—the crouched position of one looking deeply inward—that typifies the deep listening required for prayer and prayer authorship.

Creating prayer is a highly personal act, which one can only do based on one's own perceptions and questions (*my* ear, *my* mystery). At the same time, the juxtaposition of "*the* music of the lyre," as against "*my* mystery" introduces a universal element— and expands the breadth and applicability of any answer arrived at. Of course, liturgists hope to find answers not only for themselves, but for a whole community. The music of the lyre alludes to God's own voice, the sweet sounds of the Psalmist, and a singing congregation, chanting new and old prayers. And, notwithstanding the foregoing "how-to" on creating rituals, there is something mysterious about this, and every, creative process.

The response of the community is meant to validate the efforts of the liturgist(s). The assembled affirm, in God's voice, as it were, that God dwells inside the one who writes a new prayer, as well as in the midst of the community that recites it. The new prayer is thus declared to be an expression of God and the Godly. (This validation is anticipated in the context of the verses recited by the liturgist[s], since Psalms 49:4 states: "My mouth shall speak wisdom and the meditation of my heart shall be understanding.")

The literal translation "Here I am, I come" retains the urgency and immediacy of the Hebrew. It also highlights the idea that "God is right here" at the place where you incline your ear to create a prayer or lift your voice to recite one.

The word *betokhekh* ("you" in the phrase "God dwells inside you") is a feminine form of the second person pronoun. The first part of the verse (Zachariah 2:14) reads: "Sing and rejoice, daughter of Zion," Zion's daughter being a personification of the entire community. Thus, while this "feminine language" does not exclude men, it does allude to and recall women, in a way that makes any automatic mental picture of "the generic male Jew" impossible. The unspoken part of the verse also expresses the joy of the liturgical occasion.

I hope that creators of new liturgy, rituals, and ceremony will use this brief prayer, when they see fit, to celebrate their efforts. Authoring rituals and liturgies is itself a devotional act, and merits religious acknowledgement. It can also be an intimidating enterprise, and the more positive reinforcement, the better!

Click Stories

"We have all felt that tangible sensation of the tumblers falling into place in our heads, the Click! that signals a permanent recognition that the women's movement is...me. That I am one of those people oppressed, embarrassed, enraged, inconvenienced, and generally irritated by attitudes and patterns that the world would be well rid of. It is the click of tiny doors opening in the mind, and they never shut again—even though they may swing a bit in the breeze."

—JANE O'REILLY, *THE GIRL I LEFT BEHIND*[1]

The following is a selection of Jewish feminist "click stories" of the type Jane O'Reilly describes. These are contributors' stories of sudden and not-so-sudden insights on Judaism and gender.

Clicks Born of Lifecycle Experience

Like so many Jewish professional couples, we waited until our late thirties to try to have a child. After our doctor advised us that we might have difficulties, we had a positive pregnancy test on the eve of *Rosh Hashanah* (New Year). Seeing children at the High Holiday services and hearing the stories of Hannah's and Sarah's struggles to have babies resonated with our experiences. Two months later, a miscarriage dashed our hopes of becoming parents. The next *Rosh Hashanah*, the same High Holiday sights and stories were excruciating. Fighting back our tears, we left services early. The biblical message of infertility as a test of faith was insulting rather than consoling.

—BONNIE ELLEN BARON & DR. LAWRENCE BARON

377

At thirty-four, I was an assistant professor of Bible and pregnant with my first child. The baby's head would not "engage," so I had an x-ray in the fortieth week. And there was my spine, sticking into the birth canal! My doctor told me, "Go home, pack and come back in an hour so that we can prepare you for a caesarean first thing tomorrow." I displaced my anxiety, and concentrated on what I would do all evening alone in the hospital. I took novels with me, a TV guide, and—by divine providence or sheer lunacy—a file folder of Mesopotamian birth incantations that I had collected as part of my doctoral study of water imagery. That evening I did not want to be distracted—I wanted to focus on birth, and I spent the evening studying the incantations. When my mind recovered from birth and anesthetic, it clicked: Why should somebody like me, well educated in Judaism and Christianity, have to go all the way back to Babylon to find literature on birth? That was the beginning of my dedication to *Motherprayer*, to women's studies, and to Jewish feminism.

—DR. TIKVA FRYMER-KENSKY

For the first year that our *ḥevrah kaddishah* (burial society) existed, only women died in our community, which meant that only women were involved in the ritual washing of bodies. The quality of work done by the women of our *ḥevrah kaddishah* was extraordinary. In every case, the women would speak afterwards in hushed tones of being in the presence of the holy. I remember one *tohorah* (ritual washing) for the body of a young woman whom we had all loved very much. After we began with tears and prayers, we realized that we lacked a nail file to clean the fingernails of the deceased, as is required prior to immersion. We had to decide whether to send one of our members to get it, thereby disrupting the holy circle at work, or to forego the tool and continue. It seemed like a monumental decision, for everything we did was undertaken with gravity and awe.

Sometime later, a man, also beloved, also young, died in our community. Since none of the men had done *tohorah* before, it was agreed that I would be present to give instruction, while male *ḥevrah kaddishah* members and friends of the deceased washed and dressed him. I stood in the corner reading the instructions step by step. This gave me a great vantage point to see a group of men undertaking a holy task. While there was no lack of love for the man who had died, and no lack either of good hearts or of commitment, the tone was unmistakably different. "Can we do both legs at once?" one man asked. "Here, hoist him up higher!" Sheets, towels and water flew. Afterwards, several men said that, while they felt honored to have participated, they also found the task "kind of gross." And I realized, once again, how glad I am to be a woman!

—RABBI MARGARET HOLUB

It was either our first or second year at Princeton, in the early 1970s, and there was only one *Simḥat Torah* (Festival of Rejoicing in the Torah) celebration on campus—an Orthodox one. I went, and watched for a long time as the men's dancing became more and more frenzied, and as they unconsciously pushed the women up against the walls of the overcrowded room. I too longed to declare my love openly. When my pain could be contained no longer, I passed through the magic circles to the center, took a scroll from one of the men and ran outside with it as other young women followed. In the dark moist October air we danced barefoot on the wet grass with the stolen Torah until we had no breath left. Twenty years later I can still feel that moist night air on my skin.

—MERLE FELD

Clicks While Growing Up Jewish and Female

As a child, I used to read a children's book about Passover before the holiday every year. I was always struck by the picture of God seated on a throne, His long white beard and gold scepter lending an air of power and awe. As a teenager, I picked up the book again and noticed, with amazement, that the picture I had assumed to be God was actually Pharaoh, the villain of the story. The qualities which I had thought made God majestic were the same qualities which made Pharaoh tyrannical. I then realized that it was no childish mistake to misidentify the picture. How could I conceive of God in any other way when everything I had heard about God—in the prayerbook, my Hebrew school textbook, the *Haggadah* (Passover text) itself—depicted God as a male monarch? All the vocabulary that was supposed to express notions of God's transcendence—"power, majesty, might, kingdom"—evoked for me only earthbound and gender-specific conceptions. I began to understand that without a new language of metaphor, God and Pharaoh would remain indistinguishable in the minds of children and adults alike. And as long as God was a male monarch, not only was God humanized, but male supremacy was deified.

—AMY BARDACK

I was active in my temple youth group, and was delighted when the advisor and the graduating executive board approached me and a number of my friends to run for leadership positions for the coming year. The slate was prepared: Two friends named Bob would run against one another for president, and Judy and I would vie for the position of vice-president. I knew that no girl had ever served as president of our temple youth group, so was pleased when I was elected to the position of second in command. It was only when we held an event with a neighboring synagogue and I met their youth group president that I questioned the policy, for her name was Susan.

—RABBI SUE LEVI ELWELL

Although I was very active as a youngster in my Congregation Kenesseth Israel in Allentown, Pennsylvania, my parents did not want to celebrate a Bat Mitzvah (coming of age ceremony for girls) with me or my sister. But when my younger brother turned thirteen, he was forced to read from the Torah—like it or not. He hated Hebrew school, while I loved it. Although he barely made it through his part, he received a lot of money and attention. I, who was fluent in Hebrew, a budding liturgist, and a student of Judaism, never received financial reward or public recognition for becoming a Jewish woman.

—RABBI LYNN GOTTLIEB

When I was in fourth grade, my Hebrew school teacher was a crusty old gentleman, born (and ordained) in Czechoslovakia. His forbidding demeanor notwithstanding, he liked me immensely, and in later years was very proud of my achievements as a Jewish Studies scholar. Once, when my teacher was talking about God, I noticed that he kept referring to God as "He." I raised my hand and asked, "If God is neither a man nor a woman, why do you keep calling God 'He'?" My teacher replied, with a shrug of the shoulders at the patently ridiculous alternative: "What do you want me to call Him, 'She'?"

—DR. CHAVA WEISSLER

Clicks in Synagogue

I was in my mid-twenties when I first entered a synagogue to pray on a Sabbath. I was looking for "home." Hearing voices raised in song, my heart filled with joy. A friendly-looking man approached me, holding out a *tallit* (prayer shawl) for my use. I immediately recoiled, feeling as if even touching the fabric were taboo. "No thank you," I said, as I slunk down on a chair at the rear of the room. The singing voices seemed to fade away, as I could not stop thinking about the *tallit*. "Why am I so scared?" I wondered. In a moment of clarity, I realized that the prayer shawl symbolized to me all that I *thought* was "off limits" to me as a Jewish woman, all that was Jewish men's exclusive territory. Suddenly, I remembered a Hasidic saying that "the real exile of the Israelites' slavery in Egypt was that they had learned to endure it." I took a deep breath and walked over to the wooden stand where the prayer shawls hung. Holding the soft fabric, I wrapped it around my shoulders, feeling a deep warmth fill my body. I had come home.

—RABBI LEILA GAL BERNER

At our Temple's "Sisterhood Sabbath," a speaker addressed gender differences in religious observance and training and asked us how our Jewish lives might have been different if we had been born a member of the opposite sex. Several women rose and spoke about what would have changed had they been male: More religious education, perhaps a trip to Israel, loss of the pleasure of lighting *Shabbat* (Sabbath) candles with their mothers. She asked if any men would share their thoughts. Not one man spoke. Later I overheard men insisting that nothing would be different if they were born female.

—ANTONIA M. BOOKBINDER

The experience was the type of "spiritual high" that I had only dreamed of back in Cambridge: Jerusalem, the Wailing Wall, the magic of a clear end-of-summer night in Israel, prayers in Hebrew...there was an intensity, a *realness* that I had yearned for and yet never found in any Christian liturgical experience. Then one member of our group grasped my arm, shaking me from my reverie, telling me to stand up, we had to go. Unbeknownst to me, a great "black cloud" had built up behind my back, a cloud of black-coated, black-hatted *ḥaredim* (Orthodox extremists) who wanted not just to police their state-sanctioned sex-segregated prayer areas next to the *Kotel* (Western Wall), but to squash anything not to their liking that any Jews were doing liturgically. Men and women praying together?! A scandal, a perversion. One of the "black-hats" was about to attack us physically if we did not disperse, and the Israeli police stepped in. I knew then that as much as I loved Judaism, Judaism still had much *teshuvah* (repentance) to do.

—SHOSHANA BROWN-GUTOFF

My husband and I joined a Conservative synagogue. Women were active in all aspects of the synagogue, from full religious participation to administrative leadership. And yet I noticed that when I went alone (or with my children but without my husband) to Sabbath morning services, the prominent men in the congregation would never speak to me.

—CAROL V. DAVIS

I was in the synagogue where I regularly prayed, with my younger daughter Tamara who was then about eight years old. We sat in the women's section, a balcony, overlooking the activity in the men's section downstairs. I saw nothing wrong with this set-up. It was the way things were and would probably always be. I expected that the service that *Shabbat* (Sabbath) would be routine, but the *shul* (synagogue) was celebrating the arrival of a new Torah scroll. In the midst of the prayer service, the men began dancing in the aisles, singing, taking all the Torah scrolls out of the ark and carrying them to the door to greet the new scroll. The women, far above the action, had nothing to do but watch and talk to each other. My young daughter, who had been to the theater for the first time the previous week, turned to me and said, "Ma, this is just like watching a play." I was jolted by the truth of her remark. I suddenly knew that the Judaism I wished my daughters to live did not include prayer as a spectator sport. I left the *shul* that morning and never returned there again. That day I began my quest for a different group prayer experience for women.

—RIVKA HAUT

As a Reform Jewish woman I have resisted being segregated when attending services in my travels. Only in Safed did I sit behind a *meḥitzah* (partition separating women from men) at the old Ashkenazi Art Synagogue where I said *Kaddish* (mourner's prayer) for my mother, who likewise would have chafed.

But in Jerusalem's Great Synagogue, I went gleefully up to the women's open balcony. From there I could take in the whole panorama, the *bimah* (pulpit), the *aron kodesh* (holy ark), the magnificent stained glass windows. Acoustics being best in the balcony, I heard the famous male choir at its finest—truly celestial. I wondered if the men knew they had given us women the best seats in the house.

—BARBARA D. HOLENDER

The first time I opened the ark and sang *vayhi binso'a ha'aron* ("And so it was when the ark was lifted") at a women's service, I was overwhelmed. The difference between standing in front of the ark and standing behind the *meḥitzah* (partition separating women from men) is vital. Clearly, not everyone can always lead, but to know the possibility, to have a chance sometimes, changes the whole process. The intimacy with God and community that develops after the doing, the greater awareness and concentration, then becomes a regular part of every prayer service. Leading services also increases knowledge and comfort with the prayers—a direct result of having to learn how to do things. Thus, the ability to lead enriches all our prayer moments.

—NORMA BAUMEL JOSEPH

At a lecture I attended in 1979, a Conservative rabbi mentioned that he rarely "gave" women *aliyot* (honor of reciting the blessings before and after the Torah is read), and never counted women in a minyan. When I asked why, he replied that he felt that half the congregation wouldn't like it. I said that, in that case, half the congregation would *rather* have women participate. He looked puzzled and asked which half. I said that the women, in my experience, feel left out. He said that the wishes of the men concerned him more and walked quickly away.

—RENEE GAL PRIMACK

Rabbinical Clicks

Growing up as a Reform Jew in the 1950s and 60s, I had always assumed that I would become a rabbi. There was nothing in my training or upbringing that would have suggested that it would not be possible. In 1967, as a high school senior, I went to Cincinnati with the National Federation of Temple Youth to visit Hebrew Union College. We visited the historic Plum Street Temple, and heard lectures from HUC professors that made a lasting impression. What made a more subtle impression was a special meeting for the *boys* who were thinking about applying to rabbinical school. I did not attend the session, but later decided to write for information about rabbinical training. When a postcard came back addressed to "Mr. Robert Trachtenberg" (Trachtenberg being my birth name), I finally got the message. When I decided to go to rabbinical school after college I applied only to the Reconstructionist College, a new program that did not have the history of denying girls and women access.

—RABBI REBECCA T. ALPERT

I was studying Talmud and rabbinics at The Jewish Theological Seminary, years before the school opened the doors of its rabbinical school to women. Studying alongside my male peers, who were applying these courses toward their rabbinic degrees, I was often the only woman in the class. If I must say so myself, I was an excellent student. So it got my attention one day when the professor chided a male student as he read and interpreted the text at hand, saying "No, no, you must explain it so *Amy* will understand."

—RABBI AMY EILBERG

While in seminary, after three weeks of classes, I met my professor in the library. He asked me how I liked his class, and where I worked in the library. I answered that I was a rabbinic student, and that I found his class quite interesting. He responded that he had thought I had been auditing the class and was on the library staff. I responded again that that was not the case, and that I was indeed a rabbinic student. At this time, in the mid- and late 70s, many of my professors started their classes by standing at the head of the class and announcing, "Gentlemen, let us begin."

—RABBI VICKI HOLLANDER

I was meeting with a close community of high powered, successful Jewish women—a filmmaker, an artistic director, a psychologist, a writer—after the death of a friend who was a prominent Jewish feminist academic. In order to prepare for the funeral, I asked a few of the women to speak about the legacy of their friend—what they learned from her, what they would miss. Once the conversation started, an outpouring of stories, passions, and reflections emerged. There were so many offerings that these talkative, articulate, strong women were competing to speak. I was writing down their words in order to prepare a eulogy. A woman who came in late and did not know me turned to me, and said gruffly "What are you, the secretary?" "No," I answered this national figure politely. "I'm the rabbi."

—RABBI PATRICIA KARLIN-NEUMANN

In 1972 a good friend told me that she wanted to be a rabbi. It was amazing to me not only that a woman might become a rabbi, but that a woman might become a cleric in any religion! I began to think about the possibilities open to me, a religious, uneducated product of a mixed marriage. A year later I enrolled at Union Theological Seminary, a Protestant institution. Across the street was The Jewish Theological Seminary where I was also to take classes. After four years, I realized my Jewish roots were stronger and converted to Judaism. I've continued to study ever since.

—JANE BARON RECHTMAN

There is a rabbi, the sole rabbi of a healthy-sized congregation in a large metropolitan setting, who on account of her height, reserves a pair of high-heeled shoes for use exclusively on the *bimah* (pulpit), in order that she be visible behind the lectern. One day, she came upon her three-year-old son parading around in her three-inch heels. When she asked him what he was doing, he replied: "Playing rabbi!"

—RABBI ELEANOR SMITH

Clicks in the Classroom

When I was in college I spent several months travelling in Europe. A bit lonely, I especially relished meeting other Jews as they reminded me, and took the place, of family. I was invited to participate in a weekend retreat for Jewish college students from all over Europe, held in a beautiful town in the Swiss Alps. Most of the students were more interested in the ski slopes than in the Jewish content of the programming. But I found myself drawn to the lectures of an American rabbi who headed a *yeshivah* (traditional academy of Jewish learning) in Israel. There was something about him—not only his incredible charisma, but his message—

that I wanted more of. Over and over he invited us "Come, come to Jerusalem and study with me." By the end of the weekend I knew there was nothing I wanted more. I approached, a bit awestruck and very enthusiastic: "Please tell me how I can study with you in Jerusalem. I am ready to go." He smiled at me, pleased that I had heard and understood his message. He said, "I am so glad that you will come, but of course you will not actually study with me; you will study with my wife. I do not teach women."

That was an incredibly painful moment for me: I understood that there could be no place for me in his brand of Judaism. Needless to say, I never went to his *yeshivah*, nor studied with his wife. I went on to embrace a liberal form of Judaism that fully includes women.

—RABBI DEBRA NEWMAN KAMIN

The rabbi who converted me was Orthodox, and students in the Introduction to Judaism class he taught often asked why women were exempted or excluded from certain synagogue observances. "If women were included equally," he answered, "only women would go to services."

—CATHERINE HALL MYROWITZ

In the early 1980s I taught at Princeton University. Among the courses I offered was one titled "Modern Judaism." I vividly remember a class at the end of one semester in which we focused on the issue of women's ordination as rabbis. Discussing the debates then taking place in the Conservative movement, one male student loudly insisted that ordaining women was completely unwarranted and unjustifiable. "For two thousand years," he said, "rabbis have been men. Judaism rests on the power of tradition. Women can do other things. But our spiritual leaders should be men." And on he went, speaking in general, abstract terms about why women should not be rabbis until one female student, whose active participation in class had long demonstrated her Jewish knowledge and commitment, softly said: "I want to be a rabbi. Would you deny me ordination?" (The student was Debra Orenstein, now a Conservative rabbi, and editor of this volume.) The look on his face, along with his silence, indicated to all of us that he had just heard his first feminist "click."

—DR. ELLEN M. UMANSKY

I went to an Orthodox Jewish day school where classes were co-ed and the curriculum for boys and girls was identical. In the ninth grade, a new teacher came to the school and decided that the boys, for one period a day, would study Talmud while the girls would take sewing. I hated sewing. I took it in the seventh grade and sewed forty-seven button holes that year (I still remember the exact number) because we could not go onto the next assignment until the current one was completed perfectly. I never did perfect the art of handmade button holes.

Taking sewing, and being excluded from Talmud, a new, intriguing pursuit, made no sense and seemed grossly unfair. Certainly skill was not the factor that determined the separation because I was uniquely unskilled at sewing and no one knew anyone's aptitude for Talmud; it was new to all of us.

I rallied two other girls, went to the principal, and lodged our complaint. We were taken quite seriously, discussions with various rabbis ensued, and finally, we were admitted into the class. The teacher actually tutored us privately to catch us up to the boys.

—DR. CLARA FRANCES ZILBERSTEIN

Before the current feminist movement I talked with my high school counselor about becoming an attorney. He told me I would have trouble getting into a law school because I had two strikes against me: I was a woman and a Jew.

—DR. MILDRED SELTZER

I remember signing up for a course in 1980 entitled "Feminist Jewish Theology" taught by Dr. Judith Plaskow. I was incredulous that those words could be used together. What was so amazing? I think it was the willingness of women to say "We are worthy to share our images of God in full voice. We are also created in God's image."

—RABBI SHEILA PELTZ WEINBERG

Clicks in the Public Eye

I was twenty-three and newly married to a rabbi. I hardly knew what *rebbitzin* (rabbi's wife) meant and was scared to death. I had been in town only a few weeks when the president of a Jewish women's charity approached me to give the opening prayer at an upcoming meeting. I was embarrassed and stammered, "That's really my husband's department, you know." "Oh," she said, "we assumed he would write it." I politely declined.

—DR. MARY GENDLER

Once when I was a guest on a radio talk show, the host earnestly asked me: "But really, Rabbi Geller, Judaism and feminism are incompatible. Which is more important to you, your Judaism or your feminism?" After a moment's pause I responded, "And which is more important to you, your heart or your liver?" I was never invited back on his show.

—RABBI LAURA GELLER

Clicks from the Mouths of Babes

My family attended a Rabbinical Assembly conference, and the women there were mostly wives of rabbis. The youngest generation of wives hung around with our babies in the lobbies while our spouses sat in ballrooms voting. I overheard one woman report a conversation with her two-year-old daughter: "Mommy, is God married?" The mother was briefly stymied—was this the moment to talk about the *Shekhinah* (close-dwelling presence of God, associated with the feminine)? She answered, "No, dear, I don't think so." The child—who was still able to identify with the divine and for whom Mother still had primary status—thoughtfully replied, "Of course, now why would God need a husband?"

—DR. LORI HOPE LEFKOVITZ

Some years ago my daughter came home from summer camp with a picture of a very proper-looking elderly grandfather. Impressed by my daughter's burgeoning artistic ability, I said "That's very beautiful, Debbie, tell me more about it." "Well Mom, you see, they asked us to draw a picture of God." She paused in her explanation, noticing my rather startled look. This was the same daughter who wore a t-shirt to the Orthodox Hebrew Academy Day School, saying "When God created man, She was only joking." "Mom, don't get excited," she reassured me. "I know God is not an old man," she continued. "When they asked me to draw God, I handed them a blank page, but they said I had to draw something. This was all I could think of."

—RABBI SANDY EISENBERG SASSO

Alternatives to the Click Experience

When I was first asked to share my "click story," a cold wave of outsidership swept over me. The truth was, I had absolutely no idea what a "click story" was. When told that it summarized a moment or situation which brought a sudden political awakening—revelation perhaps—of ourselves as feminists in a non-feminist world, I answered that, in fact, I did not believe I had one. Of course, I could recount moments when women were not in the place I thought they should be; moments when I was the only woman in the room and felt like it; moments when I was amazed at the distance we still had to travel to get to where we already should have been. But I have always known that the world would present us with struggles that could vanquish us, not just in and of themselves, but by feeding our own anger and frustration. The trick, I suppose, is to possess the passion of the recruit with the patience of the veteran.

—RABBI NINA BETH CARDIN

We searched our memories many times over but could not recall any radicalizing moment suitable for a click story. Judaism and feminism have coexisted in each of us for as long as we can remember. Like two people holding hands they are intimately connected, even as each retains its unique character. Finding ways to express them together has been our privilege and adventure. Unclick!

—RICK E.F. DINITZ & TINA D. FEIN DINITZ

I have no "click" story. I still have a difficult time calling myself the "f" word—feminist. It conjures up, for me, images of angry women, unable to see light or humor in a sometimes dark world. I am still afraid that being a feminist interferes with my being feminine. But I am one: A feminist. It is not that anything "clicked." It is more like it crept up on me. I am a feminist because it is the only way to explain what has become fundamental to me, as a woman and as a Jew: To engage fully as a participant in my synagogue and in my community, to add my loud and urgent voice to the dialogue with Jewish text and tradition, to be counted upon and to count. In short, to be fully human.

—ROSE L. LEVINSON

It is impossible for me to single out one "click" experience—there have been too many turning points in my life to allow naming any one as the most significant. Among them, there was the first day I stood before a class and, with fear and joy, discovered that I was a teacher. My discovery of feminism brought with it the liberating recognition that my personal life, my struggles, and my angers were appropriate responses to the male-dominated world in which I live. And there was the *Yom Kippur* (Day of Atonement) service I attended—my first as an adult—where I, a casually secular Jew all my life, deeply and overwhelmingly felt absolute rightness and sureness of my Jewish identity.

—HARRIET M. PERL

My first feminist click stories are embedded deep in my consciousness—a preschool playground debate on whether women could be doctors; the girls' pants revolt in junior high; the warm approval of a liberal male shop teacher; protesting a high school class titled "Physics for Girls." By the time I was sixteen, in 1971, I was an ardent, committed, politicized feminist. It was the identity affirmation of feminism that prompted me to embrace and deepen my understanding of Judaism.

I never expected anything but controversy over feminism in my Jewish academic, seminary, and communal life. So although I could recount hundreds of tales of thoughtless and even malicious discrimination against myself and other women—past and present—none of them was a "click." Rather they were an angry threatened buzz fading now to an annoying and pathetic whine.

—RABBI JANE LITMAN

Suggested Readings

Editor's note: When I first began to solicit material for *Lifecyles*, a common response was, "But every chapter could be a book in itself!" Indeed, it could, and I hope that there will soon be at *least* one book on every subject covered in this volume. In fact, the flowering of Jewish women's literature has already begun, and served as an inspiration in creating this book.

Below are suggested readings, related to lifecycle, Jewish women, and the topics covered in this volume. The bibliographies are not intended to be exhaustive, but rather to serve as a guide for additional reading. Each chapter's suggested readings were selected by the authors of that chapter. Annotations are provided only when the subject of the book or article is unclear from the title alone.

Ritual and Life Passages from a Jewish Perspective

Adelman, Penina V. *Miriam's Well: Rituals for Jewish Women Around the Year.* New York: Biblio Press, 1990.

Cardozo, Arlene Rossen. *Jewish Family Celebrations: The Sabbath, Festivals, and Ceremonies.* New York: St. Martin's, 1982.

Geffen, Rela M. *Celebration and Renewal: Rites of Passage in Judaism.* Philadelphia: Jewish Publication Society, 1993.

Gillman, Neil. *Sacred Fragments.* Philadelphia: Jewish Publication Society, 1990.

Hoffman, Lawrence A. *Beyond the Text: A Holistic Approach to Liturgy.* Bloomington, Ind.: Indiana University Press, 1987.

Klein, Isaac. *A Guide to Jewish Religious Practice.* New York: The Jewish Theological Seminary, 1979.

Levine, Elizabeth Resnick, ed. *A Ceremonies Sampler: New Rites, Celebrations, and Observances of Jewish Women.* San Diego: Woman's Institute for Continuing Jewish Education, 1991.

Neusner, Jacob. *The Enchantments of Judaism: Rites of Transformation from Birth through Death.* New York: Basic Books, 1987.

Trepp, Leo. *The Complete Book of Jewish Observance.* New York: Summit Books, 1980.

Ritual and Life Passages from a Feminist Perspective

Beck, Renee, and Sydney Barbara Metrick. *The Art of Ritual: A Guide to Creating and Performing Your Own Ceremonies for Growth and Change.* Berkeley, Calif.: Celestial Arts, 1990. New Age, feminist perspective.

Belenky, Mary Field, et al. *Women's Ways of Knowing: The Development of Self, Voice, and Mind.* New York: Basic Books, 1986.

Chodrow, Nancy. *The Reproduction of Mothering.* Los Angeles: University of California Press, 1978.

Gilligan, Carol. *In a Different Voice: Psychological Theory and Women's Development.* Cambridge, Mass.: Harvard University Press, 1982.

Imber-Black, Evan, and Janine Roberts. *Rituals For Our Time: Healing and Changing Our Lives and Our Relationships.* New York: HarperCollins, 1992.

Josselson, Ruth Ellen. *Finding Herself: Pathways to Identity Development in Women.* San Francisco: Jossey-Bass, 1987.

Nelson, Gertrud Mueller. *To Dance With God: Family Ritual and Community Celebration.* Mawah, N.J.: Paulist Press, 1986.

Also consult Elizabeth Resnick Levine, ed., A Ceremonies Sampler *and Penina Adelman,* Miriam's Well *in the Ritual and Life Passages From a Jewish Perspective bibliography.*

General Titles By and About Jewish Women

Baum, Charlotte, Paula Hyman, and Sonya Michel. *The Jewish Woman in America.* New York: Dial Press, 1976.

Berkowitz, Elieser. *Jewish Women in Time and Torah.* New York: KTAV Publishing House, 1990. A traditional halakhic focus.

Biale, Rachel. *Women and Jewish Law: An Exploration of Women's Issues in Halakhic Sources.* New York: Schocken, 1984.

Bletter, Diana, and Lori Grinker. *The Invisible Thread: A Portrait of American Jewish Women.* New York: Jewish Publication Society, 1989.

Broner, E.M. *The Telling: A Group of Extraordinary Jewish Women Journey to Spirituality Through Community and Ceremony.* San Francisco: HarperCollins, 1993.

Carnay, Janet, et al. *The Jewish Woman's Awareness Guide.* New York: Biblio Press, 1992.

Davidman, Lynn. *Tradition in a Rootless World.* Berkeley, Calif.: U.C. Berkeley Press, 1991.

Day, Peggy, ed. *Gender and Difference in Ancient Israel.* Minneapolis, Minn.: Fortress, 1989.

Fine, Irene. *Midlife, A Rite of Passage and The Wise Woman, A Celebration*. San Diego: Woman's Institute for Continuing Jewish Education, 1988. Rituals and formulas for creating them for midlife and elderhood.

Fishman, Sylvia Barack. *A Breath of Life: Feminism in the American Jewish Community*. New York: The Free Press, 1993.

Frankiel, Tamar. *The Voice of Sarah: Feminine Spirituality and Traditional Judaism*. San Francisco: Harper Collins, 1990.

Frymer-Kensky, Tikva. *In the Wake of the Goddess: Women, Culture and the Biblical Transformation of Pagan Myth*. New York: The Free Press, 1992.

Glenn, Susan. *Daughters of the Shtetl*. Ithaca, N.Y.: Cornell University Press, 1990.

Greenberg, Blu. *On Women and Judaism*. Philadelphia: Jewish Publication Society, 1981.

Hazleton, Lesley. *Israeli Women: The Reality Behind the Myths*. New York: Simon and Schuster, 1977.

Kaufman, Deborah Renee. *Rachel's Daughters: Newly Orthodox Jewish Women*. New Brunswick, N.J.: Rutgers University Press, 1991.

Ochs, Vanessa L. *Words on Fire*. New York: Harcourt Brace Jovanovich, 1990.

Plaskow, Judith. *Standing Again at Sinai: Judaism from a Feminist Perspective*. San Francisco: Harper and Row, 1990.

Pogrebin, Letty Cottin. *Deborah, Golda, and Me: Being Female and Jewish in America*. New York: Crown Publishing Group, 1991.

Schneider, Susan Weidman. *Jewish and Female: Choices and Changes in Our Lives Today*. New York: Simon and Schuster, 1985.

Shepherd, Naomi. *Price Below Rubies*. London: Weidenfeld & Nicolson, 1993.

Swidler, Leonard J. *Women in Judaism: The Status of Women in Formative Judaism*. Metuchen, N.J.: Scarecrow Press, 1976.

Weinberg, Sydney Stahl. *The World of Our Mothers*. Chapel Hill, N.C.: University of North Carolina Press, 1988.

Also consult Penina Adelman, Miriam's Well *in the Ritual and Life Passages From a Jewish Perspective bibliography*.

Anthologies By and About Jewish Women

Antler, Joyce, ed. *America and I: Short Stories by American Jewish Women Writers*. Boston: Beacon Press, 1990.

Ashton, Dianne, and Ellen M. Umansky, eds. *Four Centuries of Jewish Women's Spirituality: A Sourcebook*. Boston: Beacon Press, 1992.

Balka, Christie, and Andy Rose, eds. *Twice Blessed: On Being Lesbian, Gay and Jewish*. Boston: Beacon Press, 1989.

Baskin, Judith, ed. *Jewish Women in Historical Perspective*. Detroit: Wayne State University Press, 1992.

Beck, Evelyn Torton, ed. *Nice Jewish Girls: A Lesbian Anthology*. Rev. ed. Boston: Beacon Press, 1989.

Haut, Rivka, and Susan Grossman, eds. *Daughters of the King: Women and the Synagogue*. New York: Jewish Publication Society, 1991.

Heschel, Susannah, ed. *On Being a Jewish Feminist*. New York: Schocken, 1983.

Kalechofsky, Robert, and Roberta Kalechofsky, eds. *Echad 5: The Global Anthology of Jewish Women Writers*. New York: Micha, 1990.

Kaye/Kantrowitz, Melanie, and Irena Kelpfisz, eds. *The Tribe of Dina: A Jewish Women's Anthology*. Montpelier, Vt.: Sinister Wisdom Books, 1986.

Koltun, Elizabeth, ed. *The Jewish Woman: New Perspectives*. New York: Schocken, 1976.

Marcus, Jacob Rader, ed. *The American Jewish Woman: A Documentary History*. New York: KTAV Publishing House; Cincinnati: American Jewish Archives, 1981.

Mazow, Julia Wolf, ed. *The Woman Who Lost Her Names: Selected Writings by American Jewish Women*. San Francisco: Harper and Row, 1980.

Newman, Leslea, ed. *Bubbe Meisehs by Shayneh Maidelehs: An Anthology of Poetry by Jewish Granddaughters about Jewish Grandmothers*. Santa Cruz, Calif.: Herbooks, 1990.

Niederman, Sharon, ed. *Shaking Eve's Tree: Short Stories of Jewish Women*. Philadelphia: Jewish Publication Society, 1990.

Riller, Carol, and John Roth, eds. *Women and the Holocaust*. New York: Paragon House, 1993.

Spiegel, Marcia Cohn, and Deborah Lipton Kremsdorf, eds. *Women Speak to God: The Poems and Prayers of Jewish Women*. San Diego: Woman's Institute for Continuing Education, 1987.

Swirski, Barbara, and Marilyn P. Safir, eds. *Calling the Equality Bluff: Women in Israel*. New York: Pergamon Press, 1991.

Wenkart, Henny, ed. *Sarah's Daughters Sing: A Sampler of Poems by Jewish Women*. Hoboken, N.J.: KTAV Publishing House, 1990.

Zones, Jane Sprague, ed. *Taking the Fruit: Modern Women's Tales of the Bible*. San Diego: Woman's Institute for Continuing Jewish Education, 1991.

Also consult Elizabeth Resnick Levine, ed., A Ceremonies Sampler, listed in the Ritual and Life Passages From a Jewish Perspective bibliography.

Chapter One: Beginnings

Cardin, Nina Beth, ed. *Out of the Depths I Call to You: A Book of Prayers for the Married Jewish Woman*. Northvale, N.J.: Jason Aronson, 1992.

Cohen, Jeremy. *"Be Fertile and Increase, Fill the Earth and Master It": The Ancient and Medieval Career of a Biblical Text*. Ithaca, N.Y.: Cornell University Press, 1989.

Cole, Diane. *After Great Pain: A New Life Emerges*. New York: Summit, 1992. After a period of infertility and many losses, Cole adopts a child.

Diamant, Anita. *The New Jewish Baby Book*. Woodstock, Vt.: Jewish Lights Publishing, 1994.

Eilberg-Schwartz, Howard, ed. *People of the Body: Jews and Judaism from an Embodied Perspective*. Albany: State University of New York Press, 1992.

Finkelstein, Baruch, and Michal Finkelstein. *B'Sha'ah Tovah: The Jewish Woman's Clinical and Halakhic Guide to Pregnancy and Childbirth*. New York: Feldheim, 1993.

Freehof, Solomon. "Devotional Literature in the Vernacular." *CCAR Yearbook* 33 (1923): 375-424. Classic essay on the themes and style of the *tkhines*, tracing their connection to contemporaneous private devotions.

Gold, Michael. *And Hannah Wept: Infertility, Adoption, and the Jewish Couple*. Philadelphia: Jewish Publication Society, 1988.

Johnston, Patricia Irwin. *Adopting After Infertility*. Indianapolis, Ind.: Perspective Press, 1992.

Klirs, Tracy Guren, et al., trans. *The Merit of Our Mothers: A Bilingual Anthology of Jewish Women's Prayers*. Cincinnati: Hebrew Union College, 1992.

Melina, Lois Ruskai. *Making Sense of Adoption: A Parent's Guide*. New York: Harper & Row, 1989. Conversations and activities for families formed through adoption, donor insemination, surrogacy, and *in vitro* fertilization.

Perlmutter, Saul E., and Shoshana Zonderman. "Preparing for Childbirth: A Ceremony for Parents-to-be." *Reconstructionist* 54, no. 2 (October/November 1988): 18-22.

Rosenthal, Rabbi Dovid Simcha. *A Joyful Mother of Children*. Jerusalem: Feldheim, Ltd., 1982.

Simons, Robin. *After the Tears: Parents Talk About Raising a Child With a Disability*. New York: Harcourt Brace Jovanovich, 1985.

Weissler, Chava. "The *Tkhines* and Women's Prayer." *CCAR Journal* (fall 1993): 75-88. The light shed by *tkhines* on the problems of incorporating women's voices into Jewish prayer in the twentieth century.

Support Groups: Jewish Children's Adoption Network, P.O. Box 16544, Denver, CO 80216-0544/(303)573-8113, is a national clearinghouse to find Jewish adoptive or foster homes for Jewish children, particularly special needs or older children. Stars of David International, Inc., c/o Susan M. Katz, 3175 Commercial Avenue, Suite 100, Northbrook, IL 60062-1915/(708)205-1200, is a support network for Jewish and partly-Jewish adoptive families.

Also consult Judith Baskin, ed. Jewish Women in Historical Perspective, *159-181 in the Anthologies By and About Jewish Women bibliography; and Gay Becker,* Healing the Infertile Family; *Jean W. Carter and Michael Carter,* Sweet Grapes; *Ellen Sarasohn Glazer and Susan Lewis Cooper,* Without Child; *and Linda P. Salzer,* Surviving Infertility *in the Infertility and Early losses bibliography.*

Chapter Two: Infertility and Early Losses

Allen, Marie, and Shelly Marks. *Miscarriage: Women Sharing From The Heart*. New York: John Wiley and Sons, 1993.

Becker, Gay. *Healing the Infertile Family: Strengthening Your Relationship in the Search for Parenthood*. New York: Bantam Books, 1990.

Blank, Rabbi Debra Reed, Rabbi Amy Eilberg, and Rabbi Marvin Goodman. "Focus on Halakhah: A Response to Miscarriage." *Women's League Outlook* (spring 1992): 14-16.

Carter, Jean W., and Michael Carter. *Sweet Grapes: How to Stop Being Infertile and Start Living Again*. Indianapolis, Ind.: Perspectives Press, 1989. Resolving the losses of infertility and choosing to be child-free.

Glazer, Ellen Sarasohn, and Susan Lewis Cooper. *Without Child: Experiencing and Resolving Infertility*. Lexington, Mass.: Lexington Books, 1988.

Kohn, Ingrid, M.S.W., Perry-Lynn Moffitt, and Isabelle A. Wilkins, M.D. *A Silent Sorrow: Pregnancy Loss, Guidance and Support for You and Your Family*. New York: Bantam, 1992.

Salzer, Linda P. *Surviving Infertility: A Compassionate Guide Through the Emotional Crisis of Infertility*. New York: HarperCollins, 1991.

Also consult Dianne Ashton and Ellen Umansky, eds., Four Centuries of Jewish Women's Spirituality, *221-222 and 282-285 and Rivka Haut and Susan Grossman, eds.,* Daughters of the King, *284-290 in the Anthologies By and About Women bibliography; and Michael Gold,* And Hannah Wept *in the Beginnings bibliography.*

Chapter Three: Welcoming Children into Name and Covenant

Barth, Lewis M., ed., *Berit Mila in the Reform Context.* Secaucus, N.J.: Carol Publishing Group for the Berit Mila Board of Reform Judaism, 1990.

Cantor, Debra, and Rebecca Jacobs. "*Brit Banot* Covenant Ceremonies for Daughters." *Kerem* (winter 1992-93): 45-55.

Conservative Judaism 42, no. 4 (summer 1990). The entire issue is devoted to *Brit Milah* (covenant of circumcision ritual).

Eilberg-Schwartz, Howard. *The Savage in Judaism.* Bloomington, Ind.: Indiana University Press, 1990.

Packets of information on naming and covenant ceremonies for girls, including sample ceremonies, are available from: Women's League for Conservative Judaism, 48 E. 74th Street, New York, NY 10021, 212-628-1600 and the Jewish Women's Resource Center, 9 E. 69th Street, New York, NY 10021, 212-535-5900.

Also consult Jacob Neusner, The Enchantment of Judaism: Rites of Transformation from Birth through Death, *43-52 and Elizabeth Resnick Levine, ed.,* A Ceremonies Sampler, *25-38 in the Ritual and Life Passages from a Jewish Perspective bibliography; Elizabeth Koltun, ed.* The Jewish Woman, *101-105 in the Anthologies By and About Jewish Women bibliography; and Anita Diamant,* The New Jewish Baby Book *in the Beginnings bibliography.*

Specifically on "Creating a Tree-dition":

Fisher, Adam. *Seder Tu BiShevat: The Festival of Trees.* New York: Central Conference of American Rabbis, 1989.

Kelman, Vicky. *TOGETHER: A Child-Parent Kit, Issue Six: Trees.* New York: Melton Research Center of The Jewish Theological Seminary of America, 1985.

Chapter Four: Adolescence

Cernea, Ruth Fredman, ed. *Jewish Life on Campus.* Washington, D.C.: B'nai B'rith Hillel Foundations, 1993.

Coburn, Karen Levin, and Madge Lawrence Treeger. *Letting Go: A Parent's Guide to Today's College Experience.* Bethesda, Md.: Adler and Adler, 1988.

Diamond, James, and Jeremy Brochin, eds. *A Handbook for Hillel and Jewish Campus Professionals.* Washington, D.C.: Association of Hillel and Jewish Campus Professionals, 1983.

Gilligan, Carol. *Making Connections: The Relational Worlds of Adolescent Girls at Emma Willard School.* Cambridge, Mass.: Harvard University Press, 1990.

Hancock, Emily. *The Girl Within: A Radical Approach to Female Identity.* London: Pandora, 1990.

Salkin, Jeffrey. *Putting God on the Guest List: How to Reclaim the Spiritual Meaning of Your Child's Bar or Bat Mitzvah.* Woodstock, Vt.: Jewish Lights Publishing, 1992.

Also consult Rela M. Geffen, ed. Celebration and Renewal, *53-70 in the Ritual and Life Passages from a Jewish Perspective bibliography; Roselyn Bell, ed.,* Hadassah Magazine Jewish Parenting Book *42-63; and Sharon Strassfeld and Kathy Green, eds.,* Jewish Family Book, *319-371 in the Parenting bibliography.*

Chapter Five: Being Single

Eilberg, Amy. "Views of Human Development in Jewish Rituals: A Comparison with Eriksonian Theory." *Smith College Studies in Social Work* 55, no. 1 (November 1984): 1-23.

Lindsey, Karen. *Friends as Family: New Kinds of Family and What They Could Mean For You.* Boston: Beacon Press, 1981.

Novack, William. "Are Good Jewish Men A Vanishing Breed?" *Moment* 5, no. 2 (February 1980): 14-20.

Peterson, Nadena, and Barbara Sofie. *Singleness: A Guide to Understanding and Satisfaction.* San Antonio, Tex.: The Watercress Press, 1987.

Also consult Sylvia Barack Fishman, A Breath of Life, *17-43, and Susan Weidman Schneider,* Jewish and Female, *300-336, in the General Titles By and About Jewish Women bibliography; and Elizabeth Koltun,* The Jewish Woman: New Perspectives, *43-49 in the Anthologies By and About Jewish Women bibliography.*

Specifically on "Standing Alone at Sinai: Shame and the Single Woman":

Broucek, Frank J., M.D. *Shame and the Self.* New York: The Guilford Press, 1991. A psychoanalytic perspective.

Miller, Susan. *The Shame Experience.* Hillsdale, N.J.: The Analytic Press, 1985. Based on interviews; Miller details how individuals experience shame.

Wurmser, Leon, M.D. *The Mask of Shame.* Baltimore, Md.: Johns Hopkins University Press, 1981.

Chapter Six: Invisible Life Passages

Specifically on "Our Silent Seasons":

Alpert, Rebecca Trachtenberg. "A Prayer on the Occasion of a Miscarriage or Abortion." *Reconstructionist* 51 (September 1985): 4.

Brady, Maureen. *Daybreak: Meditations for Women Survivors of Sexual Abuse.* San Francisco: Harper Collins, 1991.

Davis, Laura. *The Courage to Heal Workbook for Women and Men Survivors of Sexual Abuse.* San Francisco: Harper Collins, 1991.

Maltz, Wendy, and Beverly Holman. *Incest and Sexuality: A Guide to Understanding and Healing.* Lexington, Mass.: Lexington Books, 1987.

McClure, Mary Beth. *Reclaiming the Heart: A Handbook of Help and Hope for Survivors of Incest.* New York: Warner Books, 1990.

Russ, Ian, Sally Weber, and Ellen Ledley. *Shalom Bayit: A Jewish Response to Child Abuse and Domestic Violence.* Los Angeles: Jewish Family Service of Los Angeles, Family Violence Project, 1993.

Thomas, T. *Surviving with Serenity: Daily Meditations for Incest Survivors.* Deerfield Beach, Fla.: Health Communications, Inc., 1990.

W., Nancy. *On the Path: Affirmations for Adults Recovering from Childhood Sexual Abuse.* San Francisco: Harper, 1991.

Support Groups:
The Jewish Survivors Network, P.O. Box 1566, Philadelphia, PA 19105 is geared to Jewish survivors of child sexual abuse. The Center for Prevention of Sexual and Domestic Violence, 1914 North 34th Street, Suite 105, Seattle, WA 98103 / (206)634-1903, works with various religious groups.

Also consult Renee Beck and Sydney Barbara Metrick, The Art of Ritual, *and Gertrud Mueller Nelson,* To Dance With God, *in the Ritual and Life Passages from a Feminist Perspective bibliography; and Dianne Ashton and Ellen M. Umansky, eds.,* Four Centuries of Jewish Women's Spirituality: A Sourcebook, *257-265, in the Anthologies By and About Jewish Women bibliography.*

Specifically on "Eshet Ḥayil":
Levin, Yael. "'*Eshet ḥayil' bapulkhan hayehudi." Beth Mikra* 31 (1985/86): 339-47. Uses of *Eshet Ḥayil* in earlier times.

Lichtenstein, Murray H. "Chiasm and Symmetry in Proverbs." *Catholic Biblical Quarterly* 44 (1982): 202-11.

McCreesh, Thomas P. "Wisdom as Wife: Proverbs 31:10-31." *Revue Biblique* 92 (1985): 25-46.

Visotzky, Burton L., ed. and trans. *The Midrash on Proverbs*. New Haven, Conn.: Yale University Press, 1992.

― ― ―. "Midrash Eshet Ḥayil." *Conservative Judaism* 38, no. 3 (1986): 21-25.

Chapter Seven: Coming Out
Artson, Bradley. "Gay and Lesbian Jews." *Jewish Spectator* 55, no. 3 (winter 1990): 6-14.

Barber, Karen, and Sarah Holmes, eds. *Testimonies: Lesbian Coming Out Stories*. Boston: Alyson, 1988.

Fairchild, Betty, and Nancy Hayward. *Now That You Know: What Every Parent Should Know About Homosexuality*. San Diego: Harcourt, Brace, Jovanovich, 1989. Discusses issues related to coming out to your parents.

Herdt, Gilbert, ed. "'Coming Out' as a Rite of Passage: A Chicago Study." In *Gay Culture in America: Studies From the Field*, edited by G. Herdt, 29-67. Boston: Beacon Press, 1992.

Kaye/Kantrowitz, Melanie. *My Jewish Face and Other Stories, (Spinsters/Aunt Lute)*. San Francisco: Aunt Lute Books, 1990.

Klepfisz, Irena. *Dreams of an Insomniac: Jewish Feminist Essays, Speeches and Diatribes*. Portland, Oreg.: Eighth Mountain Press, 1990.

MacPike, Loralee, ed. *There's Something I've Been Meaning To Tell You*. Tallahassee, Fla.: Naiad, 1990. A volume of stories by parents about coming out to their children.

Marder, Janet. "Getting to Know the Gay and Lesbian *Shul*." *Reconstructionist* 51, no. 2 (October/November 1985): 20-25.

Matt, Hershel J. "Sin, Crime, Sickness or Alternative Life Style?: A Jewish Approach to Homosexuality." *Judaism* 27, no. 1 (winter 1978): 13-24. The entire issue is dedicated to lesbian and gay Jews.

Newman, Leslea. *A Letter to Harvey Milk*. Ithaca, N.Y.: Firebrand, 1988.

Penelope, Julia, and Susan J. Wolfe, eds. *The Original Coming Out Stories.* Freedom, Calif.: Crossing Press, 1989.

Rogow, Faith. "The Rise Of Jewish Lesbian Feminism." *Bridges: A Journal for Jewish Feminists and Our Friends* 1, no. 1 (spring 1990): 67-79. The contributions of lesbians to Jewish life.

Umans, Meg. *Like Coming Home: Coming Out Letters.* Austin, Tex.: Banned Books, 1988.

Wenig, Margaret Moers. "Welcoming Lesbian and Gay Jews into Our Synagogues." *New Menorah* 2, no. 23 (spring 1991): 14-15. The entire issue is dedicated to lesbian and gay Jews.

― ― ― . *Homosexuality and Religion.* Binghamton, N.Y.: Harrington Park Press, 1989.

Also consult Christie Balka and Andy Rose, eds., Twice Blessed: On Being Lesbian, Gay, and Jewish, 11-56; and Evelyn Torton Beck, ed., Nice Jewish Girls, 45-50, in the Anthologies By and About Jewish Women bibliography.

Chapter Eight: Marriage

Butler, Becky, ed. *Ceremonies of the Heart: Celebrating Lesbian Unions.* Seattle: The Seal Press, 1990.

Diamant, Anita. *The New Jewish Wedding.* New York: Summit Books, 1985.

Gaster, Moses. *The Ketubah.* New York: Hermon Press, 1974.

Heschel, Abraham Joshua. *The Sabbath.* New York: Farrar, Strauss, and Giroux, 1979. For creating a Sabbath that sustains the soul of a marriage, as well as an individual.

Lamm, Morris. *The Jewish Way In Love and Marriage.* San Francisco: Harper and Row, 1980. An overview of the laws written from an Orthodox perspective.

Sabar, Shalom. *Ketubbah.* Philadelphia: Jewish Publication Society, 1990.

Also consult Jacob Neusner, The Enchantments of Judaism: Rites of Transformation from Birth through Death, 53-65 in the Ritual and Life Passages from a Jewish Perspective bibliography; and Christie Balka and Andy Rose, eds. Twice Blessed, 105-151 in the Anthologies By and About Jewish Women bibliography.

Chapter Nine: Divorce

Cohen, Diane. "The Divorced Woman: Toward a New Ritual." *Conservative Judaism* 64, no. 4 (summer 1992): 62-68.

Lerner, Harriet G. *Dance of Intimacy: A Woman's Guide to Courageous Acts of Change in Key Relationships.* New York: Harper and Row, 1989.

List, Shelley Frier. "A Prayer for *Agunot.*" *Sh'ma* 24, no. 459 (October 15, 1993): 8.

Rackman, Honey. "Getting a Get." *Moment* 13, no. 3 (May 1988): 34-45.

Richardson, Ronald. *Family Ties That Bind.* Vancouver: Self Counsel Press, 1987.

Weber, Sally. "Divorce, Community, and Family." *Sh'ma* 23, no. 450 (March 19, 1993): 73-74.

Also consult Elizabeth Resnick Levine, ed. A Ceremonies Sampler, 61-65 and 71-75 in the Ritual and Life Passages From a Jewish Perspective bibliography; and Nadena Peterson and Barbara Sofre, Singleness, in the Being Single bibliography.

Chapter Ten: Intermarriage

Cowan, Paul, and Rachel Cowan. *Mixed Blessings: Marriage Between Jews and Christians.* New York: Doubleday, 1987.

Greenwood, Dru. "Will Our Grandchildren Be Jewish?" *Sh'ma* 24, no. 458 (October, 1993): 1-3.

Kosmin, Barry, Nava Lerer, and Egon Mayer. *Intermarriage, Divorce and Remarriage Among American Jews 1982-1987.* City University of New York, Family Research Series, no. 1. New York: North American Jewish Data Bank, August 1989.

Mayer, Egon. *Love and Tradition: Marriages Between Jews and Christians.* New York: Plenum Press, 1985.

— — —. "Will the Grandchildren of Intermarrieds be Jews?" *Moment* 19 no. 2 (April 1994).

Meir, Aryeh, and Marc Winer. *Questions Jewish Parents Ask About Intermarriage.* New York: The American Jewish Committee, 1992.

Mihaly, Eugene. *Responsa on Jewish Marriage.* Cincinnati, Ohio: Hebrew Union College Press, 1985.

Perlmutter, Saul. "Intermarriage and Jewish Affiliation: The Next Generation." *Reconstructionist* 55, no. 6 (July/August 1990): 18-20.

Petonsk, Judy and Jim Remsen. *The Intermarriage Handbook: A Guide For Jews and Christians.* Doubleday: New York, 1987.

Schneider, Susan Weidman. *Intermarriage: The Challenge of Living with Differences Between Christians and Jews.* New York: Free Press, 1989.

Woocher, Jonathan. "Intermarriage and Jewish Education." *Jewish Spectator* 56, no. 3 (winter 1991-1992): 12-14.

Chapter Eleven: Choosing Judaism

Bamberger, Bernard. *Proselytism in the Talmudic Period.* New York: KTAV Publishing House, 1968.

Eichhorn, David Max, ed. *Conversion to Judaism: A History and Analysis.* New York: KTAV Publishing House, 1965.

Kaplan, Aryeh. *The Waters of Eden: The Mystery of the Mikvah.* New York: National Conference of Synagogue Youth, 1982.

Kling, Simcha. *Embracing Judaism.* New York: The Rabbinical Assembly, 1987. A Conservative perspective.

Kukoff, Lydia. *Choosing Judaism: A Guide for Jews by Choice.* New York: Union of American Hebrew Congregations, 1982. A Reform perspective. Kukoff is a Jew by choice.

Lamm, Maurice. *Becoming a Jew.* Middle Village, N.Y.: Jonathan David Publishers, 1991. An Orthodox perspective.

Lester, Julius. *Lovesong: Becoming a Jew.* New York: Henry Holt and Co., 1988. Written in diary form.

Portnoy, Mindy; illustrated by Shelly O. Haas. *Mommy Never Went to Hebrew School.* Rockville, Md.: Kar Ben, 1989.

Romanoff, Lena. *Your People, My People: Finding Acceptance and Fulfillment as a Jew by Choice.* New York: Jewish Publication Society, 1990.

Scalamonti, John David. *Ordained to Be a Jew: A Catholic Priest's Conversion to Judaism*. New York: KTAV Publishing House, 1992. An autobiography.

Also consult Debra Renee Kaufman, Rachel's Daughters, *in the General Titles bibiliography.*

Chapter Twelve: Parenting

Bell, Roselyn, ed. *The Hadassah Magazine Jewish Parenting Book*. New York: Free Press, 1989.

Donin, Hayim Halevy. *Raising A Jewish Child*. New York: Harper and Row, 1977. The Orthodox approach.

Kurshan, Neil. *Raising Your Child to Be a Mensch*. New York: Atheneum, 1987.

Kushner, Harold. *When Children Ask About God*. New York: Schocken, 1989.

Levi, Miriam. *Effective Jewish Parenting*. Spring Valley, N.Y.: Philip Feldheim, 1986.

Rubin, Steven Carr. *Raising Jewish Children In a Contemporary World: The New Modern Parents' Guide to Creating A Jewish Home*. Roseville, Calif.: Prima Publishing, 1992.

Strassfeld, Sharon, and Kathy Green. *The Jewish Family Book*. New York: Bantam, 1981.

Wolpe, David. *Teaching Your Children About God: A Rabbi Speaks to Concerned Parents*. New York: Henry Holt and Company, 1993.

Also consult Susan Weidman Schneider, Jewish and Female, *371-404 in the General Titles By and About Jewish Women bibliography.*

Chapter Thirteen: Midlife

Berman, Phyllis Ocean. "Recreating Menopause." *Moment* 19, no. 1 (February 1994): 49, 72. A menopause ritual based on the *Tu Bishvat Seder* (ordered readings and meal for the New Year for Trees).

Borton, Joan C. *Drawing from the Women's Well: Reflections on the Life Passage of Menopause*. San Diego: LuriaMedia, 1992.

Brewi, Janice, and Anne Brennan. *Mid-Life: Psychological and Spiritual Perspectives*. New York: Crossroad, 1991. Primarily Christian in orientation, the ideas that correlate midlife and spirituality can easily be universalized.

Gould, Roger. *Transformation: Growth and Change in Adult Life*. New York: Simon and Schuster, Inc., 1978.

Greer, Germaine. *The Change: Women, Aging and the Menopause*. New York: Alfred A. Knopf, 1992.

Levenson, Daniel J. *The Seasons of a Man's Life*. New York: Ballantine Books, 1978.

Schoenfeld, Stuart. "Ritual and Role Transition: Adult Bat Mitzvah as a Successful Rite of Passage." In *The Uses of Tradition: Jewish Continuity in the Modern Era*, edited by Jack Wertheimer, 349-376. New York: The Jewish Theological Seminary, 1992.

Sheehy, Gail. *The Silent Passage: Menopause*. New York: Random House, 1992.

Also consult Irene Fine, Midlife: A Rite of Passage and The Wise Woman, A Celebration, *in the General Titles By and About Jewish Women bibliography.*

Specifically on "**Amidah** *and Midlife*":

Anderson, Sherry Ruth, and Patricia Hopkins. *The Feminine Face of God: The Unfolding of The Sacred in Women.* New York: Bantam Books, 1991.

Feurer, Abraham Chaim. *Shemoneh Essrei.* New York: Mesorah Publications Ltd., 1990. Compilation of traditional commentaries and spiritual insights into the *Amidah* from an Orthodox perspective.

Chapter Fourteen: Aging

Blidstein, Gerald. *Honor Thy Father and Mother: Filial Responsibility in Jewish Law and Ethics.* New York: KTAV Publishing House, 1976.

Fisher, M.F.K. *Sister Age.* New York: Vintage, 1983.

Friedan, Betty. *The Fountain of Age.* New York: Simon and Schuster, 1993.

Kramer, Sydele, and Jenny Masur, eds. *Jewish Grandmothers.* Boston: Beacon Press, 1976. A collection of oral histories of ten Jewish women who emigrated to the U.S. from Eastern Europe between the turn of the century and the 1920s.

Martz, Sandra, ed. *When I Am An Old Woman I Shall Wear Purple: An Anthology of Short Stories and Poetry.* Watsonville, Calif.: Papier-Mache Press, 1987.

Myerhoff, Barbara G. "A Symbol Perfected in Death: Continuity and Ritual in the Life and Death of an Elderly Jew." In *Life's Career; Aging: Cultural Variations on Growing Old,* edited by Barbara G. Myerhoff and Andrei Simic, 163-202. Beverly Hills, Calif.: Sage Publications, 1979.

— — —. *Number Our Days.* New York: E.P. Dutton, 1979.

Seltzer, Mildred. "Jewish American Grandmothers." In *Looking Ahead: A Woman's Guide to the Problems and Joys of Growing Older,* edited by Lillian Troll, Joan Israel, and Kenneth Israel, 157-161. Englewood, N.J.: Prentice Hall, Inc., 1977.

Also consult Irene Fine, Midlife: A Rite of Passage and The Wise Woman: A Celebration; *and Susan Weidman Schneider,* Jewish and Female, *619-625, in the General Titles By and About Jewish Women bibliography; Dianne Ashton and Ellen M. Umansky, eds.* Four Centuries of Jewish Women's Spirituality: A Sourcebook, *326-334; and Leslea Newman, ed.,* Bubbie Meisehs by Shayneh Maidelehs: An Anthology of Poetry By Jewish Granddaughters About Our Grandmothers *in the* Anthologies By and About Jewish Women bibliography.

Chapter Fifteen: Death and Mourning

Brener, Anne. *Mourning & Mitzvah: A Guided Journal for Walking the Mourner's Path Through Grief to Healing.* Woodstock, Vt.: Jewish Lights Publishing, 1993.

Goldberg, Chaim Binyamin. *Mourning in Halachah.* Brooklyn, N.Y.: Mesorah Publications, 1991. This adaptation of a classic Hebrew text is an exhaustive compendium of the details of Jewish mourning practices, with citations to traditional sources.

Harlow, Rabbi Jules, ed. *The Bond of Life: A Book for Mourners.* New York: Rabbinical Assembly, 1983. A mourner's prayerbook with commentaries, Rabbinic readings, and a guide to mourning laws and practices.

Lamm, Maurice. *The Jewish Way in Death and Mourning.* New York: Jonathan David, 1969.

Levine, Stephen. *Who Dies? An Investigation of Conscious Living and Conscious Dying.* Garden City, N.J.: Anchor Books, 1982. A spiritual approach to healing.

Metzger, Deena. *A Sabbath Among the Ruins*. Berkeley, Calif.: Parallax Press, 1992. Poetry of comfort.

Neal, Roxane. "A Well of Living Water." *Woman of Power* no. 14 (summer 1989): 74-76. A personal account of participation in a ḥevrah kadishah (burial society), including a description of the mechanics of washing the body and of the personal transformation brought about by this work.

Olitzky, Kerry, and Ronald Isaacs. *A Jewish Mourner's Handbook*. Hoboken, N.J.: KTAV Publishing House, 1991.

Rapaport, Nessa. *A Women's Book of Grieving*. New York: Morrow, 1994.

Riemer, Jack, ed. *Jewish Reflections on Death*. New York: Schocken, 1976.

Riemer, Jack and Nathaniel Stampfer, eds. *So That You Values Live On: Ethical Wills and How to Prepare Them*. Woodstock, Vt.: Jewish Lights Publishing, 1991.

Sofian, Simone Lotven. "*Taharat haMetim*: A Personal Perspective." *Journal of Reform Judaism* 38, no. 2: (spring 1991): 37-42. The author outlines a theology of commandedness from a Reform perspective and in light of her participation in a ḥevra kadishah.

Weiss, Abner. *Death and Bereavement: A Halakhic Guide*. Hoboken, N.J.: KTAV Publishing House, 1991.

Wolfson, Ron. *A Time to Mourn—A Time to Comfort*. New York: Federation of Jewish Men's Clubs, 1993.

Zlotnick, Dov, ed. *The Tractate Mourning*. New Haven, Conn.: Yale University Press, 1966. A translation and the original text of the Talmudic tractate dealing with death, burial, and mourning.

Also consult Jacob Neusner, The Enchantments of Judaism: Rites of Transformation from Birth through Death, *146-163 in the Ritual and Life Passages from a Jewish Perspective bibliography.*

Afterword: Books Related to Creating a Ritual

Erikson, E.H. *Childhood and Society*. New York: W.W. Norton, 1982. The classic discussion of lifecycle stages.

———. *Identity and The Life Cycle*. New York: International Universities Press, 1959.

Turner, Victor. *The Ritual Process*. Ithaca, N.Y.: Cornell University Press, 1969.

Van Gennep, Arnold. *The Rites of Passage*. Chicago: University of Chicago Press, 1960.

Back issues of Reconstructionist, LILITH, *and* New Menorah *magazines contain helpful material and suggestions on creative ritual.*

The Jewish Women's Resource Center, 9 East 69th Street, New York, NY 10021/(212)535-5900, offers a free listing of their materials on ritual which are available for purchase.

Also consult Elizabeth Resnick Levine, ed. A Ceremonies Sampler, *61-65 and 71-75 in the Ritual and Life Passages From a Jewish Perspective bibliography; Renee Beck and Sydney Barbara Metrick,* The Art of Ritual, *and Evan Imber-Black and Janine Roberts,* Rituals For Our Time, *in the Ritual and Life Passages From a Feminist Perspective bibliography; Irene Fine,* Midlife: A Rite of Passage *and* The Wise Woman: A Celebration *in the General Titles By and About Jewish Women bibliography; Barbara Myerhoff, "A Symbol Perfected in Death" and* Number Our Days *in the Aging bibliography.*

Glossary

Adonai: One of God's names

Adult Bar/Bat Mitzvah: Belated coming of age ceremony

afikomen: Matzah* eaten for dessert at a Passover *seder**

aggadah **(plural** *aggadot)***:** Jewish lore

agunah **(plural** *agunot)***:** Women chained to dead marriages

ahavah: Love

ahavat yisra'el: Love of Jews and the Jewish people

aliyah **(plural** *aliyot)***:** Honor of reciting the blessings before and after the Torah is read; the blessings themselves; the segments of Torah read. Making *aliyah* is immigrating to Israel.

Amidah: Standing [prayer], because the prayer is said while standing; series of blessing which is the centerpiece of every prayer service.

aninut: Period between death and burial

avodah: Temple worship; worship in general; work

avot: Ancestors or fathers; first *Amidah** blessing

badeken: Bridal veiling ceremony

bar kayyama: Viable outside the womb

*Bar Mitzvah/Bat Mitzvah (plural Bnei Mitzvah/Bnot Mitzvah)***:** Coming of age ceremony for boys/girls

bar mitzvah/bat mitzvah **(plural** *bnei mitzvah/bnot mitzvah)***:** Juridical Jewish adult

beit din: Rabbinical court

bentsh: Say a blessing

bentsh gomel: Recite prayer of thanksgiving for coming through danger in safety (see *Birkat Hagomel*)

* This word appears in the glossary.

berakhah (**plural** *berakhot*)**:** Blessing

besha'ah tovah: [May it happen] in a good hour

bikkur ḥolim: Visiting the sick

bimah: Pulpit

Birkat Hagomel: Prayer of thanksgiving for coming through danger in safety (see *bentsh gomel**)

Birkat Haḥodesh: Blessing recited in anticipation of the New Moon Festival

Brit Banot: Covenant ceremony for daughters

brit banot: Covenant of daughters

Brit Milah: Covenant of circumcision ritual

brit milah: Covenant of circumcision

bubbe: Grandmother

da'at: Understanding; intellect

dai: Enough

daven: Pray

davenen: Praying; prayer service

derash: Torah explanation

devar Torah: Torah explanation and homily

ed (**plural** *edim*)**:** Witness

ein haḥayyim: Source (literally, Fountain) of life

el elyon: Supreme God, higher being

El Maleh Raḥamim: Memorial prayer asking God to guard and keep in peace the departed soul

erusin: Betrothal

Eshet Ḥayil: Valiant woman; poem about a valiant woman found in Proverbs 31, which is sung on Friday nights

etz ḥayyim: Tree of life

galut: Exile

gematria: Jewish numerology

ger: Stranger or convert

get (**plural** *gittin*)**:** Jewish divorce; divorce document

gevurot: Vast power; second *Amidah** blessing; heroic deeds

goses (**feminine** *goseset*)**:** Dying person

Haftarah: Prophetic reading

halakhah (**plural** *halakhot*)**:** Jewish law

halakhic: Of or related to Jewish law; Jewish legal

ḥallah (**plural** *ḥallot*)**:** Braided egg bread

Hallel: Psalms of praise

hamotzi: See *motzi**

Ḥanukkah: Festival of Lights

ḥatan: Groom

haskalah: Enlightenment; wisdom

Hattafat Dam: Drawing a drop of blood from the penile area of a male convert to Judaism who is already circumcised

havdalah: Distinction-making ritual that separates Sabbath or holiday from weekday

* This word appears in the glossary.

ḥavurah (**plural** *ḥavurot*): Jewish worship/study fellowship

Hayotzer: One of seventy names of God; translated roughly as One who fashions, forms, creates

ḥayyim: Life

ḥesed: Steadfast love

hesped (**plural** *hespedim*): Eulogy

ḥevrah kaddishah: Burial society; literally, "holy committee"

ḥillul hashem: Desecration of God's name

hineni, hinneni: Here I am

hokhmah: Wisdom

ḥuppah: Wedding canopy

kabbalah: Jewish mysticism

Kaddish: A prayer sanctifying God's name, said on various ritual and liturgical occasions; more popularly, mourner's prayer

kadosh: Holy

kallah: Bride

karov (**plural** *kerovim*): Close relative obligated to mourn

kashrut: Kosher laws; fitness

kedushah: Holiness, with a connotation of exclusivity or being set apart

Kedushat hashem: Holiness of God's name; third *Amidah** blessing

kelal yisra'el: Totality of the Jewish people

keri'ah: Rending a garment in mourning

ketubbah (**plural** *ketubbot*): Marriage contract

kevurah: Burial

Kiddush: Blessing said over wine on sacred occasions

kiddush cup: Special cup or goblet used when reciting the blessing over wine on sacred occasions

Kiddush Levanah: Blessing of the moon

kiddushin: Holy matrimony

kinyan: Pulling on a handkerchief or other object to signify the transfer of ownership or the conclusion of a transaction

kippah (**plural** *kippot*): Skullcap

kittel: White garment traditionally worn on one's wedding day, various Jewish holidays, and for burial

kohen: Member of the priestly tribe

letorah, lehuppah, ulema'asim tovim: [May (s/he) be privileged to learn] Torah, to [arrive at the] wedding canopy, and to [do] good deeds; blessing offered at *Brit Milah* and naming ceremonies

mahzor: Holiday prayerbook

mamzer (**plural** *mamzerim*): Bastard; in halakhic* terms child(ren) born of an adulterous or incestuous union, not simply out of wedlock

mamzerut: Bastardy (see *mamzer*)

matzah: Unleavened bread eaten at Passover

mazal tov: Congratulations

met (**feminine** *metah*): Dead person

mi sheberach: Blessing recited on one's behalf

* This word appears in the glossary.

midrash: Rabbinic genre of lore often based on biblical texts; Rabbinic legend
midrashic: Of or related to *midrash*
mikveh: Ritual bath; ritual immersion
minyan: Quorum, usually prayer quorum
Mishneh Torah: Twelfth century law code written by Maimonides
mitzrayim: Egypt
mitzvah **(plural *mitzvot*):** Commandment, sacred obligation
mohel **(plural *mohalim*):** Ritual circumciser
Motzi: Blessing recited over bread
naḥas: Joy
niggun **(plural *niggunim*):** Wordless melody
nissu'in: Wedding ceremony
oneg shabbat: Reception following Sabbath services
onen **(plural *onenim*):** Mourner whose loved one is dead, but not yet buried; literally, bereft, and thus the bereft during *aninut**
Pesaḥ: Passover
Pidyon Haben: Ceremony symbolically redeeming first-born males, born vaginally, from Temple service
Purim: Festival of Lots
rebbe: Rabbi and teacher
refu'ah: Healing
reḥem: Womb
Rosh Hashanah: New Year
Rosh Ḥodesh: New Moon Festival; first day of the month
sandak **(female *sandakit*):** Person who holds the infant during ritual circumcision
seder: Ordered readings and meal at Passover; order
se'udat havra'ah: Meal of consolation
se'udat mitzvah: Sanctified meal
**Shabbat (plural Shabbatot)*:* Sabbath
shalom: Peace
Shalom Aleikhem: Song welcoming the Sabbath angels
Shavu'ot: Festival of the giving of the Torah
Sheheḥeyanu: Blessing for reaching a new or momentous occasion
Shekhinah: Close-dwelling presence of God, associated with the feminine
shem umalkhut: Traditional blessing formula which names *Adonai** as Ruler of the universe
Shema: Central prayer that declares God's oneness
Shemoneh Esreh: Weekday *Amidah**; literally, eighteen [blessings]
Sheva Berakhot: Seven marital blessings
shiv'ah: Formal period of mourning, usually seven days; literally, seven.
shofar: Ram's horn
shomer **(feminine *shomeret*, masculine plural *shomerim*, feminine plural *shomerot*):** Guardian
shtetl: Small Jewish town
shul: Synagogue

* This word appears in the glossary.

Shulḥan Arukh: Sixteenth century law code written by Joseph Karo with glosses by Moses Isserles

siddur: Prayerbook

simḥah: Celebration

Simḥat Bat (plural *Simḥot Bat*): Girl's naming ceremony; literally "the joy of a daughter"

Simḥat Ḥokhmah (plural *Simḥot Ḥokhmah*): Celebration of elder-wisdom

tallit: Prayer shawl

talmud torah: Jewish learning

tashlikh: Casting out, especially for the New Year's ceremony in which breadcrumbs are cast out on a body of water, signifying release of sin

tefillah: Prayer; another name for the *Amidah**

tena'im: Marriage conditions; other contract conditions

teshuvah: Repentance; return

tikkun olam: Repairing the world

tkhine (plural *tkhines*): Petitionary prayer for and/or by women, traditionally written in Yiddish

Tu Bishvat: New Year for Trees

tzaddikim: The righteous; the just ones

tzedakah: Sacred practice of charity

tzedek, tzedek tirdof: Justice, justice, thou shalt pursue.

tzelem elohim: Image of God

viddui: Confessional recited at High Holiday services; confessional before dying

yad: Hand, pointer

Yah: One of God's names

yartzeit: Anniversary of a death

yartzeit **candle:** Candle burned when a Jew dies, and annually on the anniversary of a family member's death

yedid: Loving; beloved one

yeshivah (plural *yeshivot*): Traditional academy of Jewish learning

yetzi'at mitzrayim: Going out of Egypt

Yiddishkeit: Jewishness

Yiḥud: Brief seclusion of a couple immediately after the wedding ceremony

Yizkor: Memorial service

Yom Kippur: Day of Atonement

Yom Hasho'ah: Holocaust Memorial Day

Zeved Habat: Sephardic ceremony for welcoming a baby girl; literally, gift of a daughter

Zohar: Premiere Jewish mystical text

---

* This word appears in the glossary.

Notes

Introduction

1. A discussion of standards is included in the afterword on creating a ritual.

2. Avraham Yitzḥak Hakohen Kuk's *Igrot Horiyah* 123, cited in Jacob B. Agus, *High Priest of Rebirth: The Life, Times, and Thought of A.I. Kuk* (New York: Bloch Publishing, 1972), 204.

3. Halakhic (Jewish legal) prohibitions against the wider application of the traditional blessing formula *barukh attah adonai* (Blessed are You, God) are taken up in my introduction to chapter six and in the afterword. One could translate the phrase *vekhol hamarbeh* creatively to mean not only "one who tells the story more," but also "one who tells more of the story"—e.g. one who tells women's part in the story, as well as men's.

4. A similar point is made about black women in the title and content of Gloria T. Hull, et. al., *All the Women Are White, All the Blacks Are Men, But Some of Us Are Brave* (New York: Feminist Press, 1982). See also Letty Cottin Pogrebin, *Deborah, Golda, and Me: Being Female and Jewish in America* (New York: Crown Publishing Group, 1991), 250.

5. Of course, it also literally alienates (makes alien) women from Judaism.

6. This is reflected in the language we use. Ten years ago, people spoke only of Jewish feminism; today, many speak of a feminist Judaism, as well. See, for example, Shulamit Magnus, "Re-inventing Miriam's Well," in *The Uses of Tradition: Jewish Continuity in the Modern Era*, ed. Jack Wertheimer (New York: The Jewish Theological Seminary, 1992), 331f.

7. Quoted in Gloria Steinem, *Revolution From Within: A Book of Self-Esteem* (Boston: Little, Brown, and Co., 1992), 180.

Chapter One: Beginnings

1. Avraham Gombiner, the *Magen Avraham*, a 17th century Ashkenazic authority, permits husbands to *bentsh gomel* for their wives. Ya'akov Hayim Sofer, the *Kaf Hahayyim*, a late 19th century Sephardic authority, ruled that women should *bentsh gomel* in the women's section of the synagogue, and any men who overhear should say "Amen." See G. Ellenson, *Between Woman and Her Creator: An Explanation of the Halakhic Sources* vol. 1 of *Women and Commandments* (in Hebrew) (Israel: World Zionist Organization, 1986), 136.

2. Special thanks to Nina Beth Cardin, Tikva Frymer-Kensky, Leonard Gordon, Solomon Gordon, Debra Orenstein, and Chava Weissler for generously sharing their expertise.

3. Reprinted in Elizabeth Resnick, ed., *A Ceremonies Sampler: New Rites, Celebrations, and Observances of Jewish Women* (San Diego: Woman's Institute for Continuing Jewish Education, 1991), 43.

4. Reprinted in Marcia Cohn Spiegel and Deborah Lipton Kremsdorf, eds., *Women Speak to God: The Prayers and Poems of Jewish Women* (San Diego: Woman's Institute for Continuing Jewish Education, 1987), 26.

5. Susan Weidman Schneider, *Jewish and Female: Choices and Changes in Our Lifes Today* (New York: Simon and Schuster, 1985), 120. Blu Greenberg's remarks were made at a B'nai B'rith Anti-Defamation League "Book and Author" luncheon in 1980 and are quoted by Schneider.

6. See Arlene Rossen Cardozo, *Jewish Family Celebrations: The Sabbath, Festivals, and Ceremonies* (New York: St. Martin's, 1982); and Jacob Neusner, *The Enchantments of Judaism: Rites of Transformation from Birth through Death* (New York: Basic Books, 1987).

7. Chava Weissler, trans., *Seder Tkhines Uvakoshes* (Furth, 1762), unpublished.

8. See Nina Beth Cardin, ed., *Out of the Depths I Call to You: A Book of Prayers for the Married Jewish Woman* (Livingston, N.J.: Jason Aronson, 1992); and Tracy Guren Klirs et al., trans., *The Merit of Our Mothers: A Bilingual Anthology of Jewish Women's Prayers* (Cincinnati: Hebrew Union College Press, 1992).

9. Chava Weissler, "*Mitzvot* Built into the Body: *Tkhines* for *Niddah*, Pregnancy, and Childbirth," *People of the Body: Jews and Judaism From an Embodied Perspective*, Howard Eilberg-Schwartz, ed. (Albany, N.Y.: State University of New York Press, 1992), 110.

10. Anita Diamant, *The New Jewish Baby Book* (Woodstock, Vt.: Jewish Lights Publishing, 1993), 184.

11. Rabbi Douglas Weber and Jessica Brodsky Weber, *Jewish Baby Handbook: A Guide for Expectant Parents* (West Orange, N.J.: Behrman House, 1990), 13.

12. Resnick, ed., *The Ceremonies Sampler*, 9-11, 43-46.

13 Shoshana Zonderman and Saul E. Perlmutter, "Preparing for Childbirth: A Ceremony for Parents-to-be," *Reconstructionist* 54, no. 2 (October/November 1988): 18-22.

14. These will be published in the forthcoming *Motherprayer*.

15. Zonderman and Perlmutter, "Preparing for Childbirth," 19.

16. The group includes Conservative Rabbis Cardin, Orenstein, Eilberg,

Susan Grossman, Mychal Springer, Deborah Cantor, and Stephanie Dickstein, as well as lay leader Rebecca Jacobs.

17. This phrase appears in the *Haggadah* (text of the Passover story). Other occurrences are shorter, omitting the Seraph. The *Haggadah* provides a detailed commentary on Exodus 12:12 as proof of God's sole agency. In the midrashic compendium, the *Mekhilta*, proof for the same idea is derived from Exodus 12:29.

18. Midrash *Sifre* Deuteronomy 42, commenting on Deuteronomy 11:14.

19. For references to Moses as mediator, and a scholarly discussion of this issue, see Judah Goldin, "Not by Means of an Angel and Not by Means of a Messenger," originally published in *Studies in the History of Religions* 14 (1968): 412-24. Now in Goldin, *Studies in Midrash and Related Literature* (Philadelphia: Jewish Publication Society, 1988), 163-173.

20. For Yvonne Fried.

21. In biblical law, a woman is ritually impure for seven days after the birth of a boy and fourteen days after the birth of a girl (Leviticus 12:1-5).

22. Copyright © by Merle Feld, 1983.

23. A version of our ceremony appears in Resnick, ed., *A Ceremonies Sampler*, 47-53. Rabbi Nina Beth Cardin has also written a ceremony for the acceptance of infertility (unpublished) which echoes themes from the wedding ceremony, such as the wholeness of the couple in their own right, their affinity with Adam and Eve, and their joy and gladness. It also involves the drinking of a shared cup of wine and the breaking of a glass, acts done under the wedding canopy. The former symbolizes the couple's commitment to share whatever life hands them. The latter symbolizes the shattering, and then letting go, of a dream. While breaking a glass to mark the acceptance of infertility conveys and recalls sadness, it also reminds the couple of the joy and promise they felt at their wedding. Those feelings remain vital, regardless of fertility.

24. Michael Gold, *And Hannah Wept: Infertility, Adoption, and the Jewish Couple* (Philadelphia: Jewish Publication Society, 1988), 157-161.

25. Harriet L. Parment and Judith N. Lasker, "Religion and Views on Reproductive Technologies: A Comparative Study of Jews and Non-Jews," *Shofar: An Interdisciplinary Journal of Jewish Studies* 9, no. 1 (fall 1991): 65.

Chapter Two: Infertility and Early Losses

1. The commandment to be fruitful and multiply was understood by the Rabbis to be incumbent upon men, but not women. According to Rashi and others, the Mishnah required either divorce or the taking of an additional wife after ten years of childlessness. This law is maintained by Maimonides in *Mishneh Torah Hilkhot Ishut* 15. However, it was mitigated by *aggadah* (Jewish lore). Rabi prayed for his wife's fertility, rather than divorce her or take a second wife (BT *Ketubbot* 62b). Song of Songs *Rabbah* 1:24 contains the famous story of the woman from Sidon, soon to be divorced by her husband of ten years due to their childlessness. Her husband invites her to take whatever is most precious to her when she leaves their marital house. She takes him, and they remain married.

The requirement of fertility was slightly de-emphasized later on by changes within Jewish law itself. When Rabbenu Gershom (d. 1028) formally outlawed polygamy for Ashkenazic Jews, the solution of taking a second wife in order to fulfill the commandment to be fruitful and multiply was no longer viable. This meant that the only possible solution was divorce, a solution rabbis were reluctant to enforce, due to their positive view of marriage and their valuation of marital companionship for its own sake. In his gloss on the *Shulḥan Arukh,* the Ashkenazic Rabbi Moses Isserles (d. 1572) notes that rabbis in his time and locale did not require childless couples to divorce (*Even Ha'ezer* 1:3).

2. Another interpretation of matriarchal infertility is that our foremothers, like *Niditu* priestesses, were childless by religious ordination. Savina J. Teubal, *Sarah the Priestess: The First Matriarch of Genesis* (Athens, Ohio: Swallow Press, 1984), 83.

3. Women who miscarry at this stage become ritually impure for as long as a birthing woman would, and not for the length of time prescribed for menstrual bleeding. Likewise, women who miscarry after three months do not perform *Pidyon Haben* (ceremony symbolically redeeming first-born males, born vaginally, from Temple service) for a boy born subsequently, since the miscarried fetus is considered the first issue of the mother's womb.

4. On burial at the time of "having a shape" see J.D. Eisenstein, *A Treasury of Laws and Customs* (in Hebrew) (New York: Hebrew Publishing Company, 1938), 271. Burial of a fetus or a child under thirty days old is not considered a *mitzvah* (commandment), and is not done, as a regular burial would be, on the rabbinically-prescribed second day of a Jewish holiday. For possible linkage between "having a shape" and the fifth month of pregnancy, see Minutes of the [Conservative movement] Committee on Jewish Law and Standards (October 27, 1993), 7.

5. Rabbi Stephanie Dickstein, "What Should Be Jewish Practice Following the Death of an Infant who Lives Less than Thirty-One Days?" This responsum was approved by the Committee on Jewish Law and Standards on June 3, 1992. It is not the only approved Conservative position.

6. These last two sentences are adapted from a *mi sheberakh* (blessing recited on one's behalf) for a woman recovering from miscarriage by Rabbi Diane Cohen. The rest of the paragraph is taken from the prayer for a journey and the *Hashkiveinu* (prayer in the evening service asking for God's protection).

Chapter Three: Welcoming Children into Name and Covenant

1. Most of these customs are discussed in Rabbi Yona Metzger and Nachum Langental, *In The Cycles of Life* vol. 1 (in Hebrew) (Tel Aviv: Yediot Aḥronot/Sifrei Ḥemed, 1980), 9ff. Rashi understands *Shavu'a Haben* as synonymous with *Pidyon Haben* (ceremony symbolically redeeming first-born males, born vaginally, from Temple service). However, Rabbenu Tam understands it to refer to the delivery itself (BT *Baba Kamma* 80a). The latter opinion is substantiated by the *Mekhilta Aḥariti De'avel*, which refers to a *Shavu'a Habat*, a ceremony which cannot, by definition, be synonymous with *Pidyon Haben* or *Brit*. See Michael Higger, ed., *Treatise Semaḥot* (in Hebrew) (New York: Bloch, 1931), 231. See also Aharon Oppenheim, ed., *Jerusalem in the Second Temple Period: Abraham Schalit Memorial Volume* (in Hebrew) (Jerusalem: Yad Itzhak Ben-Zvi), 1988; and Pinchas Hacohen Peli, "The Ḥavurot That Were in Jerusalem," *Hebrew Union College Annual* 55

(1984): 58-59. On *Hollekreish*, see Joshua Trachtenberg, *Jewish Magic and Superstition: A Study in Folk Religion* (New York: Atheneum, 1982), 41-42. For the text of *Zeved Habat*, see David De Sola Pool, ed., *Book of Prayer* (New York: Union of Sephardic Congregations, 1983), 417. For the root z.v.d. as gift, see Genesis 30:20.

2. Judith Plaskow refers to this verse in the title of her book *Standing Again at Sinai: Judaism From a Feminist Perspective* (San Francisco: Harper and Row, 1990). It is Moses who introduces the notion that "the people" [sic] should not go near a woman. This, in a section where he is supposedly repeating God's instructions. (Compare 18:10-13 with 18:14-19.) Moses, given the mores of his day, may have understood God's commandment "sanctify the people" to mean "stay away from women," but this is not recorded as God's statement, nor need it be interpreted as the divine intention.

3. For a counterargument that Sarah and Jewish women generally were included in the covenant God made with Abraham, see Gary Shapiro, "Sealed in Our Flesh—Women as Members of the Brit," *Ḥavruta*, no. 13 (5751/1990): 7-10.

4. The extent of the pain caused by infant circumcision is disputed; many physicians argue that because of undeveloped nerve endings in the baby's penis the procedure only causes minimal pain to the infant. There are also indications that circumcision has health benefits for men in that it correlates with lower incidence of infections and penile cancer. Female partners of circumcised men evidence lower rates of cervical cancer. Recently, the use of local anaesthetic for circumcision has been advocated by some parents, rabbis, and ritual circumcizers.

5. Traditional Jewish law makes it clear that Jewishness is passed from mother to child, but it is the father's act of entering the male child into the covenant that symbolically enables the male to become a full partner in the Jewish community. (In recent years, the Reform and Reconstructionist movements have approved patrilineal descent under certain conditions.) After age six, fathers, and not mothers, are commanded to educate their children (BT *Ketubbot* 65b).

6. The phrase of welcome is *barukh haba* (blessed is the one who comes). *Habah* is an acronym for *hinneh ba eliyahu* (Behold, Elijah comes) or *"haddevekim b'adonai eloheikhem"* (You who cling to *Adonai* your God) (Deuteronomy 4:4). It also equals eight in *gematria* (Jewish numerology)—the eight-day-old child is ready to be circumcised.

7. In the Middle Ages, in Southern France, parts of Hungary, and Belgium, it was customary to bring the baby girl to the synagogue. Typically, the naming would take place on the fourth Sabbath after the birth. In many Sephardic communities, *Zeved Habat* (gift of a daughter), a welcoming blessing for a baby girl, is recited at the first Torah reading after the birth when the mother attends synagogue. See De Sola Pool, *Book of Prayer*, 417 and endnote 17 in this chapter. In some communities, there was a festive meal to celebrate the birth, but this celebration had no connection with the naming.

8. Rabbi Daniel I. Leifer and Myra Leifer, "On the Birth of A Daughter," *Response* 7, no. 2 (summer 1973): 91-105.

9. An example of this model is the "Covenant of Life" ceremony published in the CCAR's *Gates of the House* (New York: Central Conference of American Rabbis, 1977), 114ff.

10. Mary Gendler, "Sarah's Seed: A New Ritual for Women," *Response* 8, no. 4 (winter 1974-75): 65-75.

11. Suggested by Rabbi Richard and Carol Levy, "Covenant and Redemption Ceremony for Sarah Levy" (unpublished).

12. Sharon Strassfield and Michael Strassfield, eds., *The Second Jewish Catalog* (Philadelphia: Jewish Publication Society, 1976), 36-37.

13. Rabbi Ruth Sohn, et al., "The Covenant of Washing: A Ceremony To Welcome Baby Girls into the Covenant of Israel," *Menorah* 4 (May 1983): 3-4.

14. *Pirkei Derabbi Eliezer*, Chapter 6.

15. See Philip Birnbaum, trans., *Daily Prayer Book* (New York: Hebrew Publishing Co., 1977), 562-566.

16. Adapted by Rabbi Steven Cohen from Chaim Nachman Bialik and Yehoshva Hana Ravnitzky, eds., *Book of Legends Sefer Ha-Aggadah*, trans. William G. Braude (New York: Schocken, 1992), 575. Based on *Tanhumah Pekudei*.

17. Adapted from the Sephardic naming ritual for girls, *Zeved Habat*. De Sola Pool, *Book of Prayer*, 417. A prayer of thanksgiving for the mother's recovery is traditionally recited along with *Zeved Habat*.

18. Aside from other objections to modeling birth rituals for girls after the *Brit*, this freneticism argues against birth rituals for girls on the eighth day.

19. While Israelite males were counted in the census at age twenty (the age of eligibility for military service), Levites were counted in the census from the age of one month (Numbers 3:15). The commentary *Seder Yihus Haleviim* explains that while Israelites have no independent identity before the age of twenty, being known only as the child of so-and-so, Levites are known "from the womb" as servants of the sacred. In an age when being Jewish is a choice many reject and more cannot meaningfully choose because they are ignorant, it seemed to me that we must ground a child's Jewish identity and proclaim it from the moment s/he is viable outside the womb.

20. This differs from the traditional naming practice for girls, in which the father is called up to the Torah on a day when the Torah is read anyway (Monday, Thursday, Sabbath or holiday), the reading being the normal one for that time, and the baby is named.

21. A *Simhat Lev* not held on *Rosh Hodesh* could break the Deuteronomic reading into three or, of course, use different readings entirely.

22. Since doing this, I have learned that Debra Cantor and Rebecca Jacobs, "*Brit Banot* Covenant Ceremony for Daughters," *Kerem* (winter 1992-93): 45-61, include such a wrapping in a girl's naming ceremony. On the symbolic significance of the *tzitzit* (fringes) of the *tallit*, see Abraham Chill, *The Minhagim* (New York: Sepher-Hermon, 1984), 11-24. In retrospect, I would give more prominence to the wrapping, singing/chanting appropriate verses as it is done, using a ritualized procedure for wrapping the baby—east corner to west, north to south, to indicate God's omnipresence.

23. Verses appropriate for girls can be substituted where this text is male-specific. An excellent compilation of such texts is in Cantor and Jacobs, "*Brit Banot*," e.g. "May God make you like Sarah, Rebecca, Leah, and Rachel" and verses from the Song of Songs.

24. I hope that by the time our child is an adult, lesbians and gays will have recognized ways of solemnifying their loving relationships in the Jewish community.

25. The female God language is mine. For my approach to female God language, see *"Kol Isha," Women's League Outlook* (fall 1992): 7-9, 28. For more on this subject, see Marcia Falk, "Notes on Composing New Blessings: Toward a Feminist-Jewish Reconstruction of Prayer," *Journal of Feminist Studies in Religion* 3, no. 1 (spring 1987): 39-53.

26. This blessing flowed from my own traumatic experience and was one of the most important things I said, both immediately after the birth and at the *Simhat Lev*. All births involve pain and anguish and this blessing might be meaningful to others.

27. According to folk tradition, the boy's foreskin is planted under his tree. A new tradition involves planting a piece of the umbilical cord of the girl under her tree. While both boys and girls have umbilical cords, only a girl may someday produce an umbilical cord to nourish her child. Sometimes, the placenta is planted under the tree. See Eve Jacobson Kessler's article, "New Afterbirth Ritual Takes Root in Berkeley," *Forward*, 22 October 1993, 12.

28. Based on "God's Beneficence" by Morris Silverman, *Sabbath and Festival Prayerbook*, Morris Silverman, ed. (New York: Rabbinical Assembly, 1973), 328.

Chapter Four: Adolescence

1. Carol Gilligan, Nona P. Lyons, and Trudy J. Hanmer, eds., *Making Connections: The Relational Worlds of Adolescent Girls at Emma Willard School* (Cambridge, Mass.: Harvard University Press, 1990), 10. See also Emily Hancock, *The Girl Within: A Radical Approach to Female Identity* (London: Pandora, 1990).

2. It was meant to be said at the end of an infertile woman's menstrual flow, after she puts away all signs of her period; upon a woman's monthly visit to the *mikveh* (ritual bath); and/or before fertility procedures such as artificial or *in vitro* insemination. Rabbi Nina Beth Cardin, whose work appears in Chapters Two and Three, is advisor to students in the Rabbinical School of The Jewish Theological Seminary and editor of *Sh'ma* magazine. Her prayer was adapted with permission.

3. Written during a workshop in which poet and playwright Merle Feld asked the question, "If you were to write your own *mezzuzah* (scroll placed on doorways traditionally containing the *Shema* prayer), what would it say?"

Chapter Five: Being Single

1. There is one celebration of a birthday mentioned in the Talmud. See BT *Mo'ed Katan* 28a.

2. See Rabbis Nosson Scherman and Meir Zlotowitz, *The Complete Artscroll Siddur* (New York: Mesorah Publications, 1984), 924f.

3. Naḥman of Bratzlav, *Likutei Moharan* (Jerusalem: Bratzlav Press, 1976), 1:282. The translation is mine.

4. Adapted from Daniel Chanan Matt, ed. and trans., *Zohar: The Book of Enlightenment* (New York: Paulist Press, 1983), 91f.

5. The original Hebrew prayer can be found in Rabbi Morris Silverman, ed. and trans., *High Holiday Prayer Book* (Hartford, Conn.: Prayer Book Press, 1964), 375. The Sephardic version of this prayer, adapted for the occasion and also translated by Orenstein, reads as follows: May it be Your will O God, that this year now coming upon us shall be for me and all your people, wherever we find ourselves, a year of light, a year of blessing, a year of joy, a year of happiness, a year of glory, a year of good reunion, a year of song, a year of mirth, a year of goodness, a year of salvation, a year of prosperity, a year of learning, a year of rest, a year of comfort, a year of delight, a year of gladness, a year of deliverance, a year of joyous exclamation, a year of independence, a year of ingathering the exiles, a year of accepting my prayers, a year of goodwill, a year of peace, a year of dew and rain, a year of plenty, a year in which you will guide me to walk upright to Zion, a year in which you will subdue my foes, a year in which you inscribe me for a good and happy life, a year of self-reliance, a year in which you will ward off all illness and mishaps from me, a year in which no person shall suffer loss.

The last line literally means: "A year in which no woman shall lose (by miscarriage) the fruit of her womb." For the Hebrew text of this prayer see Philip Birnbaum, *Sephardic High Holy Day Prayerbook* (New York: Hebrew Publishing Co., 1958), 589-591.

6. Plaskow, *Standing Again at Sinai*, xv. This book remains, for me, a clear statement of Jewish feminism's basic issues; the title of this essay is a respectful reference to this work.

7. Frank J. Broucek, M.D., *Shame and the Self* (New York: The Guilford Press, 1991), 3.

8. Susan Miller, *The Shame Experience* (Hillsdale, N.J.: The Analytic Press, 1985), 32-33.

9. Frank J. Broucek, M.D., *On Shame and the Search for Identity* (New York: Harcourt Brace Jovanovich, 1958), 19-20.

10. Rachel Biale, *Women and Jewish Law: An Exploration of Women's Issues in Halakhic Sources* (New York: Schocken, 1984), 64 on BT *Sotah* 20a.

Chapter Six: Invisible Life Passages

1. This young woman's comparison of her personal experience to the communal Jewish experience of the Holocaust is striking. In a recent conversation, Rabbi Debra Orenstein suggested a similar analogy, referring to Irena Klepfisz's powerful poem, "*Di Rayze Aheym*—The Journey Home," which ostensibly is about the Holocaust, but which, upon first reading, she believed to be about sexual abuse. Indeed, several feelings described in that poem are shared by survivors of the Holocaust and of sexual abuse: (a) the disturbing memory: "Too much is at stake this morning...to see what can be wrenched from unconscious crowded darkness of her memory"; (b) the shame and need to repress memory: "She is ashamed...she has forgotten...forgotten it all"; (c) the sense of aloneness and helplessness when no one will understand (or believe) what she has been through: "Whom can I speak to? she wonders...the mother...the father...the grandmother...the grandfather...the ancestors...the entire family...even the ghosts do not

understand me." Melanie Kaye/Kantrowitz and Irena Klepfisz, eds., *The Tribe of Dina: A Jewish Women's Anthology* (Montpelier, Vt.: Sinister Books, 1986), 49f.

2. Gertrud Mueller Nelson, *To Dance With God: Family Ritual and Communal Celebration* (Mahwah, N.J.: Paulist Press, 1986), quoted in Laura Davis, *The Courage to Heal Workbook* (New York: Harper & Row, 1990), 307.

3. Solon T. Kimbala, introduction to Arnold van Gennep, *The Rites of Passage* (Chicago: University of Chicago Press, 1960), xvii.

4. See "Kicked Out of my Peoplehood," *The Jewish Survivors' Network Newsletter* 1, no. 2 (February, 1992).

5. Mordecai Kaplan, *Questions Jews Ask: Reconstructionist Answers* (New York: Reconstructionist Press, 1972), 280.

6. Edward Whitmont, *Return of the Goddess* (New York: Crossroad Publishing Co., 1984), quoted in Renee Beck and Sydney Barbara Metrick, *The Art of Ritual: A Guide to Creating and Performing Your Own Rituals for Growth and Change* (Berkeley, Calif.: Celestial Arts, 1990), 9.

7. The P'nai Or Religious Fellowship has pioneered the use of movement and dance in Jewish ritual in its Sabbath prayerbook, *Or Chadash: A New Light* (Philadelphia: P'nai Or Religious Fellowship, 1982), which I co-edited with Rabbi Burt Jacobson. Another contribution in this area is Jo Anne Tucker and Susan Freeman, *Torah in Motion: Creating Dance Midrash* (Denver, Colo.: Alternatives in Religious Education Publishing, Inc., 1990).

8. Though the rituals I have designed are quite different from Rabbi Eilberg's, her work was important in stimulating my own creative process. I have incorporated some of her language and suggestions into my rituals, indicated in the text by an asterix (*). Where my approach owes a debt to hers, but differs significantly, I indicate this by writing (adapted)*.

9. Penina V. Adelman, "Playing House: The Birth of a Ritual," *Reconstructionist* 54, no. 4 (January/February 1989): 19-21, 24.

10. Adapted with permission from "Moral Choices: Women's Voices: An Interfaith Commemoration of the Roe vs. Wade Decision, January 22, 1992" (Philadelphia: Pennsylvania Religious Coalition for Abortion Rights, 1992), 4.

11. The words "who has given me the ability to make wise choices" have been added to the traditional blessing.

12. Adapted from Rebecca Trachtenberg Alpert, "A Prayer on the Occasion of a Miscarriage or Abortion," *Reconstructionist* 51, no. 1 (September 1985): 4.

13. *Mi Shebeirach* c. 1988 Deborah Lynn Friedman (ASCAP) Sounds Write Productions, Inc. (ASCAP): Music by Debbie Friedman; lyrics by Debbie Friedman and Drorah Setel. Reprinted by permission. Audio tapes and song-books by Debbie Friedman are widely available at gift shops and bookstores, and from Sounds Write Productions, Inc., 6685 Norman Lane, San Diego, CA 92120, (619) 697-6120. The traditional *mi sheberakh* for healing is found in most prayer-books, including Rabbi Jules Harlow, ed. and trans., *Siddur Sim Shalom: A Prayerbook for Shabbat, Festivals, and Weekdays* (New York: Rabbinical Assembly, 1985), 144-145.

14. Sheet music is available in *Kol Haneshamah: Shabbat Eve* (Wyncote, Pa.: Reconstructionist Press, 1989), 234.

15. Unpublished poem.

16. Adapted with permission from "Unending Love" by Rabbi Rami M. Shapiro, reprinted in *Kol Haneshamah*, 69.

17. Although the Sabbath dinner is the most prevalent setting of *Eshet Hayil*, the poem has undergone a variety of ritual adaptations at different times and in different communities, e.g. at funerals and weddings. See Yael Levin, "*Eshet Hayil*" (in Hebrew) *Beth Mikra* 31, no. 4 (1985/86): 339-47.

18. See verses 17 and 25 on her physical strength. The war-like connotations of phrases, coupled with the hymn-like structure of the poem, make *Eshet Hayil* akin both to poems in praise of valiant men and to hymns in praise of God. See Al Wolters, "Proverbs 31:10-31 as Heroic Hymn: A Form-Critical Analysis," *Vetus Testamentum* 38, 4 (October 1988): 446-57.

19. For further discussion see Claudia V. Camp, *Wisdom and the Feminine in the Book of Proverbs* (Decatur, Ga.: Almono Press, 1985), 188-91.

20. Proverbs 1:7, 2:2-5, 9:10, 15:33; Psalms 111:10.

21. Proverbs 3:15; 8:11, 18; 31:10, 25.

22. Proverbs 1:20, 8:10, 8:14, 8:35.

Chapter Seven: Coming Out

1. On lesbianism see, for example, BT *Shabbat* 65a-b and Maimonides, *Mishneh Torah Issurei Bi'ah* 21:8.

2. On the first argument cited, see Bradley Shavit Artson, "Gay and Lesbian Jews: An Innovative Jewish Legal Position," *The Jewish Spectator* 55, no. 3 (winter 1990-1991), 6-14. On the position invoking *ones*, see Daniel C. Matt, ed., *Walking Humbly With God: The Life and Writings of Rabbi Hershel Jonah Matt* (Hoboken, N.J.: KTAV Publishing House, 1993), 227f. Thanks to Rabbi Bradley Shavit Artson for discussing these issues with me and offering me the benefit of his expertise.

3. The book *Twice Blessed* explores gays, lesbians, and Jewish life, but I see a triple blessing. See Christie Balka and Andy Rose, eds., *Twice Blessed: On Being Lesbian, Gay, and Jewish* (Boston: Beacon Press, 1991).

4. The Hebrew word for Egypt, *mitzrayim*, literally means "narrow straights."

5. *Latzet min hametzarim* means, literally, to come out of narrow places. The blessing formula "let us bless the source of life" is in the feminine case and is the work of Marcia Falk. See her "Notes on Composing New Blessings," 39-53. My thanks to Rabbi Leila Gal Berner for her help with constructing the rest of the blessing.

6. Reprinted with permission. Balka and Rose, eds., *Twice Blessed*, 26-27.

7. Recently, the gay community has been engaged in debates about the practice of "outing," revealing someone's sexual orientation in public. Outing has political motives. The person who is "brought out of the closet" is usually a well-known individual whose exposure, it is argued, would help the cause of gay liberation if it were known that he or she is gay. While I do not wish to debate the merits of the practice here, it is clearly not construed as a license, in everyday circumstances, to discuss someone's sexual orientation without their permission. When someone comes out to you, it makes sense to ask them how many people know and with whom you can discuss the matter.

8. See Raymond Scheidlin, *Wine, Women and Death* (Philadelphia: Jewish Publication Society, 1986), 82ff.

9. See Leslea Newman, *Heather Has Two Mommies* (Boston: Alyson, 1991); and Julie Greenberg, "We the People: Egalitarian Jewish Education," *Reconstructionist* 54, no. 5 (March 1989): 13-16.

10. A frequent argument of those opposed to same sex marriages is that this is a slippery slope leading to the public affirmation of incestuous relationships and even bestiality. This stems from a common cultural misconception that victims and survivors of incest were participating in a mutual act. Actually, incest is a form of sexual abuse and violation and the product of dysfunction, not a consensual relationship between adults. Similarly, bestiality is a form of animal abuse, not an expression of love or caring.

11. Some gay men and more lesbians perceive the institution of marriage as part of an oppressive, obsolete patriarchal culture, and are averse to the aspects of weddings which seem to demean women. Bisexual people who are involved in opposite sex relationships often feel invisible and unacknowledged in traditional heterosexual weddings.

Chapter Eight: Marriage

1. Rachel Adler, *Engendering Judaism* (Philadelphia: Jewish Publication Society, 1995).

2. Although I wrote this paper, it really is a product of two people: Myself and my husband, Rabbi Arik Ascherman, my "covenanted spouse." Thanks also go to Rabbi Debra Orenstein.

3. Kuk, *Igrot Horiyah*, 123 cited in Agus, *High Priest*, 204.

4. Gershom Scholem, *Major Trends in Jewish Mysticism* (New York: Schocken, 1961), 227.

5. The Mishnah in *Gittin* 9:10 discusses "sufficient" grounds for a man to divorce his wife. Among these are cooking him a dish that he dislikes or finding a woman who is more beautiful than she. Later decisors of the law, however, maintained a greater compassion towards the woman's vulnerable position vis-a-vis the divorce. See Ben Zion Schereschewsky, "Divorce," in Menachem Elon, ed., *The Principles of Jewish Law* (Jerusalem: Keter Publishing House, 1974), 414-424.

6. See Judith Romney Wegner, *Chattel or Person: The Status of Women in The Mishnah* (New York and Oxford: Oxford University Press, 1988), 16; Boaz Cohen, *Jewish and Roman Law: A Comparative Study* (New York: The Jewish Theological Seminary of America, 1966), 289; Schereschewsky, "Husband and Wife," 385. *Shulḥan Arukh Even Ha'ezer* 80:15 includes women's household work as part of the husband's purchase. See also *Shulḥan Arukh Even Ha'ezer* 64:5.

7. Isaac Klein, *A Guide To Jewish Religious Practice* (New York: The Jewish Theological Seminary of America, 1979), 393. His claim is based on Louis Epstein's argument. See Louis M. Epstein, *The Marriage Contract: A Study in the Status of the Woman in Jewish Law* (New York: The Jewish Theological Seminary, 1927), 5.

8. After all, according to traditional Jewish law her wages automatically belong to him and it is she who is being purchased. An example of such an "egal-

itarian" *ketubbah* is found in Anita Diamant, *The New Jewish Wedding* (New York: Summit Books, 1985), 84-85.

9. Mordecai Kaplan, *The Meaning of God in Modern Jewish Religion* (New York: Reconstructionist Press, 1962), 6-9, 34-39.

10. Abraham Joshua Heschel, *God in Search of Man: A Philosophy of Judaism* (New York: Farrar, Straus and Giroux, 1955), 336-340.

11. A standard pre-nuptial agreement is available from the legal department of the Israeli women's organization *Naamat* (Pioneer Women of Israel), Strauss 17, Jerusalem, Israel.

12. David Davidovitch, *The Ketubbah* (Tel Aviv: E. Lewin-Epstein, 1968), 114. For versions of other ancient *ketubbot* that were more egalitarian than the accepted traditional *ketubbah* see Mordecai Akiva Friedman, *Jewish Marriage in Palestine* (New York: The Jewish Theological Seminary of America, 1980). Thanks to Rachel Adler for referring me to this and other sources on the topic.

13. For the Hebrew text and permission to reprint the English with the Hebrew, contact the authors at P.O. Box 7135, Jerusalem, Israel 91071.

14. Israelis who do not wish to have an Orthodox rabbi officiate at their wedding have three legal options. They can travel to another country (in most cases to Cyprus); sign papers of civil marriage in Paraguay through a lawyer in Israel (a procedure that costs almost as much as traveling to Cyprus); or sign a contract not recognized by the State of Israel as a civil marriage, which nevertheless allows the couple to receive some of the financial benefits that married people enjoy.

15. See Eugene B. Borowitz, *Choosing a Sex Ethic: A Jewish Inquiry* (Washington, D.C.: B'nai Brith Hillel Foundation, 1966); and Harold M. Schulweis, "Jewish Silence on Sexuality," in *Jewish Marital Status*, ed. Carol Diamant (Northvale, N.J.: Jason Aronson, Inc., 1989), 81-90.

16. Heschel, *God in Search of Man*, 12.

17. The technical legal problem is that a man could not be consecrated exclusively to one woman, since the law assumes he could marry another wife. BT *Kiddushin* 4b and Tosafot there. Maimonides, *Mishneh Torah Hilkhot Ishut* 3:6.

18. This was an important question that members of Congregation Beth Simchat Torah, New York City's gay and lesbian synagogue, grappled with for several years. Their struggle expressed itself for many years in a congregational policy prohibiting commitment ceremonies to be held in the synagogue building. This policy was successfully challenged in 1988 by Rosanne Mira Leipzig and Judith Mable. See *Lilith* 17, no. 4 (fall 1992): 14.

19. Kuk, *Igrot Horiyah*, 123 cited in Agus, *High Priest*, 204.

20. This differs from the traditional blessing in the feminization of the God language, the elimination of the notion of God as ruler, and the substitution of *kol enosh*, which is unmistakably egalitarian, for *ha'adam*, which is sometimes translated as "man."

21. Diamant, *The New Jewish Wedding*, 192-193.

22. One need not give up the receiving line entirely. It can be delayed, or reserved for the couple's parents. A bride I know was hesitating over whether or not to take time away from the receiving line in order to have *Yihud* with her

future husband. Her cantor asked an important question: "How do you want to remember the first few minutes of your marriage?" She said later, "I am so glad that we chose a holy, private confirmation over a blur of passing faces."

23. The statements by groom and bride recall the *badeken* (bridal veiling ceremony) held just prior to the wedding itself, in which the groom blesses the bride with language originally applied to Rebecca. Same-sex couples who observe *Yiḥud* following a commitment ceremony could substitute verses from the Song of Songs for these verses from Genesis.

Chapter Nine: Divorce

1. As Haut explains, Jewish men have many practical options and fewer problems when wives refuse to receive a *get*, than do wives when their husbands refuse to grant one.

2. In the eleventh century, Rabbenu Gershom decreed that a woman could not be divorced against her will. See *Shulḥan Arukh Even Ha'ezer* 119:6.

3. For example, the widely used *hetter me'ah rabbanim* (permission of one hundred rabbis). Rabbis from three different cities may grant a husband permission to marry another woman while still technically married to the first wife who is refusing to accept a *get*. They suspend, for him, the ban against polygamy. He must deposit a *get* in the *beit din* for the wife to collect when she pleases.

4. Bastards may only marry other bastards or converts. The stigma of bastardy is retained for ten generations. A *mamzer* is *not* someone born out of wedlock, but rather someone born from a sexually prohibited union, such as adultery or incest. The early rabbis were mindful of the injustice visited upon innocent children because of their parents' behavior. A *midrash* (Rabbinical legend) teaches that God takes a *mamzer* from one end of the world and unites him/her with a *mamzer* from the other end of the world. It should be noted that two Conservative responsa permit Conservative rabbis to officiate at weddings between *mamzerim* and non-mamzerim.

5. On the Sabbath preceding the wedding, the groom is called to the Torah for an *aliyah* (blessings recited before and after the Torah is read), in honor of the *aufruf* (engagement celebration held the Sabbath before the wedding). In Orthodox women's prayer groups, the bride has an *aufruf* and she too is called to the Torah. In traditional Orthodox communities, the *Shabbat* before the wedding is called *Shabbat Kallah* (Sabbath of the bride), and the bride's friends visit her. Before the wedding, the bride immerses herself in a *mikveh* (ritual bath) for the first of what will become a monthly ritual.

6. This is not the place for a discussion of the value the rabbis placed upon virginity. There are many troubling facts regarding biblical views of virginity and rape. For example, for rape of a married or betrothed woman the punishment is death (Deuteronomy 22:25). For rape of a non-betrothed virgin there is only a financial penalty, with the stipulation that, should the victim wish, the rapist must marry her and may never divorce her (Exodus 22:15; Deuteronomy 22:28). Rape is viewed not as a crime of violence, but rather as an assault upon another man's property.

7. This is in order to protect a wife from being thrown out impetuously. The husband must find a scribe and wait while a *get* is written. The hope is that by

the time he has managed to do this, his ire will have cooled and he will have changed his mind.

8. Despite the fact that today we like to think of women as being economically independent, this is not the norm in the traditional Orthodox community, where families are large and most women do not receive college educations or job training.

9. Recently, Agunah, Inc. conducted a survey of *batei din*, asking the current market value of the *ketubbah*. The responses varied from $4,000 to $20,000 to admissions of ignorance. In light of the uncertain value of the *ketubbah*, some rabbinical courts instruct women to renounce the *ketubbah* before receiving a *get*. Asking someone to renounce something of doubtful value goes against a basic halakhic premise. Yet, this additional charade often takes place.

10. There are no reliable statistics, but Israeli feminists assert that in Israel alone they number over 14,000.

11. In one case, television ownership (frowned upon in some Orthodox circles) was enough to threaten the removal of a child from the mother's custody. In another instance, a rabbinical court assigned a six-year-old boy to foster parents because the father was unfit and the mother had enrolled the child in a co-ed *yeshivah*.

12. Agunah, Inc., Get, and ICAR can be reached at P.O. Box 131, Brooklyn, New York 11230.

13. Unfortunately, this law has resulted in a bitter battle between its proponents and some major rabbinic groups (such as Agudath Israel) who insist that under this law, technical coercion is indeed at work.

14. An earlier version of this article was published as "The New Improved Jewish Divorce: Her/His," *LILITH*, the Independent Jewish Women's Quarterly 15, no. 3 (summer 1990). Subscriptions are $16.00 per year from *LILITH*, 250 West 57th St., New York, NY 10107. This article is printed here by permission.

15. Only a traditional Orthodox *get* ceremony is accepted by all movements of Judaism.

Chapter Ten: Intermarriage

1. Ariella Keysar, et al., *Highlights of The Council of Jewish Federations 1990 National Jewish Population Survey* (New York: Council of Jewish Federations, 1990), 14.

2. The use of the terms "non-Orthodox" and "liberal" Judaism merits explanation. While intermarriage has left no sector of the Jewish community untouched, the more "liberal" the community (by which I mean the extent to which individual religious autonomy prevails), the greater the likelihood of intermarriage. This means that the Reform, Reconstructionist, and Conservative movements suffer an incidence of intermarriage roughly proportionate to the scope of individual Jewish freedom granted by each. While important distinctions do exist among these three movements, each can be defined by its evolution as a result of its encounter with modernity.

3. Debra Nussbaum Cohen, "Jewish Education Linked to Observance," *Manhattan Jewish Sentinel*, 28 July 1993, 8A.

4. Eugene Borowitz, *Renewing the Covenant: A Theology for the Postmodern Jew* (Philadelphia: Jewish Publication Society, 1991), 298.

5. Carol Gilligan, *In a Different Voice: Psychological Theory and Women's Development* (Cambridge, Mass.: Harvard University Press, 1982), 23.

6. Sylvia Barack Fishman, *A Breath of Life* (New York: Free Press, 1992), 28.

Chapter Eleven: Choosing Judaism

1. This essay is dedicated to the memory of Jakob Petuchowski; and to Elizabeth Petuchowski; Bishop John Coburn; and my two best mentor friends at Episcopal Divinity School, Margaret Quill and Virginia Sapienza-Lund. God's Peace to you all.

2. By traditional Jewish law, a child is considered Jewish if the mother is Jewish. The Reform and Reconstructionist movements accept the children of a Jewish father and non-Jewish mother as Jewish (without conversion) *if* the family has committed themselves to raising and educating the child Jewishly, and if the child her/himself affirms that identity when s/he comes to the age of Jewish majority. This is quite a controversial subject in the Jewish world—too complicated to deal with in depth here.

3. For a brief summary of conversion requirements for the various movements, see Lena Romanoff, *Your People, My People* (New York: Jewish Publication Society, 1990), 261-280.

4. By this term I mean to indicate a praying community where women participate fully, sharing all ritual obligations and privileges with men.

5. You should know that some rabbis in the non-halakhic branches of Judaism (Reform, Reconstructionist) permit conversions without (for men) *hattafat dam* or circumcision, and without *mikveh*. Personally, I think this disregard of millennia of Jewish law and tradition is no favor to the convert—or to their own movement. But even in these cases, three main elements are presented: Study, ritual, and meeting with a juridical body.

6. In addition to the *Lifecycles* series, see Plaskow, *Standing Again at Sinai*, and Susannah Heschel, ed., *On Being a Jewish Feminist* (New York: Schocken, 1983).

7. According to the Rabbis, gentiles need only observe the seven Noahide laws in order to be considered righteous and merit the world-to-come.

8. Ariella Keysar, *Highlights*.

Chapter Twelve: Parenting

1. Nessa Rapaport, "Five Words for Jewish Leaders: You Still Don't Get It," *Tikkun* 8, no. 1 (January 1993): 53-54, 77. This article was prepared for one of two conferences geared for contributors to *Lifecycles*. The conferences were sponsored by the Susan and David Wilstein Institute of Jewish Policy Studies.

2. Paula Hyman, "The Modern Jewish Family: Image and Reality," in *The Jewish Family: Metaphor and Memory*, ed. David Kraemer (New York: Oxford University Press, 1989), 190.

3. Of self-esteem, Dr. Ellen LeVee, a sociologist, contributor to *Lifecycles* Vol. 2, and one of the best mothers I know told me in discussing these issues, "One of

my jobs as a mother is to make the qualities that my children have seem positive in their own eyes."

4. See for example Bronwyn Davies, *Frogs and Snails and Feminist Tails: Preschool Children and Gender* (North Sydney, Australia: Allen and Unwin, 1989), 21-42.

5. Of course, there is some negativity associated with raising girls in a feminist context, as there is, unfortunately and inevitably, in parenting, generally. It is certainly possible, too, that feminist parents could slant the feminist message to girls in a negative way, but that is rare, and a sign of sick family dynamics.

6. My thanks to Rabbi Jehiel Orenstein of Congregation Beth El in South Orange, New Jersey for sharing his insights and the work of Professor Cyrus Gordon on the linguistic connection between the words "*yad*," "*dai*," and "*yedid*." See Cyrus H. Gordon, *Ugaritic Textbook Glossary Indexes* (Rome, Italy: Pontificum Institution Bilicum, 1965), 383.

7. Rabbi Jules Harlow, ed., *A Rabbi's Manual* (New York: The Rabbinical Assembly, 1965), 6.

8. Traditionally, women recite the blessing over candles, and men, the blessing over wine.

Chapter Thirteen: Midlife

1. Martha Kirkpatrick, "Lesbians: A Different Middle Age?" in *The Middle Years*, eds. John M. Oldham and Robert S. Liebert (New Haven, Conn.: Yale University Press, 1989), 135.

2. See for example Arnold van Gennep, *The Rites of Passage* (Chicago: University of Chicago Press, 1960), 145.

3. Gloria Steinem, *Revolution from Within: A Book of Self-Esteem* (Boston: Little, Brown and Co., 1992), 246 citing a 150-nation menopause study; John B. McKinlay and Sonja M. McKinlay, "Depression in Middle-Aged Women: Social Circumstances versus Estrogen Deficiency," in *The Psychology of Women*, ed. Mary Walsh (New Haven, Conn.: Yale University Press, 1987), 157-161; Carol C. Nadelson, "Single Women in Their Thirties and Forties," in *The Middle Years*, eds. Oldham and Liebert, 118 citing P. Bart and M. Grossman, "Menopause," in *The Woman Patient* vol. 1 *Sexual and Reproductive Aspects of Women's Health Care*, eds. M. Notman and C. Nadleson (New York: Plenum, 1978); and Betty Friedan, *The Fountain of Age* (New York: Simon and Schuster, 1993), especially 472-499.

4. Steinem, *Revolution From Within*, 89. See also Joan C. Borton, *Drawing From the Women's Well* (San Diego: LuraMedia, 1992), 75.

5. Friedan, *Fountain of Age*, 144-146; and Gail Sheehy, *The Silent Passage: Menopause* (New York: Random House, 1992), 223, 226.

6. Erik Erikson first used the term "generativity" in relation to lifecycle and midlife. Erik Erikson, *Identity and the Lifecycle: Selected Papers*, Psychological Issues vol. 1, no. 1 (New York: International Universities Press, 1959); and Erik Erikson, *Childhood and Society* (New York: Norton, 1963), 67. Early on, Erikson regarded physical procreation as a pre-requisite for generativity, but he later revised that view. Still, feminists criticize him for implying that all female creativity is a channelling of the "maternal drive."

7. All of this is fed by our society's fear of aging and cult of the young female that fuels the "beauty myth" industry. Naomi Wolf, *The Beauty Myth* (New York: William Morrow and Co., 1991).

8. Germaine Greer, *The Change: Women, Aging and the Menopause* (New York: Alfred A. Knopf, 1992), 372.

9. Sheehy, *The Silent Passage: Menopause*, 145.

10. Daniel J. Levenson, *The Seasons of a Man's Life* (New York: Ballantine Books, 1978), 320.

11. Greer, *The Change*, 376.

12. Mircea Eliade, *Patterns in Comparative Religion* (New York: Shed and Ward, 1958), 267.

13. This is due to their involvement in the rituals of the Red Heifer and of healing lepers (Numbers 19:6 and Leviticus 14:49-51).

14. The Asherah in the form of a tree or sacred pole, was a symbol of the inexhaustible fertility of the Great Goddess. Though worship of Asherah was roundly condemned by prophets and priests (Judges 6:30; I Kings 15:13; II Kings 13:6, 17:9-11, 16; 21:3; 23:4-6), positive associations with the tree remained. See Raphael Patai, *The Hebrew Goddess* (New York: Charles Scribner's Sons, 1977), and S. Olyan, *Asherah and the Cult of Yaweh in Israel* (Atlanta, Ga.: Scholars Press, 1988).

15. Copyright © by Merle Feld, 1986.

16. Copyright © by Merle Feld, 1989.

Chapter Fourteen: Aging

1. Friedan, *Fountain of Age*, 87, 267, 641 n.32

2. See Wolf, *The Beauty Myth*.

3. Friedan, *Fountain of Age*, 157f, citing David Gutmann, *Reclaimed Powers* (New York: Basic Books, 1987), among others.

4. This notion of remembering was introduced to me by Joan Borton, *Drawing From the Women's Well: Reflections on the Life Passage of Menopause* (San Diego: LuraMedia, 1992), 32, citing Paula Gunn Allen, *The Sacred Hoop* (Boston: Beacon Press, 1986), 11.

5. See Savina Teubal, "Simchat Hochmah: A Crone Ritual," in *Four Centuries of Jewish Women's Spirituality*, eds. Dianne Ashton and Ellen Umansky (Boston: Beacon Press, 1992), 257-265.

6. Adrienne Rich, *Of Woman Born: Motherhood as Experience and Institution* (New York: Bantam, 1977), 237.

7. Linda Cool, "Ethnic Identity: A Source of Community Esteem for the Elderly," *Anthropological Quarterly* 54, no. 4 (1981): 179-89. See also Cool, "The Effects of Social Class and Ethnicity on the Aging Process," in *The Elderly as Pioneers*, ed. P. Silverman (Bloomington, Ind.: Indiana University Press, 1987), 263-311.

8. Rachel Zohar Dulin, *Old Age in the Hebrew Scriptures: A Phenomenological Study* (Ann Arbor, Mich.: University Microfilms, 1983), 83-84.

9. The Jerusalem Talmud recounts that Rabbi Tarfon placed his hands on the ground for her to walk on when her sandal broke. When the sages heard what he

did, they said, "Even if he would do a thousand times more, he would not have reached even half of the honoring of a parent required by the Torah" (JT *Pe'ah* 15c). Rabbi Joseph, when he "heard his [mother's] footsteps...would say, 'I will rise before the approaching *Shekhinah* [close-dwelling presence of God, associated with the feminine]'" (BT *Kiddushin* 31b).

10. The Hebrew word for "fear" refers to a commandment requiring respect and awe, rather than intimidation or a sense of danger.

11. Natalie F. Joffe, "The Dynamics of Beneficence Among Eastern European Jews," *Social Forces* 29 (1949): 238-247.

12. Cited in Francine Klagsbrun, *Voices of Wisdom* (New York: Jonathan David Publisher, 1980), 203.

13. For more on losses, see Rachel Zohar Dulin, *A Crown of Glory: A Biblical View of Aging* (Mahwah, N.J.: Paulist Press, 1988).

14. From Barbara Myerhoff, *Number Our Days* (New York: 1978), 235, by permission of Dutton Signet, a division of Penguin Books USA Inc.

15. See Sharon Kaufman, *The Ageless Self: Sources of Meaning in Late Life* (Madison: University of Wisconsin Press, 1986).

16. Myerhoff, *Number Our Days*, 256.

17. Sydney Stahl Weinberg, *The World of Our Mothers* (Chapel Hill, N.C.: University of North Carolina Press, 1988), 15, 17.

18. Unleavened bread eaten at Passover.

19. See also Allen Glicksman, "The Jewish Elderly," *The Journal of Aging and Judaism* 5, no. 1 (fall 1990): 7-21.

20. Myerhoff, *Number Our Days*, 266, by permission of Dutton Signet, a division of Penguin Books USA Inc.

21. Susan Weidman Schneider, *Jewish and Female: Choices and Changes in Our Lives Today* (New York: Simon and Schuster, 1985), 268.

22. Charlotte Baum, Paula Hyman, and Sonya Michel, *The Jewish Woman in America* (New York: Dial Press, 1976), 242.

23. Susan Starr Sered, "The Religion of Relating: Kinship and Spirituality Among Middle Eastern Jewish Women in Jerusalem," *Journal of Social and Personal Relationships* 6 (1989): 317; and Sered, *Women as Ritual Experts: The Religious Life of Elderly Jewish Women in Jerusalem* (New York: Oxford University Press, 1992).

24. Eleanor Mallach Bromberg, "Mother-Daughter Relationships in Later Life: The Effect of Quality of Relationship Upon Mutual Aid," *Journal of Gerontological Social Work* 6, no. 1 (1983): 75-92.

25. Pauline Bart, "Depression in Middle-Aged Women: Some Sociocultural Factors" (Ph.D. diss., UCLA, 1967).

26. Abraham Monk, "The 'New' and the 'Young' Aged," *Journal of Aging and Judaism* 1, no. 2 (1987): 145-165.

27. Leora Isaacs, "Intergenerational Families," *Journal of Aging and Judaism* 2, no. 2 (1987): 84-93.

28. Leslea Newman, ed., *Bubbe Meisehs By Shayneh Maidelehs* (Santa Cruz, Calif.: Herbooks, 1990); and Adele Geras, ed., *My Grandmother's Stories: A Collection of Jewish Folk Tales* (New York: Alfred A. Knopf, 1990).

29. Barbara Myerhoff, "A Symbol Perfected in Death: Continuity and Ritual in the Life and Death of An Elderly Jew," in *Life's Career-Aging: Cultural Variations on Growing Old*, ed. Barbara G. Myerhoff and Andrei Simic (Beverly Hills, Calif.: Sage Publications), 164.

30. Myerhoff, "A Symbol," 165.

31. Eva Kahana and Boaz Kahana, "Jews," in *The Handbook on the Aged in the United States*, ed. Erdman B. Palmore (Westport, Conn.: Greenwood Press, 1984), 161.

32. Leo Rosten, *Treasury of Jewish Quotations* (New York: McGraw Hill, 1970), 95.

33. Leo Rosten, *Leo Rosten's Treasury of Jewish Quotations* (New York: McGraw-Hill, 1972), 86.

34. Aryeh Kaplan, *Waters of Eden* (New York: National Conference of Synagogue Youth/Orthodox Union, 1976), 30.

35. See BT *Berakhot* 10a, BT *Eruvin* 53b, BT *Pesaḥim* 62b.

36. While the Bible does not specify that the fruit Eve ate was an apple, the image of the apple is widely used.

37. Each of us planted sage seeds in individual pots, and all of them grew.

Chapter Fifteen: Death and Mourning

1. Regarding work during *shivah* see BT *Mo'ed Katan* 15b and *Shulḥan Arukh Yoreh De'ah* 380:2, 5; 393:2. On not bathing see BT *Mo'ed Katan* 15b; *Mishneh Torah Hilkhot Avelut* 5:4; and *Shulḥan Arukh Yoreh De'ah* 381:1. On not engaging in most Jewish learning, see BT *Mo'ed Katan* 21a; *Mishneh Torah Hilkhot Avelut* 5:16; and *Shulḥan Arukh Yoreh De'ah* 384:1-4. On not attending weekday services at synagogue, see *Shulḥan Arukh Yoreh De'ah* 393:3. On not having sex, see BT *Mo'ed Katan* 21a and *Shulḥan Arukh Yoreh De'ah* 383:1. On not sitting normally, see Mishnah *Semaḥot* 6:1, *Shulḥan Arukh Yoreh De'ah* 387:1-2. For a thorough treatment of laws of mourning consult the readings in the Death and Mourning bibliography under the Suggested Readings.

2. See the Rama on *Shulḥan Arukh Yoreh De'ah* 385:3 and 389:3. See also BT *Mo'ed Katan* 22b; *Mishneh Torah Hilkhot Avelut* 6:2, *Shulḥan Arukh Yoreh De'ah* 391:1-3.

3. The Sabbath does not cut *shiv'ah* or *sheloshim* short, but a festival does. "*Sheloshim*" can refer to the period after *shiv'ah* and before the thirty day mark, as well as to the thirty day mark itself.

4. Stephen Levine, *Who Dies? An Investigation of Conscious Living and Conscious Dying* (New York: Anchor Books, 1982), 85.

5. In addition to Levine, see Elisabeth Kubler-Ross, *On Death and Dying* (New York: Macmillan, 1969); Stanley Keleman, *Living Your Dying* (New York: Random House, 1974); and, in the Jewish realm, Jack Riemer, ed., *Jewish Reflections on Death* (New York: Schocken, 1974).

6. The telling of the story paraphrases a weave of *midrashim* by Louis Ginzberg which draws on Deuteronomy *Rabbah* 11:5, II *Petirat* Moshe 383, *Likuttim* 5, 169b, and *Midrash Tannaim* 225. Louis Ginzberg, *Legends of the Jews* vol. 3 (Philadelphia: Jewish Publication Society, 1973-1966), 472 and vol. 6, 83.

7. *Ma'avar Yabbok, Sefat Emet*, 15.

8. Chaim Binyamin Goldberg, *Mourning in Halachah* (Brooklyn: Mesorah Publications, 1991), 38.

9. Victor Turner, *The Ritual Process: Structure and Anti-Structure* (Ithaca, N.Y.: Cornell University Press, 1969), 94-130.

10. On correspondence between Jewish mourning ritual and psychological need, see Anne Brener, *Mourning and Mitzvah: A Guided Journal for Walking the Mourner's Path Through Grief to Healing* (Woodstock, Vt.: Jewish Lights, 1993); Audrey Gordon, "The Psychological Wisdom of the Law" in *Jewish Reflections on Death*, ed. Jack Riemer (New York: Schocken, 1987), 95-104; and Mortimer Ostow, "Grief and Mourning" in *The Bond of Life: A Book for Mourners*, ed. Rabbi Jules Harlow (New York: The Rabbinical Assembly), 22-34.

11. Benay Lappe, *Does A Child Who Has Been Sexually Abused By A Parent Have The Obligation To Say Kaddish For That Parent? A Teshuvah* (masters thesis, University of Judaism, 1993), 30. See also *Sh'ma* 21, no. 404 (December 28, 1990) and no. 413 (May 3, 1991), both of which have several articles on the same topic.

12. The possibilities she recommends include using the *mikveh* (ritual bath) as healing waters; creating a document to supplement Passover readings, reflecting the experience of abuse/slavery, as well as feelings of liberation from victimization; designating an object (such as a picture) that represents the survivor and, over the course of eleven months following an abusive parent's death, moving a *yartzeit* candle further and further away from the object, thus symbolizing the survivor's growing independence from the abuser; using the symbols and language of *Havdalah* (distinction-making ritual that separates Sabbath or holiday from weekday) to mark a separation from one's perpetrator, or to distinguish between the perpetrator's hundred percent responsibility (for the abuse) and the survivor's hundred percent responsibility (for her recovery). Lappe, *Does A Child?*, 30.

13. Goldberg, *Mourning in Halakhah* cites *Mishmeret Shalom* who cites *Beit Lehem Yehudah*, who states in the name of *Sefer Hasidim*, "There is no halakhic basis for a daughter's reciting *Kaddish* and such a practice is ridiculous nonsense."

14. There are many occasions when women are, in fact, barred from public mourning. See Letty Cottin Pogrebin, *Deborah, Golda, and Me*, 43, 50-54 and the stories she cites there, as well as the film *Half the Kingdom*.

15. *Yartzeit* is the anniversary of a death.

16. New Year.

Afterword

1. Special thanks to Rabbi Lawrence Hoffman for lending his expertise and insight to this afterword.

2. Evan Imber-Black and Janine Roberts, *Rituals for Our Times: Celebrating, Healing, and Changing Our Lives and Our Relationships* (New York: HarperPerennial, 1992), 25f.

3. Much of my thinking on women and thresholds was shaped by a conversation I had with Rabbi Nina Cardin. I expressed that the heroics—the push, the rush—of moving from before to after seemed typical of a classically masculine

relational style, while the "in-between place," the threshold men so excitedly pass over, seemed typical of the classically feminine style. She replied, "Women *are* thresholds biologically." It was, for me, one of those astounding revelations that appears completely obvious in retrospect.

4. Victor Turner, *Ritual Process: Structure and Anti-Structure* (Ithaca, N.Y.: Cornell University Press, 1977), 95, 106.

5. These include: Jewish Women's Resource Center of the National Council of Jewish Women-New York Section, 9 East 69th Street, New York, NY 10021/212-535-5900; American Jewish Congress Los Angeles Jewish Feminist Center, 6505 Wilshire Boulevard, Los Angeles, CA 90048/213-651-4601; Woman's Institute for Continuing Jewish Education, 4126 Executive Drive, La Jolla, CA 92137/619-442-2666; Women's League for Conservative Judaism, 48 East 74th Street, New York, NY 10021/212-628-1600; National Federation of Temple Sisterhoods, 838 Fifth Avenue, New York, NY 10021/212-249-0100 ext. 350; and the Jewish Women's Studies Project of the Reconstructionist Rabbinical College, Church Road and Greenwood Avenue, Wyncote, PA 19095/215-576-0800. The library of the Reconstructionist Rabbinical College also has a "liturgy file" of creative rituals and prayers.

6. Nessa Rapaport's title essay in *The Woman Who Lost Her Names*, ed. Julia Wolf Mazow (San Francisco: Harper and Row, 1980).

7. For more on heros of the past coming into present rituals see Jacob Neusner, *The Enchantments of Judaism: Rites of Transformation from Birth Through Death* (New York: Basic Books, 1987).

8. See the discussion of traditional blessing formulas on p. 118.

9. Arnold van Gennep called the stages separation, marge, and aggregation. Victor Turner, following van Gennep, referred to them as separation, liminality, and reaggregation.

10. In "Honoring Your Liturgical Efforts Liturgically" which follows, I provide a simple prayer that can be appended to the first use of a new liturgy or ritual. This is recited in community. The commentary that precedes and follows the prayer is supplied for readers who are interested in the liturgical process, but would never be incorporated into the public reading.

11. Of course, feminist and post-modern scholarship have reminded us that even the most "objective" research reflects the authors' experience, and, often, their gender bias. See for example, Bonnie Spanier, "The Natural Sciences: Casting a Critical Eye on Objectivity," in *Toward A Balanced Curriculum: A Sourcebook for Initiating Gender Integration Projects*, eds. Bonnie Spanier, et al. (Cambridge, Mass.: Schenkman, 1984), 49f.

12. "Performance" is a term and an image commonly used by anthropologists to describe the enactment of ritual.

13. Barbara Myerhoff and Sally F. Moore call these stages creation, performance, and outcome. This is another useful anthropological version of before, during, and after. See Barbara Myerhoff, "A Death in Due Time: Construction of Self and Culture in Ritual Drama," in *Rite, Drama, Festival, Spectacle: Rehearsals Toward a Theory of Cultural Performance*, ed. John J. MacAloon (Philadelphia: Institute for the Study of Human Issues, 1984), 157f.

14. Barbara Myerhoff, "A Death in Our Time," 170.

15. The verbal root p.t.h used in terms of a riddle appears here and in Psalm 78. It is not really properly understood. The biblical lexicon edited by Brown, Driver, and Briggs lists the possible meanings of utter, declare, or propound a riddle *or* open up, expound. Most translations of this verse render *eftah* solve, declare, or the like. I prefer "open up," which refers to the process of approaching the riddle, not to the solving of it. I believe it makes better sense not just in this prayer, but in the *peshat* (simple meaning of the biblical text).

16. I use the word mystery for *hida*, despite the fact that "riddle" is the more common translation. While a *hida* can be trivial or of great import, the English "riddle" tends to have a predominantly trivial connotation. Moreover, *hida* comes to mean riddle from the root h.u.d. which means indirect, obscure, turned aside, declined—which includes the notion of the darkly obscure and the mysterious.

Click Stories

1. Excerpted from "It's Hard to Be a Feminist If You Are a Woman" from *The Girl I Left Behind* by Jane O'Reilly. Copyright © 1980 by Jane O'Reilly. Used by permission of the Wallace Literary Agency, Inc.

Index

General Index

About JEWISH LIGHTS Publishing

People of all faiths and backgrounds yearn for books that attract, engage, educate and spiritually inspire.

Our principal goal is to stimulate thought and help all people learn about who the Jewish People are, where they come from, and what the future can be made to hold. While people of our diverse Jewish heritage are the primary audience, our books speak to the Christian world as well and will broaden their understanding of Judaism and the roots of their own faith.

We bring to you authors who are at the forefront of spiritual thought and experience. While each has something different to say, they all say it in a voice that you can hear.

Our books are designed to welcome you and then to engage, stimulate and inspire. We judge our success not only by whether or not our books are beautiful and commercially successful, but by whether or not they make a difference in your life.

We at Jewish Lights take great care to produce beautiful books that present meaningful spiritual content in a form that reflects the art of making high quality books. Therefore, we want to acknowledge those who contributed to the production of this book.

PRODUCTION
Wendy Kilborn

EDITORIAL & PROOFREADING
Sandra Korinchak

BOOK & COVER DESIGN
Karen Savary, Deering, New Hampshire

TYPE
Set in Palatino and Weiss
Chelsea Dippel, Woodstock, Vermont

HEBREW
Joel Hoffman, Excelsior Computer Services
Silver Spring, Maryland

INDEXING
Anna Chapman, Arlington, Vermont

COVER PRINTING
New England Book Components, Hingham, MA

PRINTING AND BINDING
Book Press, Brattleboro, Vermont

Spiritual Inspiration for Family Life

MOURNING & MITZVAH
A Guided Journal for Walking the Mourner's Path
Through Grief to Healing
• WITH OVER 60 GUIDED EXERCISES •

by *Anne Brener, L.C.S.W.*

"Fully engaging in mourning means you will be a different person than before you began."

For those who mourn a death, for those who would help them, for those who face a loss of any kind, Anne Brener teaches us the power and strength available to us in the fully experienced mourning process. Guided writing exercises help stimulate the processes of both conscious and unconscious healing.

"A stunning book! It offers an exploration in depth of the place where psychology and religious ritual intersect, and the name of that place is Truth."

—*Rabbi Harold Kushner, author of* When Bad Things Happen to Good People

"This book is marvelous. It is a work that I wish I had written. It is the best book on this subject that I have ever seen." —*Rabbi Levi Meier, Ph.D., Chaplain, Cedars Sinai Medical Center, Los Angeles, Orthodox Rabbi, Clinical Psychologist*

7 1/2" x 9", 288 pp. Quality Paperback Original, ISBN 1-879045-23-0 **$19.95**

THE PREMIERE BOOK IN A LANDMARK NEW THREE-VOLUME SERIES

LIFECYCLES
Jewish Women on Life Passages
& Personal Milestones
Edited and with introductions by *Rabbi Debra Orenstein*

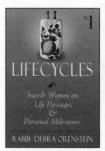

In self-aware, passionate, and insightful voices, 50 leading thinkers come together to explore tradition and innovation in personal ritual and spirituality. Speaking to women of all backgrounds, it covers the entire spectrum of life's passages, from ceremonies around childbirth to new perspectives on aging. Other topics include marriage, singlehood, conversion, coming out, parenting, divorce, and mid-life.

6" x 9", 480 pp. Hardcover, ISBN 1-879045-14-1 **$24.95**

HEALING OF SOUL, HEALING OF BODY:
Spiritual Leaders Unfold the Strength and Solace in Psalms
Edited by *Rabbi Simkha Y. Weintraub, CSW*

A source of solace for those who are facing illness, as well as those who care for them. The ten Psalms which form the core of this healing resource were originally selected 200 years ago by Rabbi Nachman of Breslov as a "complete remedy." Today, for anyone coping with illness, they continue to provide a wellspring of strength.

Each Psalm is newly translated, making it clear and accessible, and each one is introduced by an eminent rabbi, men and women reflecting different movements and backgrounds. To all who are living with the pain and uncertainty of illness, this spiritual resource offers an anchor of spiritual comfort.

6" x 9", 128 pp. (est.) illus., 2-color text. Quality Paperback Original, ISBN 1-879045-31-1 **$13.95**

Spiritual Inspiration for Family Life

IN GOD'S NAME
For children K-5

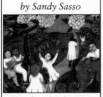
IN GOD'S NAME
by Sandy Sasso

Illus. by Phoebe Stone

by *Sandy Eisenberg Sasso*
Full color illustrations by *Phoebe Stone*

Like an ancient myth in its poetic text and vibrant illustrations, this modern fable about the search for God's name celebrates the diversity and, at the same time, the unity of all the people of the world. Each seeker claims he or she alone knows the answer. Finally, they come together and learn what God's name really is, sharing the ultimate harmony of belief in one God by people of all faiths, all backgrounds.

"I got goosebumps when I read *In God's Name,* its language and illustrations are that moving. This is a book children will love and the whole family will cherish for its beauty and power."
—*Francine Klagsbrun, author of Mixed Feelings: Love, Hate, Rivalry, and Reconciliation Among Brothers and Sisters*

9" x 12", 32 pp. Hardcover, Full color illus., ISBN 1-879045-26-5 **$16.95**

GOD'S PAINTBRUSH

by *Sandy Eisenberg Sasso*
Full color illustrations by *Annette Compton*

MULTICULTURAL, NON-SECTARIAN, NON-DENOMINATIONAL. Invites children of all faiths and backgrounds to encounter God openly in their own lives. Wonderfully interactive, provides questions adult and child can explore together at the end of each episode.

"The most exciting religious children's book I have seen in years."
—*Sylvia Avner, Children's Librarian, 92nd St. "Y," NYC*

"An excellent way to honor the imaginative breadth and depth of the spiritual life of the young." —*Dr. Robert Coles, Harvard University*

• AWARD WINNER •

For children K–4 elementary

11"x 8½", 32 pp. Hardcover, Full color illustrations, ISBN 1-879045-22-2 **$15.95**

THE *NEW* JEWISH BABY BOOK
Names, Ceremonies, Customs — A Guide for Today's Families

by *Anita Diamant*
Foreword by *Rabbi Norman J. Cohen, Dean, HUC–JIR, NYC*
Introduction by *Rabbi Amy Eilberg*

A complete guide to the customs and rituals for welcoming a new child to the world and into the Jewish community, and for commemorating this joyous event in family life–whatever your family constellation. Updated, revised and expanded edition of the highly acclaimed *The Jewish Baby Book.* Includes new ceremonies for girls, celebrations in interfaith families. Also contains a unique directory of names that reflects the rich diversity of the Jewish experience.

"A book that all Jewish parents—no matter how religious—will find fascinating as well as useful. It is a perfect shower or new baby gift." — *Pamela Abrams, Exec. Editor,* Parents Magazine

6"x 9", 328 pp. Quality Paperback Original, ISBN 1-879045-28-1 **$15.95**

PUTTING GOD ON THE GUEST LIST
AWARD WINNER

How to Reclaim the Spiritual Meaning of Your Child's Bar or Bat Mitzvah

"Best Religion Book of the Year"

by *Rabbi Jeffrey K. Salkin*
Foreword by *Rabbi Sandy Eisenberg Sasso*
Introduction by *Rabbi William H. Lebeau, Vice Chancellor, JTS*

Joining explanation, instruction and inspiration, helps parent and child truly *be there* when the moment of Sinai is recreated in their lives. Asks and answers such fundamental questions as how did Bar and Bat Mitzvah originate? What is the lasting significance of the event? How to make the event more spiritually meaningful?

"Shows the way to restore spirituality and depth to every young Jew's most important rite of passage." — *Rabbi Joseph Telushkin, author of* Jewish Literacy

"I hope every family planning a Bar Mitzvah celebration reads Rabbi Salkin's book."
— *Rabbi Harold S. Kushner, author of* When Bad Things Happen to Good People

6"x 9", 184 pp. Quality Paperback, ISBN 1-879045-10-9 **$14.95** HC, ISBN -20-6 **$21.95**

Add Greater Understanding to Your Life

JEWISH LIGHTS   Classic Reprints

TORMENTED MASTER
The Life and Spiritual Quest of Rabbi Nahman of Bratslav
by *Arthur Green*

Explores the personality and religious quest of Nahman of Bratslav (1772–1810), one of Hasidism's major figures. It unlocks the great themes of spiritual searching that make him a figure of universal religious importance.

"A model of clarity and percipience....Utterly relevant to our time."
—*New York Times Book Review*

6"x 9", 408 pp. Quality Paperback, ISBN 1-879045-11-7 **$17.95**

THE LAST TRIAL
On the Legends and Lore of the Command to Abraham to Offer Isaac as a Sacrifice
by *Shalom Spiegel*

New Introduction by *Judah Goldin, Emeritus Professor, University of Pennsylvania*

A classic. An eminent Jewish scholar examines the total body of texts, legends, and traditions referring to the Binding of Isaac and weaves them all together into a definitive study of the *Akedah* as one of the central events in all of human history.

"A model in the history of biblical interpretation, and a centerpiece for Jewish-Christian discussion."—*Dr. Michael Fishbane, Nathan Cummings Professor of Jewish Studies, University of Chicago*

6"x 9", 208 pp. Quality Paperback, ISBN 1-879045-29-X **$17.95**

ASPECTS OF RABBINIC THEOLOGY
by *Solomon Schechter*

Including the original Preface from the 1909 edition
& *Louis Finkelstein's* Introduction to the 1961 edition
with an important new Introduction by *Dr. Neil Gillman, Chair, Department of Jewish Philosophy, The Jewish Theological Seminary of America*

Learned yet highly accessible classic statement of the ideas that form the religious consciousness of the Jewish people at large, by one of the great minds of Jewish scholarship of our century.

"This is the only book on the theology of Judaism written 100 years ago that anyone can read today with profit." — *Jacob Neusner, Distinguished Research Professor of Religious Studies, University of South Florida*

"A better antidote could not be found for the still too prevalent Christian ignorance of the richness and depth of the Jewish heritage." — *The Rev. Dr. Paul M. van Buren, Honorarprofessor Of Systematic Theology, Heidelberg University*

6" x 9", 440 pp. Quality Paperback, ISBN 1-879045-24-9 **$18.95**

YOUR WORD IS FIRE
The Hasidic Masters on Contemplative Prayer
Edited and translated by *Arthur Green* and *Barry W. Holtz*

The power of prayer for spiritual renewal and personal transformation is at the core of all religious traditions. From the teachings of the Hasidic Masters the editors have gleaned "hints as to the various rungs of inner prayer and how they are attained." These parables and aphorisms of the Hasidic masters pierce to the heart of the modern reader's search for God.

"Opens up some of the more accessible realms of the Jewish inner life."
— *Eugene B. Borowitz, Sh'ma*

6"x 9", 152 pp. Quality Paperback, ISBN 1-879045-25-7 **$14.95**

Add Greater Meaning to Your Life

FAITH AFTER THE HOLOCAUST?

AWARD WINNER **THE SPIRIT OF RENEWAL**
Finding Faith After the Holocaust
by *Edward Feld*

NEW!
in paperback
Avail. Sept. '94

"Boldly redefines the landscape of Jewish religious thought after the Holocaust." — *Rabbi Lawrence Kushner*

Trying to understand the Holocaust and addressing the question of faith after the Holocaust, Rabbi Feld explores three key cycles of destruction and recovery in Jewish history, each of which radically reshaped Jewish understanding of God, people, and the world.

"Undoubtedly the most moving book I have read....'Must' reading."
— *Rabbi Howard A. Addison*, Conservative Judaism

"A profound meditation on Jewish history [and the Holocaust]....Christians, as well as many others, need to share in this story." —*The Rt. Rev. Frederick H. Borsch, Ph.D., Episcopal Bishop of L.A.*

6"x 9", 216 pp. Hardcover, ISBN 1-879045-06-0 **$22.95**
6"x 9", 224 pp. Quality Paperback, ISBN 1-879045-40-0 **$16.95**

SEEKING THE PATH TO LIFE   AWARD WINNER
Theological Meditations On God
and the Nature of People, Love, Life and Death
by *Rabbi Ira F. Stone,*
Ornamentation by *Annie Stone*

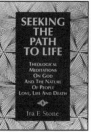

For people who never thought they would read a book of theology—let alone understand it, enjoy it, savor it and have it affect the way they think about their lives.

In 45 intense meditations, each a page or two in length, Stone takes us on explorations of the most basic human struggles: life and death, love and anger, peace and war, covenant and exile.

"Exhilarating—unlike any other reading that I have done in years."
—*Rabbi Neil Gillman, The Jewish Theological Seminary*
"A bold book....The reader of any faith will be inspired, challenged and led more deeply into their own encounter with God."
— *The Rev. Carla Berkedal, Episcopal Priest,*
Executive Director of Earth Ministry

6"x 9", 144 pp. Hardcover, ISBN 1-879045-17-6   **$19.95**

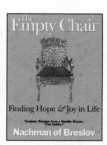

THE EMPTY CHAIR:
FINDING HOPE & JOY
Timeless Wisdom from a Hasidic Master,
Rebbe Nachman of Breslov
Adapted by *Moshe Mykoff* and *the Breslov Research Institute*

A "little treasure" of aphorisms and advice for living joyously and spiritually today, written 200 years ago, but startlingly fresh in meaning and use. Challenges and helps us to move from stress and sadness to hope and joy.

Teacher, guide and spiritual master—Rebbe Nachman provides vital words of inspiration and wisdom for life today for people of any faith, or of no faith.

4" x 6", 128 pp. Hardcover, ISBN 1-879045-16-8 **$9.95**

Motivation & Inspiration for Recovery

TWELVE JEWISH STEPS TO RECOVERY
A Personal Guide To Turning From Alcoholism & Other Addictions...Drugs, Food, Gambling, Sex

by *Rabbi Kerry M. Olitzky* & *Stuart A. Copans, M.D.*
Preface by Abraham J. Twerski, M.D.
Introduction by Rabbi Sheldon Zimmerman
Illustrations by Maty Grünberg
"Getting Help" by JACS Foundation

A Jewish perspective on the Twelve Steps of addiction recovery programs with consolation, inspiration and motivation for recovery. It draws from traditional sources, and quotes from what recovering Jewish people say about their experiences with addictions of all kinds. Inspiring illustrations of the twelve gates of the Old City of Jerusalem.

Experts Praise *Twelve Jewish Steps To Recovery*

"Recommended reading for people of all denominations." — Rabbi Abraham J. Twerski, M.D.

"I read Twelve Jewish Steps with the eyes of a Christian and came away renewed in my heart. I felt like I had visited my Jewish roots. These authors have deep knowledge of recovery as viewed by Alcoholics Anonymous." — Rock J. Stack, M.A., L.L.D. Manager of Clinical/Pastoral Education, Hazelden Foundation

"This book is the first aimed directly at helping the addicted person and family. Everyone affected or interested should read it." — Sheila B. Blume, M.D., C.A.C., Medical Director, Alcoholism, Chemical Dependency and Compulsive Gambling Programs, South Oaks Hospital, Amityville, NY

Readers Praise *Twelve Jewish Steps To Recovery*

"A God-send. Literally. A book from the higher power." — New York, NY

"Looking forward to using it in my practice." —Michigan City, IN

"Made me feel as though 12 Steps were for me, too." — Long Beach, CA

"Excellent–changed my life." — Elkhart Lake, WI

6" x 9", 136 pp. Quality Paperback, ISBN 1-879045-09-5 **$12.95**

RECOVERY FROM *Codependence*
A Jewish Twelve Steps Guide to Healing Your Soul

by *Rabbi Kerry M. Olitzky*
Foreword by *Marc Galanter, M.D., Director,*
Division of Alcoholism & Drug Abuse, NYU Medical Center
Afterword by *Harriet Rossetto, Director, Gateways Beit T'shuvah*

For the estimated 90% of America struggling with the addiction of a family member or loved one, or involved in a dysfunctional family or relationship. A follow-up to the ground-breaking *Twelve Jewish Steps to Recovery.*

"The disease of chemical dependency is also a family illness. Rabbi Olitzky offers spiritual hope and support." —*Jerry Spicer, President, Hazelden*

"Another major step forward in finding the sources and resources of healing, both physical and spiritual, in our tradition." —*Rabbi Sheldon Zimmerman, Temple Emanu-El, Dallas, TX*

6" x 9", 160 pp. Hardcover, ISBN 1-879045-27-3 **$21.95**
6" x 9", 160 pp. Quality Paperback, ISBN 1-879045-32-X **$13.95**

Motivation & Inspiration for Recovery

RENEWED EACH DAY

Daily Twelve Step Recovery Meditations Based on the Bible

by *Rabbi Kerry M. Olitzky* & *Aaron Z.*

VOLUME I: Genesis & Exodus
Introduction by *Rabbi Michael A. Signer*
Afterword by JACS Foundation

VOLUME II: Leviticus, Numbers & Deuteronomy
Introduction by *Sharon M. Strassfeld*
Afterword by *Rabbi Harold M. Schulweis*

Using a seven day/weekly guide format, a recovering person and a spiritual leader who is reaching out to addicted people reflect on the traditional weekly Bible reading. They bring strong spiritual support for daily living and recovery from addictions of all kinds: alcohol, drugs, eating, gambling and sex. A profound sense of the religious spirit soars through their words and brings all people in Twelve Step recovery programs home to a rich and spiritually enlightening tradition.

"Meets a vital need; it offers a chance for people turning from alcoholism and addiction to renew their spirits and draw upon the Jewish tradition to guide and enrich their lives."
　　　　　—*Rabbi Irving (Yitz) Greenberg, President, CLAL,*
　　　　　　The National Jewish Center for Learning and Leadership

"Will benefit anyone familiar with a 'religion of the Book.' Jews, Christians, Muslims. . . ."
　　　　　—*Ernest Kurtz, author of* Not-God: A History of Alcoholics
　　　　　Anonymous & The Spirituality of Imperfection

"An enduring impact upon the faith community as it seeks to blend the wisdom of the ages represented in the tradition with the twelve steps to recovery and wholeness."
　　　　　—*Robert H. Albers, Ph.D., Editor,* Journal of Ministry in Addiction & Recovery

Beautiful Two-Volume Set.

6"x 9", V. I, 224 pp. / V. II, 280 pp., Quality Paperback, ISBN 1-879045-21-4　**$27.90**

ONE HUNDRED BLESSINGS EVERY DAY

Daily Twelve Step Recovery Affirmations, Exercises for Personal Growth & Renewal Reflecting Seasons of the Jewish Year

by *Dr. Kerry M. Olitzky*
with selected meditations prepared by *Rabbi James Stone Goodman, Danny Siegel,* and *Rabbi Gordon Tucker*
Foreword by *Rabbi Neil Gillman,*
　　　　　The Jewish Theological Seminary of America
Afterword by *Dr. Jay Holder, Director, Exodus Treatment Center*

Recovery is a conscious choice from moment to moment, day in and day out. In this helpful and healing book of daily recovery meditations, Kerry Olitzky gives us words to live by day after day, throughout the annual cycle of holiday observances and special Sabbaths of the Jewish calendar.

For those facing the struggles of daily living, *One Hundred Blessings Every Day* brings solace and hope to anyone who is open to healing and to the recovery-oriented teachings that can be gleaned from the Bible and Jewish tradition.

4¹/2" x 6¹/2", Quality Paperback, 432 pp. ISBN 1-879045-30-3　**$14.95**

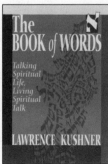

. . . .The Kushner Series

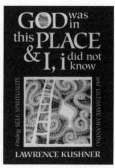

GOD WAS IN THIS PLACE & I, i
DID NOT KNOW
Finding Self, Spirituality & Ultimate Meaning
by *Lawrence Kushner*

Who am I? Who is God? Kushner creates inspiring interpretations of Jacob's dream in Genesis, opening a window into Jewish spirituality for people of all faiths and backgrounds.

In a fascinating blend of scholarship, imagination, psychology and history, seven Jewish spiritual masters ask and answer fundamental questions of human experience.

"A brilliant fabric of classic rabbinic interpretations, Hasidic insights and literary criticism which warms us and sustains us."

—*Dr. Norman J. Cohen, Dean, Hebrew Union College, NY*

"Rich and intriguing." —*M. Scott Peck, M.D., author of* The Road Less Traveled

6"x 9", 192 pp. Hardcover, ISBN 1-879045-05-2 **$21.95**

6"x 9", 192 pp. Quality Paperback, ISBN 1-879045-33-8 **$16.95**

HONEY FROM THE ROCK
An Introduction to Jewish Mysticism
by *Lawrence Kushner*

An introduction to the ten gates of Jewish mysticism and how it applies to daily life.

"Quite simply the easiest introduction to Jewish mysticism you can read."

"*Honey from the Rock* captures the flavor and spark of Jewish mysticism. . . . Read it and be rewarded." —*Elie Wiesel*

"A work of love, lyrical beauty, and prophetic insight. "
—*Father Malcolm Boyd,* The Christian Century

6"x 9", 168 pp. Quality Paperback, ISBN 1-879045-02-8 **$14.95**

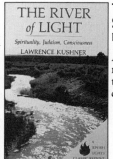

THE RIVER OF LIGHT
Spirituality, Judaism, Consciousness
by *Lawrence Kushner*

A "manual" for all spiritual travelers who would attempt a spiritual journey in our times. Taking us step by step, Kushner allows us to discover the meaning of our own quest: "to allow the river of light—the deepest currents of consciousness—to rise to the surface and animate our lives."

"Philosophy and mystical fantasy...exhilarating speculative flights launched from the Bible....Anybody—Jewish, Christian, or otherwise...will find this book an intriguing experience."—The Kirkus Reviews

"A very important book."—*Rabbi Adin Steinsaltz*

6"x 9", 180 pp. Quality Paperback, ISBN 1-879045-03-6 **$14.95**

Bring Spirituality into Your Daily Life

BEING GOD'S PARTNER
How to Find the Hidden Link
Between Spirituality and Your Work
by *Dr. Jeffrey K. Salkin*
Introduction by *Norman Lear*

A book that will challenge people of every denomination to reconcile the cares of work and soul. A groundbreaking book about spirituality and the work world, from a Jewish perspective. Helps the reader find God in the ethical striving and search for meaning in the professions and in business. Critiques our modern culture of workaholism and careerism, and offers practical suggestions for balancing your professional life and spiritual self.

Being God's Partner will inspire people of all faiths and no faith to find greater meaning in their work, and see themselves doing God's work in the world.

"His is an eloquent voice, bearing an important and concrete message of authentic Jewish religion. The book is engaging, easy to read and hard to put down — and it will make a difference and change people."
— Jacob Neusner, Distinguished Research Professor of Religious Studies, University of South Florida, author of *The Doubleday Anchor Reference Library Introduction to Rabbinic Literature*

6" x 9", 175 pp. (est.) Hardcover, ISBN 1-879045-37-0 **$19.95**

Available: October '94

SELF, STRUGGLE & CHANGE
Family Conflict Stories in Genesis
and their Insights for Our Lives
by *Dr. Norman J. Cohen*

How do I find greater wholeness in my life and in my family's life?

The stress of late-20th-century living only brings new variations to timeless personal struggles. The people described by the biblical writers of Genesis were in situations and relationships very much like our own. We identify with them. Their stories still speak to us because they are about the same problems we deal with every day.

A modern master of biblical interpretation brings us greater understanding of the ancient text and of ourselves in this intriguing re-telling of conflict between husband and wife, father and son, brothers, and sisters.

6" x 9", 200 pp. (est.) Hardcover, ISBN 1-879045-19-2 **$21.95** (est.)

Available: November '94

SO THAT YOUR VALUES LIVE ON
Ethical Wills & How To Prepare Them
Edited by *Rabbi Jack Riemer & Professor Nathaniel Stampfer*

A cherished Jewish tradition, ethical wills—parents writing to children or grandparents to grandchildren—sum up what people have learned and express what they want most for, and from, their loved ones. Includes an intensive guide, **"How to Write Your Own Ethical Will,"** and a topical index. A marvelous treasury of wills: Herzl, Sholom Aleichem, Israelis, Holocaust victims, contemporary American Jews.

"This remarkable volume will enrich all those who will read it and meditate upon its infinite wisdom." — *Elie Wiesel*

6"x 9", 272 pp. Quality Paperback, ISBN 1-879045-34-6 **$16.95** HC, ISBN -07-9 **$23.95**

Coming 1995

HOW TO BE A PERFECT STRANGER: An Ecumenical Guide to Religious Etiquette
by *Richard Siegel and William Shanken*

Explains the rituals and celebrations of America's major religions/denominations, helping an interested guest to feel comfortable, participate to the fullest extent feasible and avoid violating anyone's religious principles.

(HC) **$24.95** (est.)

LIFECYCLES 2: JEWISH WOMEN ON LIFE THEMES & CYCLES OF MEANING

Topics include identity, sexuality, spirituality, prayer, doing good, health, home, and friendship.

(HC) **$24.95** (est.)

GODWRESTLING: New Edition
by *Arthur Ocean Waskow*

Revised, Updated, Expanded 20th Anniversary Edition of this spiritual classic by one of the most creative minds in the Jewish renewal movement.

(HC) **$21.95** (est.)

Mystical Bookmark
22k Gold Electroplated Solid Brass

From

The Book of Letters: A Mystical Hebrew Alphabet
by Rabbi Lawrence Kushner
all in his own calligraphy

1¼" x 1⅞" $10.00

Why a four-pronged *shin*?

According to *Sefer HaTemunah*, one letter is missing from our present alphabet. It will only be revealed in the future. The author explains that every defect in our universe is mysteriously connected with this unimaginable consonant whose sound will create undreamed of words and worlds, transforming repression into Loving.

On the left side of the black leather Tefillin box worn on the forehead during morning prayers there is a four-pronged *shin*. Some suspect that this may be the missing Letter whose name and pronunciation must wait for another universe. Yet, nevertheless, every morning, we wear it right between our eyes.

Order Information

_____	Aspects of Rabbinic Theology (pb), $18.95
_____	Being God's Partner (hc), $19.95 (est.) OCT. '94
_____	The Empty Chair (hc), $ 9.95
_____	God's Paintbrush (hc), $15.95
_____	Healing of Soul, Healing of Body (pb), $13.95
_____	In God's Name (hc), $16.95
_____	The Last Trial (pb), $17.95
_____	Lifecycles, Volume One (hc), $24.95
_____	Mourning & Mitzvah (pb), $19.95
_____	The NEW Jewish Baby Book (pb), $15.95
_____	Putting God on the Guest List (hc), $21.95; (pb), $14.95
_____	Seeking the Path to Life (hc), $19.95
_____	Self, Struggle & Change (hc), $21.95 (est.) NOV. '94
_____	So That Your Values Live On (hc), $23.95; (pb), $16.95
_____	Spirit of Renewal (hc), $22.95; (pb), $16.95
_____	Tormented Master (pb), $17.95
_____	Your Word Is Fire (pb), $14.95

• *The Kushner Series* •

The Book of Letters
   – Popular Hardcover Edition (hc), $24.95*
   – Deluxe Presentation Edition(hc), $79.95, *plus* $5.95 s/h
   – Collector's Limited Edition, $349.00, *plus* $12.95 s/h
The Book of Words (hc), $21.95*
God Was In This Place... (hc), $21.95; (pb) $16.95*
Honey from the Rock (pb), $14.95*
River of Light (pb), $14.95*
THE KUSHNER SERIES — 5 books *marked with asterisk above*, $93.75

• *Motivation & Inspiration for Recovery* •

One Hundred Blessings Every Day, (pb) $14.95 *
Recovery From Codependence, (hc) $21.95; (pb) $13.95*
Renewed Each Day, 2-Volume Set, (pb) $27.90*
Twelve Jewish Steps To Recovery, (hc) $19.95; (pb) $12.95*

THE COMPLETE RECOVERY SET – 20% SAVINGS
5 Books *marked with asterisk above* + **Print Portfolio — $99.75**
For s/h, add $3.00 for the first book, $1.50 each additional book
All set prices include shipping/handling   **Total $** _____

Check enclosed for $ _____ *payable to:* JEWISH LIGHTS Publishing
Charge my credit card: ❒ MasterCard   ❒ Visa   ❒ Discover   ❒ AMEX
Credit Card # _____ Expires _____
Name on card _____
Signature _____ Phone (_____) _____
Name _____
Street _____
City / State / Zip _____

Phone, fax, or mail to: JEWISH LIGHTS Publishing
Box 237, Sunset Farm Offices, Route 4, Woodstock, Vermont 05091
Tel (802) 457-4000   *Fax* (802) 457-4004
Credit card orders (800) 962-4544 (9AM–5PM ET Monday–Friday)
Generous discounts on quantity orders. SATISFACTION GUARANTEED. Prices subject to change.
AVAILABLE FROM BETTER BOOKSTORES. TRY YOUR BOOKSTORE FIRST.